MARLENE DIETRICH
Between the Covers

Edited by
MICHAEL GREGG MICHAUD

"You cannot judge Dietrich on any normal scale. In the world. If you try to understand Dietrich on the normal basis — you'll never get there."

Maria Riva to journalist Diane Sawyer in 1993

Marlene Dietrich: Between the Covers
By Michael Gregg Michaud
Copyright © 2020 Michael Gregg Michaud
No part of this book may be reproduced in any form or by any means, electronic, mechanical, digital, photocopying, or recording, except for inclusion of a review, without permission in writing from the publisher or Author.
No copyright is claimed for the photos within this book. They are used for the purposes of publicity only.

Published in the USA by:

BearManor Media
4700 Millenia Blvd.
Suite 175 PMB 90497
Orlando, FL 32839
www.bearmanormedia.com

Paperback ISBN: 978-1-62933-608-4
Case ISBN: 978-1-62933-609-1
BearManor Media, Orlando, Florida
Printed in the United States of America
Book design by Robbie Adkins, www.adkinsconsult.com

MICHAEL GREGG MICHAUD

Marlene Dietrich: Between the Covers

Marlene Dietrich, a Goddess in Trousers

"What is Sex Appeal? Is it the excitement of amorous passion in men? Is it the unconscious charm exercised by every beautiful woman? Is it dangerous to those who possess it as to those who come under its fatal influence?

"Yet so fraught with misunderstanding is the subject of sex that it is almost impossible to disentangle it from the substratum of half-truths and stupid misstatement that surrounds it.

"Sex is essentially neither wicked nor dangerous. It is only the evil-minded who see in it a hideous and horrible menace. Their viewpoint is probably clouded and distorted by some of these subconscious repressions and hidden complexes we hear so much about.

"Rightly used, sex can be a great constructive force, and if in the films in which I have appeared it is shown in a discreditable light, that is an indictment of the civilization that has misused it, not of sex itself."

Marlene Dietrich, 1934

TABLE OF CONTENTS

Marlene in Song of Songs, *1933.*

"The Politics of Acting" by Michael Gregg Michaud. 1

"Will Marlene Top Greta?" by Margaret Reid. *Picture Play*, . . 44
November, 1930

"She *Threatens* Garbo's Throne" by Katherine Albert. *Photoplay*, . . . 52
December, 1930

"They're New – Hot! Marlene Dietrich – Another Garbo?". . 59
by Helen Ludlam. *Screenland*, January, 1931

"Mother" by Adela Rogers St. Johns. *New Movie Magazine,* ... 63
January, 1931

"Garbo vs. Dietrich" by Leonard Hall. *Photoplay,* February, 1931 .. 72

"Dietrich's Shadow *on* Garbo's Path!" by Clifford W. Cheasley. .. 78
Screenland, March, 1931

"Dietrich – *How She Happened*" by Otto Tolischus. *Photoplay,* .. 84
April, 1931

"*That* Garbo – Dietrich Question!" by Keith Richards. 92
Screenland, May, 1931

"*The* Perils *of* Marlene" by Leonard Hall. *Photoplay,* May, 1931 . 96

"The Romance of Marlene Dietrich" by Dr. Hans Wollenberg. 100
The New Movie Magazine, June, 1931

"Will Dietrich Stay in America?" by Dorothy Manners. 107
Motion Picture, September, 1931

"She's Not a Parrot" by Ruth Biery. *Photoplay,* October, 1931. .. 112

"*The* Extra – Private *Life of* Marlene Dietrich" by Leonard Hall. ... 118
Photoplay, November, 1931

"Dietrich's New Escort Says He's 'Just A Friend'" by Carol .. 122
Benton. *Movie Classics,* December, 1931

"The Girl with the Garters" by Lynde Denig. *Screenland,* ... 125
December, 1931

"Marlene Dietrich's Amazing Secret" by Adele Whitely ... 130
Fletcher. *Modern Screen,* January, 1932

"Dietrich Goes into Seclusion" *Modern Screen,* February, 1932 ... 135

"Will Marlene Break the *Spell?*" by Kay Evans. *Photoplay,* .. 138
February, 1932

"Marlene Dietrich Will Have Only One Great Love, Her .. 143
Handwriting Shows," by Louise Rice. *Movie Classic,* May,
1932

"Dietrich Speaks Out for Herself" by Dorothy Manners. ... 148
Movie Classic, May, 1932

"Cheasley Predicts *Domestic Changes* for Dietrich" by 153
Clifford W. Cheasley. *Motion Picture*, July, 1932

"Will Garbo and Dietrich *Be Deported?*" by Dorothy Calhoun. . 157
Motion Picture, July, 1932

"Marlene Dietrich's Husband Rushes to Her Rescue Like .. 164
One of Her Heroes" by Nancy Pryor. *Movie Classic*, August, 1932

"Marlene Dietrich Gets Kidnap Threats – Child Under 168
Constant Guard" by Janet Burden. *Movie Classic*, August, 1932

"Keeping Slim *on Her Own Cooking*" *The New Movie* 171
Magazine, August, 1932

"Is Marlene Dietrich Being *Frightened* Away from 173
America?" by Franc Dillon. *Movie Classic*, September, 1932

"Dietrich – The Lady and the Tigress!" by William E. Benton. 180
Screenland, October, 1932

"Is Dietrich Through?" by Ruth Biery. *Photoplay*, January, 1933 . . 185

"Has America Declared War on All Foreign Players?" by ... 192
Frank Cates. *Movie Classic*, March, 1933

"Dietrich Dodges Lawsuit by Ending Revolt – Future Films .. 199
to Be German-Made" by Dorothy Manners. *Movie Classic*,
March, 1933

"Marlene Dietrich Tells Why She Wears Men's Clothes!" by 202
Rosalind Shaffer. *Motion Picture*, April, 1933

"Why Dietrich Wears Trousers" by Jean Cummings. *Modern* .. 210
Screen, April, 1933

"Intimate facts about Marlene's Wardrobe" by Franc Dillon. . 212
The New Movie Magazine, May, 1933

"The Mystery of Marlene" by Elsie Janis. *The New Movie* .. 216
Magazine, May, 1933

"Is Marlene Dietrich in *Love* for the *Second* Time?" by 223
Sonia Lee. *Motion Picture*, June, 1933

"Marlene *Is Free At Last*" by Ruth Biery. *Photoplay*, July, 1933 . 229

"Is Dietrich *Indifferent* to Her Public?" by Elza Schallert. . . 235
Motion Picture, September, 1933

"Dietrich Declares Herself!" by Herbert Cruikshank. 242
Screenland, October, 1933

"War Clouds *in the* West?" by Kenneth Baker. *Photoplay*, . . 248
December, 1933

"The Strange Case of HITLER and DIETRICH" by . . . 253
Princess Catherine Radziwill. *Modern Screen*, December, 1933

"Marlene in a Rage!" by Edna Perry. *Movie Classic*, ... 258
January, 1934

"Dietrich Isn't Afraid of Mae West!" by Sonia Lee. *Motion* . . 264
Picture, January, 1934

"The Loveliest Star" by Elizabeth Wilson. *Silver Screen*, . . . 268
February, 1934

"The NEW Marlene" by Della Mason. *The New Movie* 275
Magazine, April, 1934

"You Have Sex Appeal!" by Marlene Dietrich. *Hollywood*, . . 280
May, 1934

"Why Garbo and Dietrich Lead Solitary Lives" by 284
Gladys Hall. *Motion Picture*, June, 1934

"Let Me Tell You About Marlene Dietrich" by John Lodge. 292
Modern Screen, June, 1934

"Dietrich and Von Sternberg Rumored Rifted; Ditto 297
Mae West and James Timony" by Dorothy Donnell. *Movie Classic*, July, 1934

"The Real Marlene Dietrich *Exposed*!" by Hilary Lynn. 299
Hollywood, August, 1934

"Is Von Sternberg Ruining Marlene?" by Katherine Albert. . . 305
Modern Screen, September, 1934

"Marlene Answers All Your Questions" by Ben Maddox. . . . 312
Modern Screen, February, 1935

"Marlene Dietrich" *Silver Screen*, May, 1935 318

"Marlene Looks Ahead!" by Leonard Hall. *Screenland*, ... 319
June, 1935

"I'm No Trilby, Says Marlene Dietrich" by Herbert 323
Cruikshank. *Motion Picture*, June, 1935

"What Is Dietrich's Destiny?" by Warren Reeve. 326
Photoplay, July, 1935

"Not the *Best-Dressed* – But the Most Important" by 332
Katharine Hartley. *Movie Classic*, August, 1935

"For the First and Last Time – DIETRICH TALKS" 338
by Chet Green. *Photoplay*, December, 1935

"Behold *Dietrich*" by Hilary Lynn. *Modern Screen*, ... 346
March, 1936

"The Real DIETRICH – *Unmasked*" by Ida Zeitlin. 350
Motion Picture, May, 1936

"Unlucky Lady" Marlene Dietrich Has Beauty Unrivaled .. 355
and Talent Unlimited, but No Luck at All" by Liza. *Silver Screen*, June 1936

"Drama *in the* Desert" by James Reid. *Movie Classic*, August,.. 361
1936

"Why Dietrich Waited for Donat" by Hettie Grimstead. ... 370
Screenland, February, 1937

"Projections: Marlene Dietrich" by Elizabeth Wilson. *Silver* ... 374
Screen, September, 1937

"Marriage is Enough!" by Marlene Dietrich. *Hollywood*, ... 383
September, 1937

"Dietrich Goes Light-Hearted?" by James Reid. 387
Modern Screen, December, 1937

"Oh, Give Me My Bandages and Crutches" by Duncan 397
Underhill. *Hollywood*, December, 1939

"Dietrich Rides Again" by Dorothy Spensley. *Motion Picture*, . 404
January, 1940

"Saint or Devil?" by Elizabeth Wilson. *Screenland*, ... 413
February, 1940

"Dietrich Lure" by Irving Wallace. *Modern Screen*, ... 420
March, 1940

"Dietrich and Seven Sinners" by Nord Riley. *Hollywood*, ... 428
November, 1940

"The Lady is a Tramp!" by Duncan Underhill. *Hollywood*, .. 434
May, 1941

"Marlene Dietrich" *Modern Screen*, September, 1941 440

"Dietrich, No. 1 Woman Hater Picks the World's 10 442
Greatest Women" by Marlene Dietrich. *Hollywood*, March, 1942

"What Hollywood Thinks About – Marlene Dietrich" 445
by W. F. French. *Photoplay*, April, 1942

"Dietrich Does a Strip!" by Rex Edwards. *Hollywood*, ... 456
March, 1943

"From Apple Strudel to Cheese Cake" by Constance Palmer... 460
Screenland, March, 1944

"Dietrich – The Body and the Soul." *Collier's*, May 14, 1954 . 467

"Marlene Dietrich Has the Last Word". 488

The End 492

Dietrich's Bienenstich (Bee's Nest Cake)................ 493

The Films of Marlene Dietrich 496

Marlene Dietrich on the Air 499

Notes and Sources 502

Selected Bibliography............................... 504

About the Author................................... 505

Marlene in The Devil Is a Woman, *1935.*

The Politics of Acting

"I am not an actress." Marlene Dietrich's oft repeated claim became a sort of mantra for the film star. False Modesty? Perhaps. An attempt to temper criticism? Perhaps. A contrived ploy for publicity purposes? Likely.

Acting abilities aside, she certainly had an exotic appeal, and plenty of style. She exuded a different type of sexuality in American movies. And she offered a very different type of woman to American moviegoers.

Her curious, long-distance marriage to German director Rudolf Sieber would be described today as an "open marriage." At the time, it was characterized as everything from "sophisticated," to a sham, and a "marriage of convenience." They lived very separate lives on different continents. Although Marlene dutifully and respectfully spoke about Rudi to the press, she was not shy about keeping romantic public company with Hollywood actors, directors, and "intellectuals." In truth, restrictive immigration laws in the early 1930s limited Sieber's trips to see his wife in Hollywood to periodic, short visits. Even Marlene's time in the United States was limited to her contractual acting duties. When a film engagement was completed, she, too, had to leave the country. This constant travel was the reason she didn't buy a home in California until she became a citizen, and also complicated her parental responsibilities to her only child, who traveled frequently between her mother in North America and her father in Europe.

On April 1, 1930, Marlene, accompanied by her maid Resi – whom she hired after the woman worked as her dresser on the Berlin movie set of *The Blue Angel* – embarked on the transatlantic ocean liner SS *Bremen* bound for New York.

In the early morning hours of April 1, she wrote to Rudi, "Miss you. Lonely. Regret trip already." Later that morning she wrote, "Boat rolls. Bad weather. Strong winds. Alone in mid-ocean when I could be at home and happy." The trip was defined by inclement weather. Resi actually vomited her false teeth overboard in a wave of seasickness. Marlene arrived in New York City on April 9. The next day, she began a tiring, four-day railroad trip to California.

On April 14, she wrote to Rudi, "Well, the 'Great Find of the Century' is in Hollywood. I am in a pretty little house that Jo [director Josef von Sternberg] rented for me in Beverly Hills, a residential section not far from the studio. Arrival in Pasadena went well. Flowers, and a green Rolls-Royce, a gift from the studio. I have two maids so Resi will have companionship if she will learn a few words of English. Jo opened a bank account for me with 10,000 dollars from the studio. He showed me how to write a check. I enclose a sample for $1,000. My first check. Don't frame it. Spend it. Here there are blue skies, and the weather is unbelievably mild after Berlin. Tomorrow we start work on the costumes. One of them will be my own top hat, white tie, and tails that Jo saw me wear in Berlin at that party. I will be told my lines day by day, in fact, line by line. So, with nothing to learn, I have little to do. I cut flowers and I read. I am glad to be making all this money and I am looking forward to making another film with Jo, but homesickness nags me. Love, kisses, M."

Days after arriving in Hollywood, preproduction began at Paramount on her first Hollywood film, *Morocco*. Her days were filled with hairstylists and make-up artists assigned to transform her into a glamorous Movie Star. Costume designer Travis Banton worked very closely with the actress, creating stunning gowns, literally sewed around her body. Banton was gay. Marlene embraced his wit, friendship, and remarkable talent, and collaborated with him on many of her most memorable movie costumes. The two became close friends and allies at the studio. All her "remodel" was supervised by director, and image-maker, Josef von Sternberg. Dietrich's life, and Hollywood for that matter, would never be the same again.

But who was this "Great Find of the Century"? And where did she come from?

Louis Dietrich was a Prussian officer. He was a playboy whose exploits often embarrassed his privileged family. After being considered, and ultimately rejected, by many eligible young women for marriage, his family arranged a chaperoned meeting with the young daughter of a successful Berlin jeweler. Josephine Felsing was educated, and a good candidate for marriage. Her family encouraged their daughter to accept Dietrich's proposal. The union seemed a mismatch, but the couple married in December, 1898. The bride was twenty-two, and the groom was thirty. They moved into a comfortable home in the picturesque nearby town of Schoneberg.

In 1899, Josephine gave birth to a daughter named Elisabeth. Louis had little interest in a traditional marriage, and even less interest in being occupied with an infant. He moved to a separate bedroom where he entertained his mistress, while his dutiful wife tended to their newborn. On December 27, 1901, Josephine gave birth to a second daughter named Maria Magdalena. Elizabeth was affectionately called Liesel, and Maria was called Leni. Although he provided a comfortable home and the necessary amenities, Louis was not attentive to his wife and daughters. Leni thought her father would have preferred to have sons.

The girls were privately tutored, and studied French and English. They took piano and violin lessons before entering public school. Louis hired attractive young tutors for his daughters' studies – and his own amusement. The sisters would attend the Auguste-Viktoria Girl's School from 1907 until 1917.

Louis's family liked Josephine. To make up for his lack of attention, they spent as much time as they could with her and the children. Impressionable Leni was especially fond of her Aunt Valli who was married to her father's brother, Otto. Valli was rich, stylish, independent and very outspoken, making her a very different female role model for her young niece. She smoked and drank freely with the men, which "respectable" women of the day did not do. She spoiled the girls with gifts when she visited. She gave a handsome, leather-bound diary to Leni and encouraged her to record her every thought. Leni kept diaries for the rest of her life, recording her innermost feelings, prejudices, annoyances, and grudges.

Like good German young women, Liesel and Leni learned to sew, mend, clean and cook. Otherwise, the girls had little in common. Liesel was studious and behaved properly. Leni was curious and bright, but bored with the strict discipline of school. She had an independent streak, and was more interested in romance and chasing boys. She recorded her exploits in her dairy, and when she was thirteen years old, she decided to rid herself of childhood. She began by changing her name. She practiced writing different combinations of Maria Magdalena, and decided upon "Marlene."

World War I erupted in July, 1914. Within days, most European countries had declared war on one another. In August, Louis was

Liesel, Josephine, Louis, and Marlene.

sent to fight on the Western Front. He was seriously wounded in September. After spending a month in the hospital, he returned to the battlefield. At first, Berliners thought the war would only last a few months, but the battles dragged on. Marlene's parlor became a meeting place for grieving war widows dressed in black. Maria Riva wrote in her biography of her mother, "Liesel would cry in sympathy for those black figures bent in sorrow. Leni, never a lover of stark reality, continued to see life from her own perspective." Despite the bleak mood, she ignored the looming horror of a protracted war, and wrote in her diary about the many teenage boys who flirted with her. She looked forward to visits from Valli, who swept into their house with enough panache to distract attention away from the real world drama. She gave Marlene silver jewelry and cigarettes, and taught her how to apply makeup and style her hair. Tragically, the war came home when Uncle Otto was killed in battle in December, 1914. Valli was the first war widow in the family.

Louis was sent to the Eastern Front in June, 1916. Within days, he was killed. Valli delivered the news to Josephine and the girls. Liesel was grief stricken. Marlene was stoic. She did not accept her father's death. War rations and a meager widow's pension made it impossible for Josephine to maintain their home. In October, the family moved into a small apartment in the town of Dessau. A few months later, Marlene's Uncle Max was killed in the war. The loss of relatives and family friends didn't outwardly affect Marlene so much as the rationing of everything from food to clothing to fuel. She had lived comfortably while her father was alive, but the sacrifices her family had to make to survive after his death vexed her. "During the war all we had to eat was turnips, just turnips, nothing else. After a while, everyone's skin turned yellow – but not mine," she recalled.

Eduard von Losch had been Louis Dietrich's best friend, and a trusted confidante to his family. He was an aristocrat, and first lieutenant in the Grenadiers. In the winter of 1916, he proposed marriage to Josephine. In early 1917, they married. Liesel deeply mourned her father's death, but accepted her new stepfather. Marlene all but ignored her mother's marriage to von Losch.

The family moved to a beautiful house in a fashionable area of Berlin. Marlene finally had her own room – a small space in the attic. In spite of wartime shortages, von Losch provided well for his new wife and stepdaughters. There was money for Marlene to take violin lessons. She loved learning to play the instrument, which was a gift from her Aunt Valli, and appreciated the attention paid to her by the young men in class.

Marlene's teenage sexual awakening was not limited to a consuming interest in boys. Her romantic attraction to girls became apparent in the summer of 1917. "I am starting to love Margaret

Rosendorf from Liesel's class – otherwise my heart is very empty," she wrote in her diary. "It's so much nicer if one has someone – it makes you feel so pretty."

Eduard von Losch was ordered back to his infantry regiment. Josephine was distraught, but he assured her that he had made all the financial arrangements to care for her and the girls in the event of his death. In July, 1917, Josephine took her daughters for a summer holiday in Liebenstein. The retreat was boring for Marlene. She complained about the many unsightly poor people living nearby, and the French prisoners of war who were constructing a building next to the hotel where they stayed. She considered these intrusions to impose upon her holiday mood. The most important thing that happened during their stay in the historic German village concerned the introduction of fifteen-year-old Marlene to Countess Gersdorf, a young married woman. The precocious teenager fell in love! She wrote, "My heart is set on fire! I am dying of love for her, she is beautiful like an angel, she is my angel. I would like to hold her hand and kiss it wildly until I die. She does not know how great my love is. She thinks I only like her a lot, as Liesel does. But this time it's really passion, deep, deep love. My sweet Countess. She is so beautiful!" Marlene spent as much time as she could with the young woman who gave her expensive, imported gifts. Marlene was bold and unconcerned with appearances. The relationship became the subject of tea-time-talk and gossip, and once Josephine caught wind of what was happening, she cut their holiday short and quickly returned to Berlin with her daughters. Broken hearted at first, Marlene soon pursued other potential suitors.

In September, 1917, von Losch was killed at war. Josephine was two times a widow at the age of forty. Liesel cried for days. Marlene barely acknowledged his death, and never mentioned it in her diary. In the fall, she appeared in her first school play, *The Governess*. She played the role of a man, wearing trousers and her mother's riding coat. She enjoyed the attention being on stage afforded her.

Since she was a little girl, Marlene had enjoyed going to the cinema. She especially liked the films of Henny Porten, Germany's first major female movie star. She wrote effusive fan letters to the actress, and hovered around Porten's Berlin home to present her with flowers whenever she could intercept her outside her front door.

Marlene's ability to emotionally block out any negative influences or experiences was tested that winter. Typhus swept through Germany. Many people died. In Berlin, with temperatures below freezing, corpses were left outside on the icy sidewalks to be collected by so-called "death wagons." Marlene continued to limit her diary entries to her infatuations and unrequited loves, but the horrors of the day affected her. In the summer of 1918, she fell ill and was confined to bed for months. Years later, her daughter wrote, "…considering her exaggerated romantic character, she was suffering from depression."

Armistice was declared on November 11, 1918, ending four years of one of the deadliest wars in history. In the weeks leading up to the treaty, Germany was in turmoil. Shell-shocked soldiers were shooting each other, and people – exasperated by worthless currency, and the lack of food and other essentials – were rioting in the streets. Marlene and her family stayed in their house for safety, with more than adequate provisions. Millions had perished in the war. Berlin was overrun with women, many widowed, others anxious for reunification with their husbands and sons, trying to find a way to survive and feed their children. She wrote in her diary, "Why must I experience these terrible times? I did so want a golden youth and now it turned out like this! Maybe soon a time will

Marlene, 1918.

come when I will be able to tell about happiness again – only happiness."

Conditions in Berlin continued to deteriorate. The streets were filled with beggars, homeless people, and war veterans suffering from post-traumatic stress disorders. And yet, surrounded by despair, Marlene was more concerned about her less than satisfying romances. She had little patience for her sister and mother, and believed she was in a different class than either of them. She thought of them as intruders in a world she was determined to create for herself. She wrote, "Both of them are so dry and calculating. I am like a black sheep of the family to them." In April, 1919, she begrudgingly allowed her sister and mother to accompany her to the premiere of Henny Porter's latest film at the Mozart Theatre. Marlene wrote, "I was so looking forward to going alone. I'm sure I made myself too pretty, and like a doll one wants to keep on kissing. I'm sure that's what a few other gentlemen thought, too." Several days later, she wrote about falling in love with a boy again. "I wish I were more superficial," she opined. "It would be wonderful to enjoy the moment without thinking about the future."

Eduard von Losch's generous annuity made it possible for Josephine to live comfortably, and safely. Fearful of the dangerous living conditions in Berlin, Josephine moved her daughters to the mineral hot springs of Bad Pyrmont. They spent the summer at the resort on the Emmer River, and Marlene entertained many young men. She became intrigued by the American soldiers resting in the area. She was seduced by their brazen forwardness, and chocolate biscuits. She flirted and danced with U.S. officers who frequented the cafes and dancehalls. The family returned to their Berlin home at summer's end, but spent weekends in the nearby town of Springeberg in Brandenberg. There, Marlene often slipped away from her mother's watchful eyes and romanced numerous boyfriends. She wrote, "Saturdays and Sundays I kiss enough for the whole week. I really should be very ashamed. Of course, I can't expect respect. I can't help it. It is not my fault if my romantic nature has no limits. Who knows where I will end up."

Unable to control her willful teenage daughter, Josephine sent Marlene to a boarding school in Weimar in 1920. The historic city was a cultural center with numerous schools providing education in visual, literary, and musical arts. Marlene bemoaned her banishment, and wrote, "If only someone would come to take away my longing. I wish someone would come and, with his love, make me happy and so content that I would forget all the tears shed for past loves. I am so unhappy because I don't have anybody who loves me. I am so used to being loved."

Her time in Weimar provided the opportunity to work on her musical skills. It also gave her enough privacy to explore sexual intimacy. However, her experiences with sex were awkward and unsatisfying. She attracted the attention of Albert Lasky, the conductor of the Weimar opera. He invited her to a costume ball, and under some pretext, convinced her to return with him to his home at the end of the evening. She recalled, "I went to his house, took off all my clothes, and sat on his sofa while he played the piano." She did as she was told, which included wearing her white wig to bed. The experience was forgettable.

Marlene studied violin at the school with Professor Reitz, a handsome older man. The teacher was soon smitten with her, and despite her mother's protestations, the school headmistress did not monitor their budding, and inappropriate relationship. After her Christmas holiday, Marlene returned to school, and into the arms of her waiting professor. Mr. Reitz had sex with her on the music room couch. Years later, Marlene told her daughter Maria, "He groaned, heaved, panted. Didn't even take his trousers off. I just lay there on that old settee, the red plush scratching my behind, my skirts over my head. The whole thing, very uncomfortable." Despite, or because of, her ill-conceived affair with the professor, she was not accepted for further music training at the Academy of Music. During her later life, she claimed a physical injury ended her music career.

Leisel graduated university, and found work as a teacher. She continued to live with her mother, and contributed to the household. Marlene's ambitions were less conventional. Her role in the school play, *The Governess*, had piqued her interest in performing. Against her mother's wishes, she applied to the renowned Max Reinhardt Acting Academy. She was never accepted as a full-time student, and she never personally studied with Reinhardt, but she did manage to appear in small roles in numerous productions at Reinhardt's Deutshes Theater. She studied dance and movement, and accepted any role she was offered. She was enthusiastic, and her discipline and tenacity served her well. She became a favorite of the stage managers. She also became a bit of a thief, appropriating all the costumes, shoes and accessories provided for her use on stage.

For a time, she toured as a chorus girl in Guido Thielscher's *Girl-Kabarett* vaudeville revue. She also performed in several Rudolf Nelson legendary musical/comedy revues in Berlin.

The German film industry was centered in Berlin. Marlene was determined to break into film acting, and played her first tiny credited role in the 1923 movie, *The Little Napoleon*. She then auditioned for the part of "Lucy" in a romantic drama titled, *The Tragedy of Love*, starring Emil Jannings. She fashioned a costume from the clothes in her closet, and arrived for the audition wearing a flapper dress, high heels, a ragged feather boa, and long green satin gloves. Rudolf Sieber, the associate producer. noticed her. He was taken by her spunk – and memorable green gloves – and cast her in the role. Sieber was beginning his career as a producer, director and writer in German cinema. He was smitten with the pretty, young woman. Marlene recalled, "He looked at me and I couldn't believe it! He was so beautiful! His blond hair shone. A little assistant director in real tweeds? Right away, I knew I loved him!" Marlene surely appreciated the opportunities that could be afforded her by an ambitious young filmmaker. And marriage would free her of Josephine's ever-watchful eye, and controlling ways. After a whirlwind romance, the couple married on May 17, 1923. Marlene was twenty-one and Rudolf was twenty-seven.

The City of Berlin became a morass of freewheeling immorality, and was known as the sin capital of Europe in the 1920s. Germans and visitors alike flocked to the city to enjoy the freedom, the wild night life, the bohemian lifestyle, prostitutes, nightclubs, and explicit sex clubs. Transvestites and homosexuals populated the city, giving it an air of sexual "anything goes." Marlene and her friends loved the scene, and she spent many evenings mingling and drinking with gay men and flamboyant transsexuals. She said, "Only pansies know how to look like a sexy woman!" She and her husband Rudi frequented secretive cabarets. Rudi instructed his tailor to create a man's evening suit for his wife. They danced the nights away with abandon – Rudi in his fashionable three-piece suits, and Marlene in top hat and tails.

Josephine was unimpressed with her new son-in-law, and the lifestyle he and her daughter embraced. Still

Marlene in Berlin cabaret.

attempting to keep an eye on Marlene, Josephine found a spacious apartment close to her own home for the couple.

Marlene became pregnant in 1924. She had desperately wanted a baby, and was thrilled by the news. However, her pregnancy was a profound game-changer in terms of her marriage. In a curious replay of her parent's relationship following her own birth, she told her husband there would be no more sexual contact between them! She preferred romance to actual sexual relations anyway, she explained, and Rudi was permanently moved out of their bedroom to a small alcove where he slept. Their daughter, Maria, was born on December 13, 1924. From that day forward Marlene was known as "Mutti," and Rudi as "Papi," not only to their daughter, but to each other. This life-changing event profoundly changed the way Marlene considered her husband's role in the family. She loved him and respected his advice, always calling upon him for help, but rather than a husband, Rudi became the father figure she never had as a child.

Marlene worked steadily in German silent films, and appeared on stage in numerous productions including *Pandora's Box*, *The Taming of the Shrew*, and *A Midsummer Night's Dream*. She also performed in cabarets and musical revues. Rudi worked in many different capacities in the Berlin film industry including directing, writing, producing, and casting. Still, the couple struggled to survive with a new baby. Josephine helped them pay their rent, and often cooked for the couple at Marlene's request. She delivered the prepared meals, but was rarely invited to stay for dinner by her daughter. While Marlene enjoyed her burgeoning show business career, and developed a certain level of celebrity in Berlin, her sister Liesel had a tougher time of it. She gave up her teaching job when she married a man Marlene characterized as a "low-class rotter," and gave birth to a son. Thereafter, Marlene infrequently saw her sister, or her nephew.

Film and theater work drew Marlene to Vienna in 1927. She left her family in Berlin, and stayed in Austria for many months. At her urging, her friend Tamara Matul frequently visited Rudi and Maria. Tamara, known as Tami, was a pretty Russian refugee. She was a trusted friend. The actress had more in mind than simply finding someone to keep her family company, however. With Marlene's approval, Tami soon became Rudi's life-long mistress.

When Marlene returned to her family, she brought with her a new talent – playing a saw she clamped between her legs – and a new "friend," Austrian actor, singer, and filmmaker Willi Forst with whom she starred in the 1927 silent film, *Café Elektric*. The twenty-four-year-old Forst was just the type of male friend she preferred; he was handsome, stylish, charming, witty, talented, and bisexual. He was a frequent house guest, and enjoyed dinner and parlor talk with Marlene and Rudi. In a short time, Forst was replaced as the dinner-guest-of-choice by the Austrian tenor and film actor, Richard Tauber. Tauber cut a dashing figure with his hand-carved walking stick and ever-present monocle in his right eye. He had recently recorded a number of songs with the assistance of the Russian-born composer, Mischa Spolianksy. Marlene's introduction to Spoliansky by Tauber was professionally serendipitous.

On May 15, 1928, Marlene first appeared in what would become a long-running, acclaimed musical revue titled, *It's in the Air*, with music by Spoliansky, and lyrics by Marcellus Schiffer. The show consisted of twenty-four short stories with music set in a Berlin department store. In one memorable number, she shared the stage with Margo Lion, a popular French cabaret singer, who was the wife of Schiffer. The two actresses performed the song, "When My Best Girlfriend," in duet. They danced a foxtrot together while they sang the humorous and suggestive song with undeniable lesbian undertones. They cooed together to the delight of the audience, and wore oversized corsages of violets – the "code" flower at the time for lesbians. "When My Best Girlfriend" became a lesbian anthem in Weimar Germany in the late 1920s and early 1930s.

The following year, Marlene made three films, and returned to the Berliner Theater stage in another revue written by Spoliansky, titled, *Two*

Marlene and Margo Lion in It's in the Air, *1928.*

Marlene, Ana May Wong, and Leni Riefenstahl at the Pierre Ball, Berlin, 1928.

Neckties. Rudi, whose career slowly sputtered to an end, and Tami were left to care for young Maria while Marlene worked on movie sets during the day, and performed onstage at night. One evening, the Austrian-born director, Josef von Sternberg (who had achieved success making American films), was in the theater audience. He was impressed with Marlene, and invited her to test for the role of "Lola" in a film he was about to begin, titled, *The Blue Angel*. Renowned German actor Emil Jannings was cast as the leading man.

Upon first meeting, Marlene was unimpressed with von Sternberg. She all but dismissed him and the idea of working with Jannings, as well. But her husband exercised his usual level-headedness, and convinced her to answer the call to audition for the part of a waterfront whore. When she returned home after her audi-

Marlene and her daughter, Maria, 1928.

tion at Ufa Studios, she couldn't say enough good things to Rudi about the director. Marlene was surprised when she was cast in the supporting female lead role in *The Blue Angel*. Her salary was a whopping $5,000. *The Blue Angel* would be the first full-length talking movie filmed in Germany. To add to the excitement, and production challenges, the film would be shot in German and English at the same time.

During production, von Sternberg became the Sieber's frequent dinner guest. By that time, Tami, Rudi's mistress, had settled into the house, helping care for Maria and cooking and housekeeping for the family. Marlene developed a strong respect for the director, and was willing to do what he asked most of the time. She insisted on using much of her own clothing for her character in the film, and instructed her daughter and Tami to ferret out appropriate "street-walker outfits" from her extensive closet. She followed the imperious directions of von Sternberg. Occasionally she made her objections known to the director, but more frequently to her husband. "That von Sternberg is absolutely mad," she complained to Rudi, after a particularly challenging day on the set. "This film is a disaster! It will never work!"

The iconic scene of Marlene sitting backwards on a chair with her legs spread took days to complete to von Sternberg's approval. The camera, she complained, was pointed at her crotch. She acquiesced, but expressed her displeasure to whoever might listen to her. "Why don't you let me sit on something else," she asked the director. "How many times can one be erotic with a chair?" She told her husband, "This whole thing is *impossible*! I am ashamed to walk on the set!"

She thought the sets were all wrong, and the lighting was unflattering. "Papi, *you* made me do this abortion," she said to Rudi. "It's all so ugly! He has big fat women sitting all over on the nightclub stage. Any day now it's going to collapse under all that blubber, and I'm going to break my neck! And the smoke! You should see the smoke! Thick, like fog! Why bother with all the work on the costumes when all you will be able to see is those big, fat shapes behind the fog!"

Perhaps her loudest complaint was about the lack of a script. The actors were given their lines on the day of each shoot. There was no time to rehearse. They were coached on the set. Rudi patiently listened to her rants after long days at the studio, but always encouraged her to follow von Sternberg's commands.

She balked at a song she was supposed to sing in the film. She flew into a rage and complained to Rudi, "But the song, the one that *everybody* loves, something about 'moths and flames' and 'I can't help it that all men want me' – that one is terrible! Thank God, once *The Blue Angel* is finally finished, I will never have to sing that *awful* song again!" That "awful song" was "Falling in Love Again."

Director Josef von Sternberg and Marlene.

Marlene's leading man, Emil Jannings, was often the target of her complaints. Although he had made a film in America, he struggled with the pronunciation of many English words. Marlene's English was good, but her accent was heavy at times, still she made fun of Jannings mispronunciations. Her daughter later recalled, "In English, my mother always felt like a foreigner, disguise was therefore easier. Later, rarely did the real Dietrich emerge when performing in English."

After many weeks of filming, and on-again-off-again on-set skirmishes, Marlene was allowed to see the rushes shot a few days earlier. She was ordered by von Sternberg not to speak until the screening ended. She was enthralled by what she saw, and declared the director a cinematic genius. "Papi, it is still a vulgar film," she exclaimed to her husband, "but Mister von Sternberg is a god! A Master!"

Her daughter remembers that was a turning point in fabricating the myth of Marlene Dietrich. The actress began to refer to herself in the abstract. "That was the first time I heard my mother refer to herself in the third person. It was the beginning of her thinking of Dietrich as a product, quite removed from her own reality."

It didn't take long for filmmakers in Berlin to realize that von Sternberg was working on something very special, and that the film's young actress was stealing the picture away from Jannings, its established star. At von Sternberg's urging, his home studio Paramount, the production company responsible for distributing *The Blue Angel* in America, offered Marlene an impressive motion picture contract.

On January 29, 1930, Paramount sent a cable to the actress.

Marlene in The Blue Angel, *1930.*

"MARLENE DIETRICH SIEBER STOP HAVE PLEASURE TO INVITE YOU TO JOIN BRILLIANT ROSTER OF PLAYERS AT PARAMOUNT PUBLIX STOP OFFER YOU SEVEN YEAR CONTRACT BEGINNING AT FIVE HUNDRED DOLLARS PER WEEK ESCALATING TO THREE THOUSAND FIVE HUNDRED PER WEEK IN SEVENTH YEAR STOP CONGRATULATIONS STOP PLEASE CONFIRM BY CABLE STOP BERLIN OFFICE WILL ARRANGE FIRST CLASS TRAVEL AND IS AT YOUR DISPOSAL FOR ANY HELP REQUIRED STOP BP SCHULBERG VICE PRESIDENT PARAMOUNT PUBLIX CORPORATION."

At first, Marlene had no interest in leaving her family, and she felt not enough money was offered to upend her life. *The Blue Angel* was completed at about the same time the revue, *Two Neckties*, closed in Berlin. She was out of work, and Rudi's meager and infrequent earnings could not support the family. Oddly, and perhaps at the bidding of von Sternberg, Ufa decided to drop her option. She was crushed, and commiserated over what she felt was the sudden and undeniable end of her movie career.

Josef von Sternberg all but begged Marlene to accept the Paramount offer and travel to America with him to begin a Hollywood motion picture career. She was adamantly opposed, and presented an endless list of reasons why she should not go. Rudi agreed with von Sternberg and urged her to accept the Paramount offer. He assured her that Maria would be safe with him and Tami. She would be a fool, he said, if she turned down such an amazing opportunity.

After careful consideration, and much hand-wringing, Marlene decided to go to Hollywood after von Sternberg negotiated a more acceptable offer on her behalf. She was now bound to make only two films for Paramount. If she decided she wanted to return to Germany, she would be released from the contract provided she signed a document stating she would not sign with any other Hollywood movie studio. If she decided to continue work in America, her Paramount contract would be renewed providing her with a much larger guaranteed salary and a clause giving her choice and approval of her director.

On March 31, 1930, dressed in a shimmering evening gown and furs, Marlene attended the premiere of *The Blue Angel* at the Ufa owned Gloria-Palast Theater in Berlin. She joined the other cast members on the stage for prolonged bows for the enthusiastic audience. From the theater, Marlene immediately took a boat train to Bremerhaven, where she boarded the SS *Bremen*, bound for New York. As she set sail for America, she had no idea that overnight she had

Emil Jannings and Marlene at the Berlin premiere of The Blue Angel.

become the talk of the German film industry. The press raved about her performance and declared her the next "star" in German cinema.

She corresponded with Rudi and Maria daily. Once she was settled into her Beverly Hills house, she sent them many Hollywood-style glamour portraits of herself that the studio had arranged for publicity purposes. Maria recalled that she and her father barely recognized the stunningly beautiful woman in the photographs.

Jo von Sternberg took immediate control of her hair and make-up, and her wardrobe. He directed a film trailer featuring the actress for the studio Sales Department. In it, he insisted she wear white tie and tails. He maintained control of press interviews – turning most down – and wanted her to be photographed wearing trousers, convinced her "look" and her silence would intrigue the public. He was correct. Marlene Dietrich was the talk of Hollywood before ever stepping in front of an American movie camera. Her "branding" was in full throttle.

Despite the business at hand, she missed her family very much. In one letter to Rudi, she wrote about an important party at studio chief Schulberg's mansion. Neither she nor von Sternberg was interested in attending parties, but Jo thought it would be wise to attend the executive's soiree, and "create goodwill." She wrote, "To be courteous, we went. I wore my navy blazer, white flannel trousers, and a yachting cap (to create just a *little* "ill" will.)

Josef von Sternberg greets Marlene at the Pasadena railroad station.

Gary Cooper and Marlene in Morocco, *1930.*

Her independent streak set the tone for her next several years of Hollywood stardom.

In July, production began on her first American film, *Morocco*. She wrote to her husband, "Tomorrow we begin shooting. It's been amusing, all this 'the new thing from Germany' and 'Paramount's answer to Garbo' and 'The Great Find of the Century,' but now I feel a responsibility to Jo to be just that, and though I'm sure that with his help I can be, still I am nervous and apprehensive."

Marlene played the role of "Amy Jolly," a nightclub singer. Gary Cooper was her leading man, cast in the role of "Legionnaire Tom Brown." It didn't take long for her to experience being the target of Hollywood gossip columnists. She wrote to Rudi, "Gary Cooper is pleasant and good-looking. The newspapers have said Lupe Velez has threatened to scratch my eyes out if I come near him. How can I? She sits on his lap between scenes. I don't go close enough, God knows, to see what they're doing, but it looks like they are doing something that is usually done in private." Stories persisted that she was having an affair with Cooper. She was mystified by the press fabrications. She told her family she had

Marlene in Morocco, *1930.*

no interest in the man. "All Cooper can do is say 'Yup' and 'Huh?' Lupe Velez had to do it *to* him," she chortled.

Marlene's androgyny, a product of her own and von Sternberg's making, informed her early film roles. It was most memorable in *Morocco*. Her character, dressed in a tuxedo and top hot, sings "When Love Dies" in a crowded nightclub. The audience roars, and she notices a woman seated at a table who has a flower in her hair. She asks the woman if she can take it. The woman agrees. In a shocking move, Marlene kisses the woman on the mouth, and tosses the flower to Cooper's character standing nearby.

In mid-August, production was completed on *Morocco*, and she immediately went to work on *Dishonored*, her third film with von Sternberg.

With the December 5 release of *The Blue Angel*, and the December 6 release of *Morocco*, Marlene was an overnight box office sensation in Hollywood. She was nominated for an Academy Award for Best Actress in a Leading Role for the latter. Having satisfied her contract calling for two films, a few days later, she returned to Europe.

After an extended holiday with her family, she returned to New York aboard the SS *Bremen* in April, 1931. Her daughter Maria,

Marlene holds a street urchin for photographers at the London premiere of Morocco, *March 26, 1931.*

deemed old enough to travel, joined her mother. When Marlene disembarked in New York, she was greeted by fans, the press, and photographers. She also was greeted by a process server. Josef von Sternberg's wife was suing her for alienation of affections! While it was true that von Sternberg had fallen hopelessly in love with the actress, she had no such feelings for him. She was outraged, and called the director, the studio, her lawyers and her husband, and threatened to return to Germany on the next ship. Promises were made to remedy the embarrassing situation, and she begrudgingly boarded the train for Pasadena. But another problem awaited their arrival at the train station in California.

Mr. von Sternberg was waiting for them, but when Marlene got off the train holding her daughter's hand, the press was stumped. The newest, exotic film sensation in Hollywood was a mother! They asked that Maria be moved out of the photos, and Marlene threw another fit, screaming at von Sternberg and the mystified press, "First I am called a 'home-wrecker,' now I am not supposed to be a mother? This is *my* child! She *belongs* to me! No *studio* is going to dictate to me *what* I can or cannot do with my own child! They don't want her? Then they don't get me!" The director hurried them past the stunned reporters and photographers, into a waiting car, and quickly drove into Los Angeles.

Within days, work began on *Shanghai Express*. Mrs. von Sternberg's complaint was not so easily resolved, though. She soon demanded money. Marlene was concerned that the moral's clause in her contract could be exercised by the studio. Contracts required the signee to behave in a decent and moral fashion or face possible termination. To fight the gossip, it was announced that Rudi would join his wife and daughter in Hollywood. Tami would be left behind in Germany. This was the official beginning of Marlene's game of marital hide-and-seek with the American press.

Rudi dutifully posed with his wife and daughter for photographers, presenting a united front against accusations of infidel-

Tami, Marlene, and Rudi.

ity leveled against Marlene. When Rudi returned to Germany, a German actor friend of the actress arrived in Hollywood. Hans von Twardowski had starred in the 1920 film, *The Cabinet of Dr. Caligari*. Hans accompanied Marlene to many public events, and the two were often photographed arm in arm, to debunk any suspicions that she was involved with her director, and neutralize Mrs. von Sternberg's accusations. Hans was a safe diversion. He was homosexual and fled Germany for his safety shortly before the Nazi regime took power. And Marlene was a safe "cover" for Hans who was involved in a volatile romance with Martin Kosleck, a fellow German actor who also fled Nazi Germany.

Marlene, Maria, and Rudi.

Maurice Chevalier and Marlene on the Paramount lot.

While Marlene's relationship with her director was purely platonic, she had numerous romantic flirtations and love affairs with various well-known men and women including actors Maurice Chevalier, Ronald Colman, Douglas Fairbanks, Jr., John Gilbert, and Richard Barthelmess, and writer Mercedes de Acosta. Chevalier's marriage was on the rocks when he began romancing Marlene. He was a suitable escort and squired her around Hollywood. Marlene's bewitching powers were something to be reckoned with. Chevalier fell in love with her. She appreciated his "reasonable and adult" attitudes about love affairs, which she attributed to his French upbringing. And he was the perfect suitor for her because he was impotent, she claimed, which limited any unwanted intimate physical contact.

Marlene and Greta Garbo, though often reported to be involved in a bitter professional feud, didn't know each other and had nothing in common except their affairs with Mercedes de Acosta. Marlene was amused at first by Miss de Acosta's avalanche of effusive love letters, but she tired of the love-smitten writer and, in exasperation, tossed her many correspondences to Rudi for his advice on how to handle de Acosta's pronouncements of love.

Perhaps the actress's greatest annoyance with the press concerned their obsession with her "mysterious" relationship with von Sternberg. Her contract allowed her to work exclusively with the director. He was undeniably controlling with her professional and personal lives. He was the road block between his star and Hollywood reporters. Despite her impatient denials, the press persisted in characterizing her relationship with von Sternberg as one of menacing control – not unlike the characters in George du Maurier's novel, *Trilby*, the cautionary tale of a young and innocent Trilby who was seduced, dominated and exploited by Svengali.

Marlene in Blonde Venus, *1932.*

The spring of 1932 got off to a rocky start. Marlene's first legal skirmish with the studio made headlines in April. Her announced next film, *Blonde Venus*, was written by von Sternberg. Herbert Marshall and Cary Grant were cast as Marlene's leading men. Before production got underway, the studio rejected the director's proposed ending. He was outraged, and excused himself from the film. Before another director could be found, Marlene refused to work with any director other than von Sternberg. On April 26, Paramount filed suit against von Sternberg for $100,000, and threatened to replace Marlene with Tallulah Bankhead. Tallulah famously said, "I always did want to get into Dietrich's pants." The story problems were solved to von Sternberg's satisfaction after many days of negotiations. Filming began a month later.

Marlene's preoccupation with the threatened legal suit and the screenplay issues was distracted in mid-May when she received a couple of extortion letters composed of words clipped from newspapers and magazines demanding $10,000 in one, and $20,000 in the other. If she failed to pay the money, her daughter Maria was in danger of being harmed or kidnapped. Authorities from the local police to the FBI were called in to protect the star and her child. Iron bars were installed on all the windows and doors of their rented Beverly Hills house at 822 North Roxbury Drive. An electrified fence and gate were added. She hired around the clock guards. Rudi immediately returned to California to stay with his family. Interestingly, Rudi – unconcerned by his wife's romantic transgressions, struck up a close friendship with Chevalier, the three were spotted together socializing in Hollywood nightspots. The actress liked it when her admirers became companionable friends.

News about the kidnap threat was kept secret at the request of the police while an investigation was launched. Several other film stars received similar upsetting threats at the time. In early June, a peculiar "mix-up" occurred between the actress and Elsie Muller, the wife of a wealthy German importer who also lived in Beverly

One of the extortion/kidnap letters, 1932.

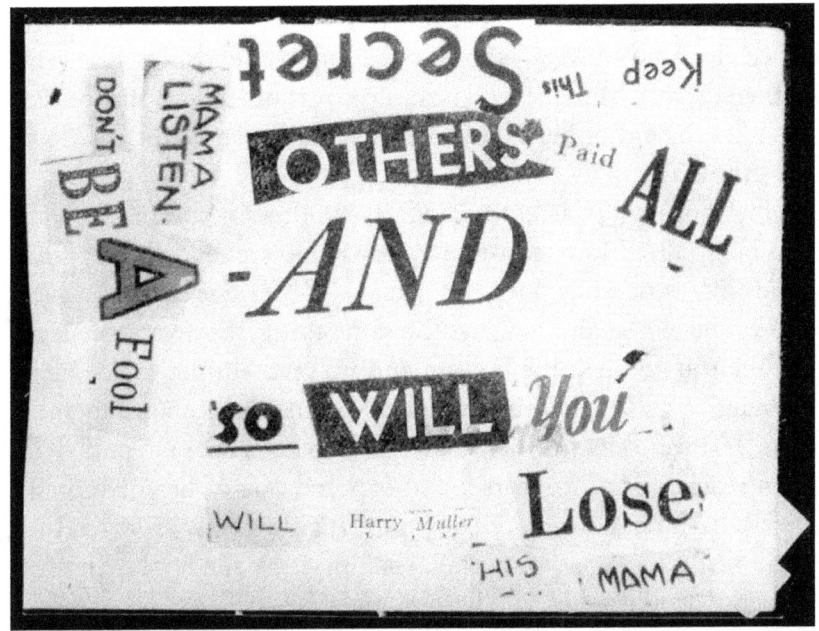

One of the extortion/kidnap letters, 1932.

Hills. They each received extortion letters intended for the other. While the District Attorney continued to investigate the threats, his office publicly reported that authorities felt the culprits were rank amateurs. On June 2, Marlene released her first statement to the press regarding the threats. "We have received threatening letters from time to time," she said, "but at the request of the police remained silent. Necessary measures were taken to safeguard the child as well as myself with bodyguards. As long as the police have given out the details there is nothing left for me to do but admit it."

When Mae West arrived at Paramount in Hollywood from New York in the summer of 1932, the press instantly pitted the two sex symbols as studio rivals. Nothing could have been further from the truth, and again, Marlene was disgusted by the antics of gossip columnists. The women were polar opposites, although both were inspired by homosexuals, transvestites and drag queens from their pasts. Mae was a comedienne and presented a comic exaggeration of femininity. Marlene's sexual appeal was defined by her daring presentation of androgyny. They were never competitors. The two actresses had adjacent dressing rooms on the studio lot. They visited each other often, sharing stories and jokes. Marlene was especially fond of Mae, who reached out in friendship. She sympathized with Marlene's disturbing extortion threat, and offered to enlist the aid of her New York gangland friends to track down the criminals.

One morning, Mae entered Marlene's dressing room when she was being fitted for a costume for a voodoo scene in *Blonde Venus*. Mae said, "Not bad, honey, not bad at all!" Marlene said, "But look, Mae. The legs again! Always the same thing, they want the legs!" "Yeah! You give 'em the bottom and I'll give 'em the top! Ducky, we have to go for the women, too. Not just the men. Remember that. If it were just the men, all I'd have to do is take 'em out!" Mae then reached into her corset and exposed one of her memorable breasts. Marlene nearly fell down in laughter. She wrote to Rudi, "She really took one out, Papi, shaking it as she spoke, the way someone would punctuate with a finger!"

The two actresses often played practical jokes on each other. Many mornings, Mae helped herself to the numerous flower arrangements frequently awaiting Marlene at the front door of her dressing room. When Marlene arrived, she'd stick her head in Mae's dressing room door and ask who had sent her flowers that morning. Mae smiled and handed over to her the cards that accompanied each bouquet. Whichever woman arrived at the studio first tried to intercept the clothing and costumes delivered to their dressing rooms for approval, or the day's shooting. They'd compare gowns and playfully argue about who was getting the best work from designer Travis Banton.

Although they were good friends at the studio, Marlene and Mae did not socialize in public. They posed together on movie sets to try to squelch stories about feuds, but to little avail. Reporters tried their best to link the two stars in any way they could. At one point, the public was intrigued when syndicated columnist Mollie Merrick posited the notion that Marlene and Mae were considering a trip to Europe together!

Marlene intended to take Maria back to Germany in October, 1932. In September, Rudi cabled his wife.

"YOU SHOULDN'T GO TO GERMANY NOW POLITICAL SITUATION DANGEROUS STOP NEW ELECTIONS HAVE RAISED DANGER OF CIVIL WAR STOP MILLION KISSES PAPI."

She felt as though she was trapped. With kidnapping danger in Hollywood, and a political upheaval in her homeland, there was nowhere to go. She escaped with her daughter for a short visit to New York City. When they returned to California, Marlene moved to a more secure location – the palatial guest house at the William Randolph Hearst estate at 321 Ocean Front Avenue in Santa Monica. Chevalier and von Sternberg took turns spending the night in Maria's room, armed with a gun.

Under pressure to produce more hit films, Marlene and

"All they ask me about is why I wear trousers," Marlene complained. *"How many times do I answer that question?"*

Marlene visits Mae West and director Raoul Walsh on the Paramount set of Mae's film, Klondike Annie, *1935.*

Marlene in Shanghai Express, *1932.*

von Sternberg disagreed over many aspects of their next two productions; *Shanghai Express* and *Blonde Venus*. Making five films together in three years had taken its toll. Their vociferous arguments were the talk at the studio. Upon release, *Blonde Venus* was a flop, but *Shanghai Express* was the highest grossing film of 1932.

Shanghai Express won an Oscar for Best Cinematographer Lee Garmes. The film was nominated for Best Picture and von Sternberg for Best Director, but lost in their respective categories. Not surprisingly, Marlene ranted about her displeasure with the outcome to von Sternberg. "That hoity-toity Academy giving its prizes for what? Like children, they have to reward each other? Don't they know when they're good? Do they have to be given a prize to know it? And over lunch! They actually go to that depressing Cocoanut Grove, with the fake nuts up those cardboard palm trees, and have themselves applauded? Terrible – the vanity of actors!"

In December, 1932, von Sternberg's contract with Paramount expired. He told Marlene that their professional relationship had run its course, and he thought she needed to move on and work with other directors. The onset battles with the actress had taken a toll on him, and his unrequited love for her drove him to despair. He told her he intended to go to Germany to pursue filmmaking opportunities. Her next film, *The Song of Songs*, was in pre-production, and he urged her to accept Rouben Mamoulian as her director. Marlene was infuriated, and felt von Sternberg was abandoning her. But she had to face making her first American film without him.

Marlene photographed by Mercedes de Acosta in Santa Monica.

On top of that pressure, she hated the script of *The Song of Songs*. At her wits end, she informed the studio that she would not make the movie.

Paramount immediately sued her for more than $180,000 – the amount of money the studio claimed had already been spent on acquiring and preparing the film – and suspended her $300,000 salary. In addition, the studio petitioned the court to prevent her from leaving the country. Within days, Rudi, von Sternberg, and her attorney's coaxed her to move forward with the film.

Her affair with de Acosta had become tiresome. Marlene thought de Acosta was obsessive, cloying, and little more than an annoyance. She called Rudi in France to complain about the situation, and he once again provided the voice of reason. But, she bitterly complained, "I must force myself to meet this Mamoulian. They say he is Garbo's boyfriend. Another thing I don't need! With de Acosta and now him – I'm surrounded by Garbo's lovers!"

British actor Brian Aherne made his American film debut as Marlene's leading man in *The Song of Songs*. Handsome, single, and well-mannered, he endeared himself to the actress when he shared his disdain for the script. They began an affair. Marlene deftly juggled a female suitor and a couple of male suitors at the same time. To complicate matters, Rudi and Tami arrived in Hollywood to watch over Maria while Marlene was occupied with the film. They all lived at the actress's rented Santa Monica house. Aherne fell in love with her, and stayed in close contact with her after the film was completed.

When her contract obligations were fulfilled, Marlene intended to return to Germany. Rudi had already returned to Europe. He wired her and warned her not to go to Germany without a new signed American film contract. The document, he reasoned, would prevent any authorities from preventing her return to the United States. She signed a new contract which provided her with script and director approval.

Rudi wired her again from his new home in Paris.

> "SITUATION BERLIN TERRIBLE EVERBODY ADVISES AGAINST YOU GOING STOP MOST BARS AND THEATERS ARE CLOSED STOP CINEMAS IMPOSSIBLE STREET EMPTY ALL JEWS FROM PARAMOUNT BERLIN HAVE BEEN MOVED TO PARIS VIA VIENNA PRAGUE STOP I EXPECT YOU CHERBOURG CABLE WHEN AND HOW MANY ROOMS AND FOR HOW LONG STOP RECEIVED FIVE PACKAGES PHOTOS FANTASTIC MAGNIFICENT I WAIT FOR YOU LONGING KISSES PAPI"

Before she left for France, another legal matter required her attention. Living with the disturbing extortion threat, and the criminal investigation which had eventually lead to organized crime in Chicago, had lingered for more than a year. On November 4, 1932, one of her bodyguards had been stuck by a truck outside her rented Santa Monica house. He was directing traffic to allow her limousine to pull out onto the busy street. In May, 1933, a sheriff made multiple attempts to serve the actress a subpoena to testify at the damages trail for her bodyguard. She skillfully alluded the process server, but eventually voluntarily appeared in court. In a classic example of journalists' impatience with Marlene, on May 4, the *Los Angeles Times* reported, "Displaying the same contempt for time-honored customs of legal procedure which she shows for accepted notions of what the well-dressed woman should wear, Marlene Dietrich of shadowland scorned the proffered paper of a process server at her Santa Monica beach home yesterday, and later swaggered into Superior Judge Sewell's court on her own initiative to testify in behalf of a member of the 'Dietrich Guards.'"

Wearing a blue serge suit, blue hat, and alligator skin shoes, she testified, "My name, it is Marlene Dietrich. I have five guards. Two for night and two for day and one to be with my child." She said she gave her guards their orders, and when asked if she was satisfied with the work of the bodyguard injured in front of her house, she said, "Oh, yes, yes." She left the courthouse as hastily as she entered, and took the train to New York, where she sailed to France.

In June, 1933, Brian Aherne wrote Marlene a letter describing his heartbreak after visiting her, Rudi and Maria in Paris. He wrote that he didn't know what to do. He had developed a respect for Rudi, and didn't want to upset the delicate balance Marlene shared with her husband. Aherne wrote, "There is one fact that stands out above all else. It is very mysterious but absolutely real – I love you. There is just no discussing our thinking further about that." As was her habit, she gave the letter to Rudi to read, and telephoned Aherne. She told him, "I don't know what is wrong with you! Sweetheart, you must be joking! All this soul searching about poor Rudi. He is my husband! What has that to do with it? You can't be that bourgeois!" Any personal relationship with Marlene Dietrich was scripted and directed by Marlene Dietrich. Years later she told her daughter, "He was in love with me! And came to Paris! A big *romantic* coming to see me, and sat frozen through the whole dinner because Papi came with us. He was *so* upset at the husband knowing about us, he rushed right back to London. Typically British!"

Aherne managed to maintain a friendship with the actress. She made a lasting impression upon him. He wrote in his 1969 autobiography, *A Proper Job*, "I saw *The Song of Songs*, which was rubbish but perhaps not quite as bad as I feared, and I cannot remember it with entire regret, because through it I made a lifelong friend who is very dear to me, Marlene Dietrich. Those of us who know her well must always regard her as one of the most extraordinary women of our time. She was and still is a great and glamorous beauty who has created from her own intelligence and cultivation a unique position in the estimation of people everywhere. A curious mixture of sophistication, complication, and simple domestic virtues, she is exceptionally well educated for a woman, well-read in several languages, innately musical, wayward, humorous, autocratic, self-reliant, and fiercely loyal to those whom she admits to her friendship."

Marlene in Song of Songs, *1933.*

Hitler was appointed Chancellor of Germany on January 30, 1933. The Nazi party immediately began to eliminate any political opposition and consolidate its control of the country. Marlene had strong political opinions, but she was careful not to speak out against the Nazi rise in Germany. She was concerned for the safety of her mother, who lived in Berlin. On September 20, 1933, the Associated Press reported that the Film Reichsfachschaft, the controlling film organization in Germany, announced ominous plans to order "pure Aryan" German film stars and film-makers to return to their homeland to participate in the "cultural rebirth" of the nation. Those who failed to return would be disciplined and barred from future German films. The command applied to all Aryan Germans no matter when they left the country. Any actors who appeared in "fugitive films" which depicted the German government in a derogatory manner, the order threatened, would be regarded as "non-Aryans." Marlene had spent three months that summer in Paris, Versailles, Switzerland, Austria, and Hungary. Once Hitler assumed power, and maintained control, she did not return to Germany. When A.P. reporters asked her as she was about to depart on a French ship for New York if the Hitler regime was pressuring her, she said, "I am an actress and never interest myself in politics." She added, "I have a long contract in Hollywood and I shall probably never again make films in Germany."

Immigration issues hounded many Hollywood personalities. Samuel Dickstein was the Democratic Congressional Representative from New York from 1923 until 1945. His family had immigrated to America from Lithuania in 1887, when he was two years old. In 1931, he became Chairman of the Committee on Immigration and Naturalization. He held the powerful position for fourteen years. His studies revealed that there was a substantial number of foreigners legally and illegally entering and living in the United States. By the thousands, people were fleeing the imminent dangers in Europe. Dickstein established immigrant quotas and strict asylum regulations. In 1934, he introduced the "Dickstein Resolution" (H.R. 198) which called for the establishment of a House of Representatives committee to investigate "un-American activities." Under the pretext of investigating perceived political threats in the form of Fascists, Nazis, and Communists illegally working within the country, a series of hearings, inquisitions and persecutions were launched. Hollywood was a prime target. The hundreds of "foreign" actors and movie-makers in Hollywood were suddenly scrutinized, and proposals were made in Congress to deport any and all "foreign" players who were working in the movie business. The long list of targets included Greta Garbo, Charlie Chaplin, Marlene Dietrich, and even Canadian-born Mary Pickford – known as "America's Sweetheart." The action forced many actors to return to their native counties, and others to quickly marry American citizens. However, the biggest box-office stars were afforded legal protections by their home studios. Marlene could remain in American to satisfy any movie contracts, but had to leave the country once her professional responsibilities were fulfilled. The rules further limited her husband's visits to America, as well. When necessary, the studio allowed her the required "down-time" between films to return to Europe to satisfy immigration requirements.

It's interesting to note, that Samuel Dickstein stepped down from office in 1945 to serve as a Justice of the New York Supreme Court. Years later, it was revealed that Dickstein was a Soviet spy while he served in the U.S. Congress. From 1937 until 1940, he was paid by the KGB for secret Congressional information about anti-Communist and pro-Fascist forces in America.

Marlene in The Devil is a Woman, *1935.*

The Devil is a Woman went into production on October 15, 1934. From the start, the production was beleaguered and suffered interference by Ernst Lubitsch, the new production chief at Paramount. After several difficult weeks of filming, von Sternberg granted an unusual interview to entertainment reporters. The headline surprised Hollywood, and caught Marlene completely off-guard.

"SVENGALI & DIETRICH in Final Split! Interviewed on the soundstage at Paramount Studio, director Josef von Sternberg stated that *The Devil is a Woman*, the film he is now shooting, starring Marlene Dietrich, would be his seventh and last picture with the great German beauty."

Within days of the news, the German consul in Los Angeles delivered to Marlene an editorial that had been printed in German newspapers. Dr. Joseph Goebbels, the minister of propaganda of the Third Reich, orchestrated the story. "Applause for

Marlene Dietrich, who has finally dismissed the Jewish director Josef Sternberg who has always cast her as a prostitute or other fallen woman but never in a role which would bring dignity to the great citizen and representative of the Third Reich. Now Marlene should come home to the Fatherland, assume her historic role as a leader of the German film industry and end allowing herself to be the tool of Hollywood's Jews!"

The actress was embarrassed and appalled by the article. Despite her professional disputes with von Sternberg, she had great respect and feelings of loyalty to the man who had made her a star.

After completing *The Devil is a Woman* in January, 1935, Josef von Sternberg was fired from Paramount. After extensive editing, the film – Marlene and the director's seventh together – was released in May 1935. It was a box office failure. Without his guidance, she made a couple of mediocre films including *Desire*, and her first Technicolor feature *The Garden of Allah*, both released in 1936.

Marlene's grandest example of star power occurred after the completion of *Desire* in January 1936. She began work on the film, *I Loved a Soldier*, playing a young servant girl who works at a famous hotel. There she falls in love with a soldier who is a hotel guest – played by Charles Boyer. The production was fraught with problems regarding the script, and arguments between Marlene and the director, Henry Hathaway, about how glamorous her character should be. A few weeks into shooting, the producer, Ernst Lubitsch, suspended production and actually resigned his position at Paramount. *I Loved a Soldier* is the Marlene Dietrich movie than never got made. After a month of finger-pointing, name-calling, and legal threats, Paramount announced that they and Marlene were on amicable terms once again.

The cancellation of *I Loved a Soldier* shook up the Hollywood elite. The entertainment press was both intrigued and angered by Marlene's antics. In June, 1936, days before leaving America to begin work on Alexander Korda's London production of *Knight Without Armor*, the actress granted a rare interview to syndicated columnist Sheilah Graham. The interview took place on the set of *The Garden of Allah* at Paramount.

"Marlene Dietrich dislikes American men, American manners, American methods of education, and Hollywood," Graham wrote. "The likes of the glamorous continental star occupy smaller space. Miss Dietrich likes to get her own way – and usually does."

Marlene seemed to unleash feelings like never before. "The American man does not possess the charm or the attraction of the Europeans," she told the reporter. "I'm not alone in this belief. Anyone who has lived abroad will say the same. Americans are rather crude in the expression of their thoughts. They lack sophistication and have no idea at all how to approach a woman.

"I am sending my daughter Maria to England or Switzerland, because there are no facilities here for learning languages. I do not wish my daughter to forget her native tongue. If I find I cannot bear her absence, I shall arrange to make several pictures with Alexander Korda in order to be near her."

Marlene told Graham she was trying to secure the services of a favored Paramount cameraman for her upcoming film in England. Graham wrote, "The actress' method of getting what she wants is extremely simple."

Marlene said, "When people refuse me something or annoy me, I do not rant, rave and make a scene. I freeze. I walk out of the production or the room. I sometimes wish I could be like the Americans and get really mad when I'm angry. The repression of feeling, the result of my European upbringing, is very bad for the nerves. Yes," she added, "I always get my way in the end."

Graham reported that the cancellation of *I Loved a Soldier* ultimately resulted in Marlene being awarded a new two-picture contract with Paramount and an increased salary. Before Marlene returned to the set, Graham asked her the meaning of glamour and charm, and how they are acquired.

"My own supposed glamour is due to good photography and good movie parts," the actress stated. "Charm consists of good manners, but you have to be born with them. They cannot be acquired."

The public's reaction to Sheila Graham's interview was mixed. Days later, actor John Boles was quoted in Graham's column. "It's unsporting to say the least," he said. "I find it difficult to understand Miss Dietrich's attitude. When she came to this country, an unknown quantity, she had a particularly good reception and was given every opportunity to make the money that has made it possible for her to be independent for the rest of her life." Many fans agreed.

In the later 1930s, Marlene helped create a fund with other Hollywood exiles to assist Jews escape Germany. "All refugees have my deep sympathy," she wrote in her 1984 book, *Marlene Dietrich's ABC*. "To lose one's fatherland by necessity or by choice is a tragedy." In 1937, she donated her salary for the film, *Knight Without Armor*, to the fund to aid refugees. While she was working on the film in London, Nazi party officials and representatives from the Film Reichsfachschaft contacted her with lucrative movie contracts if only she would return to Germany. She refused their overtures.

On March 6, 1937, Marlene appeared in the naturalization department of the Federal court in Los Angeles. She asked to become an American citizen. She filled out the necessary documents and took an oath of allegiance. She would be eligible for citizenship in two years.

Several days later, production began on *Angel*, directed by Ernst Lubitsch (who Mae West called, "son of Lubitsch," to Marlene's delight). The film was completed in three months, and released in early September, 1937. *Angel* was an embarrassing flop.

Marlene was interviewed by Jim Tully on September 16, and revealed that Hitler had offered to rename a Berlin theater after her if she would return permanently to Germany. "Mentally and spiritually, I owe the United States my first allegiance. I want to share its dangers and its joys as a citizen."

On October 6, the latest edition of Julius Streicher's *Der Stürmer*, a pro-Nazi, anti-Semitic weekly tabloid, denounced Marlene as a traitor to her Fatherland because she had applied for American citizenship. "Her association with Hollywood film Jews has made her un-German. She has become a traitor to Germany." The paper included a photograph of the actress taking an oath before a court official they identified as Jewish.

"The German-born film actress Marlene Dietrich," the story continued, "spent so many years among Hollywood's film Jews that she has now become an American citizen. Here we have a picture in which she is swearing an oath at Los Angeles. What the Jewish 'judge' thinks of the formula can be seen from his attitude as he stands in his shirtsleeves. He is taking from Dietrich the oath in which she betrayed her Fatherland."

On May 3, 1938, the Independent Theater Owner's Association printed a list of Hollywood actors they branded as "Box Office Poison." Claiming their films no longer benefited theater owners because their popularity had waned, the list included Greta Garbo, Fred Astaire, Katherine Hepburn, Joan Crawford, Mae West, and Marlene. The studios used the report to negotiate lower salaries, or terminate their contracts. Shortly after the list was released, Paramount bought out the remainder of Marlene's contract. She wouldn't appear onscreen again for two years.

Marlene entertains the troops during WWII.

In 1939, Marlene became an American citizen and formally renounced her German citizenship. She brought her husband and Tami to Los Angeles, and bought Rudi a chicken ranch in the San Fernando Valley. During WWII, she sold millions of dollars of war bonds during an 18-month tour of the United States. In 1944 and 1945, she entertained hundreds of thousands of Allied troops around the world, often placing herself in the line of fire. Perhaps the grief she was unwilling to embrace when her father and stepfather were killed in

```
                    HEADQUARTERS
                    U. S. GROUP C. C.
                        APO 742
                Office of the Deputy Military Governor


                                              8 July 1945


    Dear Miss Dietrich,

             I have your letter of June 28 relative to your desire
    to go into Berlin. While I can fully understand your reasons, at
    the present moment conditions are such that it is not possible to
    comply with your request.

             However, it is possible that at about the end of this
    month, we will be able to arrange the trip. I would appreciate
    it if you would let me know if you will still be here so that
    the necessary arrangements can be made if it does turn out to
    be feasible.

             In the meantime, I would also appreciate it if you
    would send me your mother's address in Berlin as I shall be very
    glad indeed to ascertain for you her condition and to see if we
    can be of assistance.

             I regret the delay in replying to your letter which for
    some reason did not arrive until today.

                                    Sincerely yours,

                                    [signature]

                                    LUCIUS D. CLAY
                                    Lieutenant General, U. S. Army
                                    Deputy Military Governor




    Miss Marlene Dietrich
        U.S.O. Camp Shows, Inc.
            Special Service Division
            APO 887, U.S. Army
```

WWI informed her dedication to the fighting men during the Second World War.

Throughout the war, Marlene's mother remained in Berlin. When the war in Europe ended in 1945, Marlene was reunited with her, and with her sister. Liesel and her husband had operated the local movie theater in Belsen which was frequented by Nazi officials and officers who supervised the Bergen-Belsen concentration camp. Marlene vouched for her sister and brother-in-law to protect them from possible legal action for collaborating with the Nazis. When Liesel's safety seemed assured, Marlene completely disowned her sister and her family, and never saw them again. From that point on, she never mentioned them in the press, and actually claimed to have been an only child.

During the years of her greatest movie successes, she increasingly distanced herself from the press, but never shied away from being photographed in public, perhaps understanding that a picture is worth a thousand words. The public could not get enough of this exotic film star, who projected an intriguing air of sexual fluidity and by her ability to be passive and dominant, and masculine and feminine simultaneously. Movie magazines, aware of their important role in "myth-making," did their best – in concert with the studio publicity department – to provide photos and fodder to the clamoring fans. But the more famous Marlene Dietrich became, the less she revealed about her private life.

Marlene with Irving Berlin.

MARLENE DIETRICH in "THE SCARLET EMPRESS."
A Josef von Sternberg Production
A Paramount Picture

"Will Marlene Top Greta?" by Margaret Reid. *Picture Play,* November, 1930

I suppose you would say, you naïve little thing you, that for a really good rousing article an actress fresh from European conquests would be so much caviar for even the most recalcitrant typewriter. Think of the color, the glamour, the allure of a Marlene Dietrich. All right, *you* think of it. And then for your red-hot story about sex appeal in a foreign accent, make an appointment with some Minnesota lady of the screen. Home-grown stars make better stories, because they don't balk at improving on history here and there. If they don't make good stories *au naturel,* then they make them up. Which may be an offense in the sight of God, but is a help to the poor interviewer.

Now take Marlene Dietrich. (Cries of "With pleasure!") Marlene is a foreign actress, darling of Berlin's musical-comedy stage and recently of Ufa pictures. She was imported, with considerable ceremony, by Paramount as their topper for Metro's Garbo. She is beautiful, magnetic, dashing – with a suggestion of Greta G. in her somnolent eyes and an impression of electric vitality under her composed exterior.

All of which promises copy of a torrid quality. That's what you say. But listen. "They tell me I shouldn't let anyone know I have a baby. They say it isn't romantic. But I don't understand. To me, having a baby is the most romantic thing in the world. Here – see her."

From her bag, she extracted a vanity case in which were set two pictures of a young lady of four, with yellow curls and an amiable smile.

"She is beautiful? Yes?"

Yes, she was beautiful.

Marlene and Maria, photographed by Josef von Sternberg, 1930.

"Then don't blame me," she said anxiously, "for letting people know I have her. She is the most important thing in life to me. How could I not talk about her!"

"They also tell me," she added, "that I must say I am twenty – never more than twenty. But no one would believe that. I am twenty-four, very soon twenty-five. What difference can my baby or my age make to the public, if my work is all right? I don't understand at all."

Was it for this that Paramount discovered Europe? Where are the panoplies of yesterday? We who formed exotic opinions of German stars from Pola Negri of the high-colored temperament and the grand passions are taken aback by the well-mannered Marlene. She is pictorial, but she isn't picturesque. She is no high explosive, no tornado of temperament and wiles and arrogance. She is a charming young woman, obviously well-bred and intelligent.

She didn't even start out to be an actress at all. Marlene's childhood featured no nursery theatricals with pins for admission. The yearnings of her adolescence were of another sort.

From early childhood, the little taffy-haired, violet-eyed Dietrich studied violin. Between the efficiency of German musical training and Marlene's genuine talent it was soon apparent that here was no ordinary prodigy. Herr Dietrich was an army officer, which position entailed frequent trips away from their native Berlin; but no matter where they were, the best music master available was always engaged for Marlene.

At sixteen or so, when her dreams of the concert stage were approaching reality, a disaster blasted them. Marlene was practicing six hours daily. Stronger wrists than hers would have weakened under such a strain. To Marlene's dismay, a muscle in her left hand gave out, temporarily paralyzing the hand, wrist, and forearm. When she recovered, the doctor announced that, with infinite care, she might in a few months give one concert, if numbers were selected that would not tax her strength. But never must she attempt a season of anything so heavy as routine concert repertoire.

To the ambitious Marlene no announcement could have been more devastating. She was not interested in pretty programs of drawing-room caliber. Only such as Bach, Beethoven, Debussy would sound from the strings of *her* violin. And since these were forbidden, her career was finished before it was begun.

Ill, nervous, and utterly desolate, she was sent away to recuperate. Her own existence having lost all direction, she took refuge in reading. For months she lived in books, desperately trying to fill the long hours that had heretofore been spent richly with her violin.

"I was staying in Weimar, the town of Goethe, when I happened on a play in verse by one of our greatest German poets. One passage, 'Love and Death,' was so beautiful that I read it over and over and I found that when I said it aloud the words were so lovely they sounded almost like music. And it suddenly occurred to me that it would be thrilling to say them on the stage, before a great many people. That was when I began to get the idea that perhaps being an actress would be a fair substitute for being a violinist."

Marlene, 1928.

This birth of stage ambitions was unadulterated by the glamour the theater has for children. Marlene had seen no plays in her life – had heard only concerts and the opera.

"When I got back to Berlin, I found out about Max Reinhardt's school of the theater. I took 'Love and Death' to him and asked if I might read it for him. He listened and afterwards was kind enough to encourage me."

So that is how Marlene became the first Dietrich to go on the stage. The feat was accomplished only by the stubbornness of youthful determination in the face of parental disapproval. Her family, horrified that their name should become the property of the theater, forbade Marlene the use of it. This taboo followed their refusal to let her go on the stage at all. The whole thing ended in the gentle Marlene's becoming an actress under her own name, her thwarted family looking on in despair and displeasure.

There followed two years of the usual struggles and discouragements that will occur in the best-regulated careers. Marlene's only comment on this black period, which would furnish other stars with material for several sob stories, is 'It was not easy.'

But after an apprenticeship in small parts, she finally attained to a role in the German production of *Broadway*. From this she went into a musical comedy and Berlin sat up to take notice of a beautiful new songstress.

For the next three years, the Dietrich name appeared alternately on theater programs and on the screen. But by now Marlene's family were beginning to feel a bit proud of her success. Two of Marlene's pictures to be released in America were *I Kiss Your Hand, Madame* and *Three Loves*.

"But I didn't have very much success in pictures," she said. "When films were silent, they thought a girl should be very beautiful on the screen. And my nose was funny and my mouth was too big, and directors always got annoyed because I couldn't open my eyes wide. But after talkies came in, they decided I might do better, because when players talk you don't notice their faces so much."

Be that as it may, it is a pleasure to notice Marlene's face – silent or audible. And as a matter of fact, you can't help noticing

Marlene in The Blue Angel, *1930.*

it. Marlene's particular brand of magnetism, which has nothing to do with sex appeal as demonstrated by our Miss Bow, is inescapably potent. For all her quiet unobtrusiveness, Marlene's presence is acutely felt, even in a crowded room. She is gentle, completely without affectation, and rather shy, yet her superb vitality, both mental and emotional, is the thing about her one remembers most vividly.

Josef von Sternberg, one of Paramount's megaphone aces, saw her on the stage during his recent visit to Berlin. Without so much as a test, or any of the customary preliminaries, he engaged her for the leading role opposite Emil Jannings in *The Blue Angel*, a Ufa picture which von Sternberg filmed during his vacation. Revealed in this as obviously a sensation, Miss Dietrich was signed by Paramount.

She had been in Hollywood three months. How did she like it?

"It is very pretty," she said, in tones she tried to make hearty. "Perhaps I haven't been so happy here because I haven't been working – there's been too much time to think about my little girl and my husband and my family. I am so lonely I think sometimes I just cannot stand it anymore."

"But there are a great many of your compatriots here, Miss Dietrich."

"Yes, but you know you don't like people indiscriminately, just because they are countrymen. Mr. von Sternberg has been awfully kind, but I am so homesick. I go to a few parties, but I like gay people – and here they just drink cocktails and never laugh."

She has a house in Beverly Hills, presided over by her German housekeeper. She prefers living in a house to an apartment, but is nervous, having taken to heart the general trend of our newspapers. Every night she goes through the house, locking and relocking doors and windows, lest some enterprising gangster, with a well-filled revolver, might be lurking about.

Days prior to the commencement of her picture were spent principally in writing long letters home.

"I write to them every day and I wait for the postman to come. Mail is so terribly slow coming all that distance. And now my baby has gone to the seashore for the summer and I'm worried. I write to her nurse and my mother not to forget to watch her so she doesn't get sunburned. She loves the water and the sun, and

Marlene, 1930.

I'm so afraid she'll get burned and be ill."

Marlene's husband is a film director in Berlin and his business prevented his accompanying her to America.

"And I didn't want to bring my baby to a strange country and a strange climate that might not be good for her. But this is terrible.

"I've never been separated from her before, and I'll never do it again. The other day I talked to her on the telephone and she was so excited and so sweet."

Because of her ties in Germany, Marlene would sign with Paramount only for six-month intervals. She planned to return to Berlin for a Max Reinhardt production in October. She was marking off the intervening days on the calendar. After you see *Morocco*, the initial Paramount-Dietrich film, you will be marking off the days until March, when she comes to America again. This time, you will be praying, with her baby so that she will be more content and stay for good, thus providing us with a new star of no little candle power.

Margaret Reid was an actress and entertainment journalist. Her work appeared in American and British movie magazines in the early 1930s.

Marlene in Morocco, *1930*.

"She Threatens Garbo's Throne" by Katherine Albert. *Photoplay*, December, 1930

Marlene, 1930.

When the first close-up of Marlene Dietrich flashed upon the screen at the Hollywood preview of *Morocco*, a woman sitting just in front of me said, "Why – why, it's Greta Garbo!"

A girl a few seats away turned to her companion and said, "Oh, who is that girl? She's so like Garbo, only – only she's prettier."

And thus an entire campaign of publicity fell about the heads of the Paramount staff. For weeks they've been sending memos insisting that their new German find, Marlene Dietrich, never be mentioned in the same breath with Garbo.

Because of the fact that she talked about her baby during her first interview they declared that she should have no more interviews, but when it was pointed out that this was the Garbo policy at another studio they opened up their hearts and allowed members of the press to see her.

Paramount is fearful lest Marlene be killed, professionally, by the Garbo comparison. They have still clearly in mind the sad cases of Mary Miles Minter, "the second Mary Pickford" – Paul Muni, "the second Lon Chaney," and all the various "second Valentinos." Rightly they should be worried. Since, so firmly implanted in the fan heart is Garbo, that even the suggestion that anybody else could be like her means a fight to the finish.

The same woman who had believed, at first glance, that Marlene was Garbo later said, when Dietrich appeared in a white sports coat and a beret pushed back off her forehead, "Oh, she's trying to imitate Garbo!"

How the fans will react, how they will accept this strange and glamorous girl who threatens Garbo's throne, remains to be seen. It depends upon just how much hysteria Garbo has inspired. And that, take it from me, is a lot of hysteria.

There is a story in *Morocco* itself. Directed by the little genius, von Sternberg, it introduces the new technique, for it is a silent picture with incidental dialogue. Scene after scene is playing without a sound. When you've left the theater it is difficult for you to remember that a word has been spoken.

It is Gary Cooper's starring picture – at least that is what the title sheet tells you – yet Dietrich has two reels of footage to Gary's one. Von Sternberg, you see, believes that Dietrich is the new sensation. When he discovered her in Germany he said, "Thank God, you're not like American actresses. You can make more than three faces." He not only gave the picture to Marlene; she took it!

At the risk of having all the Garbo fans bear down upon me in a body, I must say that Dietrich has the same fatal allure as the melancholy Swede, the same deeply vitalized, mysterious quality, the same ability at that utter calm which bespeaks a raging torrent beneath, and yet, oh, I must say it, along with the girl at the preview – she is prettier, fresher, she is, somehow, more attractive. The

Marlene in The Blue Angel, *1930.*

loyal Garbo fans will rail against her. They will hate her because they will be jealous of her and the sure steps she is taking to the Garbo mountain of silence.

What is this strange girl like, really? What does she possess that gives her the quality Garbo has? Whence does she come?

Like Garbo on the screen, with that long face with the shadowed cheeks, that deep, throaty voice, Marlene is almost nothing like her physically in real life. Her face is round, her nose turns up, she smiles!

But emotionally she has much in common with Garbo. If Oscar Wilde is right and "there is no mystery so great as misery" then Marlene Dietrich is mysterious. She is by far the most glamorous and enchanting woman who has come to Hollywood since the white flame from Scandinavia arrived.

Humble she is, as a great astronomer who knows how little all his knowledge avails. She is unhappy as a lyric poet.

During one of the coldest months the *Morocco* company went on location. At the end of one day Marlene had to do a scene in which she walked across the sands. She was to walk a quarter of a mile and a whistle was to tell her that the scene was over. But somebody forgot to blow the whistle. She walked on, for a mile, and then fainted.

They found her and brought her back and when she came to she was crying. The mascara was spoiling her make-up. She opened her eyes. "Oh, I'm so sorry. I have another cloze-up to do."

"It is not a cloze-up," said director von Sternberg, "it is close-up. Say it properly!"

Marlene repeated it. "Close-up."

Von Sternberg will not allow her to use an accent in films. Therefore, she does not memorize her lines until she comes on the set. Then von Sternberg says them for her. She repeats after him and does them exactly. She must remember those lines, in good English, too, translate them mentally into German and do emotional work before the camera. She speaks with a decided accent away from the microphone.

Again, on location, she was doing a scene and her teeth chattered so she could not go on with it. At last she said, "I know that I am nobody. I know I should ask for nothing, but perhaps if I had a warm cup of coffee I could then do my work."

There is no telephone in her dressing room. She has not dared to ask for one.

She wanted to see Joan Crawford, one her screen crushes, and when she discovered that they had the same manicurist she waited for over an hour in the beauty shop one day when Joan had an appointment. Crawford did not arrive and Marlene was broken hearted. Yet when one of Joan's friends suggested that a meeting might be arranged Marlene said, "Oh, no, she would not want to see me. Why should she want to see a German girl who would only gape at her beauty – who would sit speechless with wonder and awe?"

Marlene is miserable in this country – except when she works. When there is no work she sits alone and reads or plays the radio. And thinks about her young husband, a director of German films, and her baby, whom she adores. She carries in her bag two pictures of the child in tiny silver frames. Weekly the mother and little daughter exchange phonograph records of their voices.

Marlene is as lonely as all who seek and do not find. Hollywood is too big for her. Its people are too hearty. Parties, she does not like, since the women – "dey talk of their jewels only. 'See this bracelet?' they say. 'A friend he gave me that. This ring? See, another friend he gave me that!' Dey talk of such things. I would rather be alone and miserable than to talk of such things.

"I try to find with the women here warmth and understanding. I do not. They talk of their bracelets and rings. Perhaps I do not know them well enough."

She would like a little house right on the Paramount lot where she could stay the whole time and not make the trip from Beverly Hills to the studio every day.

She goes to see pictures, not as a person who is connected to them, but as a devout fan. She wonders at the beauty and talent she sees upon the screen.

"The girls here," she says, "they are pleased with themselves. They think only of the good things about themselves. Me – I do not like myself. My nose, it turns up at the end. My shoulders, they are too broad. My mouth, it is too big. I think always how bad I am. I see myself upon the screen. I wish I had not done it so. I am very bad, I think. I ask Mr. von Sternberg if he will take the scene over again. He will not. Von Sternberg he does not – how you say – do retakes."

The sunshine saps her vitality. Scientists call her type "heliophobe." On rainy days or in a deep fog, only, is she happy. "I could not have my baby here with me," she says. "She would not be well with so much sunshine."

She is the only foreign actress who has been brought to Hollywood for English versions, primarily, since the talkies began, but von Sternberg, like another director, with another young actress, saw in that poignant, mobile face some strange and wondrous beauty.

Music was to have been Marlene's life and, while studying to be a violinist, she strained her hand. They said she must not lift a bow for six months. Then she went to Max Reinhardt's school of drama. She recited a little poem she loved and he admitted her. From there she stepped to the stage, playing a leading role in the German version of *Broadway*, and in several musical comedies. She had small roles in pictures. Usually she was a gay, hard-boiled gal.

She married then, and when her baby was born, gave up her career until von Sternberg went to Germany to direct Emil Jannings in *The Blue Angel*. Her heart broke when she knew that she

Marlene in Berlin, 1928.

must leave her baby for six months. She is going back to Europe for the child's birthday and the Christmas holidays.

She is beautiful, with a complexion so perfect that you want to spend the next year in a beauty shop. Her eyes are blue, her hair reddish golden.

I wonder what Garbo thinks, if she has seen this strange woman so emotionally like her, on the screen. I wonder if she fears a rival.

Marlene says, "When I work, when I am busy I do not think. I put on make-up. I see other actors with make-up on. I like to see the faces I know so well on the screen. I stare at people like a rude child for I think them so beautiful. I go on the set. I work, work, work. I love that.

"It is when I am alone that I wish – oh, I wish for my baby, my home, for rain, for good music, for people who – who do not talk about their bracelets and rings."

Katherine Albert (1902-1970) wrote for newspapers and magazines before getting a job in the MGM publicity department. She was assigned to work with Great Garbo, with whom she didn't get along. In 1928, she became a contributing writer and editor at *Photoplay* magazine. She was married to television writer Dale Eunson (1904-2002) and, beginning in the 1950s, often collaborated with him on television scripts for numerous programs including *Climax*, *Wagon Train*, *The Deputy*, *The Rifleman*, *Leave It to Beaver*, *Run for Your Life*, and *Ironside*. She wrote numerous screenplays including *On the Loose* (1951), *The Star* (1952), *Sabre Jet* (1953), and *Gidget Goes to Rome* (1963). The couple had one daughter, actress Joan Evans (1934 -).

"They're New – Hot! Marlene Dietrich Another Garbo?" by Helen Ludlam. Screenland, January, 1931

Marlene Dietrich, shy, sweet, a little frightened, brings a breath of old-world romance to sophisticated Hollywood.

It is not a wise thing to promise too much in advance. But the girl you will see on the screen in *Morocco*, Marlene's first picture in America, will be a very different girl from the one Paramount sees every day. The girl in *Morocco* will be La Dietrich. The girl I am telling you about is just Marlene.

She met me at the studio and we were ushered into what is called the "interview room," a new thing in studios. A room set aside for conferences when occasion demands. We were both a little awed by the stiff formality of this place. She sat huddled in an enormous chair swathed in a luxurious mink coat and wearing a glad little cherry-colored hat. She slipped the coat off as the warmth of the room made it uncomfortable and pulled tight about her shoulders a huge cherry silk scarf. Her face was pale: no make-up on the clear skin. Tendrils of red-gold hair relieved the severe line of her hat. Her beautiful, sensitive mouth was cherry red: so were the tips of her fingers. Hat and scarf and lips and finger tips made up a symphony of color against the somber background of the fur that was quite bewitching.

Marlene Dietrich is the daughter of an army officer. Her parents planned a musical career for her and sent her to a private school where she studied violin and piano. She likes to play the psaltery, a rarely-used instrument these days. She speaks both French and English. Later she trained for the concert stage but an injury to her wrist laid her up for several months and during this time she became interested in the stage. Her parents did not approve, but she had found her vocation and finally persuaded them to her way of thinking. She entered Max Reinhardt's school of drama which began her theatrical career. Her first role was a German version of *Broadway*.

I asked her whether she came to America with Reinhardt a few years ago when he staged his lavish productions at the Century Theater in New York. She laughed. "No, I did not come. I had married by that time and I was very busy having my baby. That took two years of my life, which," she added quickly, "I was very happy to give."

The casual way the modern American business or professional woman disposes of this event amuses Miss Dietrich, "I think it is marvelous," she said smiling. "American women do things so easily – and they turn out just as well. We are much too serious in my country. When I think how careful I was of myself those times I must laugh. I wouldn't be in a room where people were smoking for fear the impure air would harm her. And I ate such nourishing things, such good soup and beer and everything that would make her grow. And after she came I was just as careful. Oh, I grew *that* fat!" she laughed delightedly and stretched her arms out as far as they would go. She never touched wines during that time, only beer, and after two years of abstinence she found she didn't like them, so unlike most foreigners, our so-called prohibition laws were no trial to her.

"I show you her picture," she said, extracting a little silver object from her purse which looked like a compact but opened, revealed two snapshots of a darling baby girl, about four years old.

In spite of the fact that she loves to work in America, Marlene is very homesick for her baby and her own fireside. It was a bitter blow to her when Paramount decided to have her make her second picture immediately. "But then I shall be home for Christmas. Oh, I never could stand being away for Christmas!

"I make records for her. There is a marvelous place here which records the voice almost perfectly. That is the way I write my letters to her and she makes records and sends them to me. The other night I called her on the telephone. She asked me where I was and I told her I was in bed. She wanted to know why and whether I was ill. I told her that I was in bed because it was night. It was noon in Germany and she couldn't understand how it could be night where I was!

"When I left home my family cried and the baby comforted them. 'Why do you cry?' she asked, 'Mama will come back. People who go must always come back.' What a happy philosophy! Happy for me, too, because if she had made a fuss, I never would have left her.

"I was so different. When I first went to school I used to cry so hard the man at the door would telephone my mother at recess and she would come and comfort me. Imagine! Only two blocks away from home and homesick! That is why it is hard for me to make new friends here. It is just my nature. I used to go to school crying and singing a song that started with these words, 'He is happy who forgets all that he cannot change.' Six years old, and I sang that!"

Twice before, Hollywood tried to lure Miss Dietrich and twice she refused. When Paramount, through Josef von Sternberg, offered her a contract, she accepted. She had appeared in a picture in Germany under his direction and opposite Emil Jannings, called *The Blue Angel*. She had confidence in von Sternberg and he had told her so much about the marvelous studios in Hollywood that she was eager to work in them. "Here there is everything to make a fine picture. If I am not good, then better I never try again.

"In silent pictures it was hard for me. My nose was always something the matter with it, or my chin was wrong or my cheek or something!" she laughed. "In talking pictures those things are not as important as they used to be.

"When I am working I am always very happy. I never care how many hours I am in the studio. Everything is interesting to me. It is only when I am not working that I am unhappy. I used to go to parties when I first came out here; everyone was so very kind to me. But at parties, no one seems to be having a really good time. There is much laughter, beautiful women and handsome men, but the laughter doesn't seem to come from the heart. Or maybe it is because I am out of tune; anyhow, I stay home now.

I brought with me my maid from home and in the evening we sit together and turn on the radio and read and I feel like a very old lady. Sometimes on Sundays we have a picnic. Because I cannot bear to stay at home on Sundays. We go to the beach and swim and lie on the sand. But without my family and friends it isn't fun. It makes me miss them more because I want them to enjoy it with me.

"When I come back after Christmas, though, I know I shall be happier. Things out here will be familiar and I won't feel as if I were coming to a strange land. When I am really transplanted I shall make friends, perhaps. I don't do that quickly," she said with her shy look.

Now you may not like La Dietrich when you see her in *Morocco*, but the bets are in her favor out here, and the wise boys have been trained to anticipate what the public will like. She is often compared to Garbo, a fact that upsets her very much. "How can they say so? We are not at all alike. Garbo is a great artist." She doesn't realize that some people think she is one, too.

Garbo is her favorite actress and she has as much hero worship for the Swedish siren as her own fans have for her.

Helen Ludlam (1889-1981) wrote Hollywood star profiles and interviews for movie magazines throughout the 1930s. In later life, she worked as an actress. She appeared in *Annie Hall*, and *Summer Wishes, Winter Dreams*, among others.

"MOTHER, Marlene Dietrich, the Newest Screen Personality, Finds It Isn't Easy to Combine Motherhood and Acting" by Adela Rogers St. Johns.
New Movie, January, 1931

Above all things in motion pictures, I love an *actress*.

I am of the old school and cannot be convinced that the display of an attractive personality is acting.

I do not object to it, of course. It comes within the laws of entertainment. We, as a nation, love personalities, exploit them and respond to them, in politics, business, athletics and the arts.

But I do want them called by their right names. And the presentation of personality, over and over again on the screen, is *not* acting.

I love acting. Love to see it. So, I believe, do the vast majority of people who remain content with personalities because they see so little acting that they forget what it is like.

They are going to see some of it now. Believe me!

Marlene Dietrich is an actress.

In my opinion, she is a very great actress. She is going to knock American audiences right off their seats and have them, as Wilson Mizner would say, gasping in the aisles. As Pola Negri used to say, "Here is great artist." I admit I am all excited. It happened all in one day and without any real warning, because I have long since ceased paying any attention to the ravings of a studio anent a new foreign importation. They arrive by the carload and go back the same way and they are as quickly forgotten.

But the day I saw *Morocco* and met Marlene Dietrich was a great big breath of heaven. Twenty-four hours of real thrills, which I had given up expecting in these colorless, mechanical days of the talkies. Now that I have seen her act, and met her as well, I may confess that it's been hard, woefully hard, trying to be enthusiastic about

Marlene in Morocco, *1930.*

the smooth, bland, too-competent and too-conscious charms of our modern youths and maidens of Talkieland.

I have, even in print, yearned back toward the good old days.

Then – Marlene Dietrich.

I haven't had such a kick since Pola Negri descended upon us like a gorgeous tornado some years ago. Pola shook Hollywood to its foundations.

In the morning I saw *Morocco*, which is Marlene Dietrich's first American talkie. Into my vision moved a woman who left me breathless, who stirred me as no actress on the screen has stirred me since I saw Pola Negri in *Passion* ten years ago.

A woman who showed me on the screen all the phases and emotions of a consuming passion. The little projection room grew tense with it. I felt myself swept along upon its tide toward the inevitable end as the music of Wagner sweeps me.

I had no time to think of the story, to judge whether I liked it or didn't like it, no time to criticize this woman's technique or appearance or personality.

It was as vital as looking upon a storm in the mountains, or a great murder trial. You have nothing to do with it, no opinion of its place in the scheme of things. There it is – life. And there she was, living, suffering, loving. The heart followed her as resistlessly as the eyes. Bad woman – good woman? How can you tell? A human being, handled roughly by Fate. A fiery, lovable, dynamic, mistaken, pitiful, alluring figure. Right or wrong, something *real*. Every breath she drew you drew with her. She made you *believe* that woman.

She lifted Gary Cooper up with her. All his possibilities became actualities.

The Paramount Studio, which regards me as hard-boiled, cynical, critical and cold-blooded because I cannot get excited about the immature and routine flutterings of machine-made stars, decided to give me a special medal when I came forth, white, tear-dimmed, speechless.

"I've just seen an actress," I said.

Five minutes after I met Marlene Dietrich I realized that she was even greater than I thought.

Because it was her acting.

Marlene Dietrich is no more like the elemental, violent, fascinating woman of *Morocco* than the gentle, sensitive Duse was like Camille.

To me, Duse was the greatest actress who ever lived. I have resented, bitterly, openly, and often, the comparison of any living actress to the immortal Eleanora. In a very small whisper, let me say that if time and fate are good to her, this German girl might one day be allowed a very small corner of the Duse mantle.

I was still quivering with exaltation when I met Marlene Dietrich. The rest of this interview with the star of *Morocco* belongs by rights in the magazine of the Parent-Teachers Association.

We talked for an entire afternoon, interrupting each other, laughing, shedding womanish tears, getting all worked up – without a single change of subject.

Marlene in Morocco, *1930.*

We talked about children. Bearing them, having them, loving them.

I never saw anyone so mad about children, so proud of motherhood, so agonized over separation from a child.

"I wish I had twelve of them," she said. "Always, I have liked to think of a long table, with children on both sides, all mine, and me at the top.

"Sometimes I wish I am not an actress. It is difficult. In America you women have babies – poof, like nothing. Norma Shearer has a baby and hardly is it noticed. Me? Oh, while I wait for it I can do nothing else. I hardly dare to breathe. I must not have one thought that can go inside of that baby-which-is-to-come. Then – six months I nurse my baby. In America it is so that one does not nurse the little baby. You give it out of a bottle, eh? Maybe. I could not do that. Oh, how I cried when the doctor says, put the little baby on a bottle. That is a sad moment, is it not?"

I studied her while she talked and was more and more surprised.

There is an unusual simplicity about her whole appearance. Her expression is sincere and her manner gracious and a little shy. Very little make-up, less, indeed, than I have seen on any woman in public in a long time. She wore a gorgeous brown suit trimmed with two baby foxes, but without that air of smartness which makes so many American women look exactly alike. No mannerisms, no tricks. A rather deep voice which is remarkable for its lack of accent, since she arrived from Germany only eight months ago. A big girl, beautifully and strongly built, with long, slim legs, expressive hands.

There she is. You can take her or leave her. Plainly, she hopes you will like her. Her ways are neither conciliatory nor antagonistic. Simple, sincere, natural.

That's what she is. A simple, sincere young German woman, well-bred, well-educated. A sweet mouth, a clear skin, nice blue eyes, and hair that is nearer red than gold. You wouldn't call her beautiful.

"I miss my baby so much," she said, quietly. "I am very lonely here. I wish I did not have to stay. Now, I do not sleep nights anymore because very soon I go back to Berlin and my little girl. You would like to see her picture? They are little ones, but I have not the big ones here at my dressing room. Some time you come to my house in Beverly Hills and I show you lots of the big ones – and when she was a little baby."

From her brown bag she took a small silver case. I opened it and looked at an exquisite, fairy-like little thing, with golden curls floating about a round face.

"On her birthday, December 12, I am back in Germany," she said. "For Christmas I stay there six months. Then – I come back for six months."

"How did you get the courage to come in the first place and why didn't you bring her?" I asked.

She made a quick gesture, hands open, palms up. "I cannot bring her. It is better that I ache with loneliness for her than that she be in a strange place and this too warm climate. I am afraid here she loses the red apples in her cheeks. There – is her father, her grandmothers, her little cousins, her home and her garden. Maria is only – oh, when I get home she will be *five*! She was but a little past four when I left. How quick they go! And I have missed so many days."

Her face fell. But she brightened again.

"In her letters which she tells her papa how to write to me, each time she tells me she is still little. She knows I am afraid she will grow. So she says, 'Mama, darling, I am still little. I am the same. You will see. I do not grow more than I can help!'

"You see it was Maria herself who has made me come to America.

"For a long time they talk and they talk and they talk to me that I should come for pictures. In silent pictures they want me to come, but I say no. Then Mr. Joseph von Sternberg, who directed *Morocco* and is the greatest director in the world, came to Berlin. He had seen me in a musical comedy in Berlin. I was educated for music you know – at Weimer."

I said I had once studied at the conservatory in Leipzig, and she came quickly and took my hand.

"You were there? You know then? I was happy, too. First I am at the pensionart – where one learns to cook and keep house. Then I got to study music.

"So – Mr. von Sternberg cast me with Mr. Jannings for a picture in Germany. Once more they start – talk, talk, talk all day. I shall come to America. I say, 'No, no, certainly not.' I cannot leave my Maria.

"It makes me nervous and unhappy. I love my work. Money – I care for that only that one may live nicely and that Maria may be safe. You know. One night I came home from the studio. All day they talk to me. My husband, even, who is also a director in German pictures, he thinks I should do it. He feels they should not hold me back from the great career they talk about. I am crying.

"Maria – she is only four – comes. 'Mama, cry here,' she says. And I put my head on her little shoulder and cry and cry. When I have stopped and she holds out her little dress and says proudly, 'See, my mama makes it all wet on my shoulder.' Then she looks at me and says, 'They talk to you more about America. One sees that.'

"I said yes. So she goes to the telephone, so little, and she calls up Mr. von Sternberg at his hotel. She likes him very much. She says, 'Is it right that my mama should go to America and will she come back soon?' He told her yes, and said how great things awaited me across the ocean. She comes back and says, 'Mama, you must go to America. I will wait here. You will come back soon and I will be a good girl. Only before you go, you must buy me a little doggie. Then I will think about him and not be so lonesome for you.'

"The day I left everybody cried but Maria. She had her new doggie, a little white Sealyham, so cute. She looks at the nurse, and the servants – who are kind enough to love me – and her papa and grandmamma, all crying. Then she dances to me and says, 'You must all stop crying. What is this? She comes back! Soon she comes back. How proud we shall be, no?'

"If, that last moment, she had said, 'Stay here, mama,' I would have stayed. Oh, yes. No one could have made me go then. So I come, for six months only.

"Now I go back for six months. Maybe I come again. I have said so. Unless Maria asks me to stay. All the time I am here we make phonograph records for each other. At night I do not go out to parties. I am very lonely. I sit and play over and over those little records where my Maria talks to me. She has learned some English words now and she says them in the records.

"When you are a mother everything becomes clearer to you. My mother – she was a very good mother. Very careful. My father, he was an army officer. So, of course, he was killed early in the war. Mother thought she must be everything to us. Always she made me study English, French, music – to make something of myself. Sometimes I grew so angry. Why is that? I felt she – bossed me too much. 'Do not take cold. Come practice your music. Here is your English teacher.' I grew so cross.

"The minute my baby was born I understood all. I loved my mother much more than I had ever loved her before. She wished to come with me. But a mother cannot be spared. My baby – my husband – my sister and her children. All revolves in this world around the mother. Is that not so?

"Then, too, I have two babies, really. My husband, he is very young. Men are younger than women. I have told Maria when I leave always she must sit with her papa while he eats dinner, always she must be at the door to greet him. While I am away, who else has he but his little one? She will do it. No one in the world understands men like she does.

"We are so close. If somebody does wrong or forgets in the house she will say, 'Mama, next time you tell me and I write it down.' She cannot write, but she says that. She knows what to get for me, what I need. No one understands so well. Like an angel.

"This summer they have taken her to the North Sea. When she saw the ocean she runs down and stands by it and holds out her little arms and sings songs to me across the water. She thinks maybe I can hear. Maybe – I can.

"It is not easy to be a mother and an actress. I wish now to have another baby. But that means for me, two years out of my work. Why not? But once you are in the thing, it is like a squirrel cage. So hard to get out. I love my work, too."

I told her what I thought of her work.

"That is kind," she said. "Most of it is Mr. von Sternberg. The actress is part. The director is part. Fifty-fifty, as you say. You must give to him much credit. Without him I could not do it. I know. When I am working it is not so bad.

"I have a house in Beverly Hills. When I first arrive I see all those sweet, lovely little houses. So clean, so pretty. I say, 'I must have one. I must have one.' But never again. A home is not a home alone. I am afraid. I get a little dog, then a great big dog. I have my German maid. But – I am afraid and lonely. I play the radio. I write letters. I listen to my records. But no home is home without a child.

"Next time, I work in New York. Then I can get on the boat after each picture – and be home quickly. That will be alright. Only four days. Then I will be happy. Now – it is nice I am a success. I am grateful if it should be so. But – Maria is my happiness. I go to her."

I think in time Maria will be very proud of her mother.

When she is older she will be glad that she could make her baby sacrifice.

She will be proud to be the daughter of so great an artist as Marlene Dietrich. That's a lot. It's a wonderful thing for a little girl to be proud of a fine mother who is also a great actress.

Adela Rogers St. Johns (1894-1988) was a journalist and novelist. She joined the writing staff of *Photoplay* magazine in 1919, and was known as "The World's Greatest Girl Reporter" in the 1920s and 1930s. She earned a respectable reputation for interviewing and profiling Hollywood's biggest stars for movie magazines and other periodicals. St. Johns was also a screenwriter with nearly two dozen silent films to her credit. Her other screen writing credits include, *What Price Hollywood?* (1932), *A Woman's Man* (1934), *The Great Man's Lady* (1942), *That Brennan Girl* (1946), and *The Girl Who Had Everything* (1953), among others. Her many novels include, *A Free Soul*, *The Single Standard*, *The Root of All Evil*, *Tell No Man*, and *Field of Honor*. Her autobiographical works include *The Honeycomb*, *Some Are Born Great*, and *Love Laughter and Tears: My Hollywood Story*. St Johns was awarded the Presidential Medal of Freedom on April 22, 1970.

"Garbo vs. Dietrich" by Leonard Hall. *Photoplay, February, 1931*

Is that thunder, mother, that is shaking the plaster down into my bean soup?

No, my child, it is the guns!

The battle of Greta Garbo and Marlene Dietrich – one of the most ferocious in the history of the screen – is not raging.

And nobody started it!

Heaven knows Garbo didn't. She's been toiling on the sets and retreating to her guarded castle in the Santa Monica hills. As far as we know, the gorgeous Dietrich, to her, is still an unconfirmed rumor.

Dietrich didn't. She's a jolly German girl, even more beautiful than sin, who was lured to this country, trained and groomed, and pushed before the camera. Paramount didn't fire the first gun – on the contrary, it fought for peace by demanding that their Miss Dietrich and Metro's Miss Garbo never be mentioned in the same ten breaths. Metro, of course, merely sat out in Culver City, smiling the smile of the Sphinx.

Yet the battle that no one started screams and thunders across this fair republic.

There is an old and toothless gag to the effect that it takes two sides to make a fight. This is strictly the old hooey, or, in the original Latin, the *phonus bollonus*.

In the case of any argument, bickering or brannigan in which the name of Greta Garbo appears, only one side is sufficient to make a battle of major proportions. That, of course, is the side of the Garbo maniacs, to whom the Beautiful Swede is only one hop, skip and jump from downright divinity – and sometimes not even that.

The history of the first skirmishes of the Garbo-Dietrich battle is brief and pointed.

Director Josef von Sternberg "discovered" – for the American screen – and brought to this country, the very beautiful German musical comedy and screen actress named Marlene Dietrich. The moment her first pictures appeared in the American press, there was a flurry. She bore a distinct resemblance, from some angles, to the current queen, Greta Garbo. She also resembled, in profile, the late Jeanne Eagles.

The Garbo-maniacs, raving mad in their idolatry, issued from their caves and began growling.

Marlene on the set of Morocco *at Paramount Studios, 1930.*

In due time, Miss Dietrich's first American-made talkie appeared. *Morocco* was a labor of love and justification on the part of Director von Sternberg. With infinite pains he had trained, rehearsed and projected his German find.

No question about it – Miss Dietrich showed definite Garboesque symptoms, at least in the minds of the Garbo fans. The critics remarked on it. The low growls of the Garbo devotees became shrieks, then roars.

The beautiful German girl, new to the madnesses of Hollywood, lonely for her husband and little daughter in the Fatherland, just trying to make good for God, for country, for von Sternberg, and for Marlene, became the focal point of a vocal and epistolary storm that is wrecking bridge games, tea fights, family gatherings and erstwhile happy American homes all over the nation.

A couple of months ago *Photoplay* stepped into the hornet's nest. We printed an informative story about Miss Dietrich. It was entitled "She Threatens Garbo's Throne." It described the Prussian Peacherino, and definitely hinted that a potential rival to the solitary Swede was now on deck – another beauty, bursting with a similar allure, possessing more than a dash of screen mystery, and with a talent both wide and deep.

Bang! Sumter was fired on! The Maine had been sunk! The fatal shot was heard again at Sarajevo! Sheridan was at least thirty miles away! And the author, Katherine Albert, ran for her private cyclone cellar.

The Garbo-maniacs, to whom any mention of an actress in the same wheeze is sheer blasphemy, seized their pens, and clattered their typewriters like so many machine guns.

Hear some shots from the barrage that has fallen on this trembling editorial dugout in the past month.

From Miss M.L.K. of Detroit, Michigan, "The woman to compete with Greta Garbo will not be born! Garbo to us is not a woman – she is a goddess. There will be one Garbo. Down with the imitators! Vive la Garbo!"

From Miss J.D.W. of Chicago, Illinois, "Garbo's subjects are legion. If she ever descends from the throne, that throne, like Valentino's, will remain vacant! Long live the Queen, Miss Greta Garbo!"

A Garbo-maniac situate in Meridian, Mississippi takes her fiery pen in hand, "This Marlene Dietrich may be a good actress, a beautiful woman and all that, but please understand right now that no one can be compared with Greta Garbo. Anything she does is all right with me – and fifty million others. She is the greatest and most wonderful woman of all time!"

You can gather, from this tiny assortment from a great batch, the divine madness that grips the true worshipper of that amazing Swedish girl. Let us turn to the less perturbed section of the populace – the milder spirits whose judgement is settled and whose souls are more serene.

Mr. J.V.K. of Cumberland, Kentucky, pours some oil on the roiled and stormy waters. "How could anyone get mixed up on this Garbo-Dietrich situation? Both Dietrich and Garbo can speak the same language, have the same likes and mysteries. Why not let them alone and let them become friends? Garbo is so much like Marlene Dietrich, and Dietrich so much like Garbo that I am sure they would become fast friends."

A hopeful note is struck by Miss E.B. of Henderson, Texas. "I believe all the Garbo fans will like Miss Dietrich. She isn't trying to take Garbo's throne. She merely wants another one beside it."

And Mr. J.B. of River Forest, Illinois is a little bored with it all. "Why this everlasting bringing-up of the 'new menace to Garbo's throne' idea? But since another 'new menace' has again come up, let's give the new girl a break. I am, of course, also a Garbo fan. But I'm not a narrow-minded maniac. Let there be one God, one Caesar, one Lincoln, one Napoleon, one Mickey Mouse, *one Garbo*. But why not also *one Marlene Dietrich*?"

And Mr. J.B. strikes the keynote! He points the way to peace! Why not one Dietrich, indeed?

After all, can Marlene help it if she looks something like the Queen of Culver City?

Is Hollywood only large enough for one beautiful girl who employs restraint and whose screen personality is alive with the glamor that gives certain actresses of stage and screen their true greatness as public magnets?

I answer my own question. Certainly not.

And may I point out that the tricks, attitudes and methods of la Dietrich are less Garboesque than they are European? Let us, in this moment of armistice, remember that Garbo is the only European trouper to attain great Hollywood eminence since Pola Negri's time, and that's long ago, as *tempus fugits*.

But there's no need of getting deep-dish about this war. We should get the boys and girls out of the trenches by Lincoln's birthday – nay, they should be out now, cooling off their fevered typewriters and turning to the productive arts of peace.

Miss Dietrich's *Morocco* was a hit. The country's fans and critics gave her a nice sendoff. They welcomed her as a distinct personality – a fresh gift to the American screen. Great Caesar's perambulating ghost, isn't the American motion picture big enough to support two foreign ladies who drip personality, even though one is a tweedish Swedish divinity named Garbo?

Marlene in Morocco, 1930.

As soon as Marlene had finished *Morocco*, she was set at *Dishonored* by the ardent von Sternberg, this time with big Vic McLaglen opposite. This done, she set off for Germany to see her little daughter, for whom she had been pining. She left behind her the dawn of a first-rate American reputation, born amid the thunders and alarms of a one-sided war.

God willing, she'll be back – back, I hope, in peace. She's a fine actress, this lush Teuton with the slumberous eyes. We need her. Even the Garbo-maniacs need her, as they'll realize as soon as they cool off and discover that Marlene is no copy-cat trying to steal thrones at night. Garbo is Garbo and Dietrich is Dietrich, and thank Heaven for both. That's the attitude, and that is what will happen.

You are cordially invited to attend a big shenanigan I am promoting for the spring drinking season.

It is to be held at Madison Square Garden in New York City – a banquet seating as many as can be herded in. At one end of the table will be a throne for Greta Garbo – at the other a throne for Marlene Dietrich. Each will be exactly the same size, and contain as many diamonds, rubies, emeralds and sapphires.

A hundred flappers, dressed in white and carrying olive branches and autographed photographs, will attend each monarch. In between will be Mr. and Mrs. John H. Fan and the little Fans. Each will have one eye on Marlene and one on Greta, who will both be smiling, whatever the cost.

Paramount will furnish a band to play at one end of the hall – Metro-Goldwyn-Mayer will hire one to tootle at the other.

At the proper moment, I shall rise with a glass of pop in each hand. Bowing simultaneously to both thrones (a very good trick if I can do it) I shall propose a toast, "The Queens, God bless them!" and will then drink from both tumblers at once. (Another good trick. I learned it in India from a Swami.)

And you all will drink it too – even the wildest of you Garbomaniacs.

Hush now – nobody's trying to steal your baby's throne!

Leonard Hall (1896-1946) was a columnist, lecturer, and author. In 1930, he was named managing editor of *Photoplay* magazine.

"Dietrich's Shadow on Garbo's Path!" by Clifford W. Cheasley. *Screenland*, March, 1931

Marlene, 1931.

Most movie-goers by this time have had the opportunity to view Marlene Dietrich, the subject of *Screenland*'s cover this month, in her two successes, *Morocco*, and *Blue Angel*.

Similarly, we have all had plenty of opportunity to read the opinions of many writers who have coupled the names of Dietrich and Garbo and have attempted to gauge the future destinies of these two outstanding players.

Those more interested in Garbo have taken issue with the newly made Dietrich fans, and so it seems just the right thing to turn to the ancient science of Numbers, which is widely known under the name of Numerology, with the hope that such cold calculating things as numbers, which are bound to hold ideas so much more impersonal than those we are hearing expressed by either side, may reveal just how well founded is this controversy, what real basis there is for making the comparison in the first place, or whether it is just another publicity stunt.

The numbers in the birth names and dates of these personalities will give us the exact truth of the whole matter, telling as they do whether the inherent talents and abilities are of the same or of a different quality than that suggested by the style or portrayal which both Garbo and Dietrich seemed to have been directed to assume.

Since Garbo came to Hollywood she has maintained a style of acting that has remained unique. A style that seemed to have no precedent and unlikely to be duplicated even in part, until Marlene Dietrich came along.

Immediately a comparison was to be expected. Both come from life in Europe and bring with them all that this means in the field of drama, whether portrayed on the screen or the stage.

Just what does this mean? Why, first of all, an entirely different set of life values than they could have received in modern America. Secondly, religion is taught in the grade schools of the countries where they were born and raised, instilling the mental habit of reverence if not any definite religious belief. Thirdly, a kind of discipline in the home was enjoyed, where young folks must take second place to their elders, where correction and often discouragement await the youthful impulse toward careless expression. Thus early expression denied is driven deeply into the nature and in the cases of the really talented is made a hard-rock formation upon which a capacity for portrayal of human emotions reaches to greater heights in maturity. Not hard to create a Garbo or a Dietrich type with such a background, whereas in the new world of America, where the circumstances of birth, child training, education and opportunity are devoted to bringing youthful impulse to the surface, the same creation would be utterly impossible.

In applying the scale of measurement used by Numerology to the name and dates of Greta Garbo and Marlene Dietrich a numerical basis for some comparison is immediately observed when we note that the "Ideality" number in each name is the mysterious, mystic, subjective 7, which always plays such an important part in the temperament of most successful stage and screen people.

This number 7 appearing where it does, enables me to say that both Garbo and Dietrich share an outlook upon life that is aloof, poetic, slightly indifferent to ordinary social values and human interests, but keenly alive to what is deepest in art, in mysticism; to the joys of thought and meditation and of being alone.

The fact that their sense of values is different from most of the people they are thrown with, causes them to be little understood and like all those who have 7 for the "Ideality" number, it is too much trouble for them to explain, for they have learned that the more they attempt to explain their mental positions, the more they are likely to be misunderstood and ridiculed. Seven being a very shrinking and sensitive number causes them for their own peace of mind to protect themselves behind a veil of deeper silence, and outer pleasantness that while it does not mean a thing, at least keeps them out of useless arguments!

Analyzing a little more closely the number 7 which is the "Ideality" number of both the names of Garbo and Dietrich I see, however, that there is a small difference in the value of the individual name numbers which I added together to produce the total of 7. In the case of Greta Garbo, the "Ideality" 7 is arrived at through the addition of 6 and 1, making 7, and in the case of Marlene Dietrich by 11-5, making 16 or 7.

According to Numerology this is where the parallel between these two players would begin to diminish, for at 7 arrived at by 11 and 5 has more fun, ingenuity and resourcefulness hidden in it than a 7 arrived at by a 6 and a 1.

There are basic moods, ideals and likes shared by Garbo and Dietrich, which will give to both their portrayals a common undertone of poise, repression, sensitiveness, refinement and mystery largely derived from inhibited fears of the number 7. But deep in the eyes of Garbo, we shall find a sadness, moodiness, indifference, whereas it will take all the best directing to suppress a hidden twinkle of fun from the eyes of Dietrich, who really gets more satisfaction out of comedy than out of tragedy.

Now let us take our yard stick of numbers and measure and compare the outer general temperaments of these two favorites and see just to what degree the comparison wished upon them by producers and an adoring public is excused in this angle of their personalities.

Greta Garbo, who at birth was given the name of Greta Gustafsson, started in life under a number 3, and, although to her modern public with the name of Greta Garbo, she has had her greatest success under the number 4, it is to the original "Expression" number of 3 that we must refer to explain her personality, her ability to express her talents and to come into a position of prominence.

Marlene Dietrich has had her success under the "Expression" number 9 and a contrasting explanation of these two expressions is of interest to the student of character by numbers and also to the movie-goer who sees in the personality of his favorite the effect of the cause to which the numbers are the key.

Three and 9 are both odd numbers, which bring them into the same class which is that of the artistic, expressive, indicating success and progress in dealing with the public upon a sympathetic, social and artistic basis.

Nine, however, is 3 times 3, but let us not jump to the conclusion that this means that Dietrich is 3 times as good as Garbo in her expression. The real meaning is that the expression of Dietrich under the name she uses is three times as broad; has three phases to Garbo's one. The roles that Dietrich will be able to portray will be of a greater variety than those through which Garbo would find her success.

The number 3 is more distinctive, more distinctly a type, and as such must be limited somewhat to its own class or else its success is quickly affected; whereas, the 9 is more general, capable of the portrayal of human emotions over a much wider sphere. It has the capacity to express the whole gamut of human feeling from refinement to vulgarity, from comedy to tragedy, and in this expression to give the impression really of living and being the character. There is nothing cold about number 9.

The number 3 is a high ideal of its own type. The number 9 is cramped in its expression when it is forced to be limited to any particular style. A 3 personality acts with reserve and gives not over-generously of itself, but a 9 personality can take on almost any personal mood and express all, with about an equal degree of feeling which is often too extravagant. Its tendency is to give of itself too freely and without reserve.

In the consideration of the comparative value of the numbers 3 and 9 we see where the similarity between Garbo and Dietrich is much less in the expression of their talent than in their viewpoints of life and their deeper natures. With much of the same indifference and inner detachment from their circumstances which both of these women possess, Dietrich will be the more able to appeal to a wider public, to touch the heart in a greater variety of ways which the masses will appreciate easily: whereas, Garbo will continue to hold a rather exclusive place upon the screen.

Marlene Dietrich was born on December 27th which indicates that she came into life under a vibration which through the medium of her associations, opportunities and circumstances would tend to force her into artistic life, to train her for public expression, and in her own development to overcome considerable fear, reticence and sensitiveness which as a child she must have shown to a large degree.

All activities not directly concerned with preparing her for a public life but which might have been accepted as a logical part of her environment, would have to give way to the supreme attainment of success in expressing her personality. She trained to be a musician, but as a musician she would have been hiding herself behind the more impersonal art of music, and so conditions arranged themselves in a so-called "accident" and discouragement, to make acting her vocation and music her hobby.

Considering these influences which pointed to her destiny in public success where her personality would be the main feature, together with her deeper impulses which are more creative, individualized and aloof, than co-operative or domestic, any marriage which she would make prior to her middle life, unless it directly advanced her public success, would run the risk of proving unhappy.

During the year 1931 Dietrich will be found giving a good deal of attention to the emotional phases of her life and to gaining her practical and mental freedom from certain unsatisfactory situations which during the past year and a half have occasioned her some worry.

Her immediate public success is affected favorably by the number 8, which commenced in October of 1930 to launch her into the two most successful years of her career. Under these favorable influences which remain through 1931 and most of 1932, we shall see Marlene Dietrich in bigger and better roles.

A Numerological summary of the numbers of Garbo and Dietrich can bring the reader to a conclusion that it will be better all-around if the personality of Dietrich is removed from any false position between the sun of success and Garbo, in which popular fancy may have placed her.

The number 7 which both share as the keynote of their deeper viewpoints would be unlikely to create any personal jealousy, for each has a better understanding of what they really are than is always apparent through the interviews given for publicity. Both having this understanding they are self-sufficient in their opinions of themselves and cannot be bothered by possible competition.

As a shadow on the path of Garbo, the public will never know the capacity of the real Dietrich. Numerology would rate her as an extremely versatile actress who could only be disappointing if cast for any one role.

Clifford W. Cheasley was a world-renowned expert in the field of Numerology. He consulted with "high society" and celebrity clients, and established a successful business, Human Engineering Associates, on Fifth Avenue in New York. He was a columnist, and authored several books about the subject including *What's in Your Name? The Science of Letters and Numbers* (1916), *Numerology* (1926), and *Numerology: It's Practical Application to Life*. Cheasley was a popular figure in Hollywood during the late 1920s and early 1930s.

"Dietrich – *How She Happened*" by Otto Tolischus. *Photoplay*, April, 1931

By the time this article appears Marlene Dietrich will have started back to Hollywood to resume her picture making, but she has left behind considerable amusement here over the frantic efforts of the sages of Hollywood to peg the exquisite, exotic and elusive star, its latest sensation, to one of the few standardized types to which every respectable American movie beauty is supposed to belong.

But apparently Marlene won't stay pegged, for she is not an American girl, but a European woman.

The closest these sages have got to a classification has been to say that she is another Greta Garbo, which is true as far it goes. It goes no further, however, than to say one Chinaman is like another.

True, both are European. True also that both are blonde and Nordic. That increases the resemblance, but there it ends, too.

America still produces the most beautiful girls in creation. They are not only beautiful, but upstanding, self-reliant, free, fearless, and superior to mere man. They glitter and sparkle, with the beauty of rare gems. And that goes for all of them – from sixteen to sixty.

Europe, on the other hand, is still a man's country. The female of the species is still the Submerged Sex. "Americanized" girls are few – and frowned upon. The European woman is, outwardly, at least, not upstanding, nor self-reliant, free or independent. She does not flaunt her superiority to men.

Girls in particular are nothing much in Europe. They are merely incomplete women – chicks who stray at times, but who really belong under the wings of some mother hen. The European man dominates the woman, and the European woman dominates the girl.

But a subtle training has helped to equalize things for the European woman. Unable openly to challenge man's dominance, she is brought up from childhood to gain her ends through man by methods which would be known in America as the "clinging vine" system. It means making man her prime concern. Her weapon is her femininity, her weakness, her strength.

And so, the difference between Marlene Dietrich and American movie stars is the difference between two continents. Not all European women are Marlene Dietrichs, but Marlene Dietrich could only be a European woman.

For Marlene Dietrich is, in a sense, the sublimation of European Femininity, with wish-fulfillment of European girls. "Sex appeal" is the American word for it, but that is only one side of it. Marlene is reputed to have the most beautiful legs in filmdom, but somehow one does not think of Marlene Dietrich as merely a pair of legs.

She is primarily a woman in the comprehensive, all-inclusive sense.

"She is all women in one," an American writer said.

A European would have said that she is wife, mother and sweetheart, all in one, and would have paid her therewith his highest compliment.

Patrician, continental upbringing and a continental background made Marlene Dietrich what she is. Only through them can she be explained.

That soft, seductive beauty which is not "vampish" at all, and is independent of the beauty parlor; the supple figure which, for American standards, is really somewhat overweight; the soft, cultivated voice, her unassertiveness, patience and eagerness to please, so favorably noticed in Hollywood; above all, those eyes that can light up in a saucy smile and then hide behind simmering veils that seem to hold all the mysteries of womanhood – all that is continental, European, and yet unique.

Have you noticed the resemblance between the look in the eyes of Marlene Dietrich in some of her photographs and those of Mona Lisa, Leonardo da Vinci's master painting?

That look, too, is the sublimation of European womanhood.

Translated into American, one might say Marlene Dietrich is the girl with the Mona Lisa look and the beautiful legs.

In an age when in America, too, the flapper and the jazz baby have had their day, when hair and skirts are longer, and Florenz Ziegfeld demands rounder revue girls; when, in a word, a more feminine touch is the fashion, Marlene's overwhelming success seems not unnatural. Rather it may be accepted as significant of the trend of the times.

Not all European stars, of course, have been all gentle femininity. Bohemian upbringing and success may have spoiled them. But Marlene is not spoiled – at least, not yet.

For the theater and the movie studio is merely one side of her life. In private life she is Mrs. Rudi Sieber, the wife of a German movie producer, and the mother of a charming five-year-old daughter, Maria. She loves her beautiful Berlin home where her mother lives, too, and Paramount was able to lure her to Hollywood only on condition that she could return home to husband and child for a prolonged vacation every year.

Her first vacation from her American triumphs brought her home in time for Christmas. All fashionable Berlin was cavorting at winter sports places in Germany and Switzerland. Marlene stayed at home, banished all professional cares, refused all interviews, accepted few invitations and devoted herself to mother, husband, child – and cooking.

"They won't let me photograph myself with my daughter anymore," she explained laughingly when I finally saw her. "They think it's enough if I just mention her. The idea! She's the most wonderful child in the world!"

Just the same, Marlene obeys orders. The photograph of Marlene and her daughter printed here has been obtained from other sources without her knowledge.

But Marlene is not just a German *hausfrau* by any means. She is an accomplished musician, and she loves sport. She likes to speed through the country in an auto, she loves tennis, and she is a good swimmer.

Like many another girl, Marlene came to the stage through the lure of the forbidden.

She was born in Berlin on December 27 – never mind the year – as the daughter of patrician parents. Her father was Major

Dietrich of the German Army. He died before the war. Her mother, nee Felsing, comes from a substantial merchant family of Berlin, and Marlene's uncle, Herr Conrad Felsing, is owner of three fashionable jewelry shops in Berlin's three most fashionable shopping streets.

After the death of her first husband, Marlene's mother married Herr Rittmeister von Losch, member of the German nobility and captain of the Death Head Huzzars of Danzig, whose regimental chief was then the German crown prince. Captain von Losch fell on the battlefield during the war.

Through the peace treaty of Versailles, Danzig was detached from Germany and is now a free city under the supervision of the League of Nations, but within the Polish customs union. This change of Danzig's sovereignty possibly accounts for the reports that Marlene Dietrich is not a German.

But she is a Berlin girl. Marlene says it proudly. Her name, incidentally, is a contraction of the names Maria and Helene.

She passed her childhood under the strict regime and in that sheltered manner which was typical in German patrician and especially officer families before the war – rigid family discipline enforced by the father, careful isolation from too much contamination with the world enforced by the mother, submergence of self in worship of the male members of the family, enforced by her own inherited instinct.

What she remembers most of her childhood is that she seemed to be constantly moving from one garrison to another. Garrisons are usually in small towns. Thus, though born in a metropolis, Marlene really grew up a small-town girl.

She didn't attend theaters. Theaters were still considered wicked. They were strictly taboo for girls.

Of course, this merely roused her curiosity, but declamation of school poems was considered the only proper outlet for her desire at self-expression.

Her Uncle Conrad, however, related that Marlene was always an exceptionally bright girl, and precocious at mimicry.

"Her imitations of people and early attempts to impersonate literary characters used to provide a lot of amusement for the family," he says.

But even the thought of a stage career would have been heresy. What an "accomplished" girl of a "better" family had to know, of course, was music. So Marlene studied at the College for Music in Berlin under the famous Professor Flesch, and was then sent to a girls' finishing school at Weimar.

Here she learned English and French and continued her music studies, becoming an accomplished violin player. Also, she began to come out of the shell of the small town girl and develop into that vital personality that one can now feel smoldering below the outward calm. Now that she is famous, school friends recall that she was the leader in many a school prank.

Her actual turn to the theater was largely accidental. Through too much violin practice she strained her hand and was forbidden to touch a violin for six months. During that time, too, she and her mother moved back to Berlin.

Having nothing else to do, she decided to try out for the stage. Her mother didn't think much of her talent, but she argued that either she had some talent or she didn't, and the best man to tell her that would be Max Reinhardt. So to Reinhardt she went.

He accepted her for his stage school at the "Deutsche Theatre." After six weeks she had her first engagement – in Shakespeare's *Taming of the Shrew*.

The movies were going big in Germany and, of course, the girls filmed as well. That is, they played extra parts when they got a chance. Joe May gave Marlene her first real chance on screen in *Tragedy of Love*.

Then she played on the stage again for Director Barnowsky in *Rubicon*, where she was successful enough to win an engagement at the Prussian State Theater in *Duel on the Lido*.

After that she played for Reinhardt in *It's in the Air*, a musical comedy. This was her first real success. Then she stopped for a year and a half.

"Why?" I asked.

"Oh," she answered, "I had married and I was having a baby, a most wonderful baby, and I didn't have any time for anything else."

She came back to the stage again in *Broadway*, which she played both in Berlin and Vienna. Then she really broke into the movies. That, also, was an accident.

Robert Land had seen her in *It's in the Air*. He gave her a little part in one of his films and liked her work so well that two weeks later her gave her the leading role opposite Harry Liedtke in *I Kiss Your Little Hand, Madame*. That was in 1928. It became her first movie success.

After that she changed off between film and stage. First she played with Fritz Kortner in the movie, *Three Loves*, which ran for six weeks at the Playhouse in New York, as well. Then again on the stage for Reinhardt in Bernard Shaw's *Misalliance* in Berlin. Then Maurice Tourneur gave her the leading role in the film, *The Ship of Lost Souls*, and later she played in George Kaiser's revue, *Two Cravats*. That proved an extraordinary success and got her a Hollywood contract – again by accident.

For Josef von Sternberg had just come to Germany to direct *The Blue Angel*. Emil Jannings' first all-talking picture, which was to be made in both German and English. Originally he had hoped to use either Gloria Swanson or Phyllis Haver for the leading feminine role opposite Jannings, but Miss Swanson refused, and Miss Haver had retired to a happy domestic life as the wife of William Seeman, wealthy executive of Seeman Brothers, big American food corporation.

So he searched for the type he wanted, but with little success. He dropped into the theater where *Two Cravats* was playing, weary after a long day of vain searching and almost at the point of returning to America. He was late and missed part of the first act, but he arrived just in time to hear Marlene cry in English: "Three cheers for the gentleman who has won the grand prize!"

They were the only English words she spoke in the whole show, but they immediately arrested von Sternberg's attention. He saw in her just the actress he wanted and sent his card back stage that night, made an appointment for her to see him the following day at the UFA Studio, and she was signed for the part in *The Blue Angel*.

She scored a pronounced success, and von Sternberg knew he had made a real discovery, but Marlene objects to the impression in some quarters that it was her success in *The Blue Angel* which won her a Hollywood contract.

"I had my contract in my pocket long before that film was finished," she says, "and on the opening night of *The Blue Angel* I left for Hollywood."

Her fame hasn't turned her head. To hear Marlene tell it, it was all just work – and a few lucky accidents. She sincerely believes it and takes her success calmly.

She doesn't even believe that her "type" or her special attractiveness had much to do with it.

She repudiates the "European woman" idea put forth at the beginning of this article.

"Good work will win," she says. "Type? Why, there are many types in Hollywood, and the American girl type is the most successful."

What she says about work she means. Work is part of her life.

She frets at idleness. Also, she doesn't believe that she did it all herself.

"All depends on the director," she says. "It is wonderful to work for a genius like von Sternberg."

She isn't wedded to the movies for good. She admits the talking pictures give one great opportunities, but she still has a love for the stage.

With a director like von Sternberg, she feels she could make a hit on the stage again.

Her family adores her.

Her skeptical mother has long since seen the error of her first view regarding her daughter's talent, but she also takes success calmly.

In fact, she accepts it almost as something due a daughter of hers, and doesn't say much about it.

She busies herself presiding over her daughter's home during the latter's absence, and taking care of her grandfather.

Herr Sieber – he's almost embarrassed at his wife's fame however proud he may be of it. It keeps him busy warding off innumerable requests for interviews, pictures, invitations and other burdens of fame. For Marlene insists on having her vacations to herself and won't be bothered.

She doesn't understand why the world should be so much interested in her. She feels that everything that can be said about her has already been said, and she shies away from interviews when at home.

The fact that she had to submit to interviews almost daily while in America she offers as reason enough why she should want to spend her vacation at home without this torture, especially since she will have to go over it again when she returns to America.

Uncle Conrad is the only one more communicative.

"Of course, the whole family is very, very proud of Marlene and her success," he says.

"But," he adds, musingly, "I wonder whether all that makes people really happy. Marlene is so terribly busy and she is away from her family so much – I wonder!"

But Marlene isn't wondering at all.

Marriage and a career?

Why should they interfere with each other?

"I love both," she says, "and I am going to make a success of both."

Otto D. Tolischus (1890-1967) was a Prussian-Lithuanian-born *New York Times* journalist. He won the 1940 Pulitzer Prize for Correspondence for his writing in Berlin during WWII. He authored several books including, *How Hitler Prepared: On the Propaganda Front, On the Military Front, and on the Economic Front* (1940).

"That Garbo-Dietrich Question!" by Keith Richards. *Screenland*, May, 1931

You'd think that with Marlene safely launched, and Garbo sailing smoothly along, everything would be all right. But no – the Dietrich adorers and the Garbo defenders are still at it. And while they're at it, we might as well join in with the query, "Body or soul?"

If all you fans were as much concerned with the art of these two stars as you say, there wouldn't be any argument at all, for the respective techniques of Garbo and Dietrich are as different as they can be. It's only in their physical resemblance that there is really any basis for comparison. And if you are going into *that* –

Garbo's face is more classic. And colder. There are absolutely no other eyes like hers. They are incomparable. Dietrich's face is more whimsical – and warmer. Her eyes are impish, mocking, rather than cataclysmic. Greta's, in fact, might be the face that launched a thousand ships. Marlene's face changes with her moods. One minute, it's Mona Lisa's; the next, a naughty little girl's. Fascinating. But not the marvelous mask of Garbo.

Then there is the matter of legs. And here Marlene has everything her own way. She can afford to show her gorgeous underpinnings any old time – and does. In *Morocco* she wore some scanty costumes; there was scene after scene to show the symmetry of the Dietrich pins and pedals. In *The Blue Angel*, too, director von Sternberg was evidently bent on proving that his star-discovery can always get a job with Mr Ziegfeld if she tires of the screen. Marlene Dietrich has showgirl contours – if recently acquired; in her earlier German films she was too plump for American taste. Garbo is no Ziegfeld candidate – and here her admirers will probably rise in a body and shout, "She can be anything she wants to be!" And there's some truth in that. If for some reason Greta wanted to be accepted for a Follies she would give an illusion of such beauty

Marlene in Dishonored, *1931.*

of body that she would be as perfect as the conventional Follies girl – and a whole lot more interesting.

Dietrich and Garbo have never met. Dietrich finished *Dishonored* right after *Morocco* and sailed for Germany to visit her family. Those last weeks on the set were hectic, for Marlene was in a continuous anxiety that the picture would not be finished in time for her to get home for her baby's birthday. There was a day for which she was almost prepared to wreck the picture, bust her contract and jeopardize her whole career in order to get back. On this occasion, at least, Marlene knew that woman's place was in the home.

Here it may be mentioned that Marlene's husband is said to have been more successful in Germany than his wife, better known, and receiving a bigger salary. His name is Karl Seibert. Incidentally, Paramount is trying to land a job for Marlene's hubby so that Marlene won't have to be running back to Germany to visit her husband and baby.

In spite of her anxiety about the baby's birthday, Marlene was a merry soul on the set during the filming of *Dishonored*. In one scene she wears a short frock (those legs, eh?) and she came bouncing in like a kid excited over her first party dress. She had any amount of fun with Lew Cody, also in that picture. Lew proving a sympathetic confidant, and soothing factor, when things seemed to be delayed.

When Marlene left Hollywood to return in April, it was a front-page story. When she had arrived in New York a few months before there was not a ripple of excitement. But at the boat when she left, crowds assembled at the pier at midnight, begged autographs, blew kisses, and generally raved.

A German picture of Marlene's that appeared in New York about a year ago created almost no attention. Hollywood does things better. Von Sternberg, the director, saw her in a Berlin musical comedy and captured her for *The Blue Angel* with Emil Jannings, after Jannings had left Hollywood in eclipse, because of the talkies. This *Blue Angel* was shown the same week Paramount's *Morocco* was released, so that she jumped into stardom.

Rumors abound about Dietrich. It is variously claimed that she is really an American-born German girl, just as Emil Jannings was born in Brooklyn; that she lived in San Diego and won a beauty contest there; that she had played numerous extra and atmosphere roles in Hollywood without anyone discovering her before going to Germany; that she originally studied to be a violinist, but hurt her wrist and so drifted to the stage in Germany; that her foreign accent is a clever pose and that if one listens attentively, she will be heard to relapse into good American. But I haven't been able to verify the San Diego beauty contest story, if true. I mention it only to show how Dietrich is continually discussed over Hollywood dinner tables.

While in Hollywood Marlene lives quietly with a cook, a maid, and a Rolls Royce! She is absurdly fond of toys and owns a woolly toy dog on which she lavishes much affection. She loves buying American dolls and toys for the baby. She has a gay sense of humor which is always on tap, even when she's worried. In Hollywood, she has become "Dutchy" to all her friends. She carries a portable phonograph around with her, and she is perfectly piggy about strawberries.

All of which is different from Garbo. Garbo keeps very much to herself, and these days she goes straight from home to the studio, and back again the moment work is finished. She rarely chats on the set and has a perfect horror of strangers. For quite a while now it has been impossible to get Garbo to a party. As for interviews, she still avoids them as though they had the plague.

Still, there is a human side to Garbo. When she first came to Hollywood, she was a constant visitor at the home of Frances Marion, the Fred Thompson castle high on a hill. Then she became just dear Greta, and was simply darling with Frances's children, who adored her. She would scamper around and play with them like a kid. She loved the horses, too, seemed to have a spiritual communion with them, which they understood.

This Greta could sit placidly for hours, admiring a summer sunset, reveling in a summer night, from that gorgeous garden. Frances said she seemed to become a part of nature itself, actually to have spiritual communion with the universe. This was in the days of Frances' widowhood. They don't see so much of each other now.

So the Greta she prefers to show to the world is not necessarily the real Greta. In those realms in which she differs from Marlene Dietrich, she is a very distinct personality, and there is room for both of them. Off the set, Greta is indifferent to her personal appearance, whereas Marlene is smart in appearance always – which somewhat agrees with the American-born theory.

However, her biography at the studio sets forth that she was born in Berlin on December 27th (no year mentioned!), her father having been an army officer who was killed in the war. Her mother still lives in Berlin, and she is an only child. She was educated at private schools, proved good at languages, and later studied violin for the concert stage. The injury to the wrist spoiled that, hence her entry at the Max Reinhardt School of Drama, which soon supplanted concert work ideas. Her very first part was in the German version of *Broadway*. Then came musical comedy and the discovery that her singing voice was unusual. Her first pictures, both released in this country without creating the slightest stir, were *I Kiss Your Hand, Madame* and *Three Lovers*. UFA productions.

Garbo, as we know, is now about 23, going on 24. Dietrich might be about 26 or 27, yet has younger manners in public. Garbo can only be playful in private, Dietrich is naturally playful.

In the meantime, Hollywood won't be quite happy until they have seen these two together. One pictures Garbo being a little formal and polite, and Dietrich magnificently giving Garbo subtle homage. Marlene is like that. She can afford to be.

Keith Richards was a Hollywood publicist and frequent contributor to movie magazines.

"The Perils of Marlene" by Leonard Hall. Photoplay, May, 1931

What's to be done about Marlene Dietrich's legs?

You may reply, "I thought they were all right," or "Just look, and like it!" But that is flippantly begging a very serious question that confronts the motion picture world today.

With *Dishonored* – her third picture – snapping on the screens, Marlene is now definitely set as a hot box-office pet and star of the first magnitude. The same picture poses the problem that we must face if we are men and not mice.

You may and will say that America was made Marlene-conscious and Dietrich-hungry by her beauty, her talent, her colossal press-agenting. I say that her tremendous overnight popularity and appeal was not fatally hurt by the pictures of her that were spread across the United States – pictures showing her wearing a feather boa, a yard of velvet and a slow, cool smile.

Those lovely legs bellowed from billboards, they leaped at the beholder from newspapers and magazines. They spoke more eloquently than the rantings of seven-hundred foaming press agents.

The Twin Perils of Marlene began, with *Morocco*, as a lure and a delight. They smote us in *The Blue Angel* – in which all her costumes together would not furnish decent raiment for four orphaned midgets.

But in *Dishonored*, owing to the mistaken generosity and zeal of the talented Herr Direktor, Josef von Sternberg, they constitute an overdose of sex appeal, a plethora of beauty and a definite menace to the future sound and solid career of the Belle of Berlin.

Let me remind you.

The picture opens with a close-up of two silk-clad legs. No more was necessary. The crowd of devotees in the theater sighed aloud, "It's Dietrich!" Those ineffable, unmatchable understandings,

Marlene with von Sternberg on the set of Dishonored, *1931.*

twinklin' in the rain! We'd have known them in the dead of an African night!

The length and breadth of the picture was dominated, ruled and obsessed by the superb stems of Marlene Dietrich! When she and Victor McLaglen, rival spies, faced each other and life and death were in the balance – the eyes strayed from the pistol-point to the legs of Marlene, carelessly revealed with such exquisite care by a director who knows his selling points.

They were displayed from end to end in *Dishonored*, for any reason or none save their own virtues. They dominated every dramatic scene in which they appeared, and they appeared in them all. They were, in fact, the stars of the piece – and the rest of Marlene and all the huge, hairy McLaglen were forced to divide what slim honors remained – with a bow to von Sternberg.

For a time, I didn't know whether I was looking at a spy drama or a hosiery show.

And who can forget the picture's end?

Dietrich, nonchalant as only a lady spy can be when she knows the rifles are loaded with blanks, faces the firing squad. The fatal drum starts the long roll. The troops draw a bead on that fair, alabaster brow.

Then, as the word of command trembles on the officer's lips, Marlene reaches down, hikes her skirt up to here, and adjusts one silken stocking! The soldiers shudder, but they know their duty! In fact, they, and not the victim, should be blindfolded!

Blooie! A ragged volley rings out, and Marlene is gathered to her fathers. Thank God she died with unwrinkled hosiery – can you imagine her hurled into eternity with one stocking bagging at the ankle!

Not Dietrich! Not if Joe von Sternberg knows it!

Now, I submit that this is all very pleasant. I'd fare rather look at Marlene Dietrich's legs than at the Taj Mahal by moonlight, or even at a fat lady slipping on a banana peel and coming down.

But I further submit that Dr. von Sternberg – discoverer, director and artistic exploiter of the glamorous Potsdam Peacherino – is definitely threatening the artistic advance of this star by overemphasizing those portions of the lady which lie below the Adam's apple.

In short, she is spending the time draping herself on chairs, divans and four-posters that might be devoted to showing us what a great actress she is.

Von Sternberg is to blame. He saw Marlene Dietrich's legs first and gave them to the American gaze, and we are all in his debt for it. But he is now in a fair way to show them off until, in her next picture, we are apt to say, "Oh, yes – there are Dietrich's legs again, and very nice, too! Now, baby, let's see some of that swell acting we hope you can do."

And if we don't see it, we're very apt to gallop down the block to the next tent!

I'm for Dietrich – and Dietrich's legs – till Pike's Peak's a dimple. But, in the name of the American motion picture public, I presume to warn Herr Doktor von Sternberg that, just as pigs are pigs, legs are only legs, be they ever so magnificent. Be they ever, in short, Dietrich's.

I further announce that when I see Marlene Dietrich play a great drama magnificently, dressed from shoulder to toe in a suit of opaque blue union overalls, then will I get up on my seat and howl that I have seen one the greatest dramatic actresses on the screen. As it stands today – this early in the game – we can't see the genius for the legs. The trees for the limbs, that is.

"The Romance of Marlene Dietrich" by Dr. Hans Wollenberg.
The New Movie Magazine, June, 1931

One does not ask any woman – and above all an artist – how old she is. At the utmost one may guess and with Marlene Dietrich one does not go wrong, if one assigns her birthday, which she celebrates on December 27, to the year 1905.

Marlene Dietrich is not her right name; she was born the daughter of a German nobleman and army officer and was baptized as Marlene von Losch. Her mother was not of the nobility, but was a member of a well-known and respected family by the name of Felsing.

In the formerly imperial Germany it was against tradition for a member of a family of nobility to go on the stage; perhaps it was this consideration which decided her, after the War, to drop her parental name and call herself Marlene Dietrich, a name which also belonged to her family.

She lost her father quite early; her mother is still living and has her home in Berlin on the same street as her daughter. They are devoted to each other

Marlene Dietrich grew up in Berlin, where she received a careful education. Besides attending the Auguste Victoria Lyceum (one of the foremost schools for young girls in Berlin), she had many private tutors at home, especially for languages, and thus it happened that she learned to master English and French, as well as her mother tongue. At that time no one guessed what wonderful help this knowledge of languages would be for her career as a star of the talking films. The fact that her only sister, slightly older, is a student of philosophy proves that the von Loschs were strong for culture and education.

It is customary in Germany's best families for the daughters to attend a finishing school (Pensionat) after graduating from the

Lyceum. And so we find Marlene finishing up the study of music at Weimar, the city of Goethe, ancient culture and artistic impressions.

This was her first step toward Art.

Marlene von Losch had natural musical talent. She plays the piano, and besides having her voice trained, she was quite fascinated with the study of the violin. While speaking of her remarkable musical talents, it must be revealed that she can play other instruments beside those mentioned above, and that she derives a special pleasure from playing on the "musical saw," which she manipulates very skillfully.

But in spite of this love of and gift for music, this art was not destined to become her fate and the stepping stone to her fame. For, when she left Weimar and returned to Berlin, she discovered that her strongest ambitions and desires leaned toward the stage.

What was she to do? The greatest shining light in the theater firmament, as everyone knows, is Max Reinhardt. In connection with his various theaters, Mr. Reinhardt also conducts a theater school where young talents are discovered and trained, and are then offered opportunities as actors in his theaters. It is in this school that the brightest careers of the German stage have made their beginnings. No wonder that the dream of every stage aspirant centers in being admitted to Reinhardt's "Theaterschule," a wish that is not easily gratified, as the selection of artists is very strict and the doors of this school open only to those of most extraordinary talent and ability.

One of Reinhardt's most important co-workers, Berthold Held, is the director and a teacher of this school. He himself gave me the following interesting account of Marlene Dietrich's first steps towards the stage.

"It is now eight years since Marlene Dietrich presented herself to me in company of her mother; a young girl, like so many others, with an unquenchable desire to go on the stage," he said. "Of course, this meant a test, for only such pupils are accepted who convince me from the first of their ability. Twice she put in appearances to recite for me; something of literary value which would enable me to judge her existing dramatic talent. The fact that I accepted her as my private pupil is proof of her ability.

"I started the study of famous parts from classical plays with her. I remember well that I studied with her the role of Princess Eboli from Schiller's *Don Carlos*. This private course lasted but a few months; but within that time there occurred an incident which affected her future life. To give her an opportunity to cooperate in a film as a super, I took her to the UFA Studio and thus she made her first acquaintance with the movies, with Klieg lights and camera, if only at a distance, as a small unknown super. But she also made another important acquaintance at the UFA Studio; for I, myself, introduced her to the director and I noticed at once, that in the first second of their meeting there was a mutual interest between them. You might call it love at first sight. The fact is, that one year later this director and manager, Rudolf Sieber, became, and what is more, is still her husband.

"This sympathy helped her career along, for already on the following day she was advanced to an extra, sitting in the first row, with a monocle in her eye, instead of being in the background as a super.

"Incidentally, it is quite interesting to note that on that same day, I took another lady to the UFA Studio, for whom this same day proved to be of no less importance; she became the wife of Ernst Lubitsch later on.

"At that time I had already gotten the impression that Marlene's interest in the film was far greater than that in the stage; her career proved it. The last time I met her was a year and a half ago. It happened before her engagement and big success in *The Blue Angel* at the UFA, under the direction of von Sternberg. Although at that time she could already look back on several film successes, she told me that artistically she felt dissatisfied, had not yet been able to develop in the right direction and was anxious to accomplish something totally different. It was obvious that she was suffering from unsatisfied and strong artistic ambitions. Very shortly they were to find surprising satisfaction." That is the story of Marlene Dietrich's teacher who directed her first dramatic steps.

Now, let us go back to her career. After her studies with Berthold Held there was a pause and then we see her in her first small parts on the stage, but at first-class theaters: at the Deutsches Theater with Reinhardt, in the Kammerspielen, at the "Staats-theater." But she did not remain long in Berlin; she was anxious for bigger parts, for further artistic development. We see her again in Vienna at the Kammerpielen in a role in *Broadway*, then in the *Schule von Uznoch* under Reinhardt.

After a pause of some duration, she returned to Berlin where Viktor Barnowksy, Max Reinhardt's most important rival as a director, engaged her again for *Broadway*. She does not yet belong to the stars, but she is beginning to draw attention as a gifted actress.

And then it happened – her big stage success! The Komodie, one of Reinhardt's famous theaters in Berlin, produces a charming revue in 1928 with the title, *Es Liegt in der Luft (It's in the Air!)*. Marlene Dietrich has one of the principal parts and is triumphantly successful. Suddenly she belongs in the front row of the Berlin theater world. Her charm, her singing and her dancing are big assets and establish her success. Her song hit, "Wenn die Beste Freundin mit der Besten Freundlin" ("When the Best Friend with the Best Friend"), from this revue is still remembered by Berlin theater-goers.

And naturally now she draws the attention of the film world. This is what her first director, Robert Land, has to say about her discovery for the movies, "I saw and heard Marlene Dietrich in 1928 in the revue, *It's in the Air*, and was fascinated. I said to myself at once that this artist was made for the films, and I asked her to call on me to talk things over. She came, but said at once that it was of no use, that she had been in about thirty pictures and had gotten nowhere; that she had never been selected for a principal part and probably was not suited for it. All that talk did not discourage me. I asked her to drink a glass of water to notice her natural motions. My impressions of this confirmed me in this intention to win her over for the talking pictures. Trying to persuade her I said, 'People will say that you resemble Greta Garbo, but do not let that irritate you.' At last I engaged her for a small part in the picture, *Prinzessin Olala*, and her debut encouraged me to select her for the principal female part in my next picture, *Ich Kusse Ihre Hand, Madame (I Kiss Your Hand, Madame)*, opposite Harry Liedtke, one of the most famous German movie stars.

"It was only gradually, after everything went well, and she scored a big hit in *I Kiss Your Hand, Madame*, that she gained her assurance and self-confidence.

"Marlene Dietrich is a dear and grateful person; we are still great friends. She is very charitable and kind hearted. I have known her to befriend poor fellow-actors, who were in need; pick them up from the street to take them home with her, feed them and give them money. Incidents like that which emphasize the kindness of her heart are far from being exceptions."

Other film engagements followed. Her first vamping part was in *Die Frau, Nach Der Man Sich Sehnt (The Woman One Longs For)* and the fact that such a celebrated director as Kurt Bernhardt selected her for the part is direct proof of her ability.

Soon after that she was offered a leading part by Maurice Tourneur, when he produced *Schiffe der Verlorenen Menschen (Ships of Lost Men)* a big production, similar to *Die Insel der Verlorenen Schiffe (The Isle of Lost Ships)*. A picture from it, reproduced in *New Movie*, shows Marlene Dietrich from an altogether different angle.

Then came another small film and while between times she appeared again on the stage, her film career would not progress enough to satisfy her unbelievable ambition. That was the time of her depression, of which her teacher Berthold Held was telling, until in September, 1929, UFA selected her to play the principal part in *The Blue Angel*, opposite the great Emil Jannings. How, after that, Jesse L. Lasky engaged her for Paramount and how her world fame spread, is well known.

Less known, however, than her film career is her private life; her motherhood is not less important to her, perhaps even more so than her career, and her mother love a still stronger feeling that her ambition.

For seven years, Marlene has been happily married to Rudolf Sieber whom she met at the UFA Studio when she was still an obscure super and I think we can safely say that all rumors of divorce intentions are groundless. They have a daughter, now five years old, by the name of Maria, but whom everyone knows by the name of Heidede, a pet name which her mother gave her.

Marlene Dietrich.

Outside of her work, Marlene Dietrich says that her child holds her whole interest. She does not indulge in sports of any kind and has no particular hobbies. Her "one and all" is her Heidede. When the baby arrived, she refused every engagement and every stage activity. There was a pause of about a year and a half between her last engagement in Vienna and the taking up of her stage career- and this interlude was given over wholeheartedly to motherhood. And just as she herself received a careful education through the efforts of her parents, so does she see to it that her own child receives a thorough education, and the child already speaks French and English, as well as German.

Dr. Hans Wollenberg (1893-1952) was a German film jurist and critic. In 1920, he became the editor of the German film magazine, *Lichtbild-Buhne*. He produced several silent films in Germany. In 1938, he fled Hitler's Germany and made his way to Great Britain. He established himself as a film publicist and lecturer, and published the comprehensive, 1948 study, *Fifty Years of German Film.*

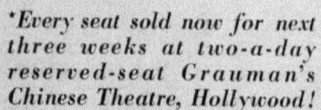

"Will Dietrich Stay in America?" by Dorothy Manners. *Motion Picture,* September, 1931

Something terribly important has happened to you, Marlene Dietrich!

It isn't possible to look at you without seeing it – or to be with you without sensing it.

Something has happened to your spirit. Whatever it was that was holding you in moody bondage a few months ago, when I first talked to you, is loosened. You seem five years younger than that first woman I met. That sullen droop of the shoulders has gone.

And somehow I can't forget that all that separates that homesick, spiritless Marlene of yesterday from this newer, fresher Dietrich is that trip of yours back to the country and people you had longed for!

What happened in Germany, Marlene, that is causing you to reach out your arms to Hollywood as though you realized for the first time what it really holds for you? What happened that makes you switch on that tricky little radio, cleverly concealed in a clock in your dressing room, and tap your feet and sway your body to the tantalizing jazz? Your mouth laughs. And your eyes laugh, now. You even stretched out your arms to the sunshine pouring in at the windows of your elaborate new studio suite and exclaimed, "Dott sunshine – I love it! I used to hate it – but now I love it!" And then you hummed a strain of the hot jazz melody under your breath.

I have always thought you were beautiful, but there is something electric about your beauty now – as though a light had been turned on around you. You looked startling in your red-and-white sports costume from the top of your fine blonde head to the tips of your red-and-white sport sandals. But even more startling was what you are.

I hardly knew you. You see, I remembered you so vividly from that first meeting of ours, sitting dejectedly in that little office in the publicity department – hating Hollywood, and homesick and lonely for Berlin and your baby. You were weary of waiting for your first picture to go into production – weary of uneventful evenings with your ear glued to the radio for lack of better entertainment, but even more weary of having nothing to think about. You smoked innumerable cigarettes and shrugged your shoulders now and then. The only flicker of interest that crossed your face was when you talked of going HOME after the two pictures, *Morocco* and *Dishonored*, were finished. You said, "Berlin! Sometime I am so lonesome for it I can almost *feel* it!"

The ballyhoo that greeted your debut in *Morocco* and the repeat success of *Dishonored* brought you greater fame than I think you had dared to believe possible. America went "Dietrich-dippy." You know that, Marlene. But with all the adulation of this country, I think that deep in your heart you were planning to gather the real fruits of your victory from your own people.

You went back in a blaze of American approval. In two short cinematic jumps you had landed on a pedestal where you were compared to the great Garbo. New York went crazy about you, wined, dined, courted you. The most famous critic of them all called you "the woman America and I are in love with." I think you loved the thrill and excitement of it – but always there was that impatience to be back among your own again, particularly with your little Maria.

What happened at home, Marlene, that makes you so radiantly glad to be back on the soil you had been so eager to leave that you had had a clause inserted in your contract permitting you to return home between every two pictures?

Yesterday you spoke very briefly about that homecoming. "It was very cold in Berlin. The winter was bad – so many wet, dreadful storms. Funny, but I found myself missing this eternal sunshine of Hollywood." There were other things you did not dwell upon. The reports from European papers, for instance, that Dietrich was not the artistic success in *Morocco* and *The Blue Angel* to Europe that she was in America. As one writer put it, "Marlene may have knocked American audiences into a cocked hat with her imitation of the Garbo technique in *Morocco*, but Gary Copper stole all the honors in Marlene's own Berlin."

Too, there were the thinly-veiled snickers concerning your intended reception of Charlie Chaplin when he arrived in Berlin. According to the papers the luscious Dietrich had been pushed aside, shoved out of the picture and generally ignored by the frantic crowds that came to do homage to Chaplin.

If this is true, it must have hurt and puzzled you. Fast-moving America had lifted you upon her broad shoulders. Is it true that Germany turned hers on your fame?

This new excitement and interest of yours must have begun after you gathered up your little girl and sailed back to the country that has adopted you. If Europe had turned an indifferent, though hardly, cold shoulder, New York pranced in reception. Interviews, flowers, theaters, parties in your honor. You told me with a laughing gleam in your eyes, "Sometimes I did not go to bed all night. I lose twelve pounds in *ex*-citement!"

New York! And your name high in electric lights again! New York in hurrahs for Dietrich!

Then the triumphant tour across the country, where at every important stop you were met by newspapermen who rushed your name into more headlines.

Then Hollywood – where you are Queen of a great studio. The excitement of studio plans. The dressing room they proudly escorted you to, especially designed and decorated by Josef Van Sternberg during your absence. The thrill of settling yourself and your baby in a new home in Beverly Hills. No wonder you tell everyone you meet that you are seeing Hollywood through different eyes!

Truthfully, I think the secret of it is that you are delightedly happy to be back where you are important and loved again. As you said, "It is goot to be back! Before, when you talk to me I vas – I *vas* – very unhappy. I am afraid I said many bad things about Hollywood. That it was dull and uninteresting, yes? That was because I was lonely without my baby. I felt strange and lonely with nothing to do.

"I used to stay here at the studio, hoping something would happen. I used to sit in the publicity department, looking at pictures and watching the hands on the clock to see if it was time for lunch, or time to go home. Now, I am so busy it takes me three hours to get out of my house. I fly around like *crazee*. Instead of waiting, I have to hurry very fast to get out of my house and be here on time for things planned for me. This morning it took me three hours to get out of my house, I have so much to do. Before, it would have been three minutes.

"Before, I grieve for my baby. Now I play with her until I am worn out. She is so very happy in this sunshine! She even looks prettier to me than she did in Berlin."

I asked you when you were planning to go back home again. You shrugged. "Six months – a year – I do not know." Nor did you look particularly interested!

You did say that the German people seem to expect you to make a talking picture in your native language. You said that when you do go back, you may stay long enough to make a German picture for a German company.

I asked you, "And will your husband direct it?"

You did not answer right away. You turned that lovely head of yours and looked out the door at the studio gardens. Somehow, for a moment you reminded me of that sullen girl of six months ago. You shrugged your shoulders, deeply. When you finally answered, you said, "My husband? He is in Paris. No, I would not make a picture with my husband in Germany." It was not so much your words, as the way you said it, Marlene, that leads me to believe that the strongest link of yours with Berlin has been severed – now that the baby is here in Hollywood with you.

Your baby, your career, your fame, are all here in Hollywood. And for the first time, I believe that you, too, are here in spirit, as well as body.

Dorothy Manners (1903-1998) began her career as a film extra. She realized she was not cut out to be an actress, and began writing entertainment columns for *The Hollywood Citizen* and the *Los Angeles Times* before becoming a regular contributor to *Motion*

Picture magazine. In 1935, she became the assistant of legendary Hollywood columnist Louella Parsons, and later a long-time columnist for Hearst Corporation publications. During the 1960s, she was a frequent guest on television talk shows.

"She's Not a Parrot" by Ruth Biery. *Photoplay*, October, 1931

Marlene Dietrich is angry. This charming, cultured woman of Europe is burned up in a wholly American, plebian manner.

She is on the verge of saying "to hell with it all" (or the German equivalent) and turning her back on everything over here but making pictures and caring for her baby.

Hollywood can go to; society can choose an equally warm place, and writers – well, there isn't a place hot enough for her to send them.

And it is not because of that unfortunate fuss in the newspapers started by the wife of Josef von Sternberg, the director who has guided her to success in American pictures.

That matter is referred to in Cal York's column in this issue of *Photoplay*.

Hollywood's sympathy, the friendly attitude of the newspapers and the generous reaction of the motion picture public all over the country give her sufficient assurance on that score.

No, it's all because she has been misquoted; deplorably misquoted.

That's the penalty of fame, and Marlene hasn't become inured to that yet.

For example, Ruth Chatterton was kind to the Paramount newcomer. They interchanged daily visits at the studio; became mutual admirers. Marlene thought – so did Ruth – that they were two who might be screen rivals but could be personal cronies.

While Marlene was in Germany, she read disgusting things Ruth was supposed to have said about her. She also read that Ruth refused to speak to her at the opening of *Morocco*!

"I could smile at that. Nobody spoke to me but Mr. Zukor and Mitzi Green. They said it was a good picture."

Fortunately, neither Ruth nor Marlene believes everything that is printed. They are so friendly that Ruth went to a writer and

Josef von Sternberg and Marlene on the set of Dishonored, *1931.*

begged her not to print any more unkind things about Marlene! But word has circled the globe that they are mad-dog about one another.

On the way back to Hollywood, Marlene was asked if she would like to make a picture with Ernst Lubitsch. She said she did not know enough to leave the tutelage of her master – Josef von Sternberg. The story was printed that Miss Dietrich did not wish to make a picture with Lubitsch because he could not speak good English.

Marlene sent messages galore to her countryman, explaining she had been misquoted.

He understood, but she could not send messages throughout the world to insure the same understanding.

And the day after her return – with the fires of anger already sizzling – she picked up a magazine (not *Photoplay*, decidedly not *Photoplay*) and read she was a "parrot." Von Sternberg "puts words into her mouth." She repeated them. "*A red-headed parrot*," said the article!

Whoops, Agnes! She's red-headed all right, but she's not a parrot. Although a parrot might have used equally expressive language, it could never have expressed the same depth of feeling. Never!

The next interviewer who saw Marlene, walked out. "I walked out on *her*," he said. Don't let a reporter's pride mislead you. Marlene staged the exit. She acted so dumb she didn't even pull a parrot-line on him.

And the next scribbler said, "Well, if you can get *anything* out of *her*…" Clam is an old simile, but it explains perfectly the silence of Dietrich.

Enter – this writer. I thought I had an advantage. I already knew Marlene. But I didn't know *this* Marlene. When von Sternberg came in, for example, she said, "Your parrot will now put on her hat," and did a fade-out, leaving the director to carry on the battle.

Friends have told her she should not pay so much attention to misquotes. "I suppose I should laugh!" she shrugged. "Then what is the use of giving interviews at all – if I pay them no attention. I wish I could do my work, and say nothing."

But that means she is copy-catting Garbo. And she's as anxious to live that down as she is to be quoted correctly.

It's really a serious problem to Marlene. Doubly serious now because she returned to Hollywood determined to be happy. This time she had intended to enjoy Hollywood – not hate it as she did during her first eight months of American pictures.

"Why, the whole time I was here before, that same tree stood outside my dressing room door and I never saw it. But now – I am able to see what is around me. I love it. I want to be happy here. And I thought I could. *I have my baby!*"

It is true – Marlene was ready to sacrifice everything *before* because her five-year-old daughter, Maria, was in Europe. She is so devoted to the child that I do not think it is a stretch of imagination to say she has a mother complex which would interest our most astute psychoanalysts.

To prove it, she had just secured a foothold on the German stage when she discovered she was to have a baby. She retired for two years. The first year was necessary; the second wasn't. She nursed the baby for an entire year. The doctors warned her it might spoil her figure.

"Let it. I must nurse my baby as long as I can," was her answer.

She wanted to stay home continuously to care for the baby. But some force within her pushed her relentlessly on.

But she had tasted stage life and she could not – once the baby no longer needed her for actual sustenance – forget it.

It was hard to get back. Marlene has had remarkably few struggles in life, but this return to the footlights was not easy. Max Reinhardt finally turned the trick for her. Musical comedy in which Herr Josef saw her. Then America *without* her baby.

Ah, one would have to be a mother like Marlene to comprehend those eight months of torture. The two little lost teeth of the child were sent to her; she slept on them. They talked long distance, they babbled daily. And still the nausea of discontent continued.

"And when you arrived home?"

Marlene's face lit as though an electric light had been snapped on within her; her eyes glowed with excitement.

"When I got home at last, I found my home exactly as I had left it. Nothing was different. That is because I was not different. Eight months over here has not changed Marlene Dietrich."

And that really is the amazing part of this woman. Hollywood usually touches its newcomers with a sure hand. Sometimes it paints with bold strokes; sometimes with deft subtleness. But it has always left some mark upon its captives.

"Divorce?" Her eyes widened. "People say I will get a divorce? But that is as funny as to say I would leave my baby. My baby and husband are altogether. They are one with the other.

"Of course, it is more expensive this way. It costs me much money. My contract must be for six months in this country and six months in Europe. It is natural they do not want to pay me. But is the best we can do."

To understand Marlene, you would have to know the psychology of European women. She is a true daughter of German routine and German traditions. While she was home she lost twelve pounds.

"When I am happy I always lose weight. I go so much. I dance every night; I see all the excitement. Here I live in a house very quietly – I already start to gain. It is strange," the lights in her eyes change to shadows, "but when I become just a little unhappy I gain weight."

Josef von Sternberg is amazingly frank in his interest. "I think I will get sick on this next picture (which will probably be a German one made from a story Marlene brought back from the homeland) and stay away two weeks and let her direct it," he says. "She almost directed *Morocco* and *Dishonored*. No, I mean it.

"The entire stage scene in *Morocco* was her idea. The songs were hers and it was the best scene in the picture.

"A parrot!" He laughed. "I am going to make very few more pictures. I am going to retire. Yes, you can print it. I have few more stories left in me and I am ready to take a long rest. I shall recommend that Marlene direct, then.

"She spent hours every day in Europe hunting for stories, not only for herself but for Paramount to produce with other players. The only thing I put in her mouth is good English."

And Marlene is so afraid of von Sternberg's harsh criticism on her pronunciation of English that she tries to get away with firing German at him.

For no matter how she improves in English pronunciation, he is never satisfied. He criticizes her in loud tones – until she shivers, but doubles her efforts at perfection.

The result – you would scarcely know today that she is foreign – except from her psychology; most certainly not from her diction.

Ruth Biery was a newspaper writer before becoming a Hollywood columnist and regular contributor to *Photoplay* and *The Modern Screen Magazine*. Her multi-part biographical profiles of Mae West, Jean Harlow, Carole Lombard, and Greta Garbo established her as a respected show business journalist, and a writer who was not afraid of controversy.

"The Extra-Private *Life of* Marlene Dietrich" by Leonard (Old Snoop) Hall. *Photoplay,* November, 1931

Marlene Dietrich is essentially a "home girl." The famous German star, shy and retiring in company, which she seldom is in, said today, "I am happiest among my kiddie. Also among my hubby and my book. I am also extremely happy among my sauce pan. *Ach,* you should taste my *pfann-kuchen und kartoffel-salat.* Also, my *strudel.* I am very, very happy among my strudel. And I like to be alone!"

As one of the leading sneakers of Hollywood, known to the police as "Key-Hole" Hall, I went on the prowl. Today I can present to you, for the first time anywhere, a verbatim account of twenty-four typical hours in the life of Marlene "Legs" Dietrich. (Not to be confused with "Legs" Diamond.)

The Dietrich Day (and every day is Dietrich day with me!) –

8 A.M. – Marlene is awakened by three photographers, under the bed, quarreling over who shall get the first snapshot of the star putting on her mules. Bathes, her small daughter washing her back and her husband handing her the so-and-so's while she dresses. Breakfasts, discovering a cameraman disguised as a grapefruit and another as a sliver of burned toast. Expresses pleasure when told that a cameraman has fallen down the chimney during the night.

8:30 A.M. – What is known as "Dietrich's Quiet Hour." On the lawn before the house massed military bands play "*Deutschland Uber Alles* Except Hollywood," Miss Marlene playing the bass drum with her knee-caps. Other numbers are "I Used to Love Louisa 'til Marlay-nah Came Along" and "If You Snap My Garters, I'll Snap You on the Nose." Dietrich then boards three Rolls-Royces and pushes off for the studio. She would be unaccompanied if it were not for twenty motor-cycle cops and ten cameramen on trucks. The star obligingly stands on her head, puts her feet on the windshield and juggles four Jonathan apples.

9 A.M. – Slightly burned about the face by a premature explosion of flashlight powder. "Poof! Idd iss nudding!" she tells the press. "Only my face!"

9:30 A.M. – Delivers a ten-minute address to a delegation of rotogravure section editors on "Your Knees Know."

10 A.M. – Radio speech over a network of 150 stations, from the studio. "I luff my husband and my leedle girl," Miss Dietrich says in part. *Herr* von Sternberg – *ach*, he is a genius! Such a great director! I luff my husband and am happiest among my schnitzel. I want to make great pictures for the American people. I luff the American people, and my husband and my leedle girl!"

10:30 A.M. – On the set. Mr. von Sternberg is directing her in "Below the Equator." Her costume is an old peach basket. "Now, Miss Dietrich," he calls softly, "the left ankle, please!" Now the right knee-cap. Quiver it gently! Give me anger with the left knee, Miss Dietrich!" Several susceptible young prop boys faint dead away.

12 Noon – Luncheon as guest of honor of the Dairymen's Association, Miss Dietrich speaks on "Better Calves."

1 P.M. – Back on the set. Miss Dietrich is now wearing a cherry colored sunbonnet with coral piping and an insert of turkey-red fichu. The scene is a night club in Panama City. Marlene is playing twenty-four Albertina Rasch dancing girls, thus showing no less than forty-eight perfect Dietrich legs at one and the same time, thus breaking the record held for forty years by a New York City octopus. "I can't stand it," screams an assistant director. Cinematographer Lee Garmes has sixty-six cameras focused on the set, some of them shooting through lace, cellophane, cob-webs and an old pair of overalls he found somewhere. "Umph!" said Director von Sternberg. "A great day!" He dismisses the troupe by firing a field-gun and running up the von Sternberg house-flag.

2:30 P.M. – Retakes of scenes showing Miss Dietrich's brow, ears, neck, elbows and torso. These were taken by error and an assistant director while Director von Sternberg was out seeing a lady about an Airedale. Scenes are substituted displaying Miss

Dietrich's knees, thighs, ankles, arches (far from fallen), great toes, and shin-bones. "Looks like a great audience picture!" murmurs the crowd, now numbering 7,000.

3 P.M. – Miss Dietrich poses for still photographs at the studio. Among the poses shot is one with Miss Dietrich with an arm around her little girl, while her little girl has her arm around her daddy and her daddy has an arm around Mr. von Sternberg's throat.

Other poses: Director von Sternberg holding Marlene with one hand and her husband with the other, while the little girl rides a high bicycle.

Miss Dietrich standing on her head holding von Sternberg on one foot and her husband on the other, while the little girl waves the German and American flags.

Director von Sternberg playing a bassoon, Marlene a left handed oboe, her husband a swinette and the little girl a kazoo.

All four singing "Down by the Old Mill Stream."

4 P.M. – Miss Dietrich receives a deputation from the American Association for the Prevention of Bare-Legged Women. "I promise to wear sheer opera-length hosiery whenever the part permits," says Miss Dietrich. Thanksgiving by the chaplain, and grand display of fireworks on the lawn.

5 P.M. – Miss Dietrich, wearing shorts, plays nine holes of golf. She is alone save for six caddies, her husband, her little girl, Mr. B. P. Schulberg, fourteen cameramen (seven movie and seven still) and the Fourth Infantry, California National Guard. She takes ninety-nine.

6 P.M. – A half-hour nap. Flashlight Drill by Photographer's Union on the lawn.

6:30 P.M. – Marlene dresses for dinner, or *abendessen*. She chooses, for the occasion, a tulle butterfly net trimmed with mauve cellophane, hip length, with insertions of sheer plate glass. "Let's eat!" she says, and the Grand March to the eating-room forms and sets out.

7 P.M. – Dinner, served by cameramen and reformers disguised as butlers and busboys. A plate is served and exposed with each course. Seventy-four guests, including officials of film and cam-

era companies, newspaper and magazine publishers, her husband and her little girl. Miss Dietrich responds to the toast – "Down with Long Skirts, A Menace to the Health of American Women." (Cheers and flashlights.)

9 P.M. – Private film showing in drawing room. Preview of new D. W. Griffith epic, "Legs Through the Ages."

10 P.M. – Bed. Platoon of police drive cameramen from bedroom, house, grounds and county, at pistol point. "I luff to be alone," murmurs Marlene, as the Sandman approaches at the end of another quiet, sheltered day.

"Dietrich's New Escort Says He's 'Just A Friend'" by Carol Benton. Movie Classics, December, 1931

Hollywood used to recite a little nursery rhyme that ran, "Everywhere that Dietrich goes, von Sternberg's sure to go." The reference was to the sensational Marlene and her shaggy-haired director, seldom seen in public without one another. Now they have been joined by a third – Marlene's former leading man in Germany, a good-looking young chap named Hans von Twardowski. And Hollywood has begun to chant only the end of the nursery rhyme – "von Sternberg's sure to *go*."

The newest "von" in Marlene's life didn't come to Hollywood to woo fame as the Dietrich escort, but to act in American movies. You'll probably have your first glimpse of him in *Grand Hotel*. In that projected production, MGM hopes to outdo itself, overcome some temperamental differences, and give you not only two, but four stars in one picture. Imagine – if you can – the mysterious Garbo, the flaming Crawford, the romantic Gilbert, and the virile Gable all on the screen at the same time! And for good measure, as the fifth principal character in the Vicki Baum story – the doomed invalid "Doctor Otto" – the big, blond and handsome newcomer named Hans von Twardowski. There's a lot of talent for you!

Before Marlene was "discovered" by Josef von Sternberg in Berlin, she and von Twardowski had played together on the stage and in several motion pictures – one of which, translated, means, "I Kiss Your Hand, Madame."

"She was not an unknown as people here seem to think," explains Hans in his careful English. "Already she was quite famous. Much more famous than was Garbo in Europe. Dietrich was the star in the revue in which Mr. von Sternberg saw her the first time."

Twardowski has been in Hollywood since December, having been imported to play in foreign versions. But he has been studying

Marlene with Hans von Twardowski.

English, with the result that he now has a year's contract with MGM and the prospect of being in the amazing cast of *Grand Hotel*. Surprisingly enough, he gives the credit for his progress to none other than Josef von Sternberg.

"Mr. von Sternberg has help me so much," he says. "I don't know how I should have learn to speak the English without him. With Marlene, too, he works always to make her speak without the accent. Now she talks English so well people say, 'Pooh, she is not a German.' But she learned English when a child from a British nurse. When I came to America, I could only say 'yes' and 'no.'"

Hollywood rumor has it that Marlene's studio looks approvingly at her new escort, particularly since Mrs. Rizza von Sternberg, estranged wife of their brilliant director, has brought suit against Marlene for alienation of affections – a suit that the star is fighting bitterly. However, the suit has seemed to make little difference to either Marlene or her director – for von Sternbeg usually makes a threesome when she and von Twardowski are seen together. Von Twardowski laughs at the hint of romance either between himself and Marlene, or between Marlene and von Sternberg.

"We are friends," he declares. "In Berlin, I am often visitor at the home of herself and her director-husband, Rudolf Sieber, who is also my friend. Anyone who knows the Sieber's at home knows how foolish is any talk that they are not happy together. When he came to visit her this summer, we were four good friends together – von Sternberg, Rudolf, Marlene and I. Among ourselves we laugh at the lawsuit Mrs. von Sternberg brings.

"This lawsuit, it is unkind. When Mr. von Sternberg made *The Blue Angel*, every actress wanted to play the heroine. In this country, it was just a picture; but in Germany it was the rage. There were streets named "Blue Angel," and restaurants. Women wore "Blue Angel" hats. It was natural that Mrs. von Sternberg, who was an actress, should want to play the heroine herself, *nicht?* But there is nothing – nothing at all – to this gossip of romance between Marlene and von Sternberg. I am welcome at her home here; I should know.

"Marlene is lonesome for her husband. She has no friends in this country. She never goes to parties. In Germany, also, she lives very quietly. Few people know her. But sometimes she must go out, *nicht?* So her director, the only one she knows, goes with her. And now I – an old friend of her own country – take her to picture openings."

Marlene will go abroad for Christmas, just to see her husband, Hans von Twardowski explains. Also, perhaps, she will leave her little girl in Germany, for Maria is now nearly old enough to go to school and Marlene wants her to grow up in German ways. Upon Marlene's return, Hollywood whispers, there might be a part for Hans in a Dietrich picture.

He was in the first great German picture – *The Cabinet of Dr. Caligari*. He wants still to play complex, mysterious characters – "men with secrets, strange men" – rather than simple American heroes. He likes Hollywood so well that if *Grand Hotel* shows that he has a real future here, he will become an American citizen.

[Editor's note: Hans von Twardowski (1898-1958) began his film career in German silent films. He was homosexual and permanently fled Germany for fear of his life in 1933 when the Nazi party took control of the country. He made more than 50 films in America.]

Carol Benton was a Hollywood reporter.

"The Girl with the Garters" by Lynde Denig. *Screenland,* December, 1931

Manager of the Gem Theater
Marlene Dietrich?
Sure, I remember, that German girl with the garters.
She's a good-looker, all right; but my crowd doesn't go in heavy for these dames from Europe.
Hey, Sam! They're giving us a Marlene Dietrich for Thanksgiving week.
You know, the girl with garters.
We got to think up something good to get the crowd coming.
Marlene's a hot number, sure enough; but I'm scared of the women and the kids.
Remember *The Blue Angel*, Sam, and the lace trimmings?
And how the old professor wanted to snap those garters!
Oh, here's a break!
It's a circus film: Circus stuff for the entire family.
Wait a minute, Sam. Just a minute.
I'm getting an idea. It's the big idea for your advertising.
It's big enough to cover the whole town: Men, women, children.
I've got it; all in one line.
Listen, Sam! "The Girl With the Garters in a Sweet Story of Circus Life."

Proprietor of Lingerie Shopp
Let me see the paper, Myrtle.
Humph! Don't think much of the looks of that ad.
Under Finkelsteins's, too.
Finkelstein is cutting hosiery prices.
Listen to this, Myrtle,
"Ladies' hose. Finest Quality. All shades. Formerly $2.50. Now $1.49."

The old shyster.
We got to get back at him somehow.
How about them green beach pajamas?
We'll call them Winter Greens.
Guess they'll do to sleep in.
Wow! What's this?
"Marlene Dietrich, the Girl With the Garters, Coming to the Gem."
Garters? Who said garters?
We've got a couple of crates of garters in the cellar, right now –
Pink, blue, red, orange, purple;
A garter for every leg,
"You can't look right without a garter."
"When you see Marlene Dietrich at the Gem,
Be sure of your garters."
We'll fill the window with garters!
We'll get Sam to give us a show-case in the theater lobby.
Let old Finkelstein peddle his stocking.
It's garters for us, Myrtle!
Garters for us!

Amusement Editor of the Blade
Sam promised me an autographed picture of Marlene Dietrich.
But he never came through.
That's the way with those publicity guys.
You give them the works,
And then they forget.
This time, I'd do a little forgetting myself,
Except I'm nuts about that German girl.
I don't like calling her
The Girl With the Garters, either.
She's too good for that.
She's too good for this dumb town, anyway.
Those eyes – those legs – that voice!
She sets me going, all right.
Just to look at her, sets me going.
And can she sing?

"I'm Falling in Love Again."
I'd fall in love with her. Would I?
What a chance? What a chance!
Wonder if she ever saw that piece I wrote about her.
Sam said he'd see that she got a copy of *The Blade*.
But you can't count on Sam.
Some day I'm going to Hollywood.
I'll forget all about this bum town.
I'll see her myself.
She'll talk to me and listen when I tell her the story I've written for her.
I'll tell her to can that "Girl With the Garters" stuff.
She's "The Girl with Everything!"

President of the Women's Club

The next subject for your consideration, ladies, is the report of Mrs. Doolittle, chairman of your literary and dramatic committee. It deals with the request of Mr. Solomon, manager of the Gem theater, that we place "Four Rings," starring Marlene Dietrich, on our Pink List.

As you will recall, Miss Dietrich is a German actress who appeared here in "Blue Devil" and "Algeria." I am not quite certain of the titles, but you know what I mean. There was some question about the propriety of Miss Dietrich's costume in "The Blue Swan."

Mrs. Doolittle reports the outcome of several conferences with Samuel Mayer, director of public relations for Mr. Solomon. She has the personal assurance of Mr. Mayer that the costumes in "Four Rings" are modest. Mr. Mayer even goes so far as to offer his written guarantee. Furthermore, it has been found on investigation that Miss. Dietrich is happily married and the mother of a seven-year-old daughter.

In reference to the line, "The Girl With the Garters," Mr. Mayer said that its appeal is on the side of modesty and in opposition to bare-kneed, stockingless fashions. Rather humorously, he referred to members of this club as being habitual wearers of garters.

It is the recommendation of Mrs. Doolittle that in view of these findings we place "Four Rings" on our Pink List. Will all in favor kindly raise their hands?

Thank you, ladies.

Town Beauty on Her Thirty-First Birthday
Sam had a nerve last night,
Telling me that it wouldn't hurt to take a few pointers from that
    German actress.
He's just sore because I turned him down.
He ought to get wise to himself.
Hanging around a theater don't make him a licensed lover.
He kept hinting that my looks won't last forever.
As if I didn't know it.
Personality – personality – personality!
Whoever taught him personality?
I'm sick of the word.
"The Girl With the Garters has personality," he says.
"She's got poise," says Sam.
"Every girl over thirty is going to lose out unless she gets
Personality and poise.
"Watch her eyes," says Sam.
"And the quiet way she moves."
"Remember *Morocco*? How she sweeps her eyes
Over that booing crowd in the dance hall,
And how they shut up."
"She knows she's got more stuff than any of them," says Sam.
"And the crowd backs off.
"That's personality.
"If you're got enough of it, you're okay for a lifetime," says Sam.
Whether I grow personality, or not,
It will be all the same to Sam.
For me, he's out!
He talks too much.

Sam
Yes, Boss, I've covered everything.
I've done a swell job; even if I do say so.
The whole town is talking about
The Girl With the Garters.
She's on the Pink List.
She's got window displays.
She's everywhere.
Just wait until you see the crowds.
You know me, Boss, when I let myself go.
It will be a panic.
It will be an all-time record for the Gem.
How about that little raise you were going to give me?
I've sure earned it this time.
And I may be getting married soon.
Just last night, I sold my girl on the idea of getting a personality like Dietrich's.
How about it, Boss?
What's that – what?
You just found out.
It's not a circus picture after all?!
The title "Four Rings" gave you a bum steer.
It means four marriages?
Not a four-ring circus?
Too bad – I'll say it's too bad.
But say, Boss. To get back to that little matter we were discussing.
It's okay, is it?
Five more, you say.
Well, that will help.
Thank you, Boss. Thank you!

Lynde Denig was the managing editor of the New York periodical, the *Dramatic Mirror of Motion Pictures and the Stage*. In 1918, he became the editor of *Wid's Daily*, a New York based service of film reviews. In 1921, Denig left the publication and became a feature writer for various motion picture magazines.

"Marlene Dietrich's Amazing Secret" by Adele Whitely Fletcher. *Modern Screen*, January, 1932

Dear Marlene,

They say you are heart-broken. That you're going home. To stay! It must be wretched to have your name the stuff of which headlines are made. It must be revolting to have photographs of your little girl used as illustrations for news stories in which you are sued for alienation of affections and libel. It must be humiliating to have your husband brought from Germany, as rumor has it he was, to act as a cover, proof for the public of his belief in your innocence.

All of this would be unbearable enough if it were the price you were paying for an extra-marital affair; if it were the inevitable punishment levied for indiscretions you committed either because of emotion or ambition. But those who know you best, those who work with you in the studios, insist the charges made against you in this von Sternberg fracas are ridiculous; that your interests do not lie in any such direction.

They say so much about you. And there is so much more they might say. But, of course, a beautiful courage isn't nearly as good newspaper copy as a pair of beautiful legs. Furthermore, there is doubt in a good many minds as to whether these two things are even likely to be compatible.

It's your courage I want to talk to you about now.

You were very young when life first challenged you. You had been sheltered and protected. You had been educated carefully in specialized private schools. You were seemingly unfitted for the battle. But you came through!

I can see you in Berlin playing in the German version of *Broadway*. You were in your dressing room about to go on when they brought suddenly, unexpectedly, bad news. Your father, whom you adore, was in serious financial difficulties. An army man, ignorant of the business world, he found himself in desperate straits. Through no direct fault of his own, because he had been trapped, he faced bankruptcy. His creditors had decided to take the matter to law. Your father had used all the money he had saved to keep him and your mother in their old age but it hadn't been nearly enough to stem the adverse tide. There was absolutely nothing more he could do.

That night when your cue came, you walked on the stage casually but your heart must have pounded fearfully against your side. Bankruptcy, you knew, was something no German officer could survive. It meant not only poverty but social ruin and professional disgrace.

It must have seemed ages before you reached home. There were your mother and father with bowed heads. In your mother's eyes, usually calm, were tears. Your father's eyes, usually keen and bright, were dark with worry.

"You're to stop worrying," you told them, "for there is nothing to worry about."

"You call it nothing," your father said brokenly. "I owe hundreds of thousands of marks and you call it nothing…*Liebchen*, you don't know how much money it is. You don't know the many years it would take to make that much money. And there are no years left, only days…a few short days…"

"You're not to worry," you repeated. And there was such confidence in your voice that they believed you.

"I'm going to get your creditors to wait," you explained in answer to the mute question in their eyes. "And then I'm going to pay them back out of the money I'll earn!"

The next morning a week of trying days began. It took courage and determination and a readjustment of all your values for you to approach your father's creditors. Never before in all your life had you needed to ask a quarter from anyone.

The first man you saw laughed at your proposition. Why should they wait? Threatened with bankruptcy and the consequent ruin it meant, he felt your father would move heaven and earth to settle; that your mother would sell the securities and properties representing their savings which he was convinced were hidden away somewhere in your name.

"You are wrong," you told him. 'My mother has nothing. My father's savings have gone. Press and you'll gain nothing but his ruin. Wait, and you have my word for it, you'll be paid back to the last mark."

"You will pay me back?" the man asked. But it was evident wasn't it, that he believed you? There was about you an unquestionable aura of truth which convinced him. He only questioned how you, little more than a child, planned to make so much money.

"I am an actress," you explained. "I'm only beginning my career. But already I'm getting ahead. I tell you I will pay you back!"

Likely enough that creditor felt anyone who had impressed him as you had must inevitably impress others. At any rate, when you left his great office you had his word that he would wait, that he wouldn't present his claim. But he was only one – only the first.

There were many others to see, some more lenient than he, others even less lenient. However, although it took many days for you to talk with them all, the interviews never were to become any easier. Always you had to muster your courage before you started out.

Then, at the very last, there was that grim-faced, tight-lipped broker who threw back his head and laughed in derision when you had finished talking. If he alone held out, your cause was lost. But you didn't truckle him.

"You must not laugh," you told him angrily. "If it were your daughter who stood in my position, who asked what any daughter would ask for her father's sake, then you wouldn't think it was funny.

"And if it is that you're doubting my ability to keep my promise… if it is that you're doubting my ability to earn enough money to pay you back, then it is an insult. And I demand that you apologize!"

It doesn't surprise me in the slightest that the financier immediately asked your pardon. Greek had met Greek. Men of such caliber are quick to know when they have met their match.

Your biography skims over the next few years lightly. It names the other plays in which you appeared following *Broadway* and marks your entrance into the movie studios with their heavier money bags. Nothing is said about any love affairs. Nothing is said about any beautiful homes in Berlin or in Paris or at any of the fashionable resorts. There are no tales about your furs or your jewels.

Because, for a long, long time you lived economically. I know how for years you maintained only the merest semblance of the "front" your position came to demand. I know how every week, without fail, your salary was divided…so much for this creditor, so much for that creditor…until there was barely enough left to keep you until the next check came.

There was, however, gold upon your father's sleeves. What more?

Paying back all that money took the best years of your life. It cheated you out of the intoxication of your first sensational success. It forbade you being gay and carefree. It denied you extravagance. But though you missed all of this you gained something, too. Today because of those difficult years, your spirit is stronger.

"Show me how a man treats his mother," the old wives used to say, "and I'll show you how he'll treat his wife." It amounts to the same thing, I think, to say, "Show me how a girl treats her father and I'll show you how she'll treat her husband."

Therefore, when I remember the fine way you served your father, I cannot find it in my heart to believe you would make your husband the butt of a Hollywood scandal. Were you madly and recklessly in love with Josef von Sternberg, your director, I can see you counting the world well lost and running away with him. That, yes. But I can't, for the life of me, imagine you sneaking your love in dark places, hiding behind Rudolph Sieber's husbandly confidence and trust in you.

However, aware of the courage you showed in this heretofore unpublished, secret episode from your early life I can't believe you're going to quit under fire. You don't do that…You have to go home for a little while, I know, when in April your immigration permit expires. But I, for one, won't believe it will be a final leave-taking. So I say only *Auf Wiedersehen*…

Adele Whitely Fletcher (1897-1979) began her career in 1916 in the publicity department of Vitagraph Studios in Brooklyn. From 1920 until 1924, she was the editor of *Motion Picture* magazine, and then worked in the same capacity for *Movie Weekly* from 1924 until 1931. She is credited with giving Joan Crawford her name while editing *Movie Weekly*. Beginning in 1931, and for the next forty years, she wrote hundreds of articles for *Motion Picture* and *Modern Screen* movie magazines. Fletcher also served as the editor of *Photoplay* magazine from 1948 until 1952. In her later years, she wrote four self-help books including, *How to Stretch Your Dollar*, 1972.

"Dietrich Goes into Seclusion." *Modern Screen*, February, 1932

Marlene's Roxbury Drive house in Beverly Hills.

Since the day of her arrival in Hollywood, Marlene Dietrich has fought hard, with every weapon at her command, to escape being compared with Great Garbo.

At first, Marlene loved to wear plain, tailored, mannish suits about the studio, but when she heard that this was an "exclusive" Garboesque costume, at least as far as Hollywood was concerned, she immediately took to satins to down the snicker that she was "pulling a Garbo."

But lately a development has taken place that is forcing Marlene into a Garbo tradition. In spite of what the gossip writers say, Marlene is going into seclusion!

No longer is Marlene granting interviews to the press.

No longer is she a conspicuous "first nighter."

They say Marlene has even abandoned her little circle of professional friends, including Joan Crawford and Doug Fairbanks, Jr.

How different this new seclusion is from Marlene's first eighteen months in Hollywood.

When the German girl first arrived at the Paramount studios she was the pride of the publicity department. She was the reporters' delight. In her fascinating German accent, she talked frankly of every phase of her life…her marriage…her motherhood…her career in Berlin…her deep admiration for Greta Garbo…her gratitude at her American reception. Unlike Gloria Swanson and Norma Shearer she even had no scruples about being photographed with her child.

As for keeping herself aloof from the crowds, there was none of that in Marlene. She, and her constant companion, Josef von Sternberg, were as much a feature of the Hollywood premieres as were the spotlights.

But all that is over now!

Marlene will see no one. She has become as difficult to locate for a story interview as Garbo. She has said that she might "consider" a story angle if the angle particularly appealed to her. A great many possible interview angles have been presented to her in the past few months and the statement has come back, "Miss Dietrich is not interested in talking on this subject."

What is the reason for this sudden aloofness?

Those who know her insist that Marlene has been deeply hurt by what she considers the scandal of Mrs. von Sternberg's alienation of affection charges. To no avail it has been pointed out to her that American stars have successfully weathered gossip and rumor far more scandalous than the legal difficulty in which she now finds herself. But Marlene will not be consoled by such explanation. She has the typical continental woman's slant on newspaper notoriety. In Europe, it seems, divorce actions are handled very quickly and seldom reach newspaper headlines. Marlene cannot seem to realize that in America divorces are more frequently in the headlines than are the news events of the world.

Marlene feels exactly as she would if these headlines had broken in Germany instead of America. She feels that she wants to hide away from them. Not that Marlene is hiding from Mrs. von Sternberg's charges…she vehemently denies all of them. But she does want to hide away from people who wish to discuss the case.

To a girl at the studio who enjoys Marlene's confidence, the German star said, soon after the unfortunate publicity broke – "These kind people who have been so friendly to me…what will they think now!"

Marlene seems to feel that no longer will the reporters seek her out for some friendly little story about her child…but that they would demand "love pirate" tales. She speaks frequently about returning to Germany for good.

In short, Marlene's feelings are hurt and she has gone into retirement, no matter what the gossips say about "pulling a Garbo." That, at least, is no "scandal!"

"Will Marlene Break *The Spell?*" by Kay Evans. *Photoplay,* February, 1932

It was a small, intimate Hollywood party. Everybody was having a good time, like kids on a holiday. It was all innocuously innocent and if you've never seen a Hollywood party, you don't know just how much nonsensical, silly, funny clowning goes on.

The person who was having the most fun was Marlene Dietrich. That strange, exotic face you've seen on the screen was wreathed in childish smiles. She could think up more silly stunts to do than any of the others. And she greeted every new game proposed with wild enthusiasm.

Suddenly she looked up at the door. The smile froze on her face. She sat down instantly and a curtain was pulled across her eyes. The mask she wore so immediately was the mask she wears in her films.

The others saw the sudden difference in her. They turned to the door seeking the reason for her brisk change.

Josef von Sternberg had entered the room!

And that is an incident that illustrates one of the strangest real life stories ever enacted in Hollywood – a drama fraught with the weird sensationalism of a mystery play.

The relationship that existed between Greta Garbo and Mauritz Stiller has been compared to that of *Trilby* and *Svengali*. The analogy is not quite accurate. Garbo loved Stiller.

The real *Trilby-Svengali* story, almost word for word as Du Maurier wrote it so many years ago, is being played by Marlene Dietrich and Josef von Sternberg.

And now there's a new chapter to add. This chapter concerns the struggle of Marlene to get out from under the von Sternberg influence. And the struggle of Dietrich's friends to help her shake off the hypnotic spell.

Marlene is like *Trilby* in that she does not love von Sternberg. Yet when her friends say, "If he keeps on directing you, making you play the same role over and over again, giving the same mannerisms, your career will soon be all washed up." Marlene answers, "No, he is the greatest genius of the screen."

Professionally, he has sold her the bill. Personally, not at all.

But not long ago a strange thing happened. Marlene walked into the Paramount lunch-room alone. She and her grim shadow, Josef, had lunched together every day that she was at the studio since her arrival in Hollywood. Her sudden aloneness, therefore, made Hollywood shake a puzzled head. They had quarreled – *Trilby* was chafing at the *Svengali* dominance.

For ten days they were not seen together. Those ten days may preface the complete change in a woman's character.

There was a young German actor who comforted Marlene during this time. There was also Maurice Chevalier, whose constant society Marlene sought. They lunched together and they danced together at the Ambassador Cocoanut Grove. What is more, they laughed together – a thing she never did with von Sternberg.

At first it seemed a friendship merely, and those who had Marlene's best interests at heart were delighted that she was being a human being and not the automaton that von Sternberg had made her.

She and Chevalier had their pictures taken together by a Paramount photographer. Suddenly all these pictures were recalled and destroyed. However, *Photoplay* printed one of them.

But for ten whole days Marlene was free – free from her *Svengali*.

In order to understand the strangest of all strange Hollywood relationships, it is necessary to understand the two protagonists in the drama – Marlene and von Sternberg.

Von Sternberg is the more important since Marlene, the Marlene you have known, is a figment of his imagination.

Clive Brook recalls that years ago in England he met a strange little man interested in art and *belle lettres*, who told him, "The only way to succeed is by making people hate you. I intend to bring myself to the attention of the higher and mightier ones by making them remember me as someone whom they hate."

This was, of course, von Sternberg. He has succeeded.

When he was starting out in the business, a famous director who wanted to help him said, "I believe you can be a director. In three months I could teach you to be one."

To which von Sternberg replied, "It would take *me* longer than that to teach *you* to direct."

Once von Sternberg was employed by MGM. His first picture was put into the hands of a supervisor who disliked him. The finished result was a botch. Von Sternberg was, at the time, in the midst of directing Mae Murray. When he saw the result of his first MGM attempt he walked on his set one day, turned his cameras heavenwards, took a hundred feet of film showing the cobwebbed rafters of the stages' ceiling and, with this magnificent nose thumbing gesture, left the lot never to return.

Yet there is a legend which says he used to stand in the doorway of his house upon a hill and, throwing his sensitive hands toward the lighted panorama of the city below, cry in childish ecstasy, "My Hollywood!" And that he would listen for the purr of cars coming up the hill and when he knew that he was to have visitors he would run into the house and seat himself in a high-backed chair with an erudite book (title carefully displayed) before his face.

I could go on and on recounting von Sternberg yarns, but perhaps there are enough to show you that the man is a trifle mad – yet he comes darn close to being a genius.

Finding life falling short of his fantastic ideal, he has built up in his films a world of his own, peopled with great heroic characters, women with incredible brains, women who make incredible gestures, women who behave not at all as we, who have wiped the star dust from our eyes, expect human beings to behave, but women who, if they existed, would certainly give the dish of life a French sauce of romance and color.

And now we come to Marlene.

Von Sternberg has created her in the image of these women about whom he dreams and whom he crystallizes upon a screen.

He saw her, as Stiller saw Garbo, a piece of clay waiting for his hands to mold.

But Stiller saw Garbo as an actress. What she did off screen did not matter to him as long as she loved him.

Von Sternberg does not want love from Marlene. But he, being a different type of man from Stiller, wants more.

He has tried to mold her not only as an actress, but as a person.

I remember the first time I saw Marlene Dietrich.

I thought her one of the loveliest women I'd ever known. That she was unhappy in America I knew – as Garbo was unhappy when she first came over. But she talked freely of her baby, of her life in Germany, of her husband. Von Sternberg was not there.

When he came in the room – as he always eventually comes into any room where Marlene is, he bowed politely to me and turned to Marlene to talk to her in German. She arose instantly. "I must go," she said. And shortly she left.

She is two different women. With von Sternberg she is what he has made her be, the woman who wandered through *Morocco* on a pair of ridiculously high heels, the woman who rouged her lips before facing a firing squad in *Dishonored*. When she is away from him she is a gay, happy, laughing child. The mask is tossed away, the pose in gone. She is the Marlene Dietrich of Germany and not the creation of von Sternberg of some mystic Graustarkian country.

In spite of the fact that he says she helps direct her pictures and that it makes her furious to be told he dominates her, his spell has lasted over her since her arrival in this country. And then came those fatal ten days and the spell was broken. It was during these ten days that she laughed and danced with Maurice Chevalier. And, although they are back together again, she and Josef, lunching and talking their serious talk, there is a difference. Things are not as they were.

As a person, this all affects her tremendously but it chiefly concerns her career, which is now at a serious crisis. Not even her most ardent admirers (of which I am one) can fail to see that she has (through von Sternberg) repeated her roles in every picture.

And already people are asking, "What could happen if someone else directed Marlene?"

It is in her contract that von Sternberg shall direct her pictures.

But suppose those ten days have paved the way for her, suppose she should work for another man? Undoubtedly the vague, intangible, inarticulate woman would be gone and in her stead would be a warm, alive, delightful actress – as Marlene herself really is.

Now perhaps you wonder where Marlene's husband, Rudolf Sieber, comes into all this. He plays a certain role in Marlene's life but not the starring one. Her baby is her greatest and most vital interest. Don't forget that Sieber was an assistant director who could further her interests on the screen in Germany at the time she married him.

And she loves him, of course, since he is the father of her child and that child, little Maria, is her ruling passion.

Marlene is not a strange figure. She is a woman of intelligence and charm. She takes a normal interest in having a good time. Von Sternberg has made her the thing she appears to be. But now that she is being gradually weaned away from the influence – what will happen to her? George Du Maurier's ending for his novel, *Trilby*, was not a happy one. But "Trilby" did not have the brains Marlene has.

Kay Evans was a Hollywood columnist and movie magazine contributor.

"Marlene Dietrich Will Have Only One Great Love, Her Handwriting Shows" by Louise Rice. *Movie Classic*, May, 1932

Marlene Dietrich's signature – reproduced herewith – gives the graphologist an enormous surprise. For what have all the publicity men featured in their blurbs about the German sensation? You all know as well as I do – LEGS, and not much of anything else. But ask her director and her business manager, and I am sure that they will tell you that they have found her to have a head for business and a good understanding as well.

No, I didn't mean that last characteristic as a joke, although you may think that I was guilty of a pun, which is a serious crime in this country. I mean that she has the ability to think quickly and to the point on any subject that seems to her worthwhile. Also, that she has a sudden feeling or intuition that is often of great assistance to her in outguessing the "other fellow," when trying to carry out her plans. See if your handwriting shows the little breaks in the connecting strokes of the small letters that Marlene has in her words. If so, you also have intuition and should use it to the best of advantage.

Her handwriting reveals Marlene Dietrich as a person who has enormous pride, as shown by the inflated letter formations and high capitals; and there is a dislike of fussy conventionality in every stroke of her writing. Look at the reproduction of her signature and notice the sweep and swirl of the connecting stroke between her first and last name, which is just like a high-flung gesture of defiance.

Also, notice how few of her letter-formations follow the accepted rules of writing, as she forms her letters according to her own ideas and not those of others. Therefore, she will always be happier and more successful if she is allowed to work out her own destiny as far as possible, without too much interference, either from her family or from her business associates.

Along with this energy, we find that she is by nature positive, as well as somewhat self-centered. Also, we discover a good deal of emotional generosity and extravagance, shown by the letter "a" in her first name (which is open at the top) and the wide spaces between her words. If you want to get something from her, let her feel sorry for you first, and she will be apt to work with all her might to help you with your problems.

But be careful not to give her a "sob-story" without any truth in it, or else have a shell-proof dugout near at hand when the fireworks start. She may be fooled once, but never twice, and it is a dangerous proposition to try to impose on her kindness. For she is no milk-and-water miss, who will say nothing and turn the other cheek. Look at the long ending strokes of her words and the downward ending stroke of the capital "M" in "Marlene," and then think twice before incurring her wrath.

The unevenness of her letters and the heavy pressure with which she writes show that she can be temperamental, as well as kind. Her nature is not of the regulation type. It is a fortunate thing for her that she is able to let out some of these over-emotional feelings – rather than to keep them bottled up until an inevitable explosion might wreck her life. In my work, I find too many inhibitions and repressions caused by self-consciousness and fear of what people may think. I do not find this in Marlene Dietrich's character, although there is some reserve at times, which makes her inscrutable and hard to understand. This will give her charm – especially for the male sex.

Notice the plain capitals that she uses – so free from over-ornamentation and vulgarity. This is a proof that she comes naturally by the poise and self-possession that we see in her work in the movies, in which she has had such success. This shows her ability to think clearly and plan ahead so that she can keep her balance even when she has work to do. She has many of the constructive, as well as the artistic qualities, in her nature and can put aside her emotions and temperamental qualities when sincerely interested in anything. There is a driving force that makes her almost ruthless in her willingness to give up practically anything in order to satisfy her ambitions.

Yet this love of success does not spring purely from a fondness for material rewards, such as money and fame – although there is a material side to her complex nature. It does not even arise from a desire to get her own way, in spite of the fact that she is stubborn and dislikes interference with her plans. It comes more from an urge for achievement that will satisfy her own sense of what is right.

In choosing the director of her pictures, her studio should always select someone she can respect and admire for his cleverness and power. Under such direction she should be easily managed and do excellent work. For, with her instinctive feeling for what is right and fine, whether she has had any special cultural training or not, she will dislike and despise mediocrity and pretension and will probably sulk and do poor work under a person of inferior mentality.

While she can work hard when necessary, she will also want comfort and luxury and enjoy being lazy, "even as you and I." Just as a beautiful tigress can stretch out in the sun and relax and purr like a good-natured house cat, Marlene will enjoy being waited on and petted and made much of. This quality, while it may be irritating to those who want her to do something, is in reality a very good thing for her, both physically and mentally. Otherwise, she might become too tense and excitable under the high pressure and glare of publicity under which our popular stars must live, and which has shortened so many promising careers.

Her love nature, while very ardent, has the ability to separate her emotions and affections from her interest in her work and her future success. She has the magnetism that attracts people, both men and women, through the medium of the screen – magnetism that makes her hard to forget when you have seen her pictures. This is even greater in personal contacts, and she will have many admirers and the opportunity for many loves in her life.

However, like most of the constructive type, she will have only one big, deep, and real love, in which she will give herself freely and completely. And Heaven help her, so far as her intimate personal happiness is concerned, if she is disappointed in the one she loves. If she should be disappointed, she might never show it to the world in general, or even to those who are nearest and dearest to her, because of her intense pride of which I have spoken. She might have dozens of lovers and several marriages but there would still be a wound in her heart that would never heal.

Before putting this character study aside, take one more look at the reproduction of Marlene Dietrich's handwriting and see if you cannot visualize this woman from what I have told you of her character. Just a mixture of a very human wife and mother – like yourself or Mrs. Jones, your next-door neighbor – but with something that drives her on to accomplishment in spite of obstacles and disappointments.

While she has faults and is temperamental, she has endurance and determination and can be urged on to even greater effort by encouragement. She may not always be wide in her judgement – perhaps because of her impatience and dislike of pettiness of any kind – but she is sincere, and capable of great things when she finds the right outlet for her energies. With the right pictures, she will go on to ever greater triumphs in her profession.

Louise Rice was a renowned handwriting expert. She authored several books about Graphology including, *Character Reading from Handwriting* (1927), and *By Whose Hand?* (1930).

"Dietrich Speaks Out for Herself" by Dorothy Manners. *Movie Classic*, May, 1932

Marlene Dietrich baffles interviewers, as you probably know. She answers their questions with "Yes" or "No," if possible. She just can't be persuaded to talk about herself. But here is one interview in which she does speak out at length and with frankness and a sense humor – and shows you, herself, a Marlene Dietrich you have never seen before. You may be surprised. Certainly, you will know her better.

It was just pure luck that I happened to find Marlene Dietrich in a talkative, confidential mood – a Spring fever mood. Many writers, including this one, have interviewed Marlene and have come away with the feeling that they have been evaded by the Languorous German gal who so hates to talk about herself for publication. But, this time, I sensed that this was not to happen. Dietrich, the Lady of Many Moods, was in a brand-new mood. If such a Yankee word may be applied to such an aloof foreign charmer, she was *peppy*!

In short, she looked as if she had risen early, put her blonde head out of her Beverly Hills window, inhaled deeply of the Spring morning, sung a guttural ditty or two in her bath, and arrayed herself in her gayest Spring raiment before coming to the studio to keep her appointment.

"You look like Spring flowers, or something," I remarked, because she really did.

"I feel goot," smiled Marlene, as she held open the screen door of her dressing room.

Like other interviews, I have been warned that certain subjects are taboo with Dietrich – such subjects as Hollywood's gossip about her, and the "influence" of director Josef von Sternberg on her career. At first, I remembered the warning. We skipped over the neutral subjects of current pictures – Marlene's and other stars', and of the great news value connected with the release of *Shanghai Express*; of the unusually enthusiastic reception accorded *Dishonored* by London audiences. Marlene, it developed, had seen a number of movies lately. She thought the new releases were

Marlene in Shanghai Express, *1932.*

surprisingly "goot," taken as a whole. From there we drifted to the influences that go to make up a "goot" picture – the director, the story, the acting, the camera work, the cutting, and so on.

And then, suddenly, I found myself asking a bombshell question – a question that surprised me – a question that could have been dared only because of Marlene's consistent good humor. "What do you think of all this Hollywood talk of Mr. von Sternberg's influence in your own pictures – the talk that he feels and speaks and *thinks* for you, as the Hollywood gossips are so determined to make out?"

For a moment, you could have heard a pin drop – at least, I could! But when I dared to look at her again, her smile had not faded – it had widened into a very humorous sort of old-fashioned grin! She nodded her head a couple of times, as if such talk were familiar to her.

"That's funny, very funny," she said. "Just last evening Mr. von Sternberg and I were reading a magazine with an article that told of how I was a 'Trilby' to my director's 'Svangali.'"

Marlene gave a short laugh – probably in demonstration of how she and her director had laughed over the article.

"I am sure the writer would have been disappointed to see how we laughed," she continued. "I think that maybe he thought such a story would make Mr. von Sternberg very angry. But that is because most people do not understand Mr. von Sternberg. They believe he has no sense of humor. If they could only have seen him laugh at the story! He said, 'It is too bad it is not true. Think of all the fun I could have, hypnotizing you!'

"As for me – I am truly sorry I do not know such a person as my director is supposed to be. Think how interesting it would be to know a man who could so completely control another person's destiny! How nice it would be to have such a man as a friend. One would never weary for entertainment.

"Is it not silly that writers say Mr. von Sternberg has such a weird, uncanny effect on me? It is very true that he is a tremendous influence in the direction of his pictures – but surely the critics and writers must have noticed this same influence in the performance of other players. It is not only Dietrich who responds to his direction so completely – every actor who has worked with him will tell you that he goes through a new directorial experience when he works in a von Sternberg production.

"Notice the difference in other players besides myself when they are working in one of his pictures as compared to their work with other directors. Yet they (the writers) do not say Mr. von Sternberg hypnotizes them. I believe he brings every actor he directs to his heights!" (Several months ago Marlene had told me that if von Sternberg ever made a picture with Joan Crawford, the public would be surprised at the power and sweep of her personality.)

"But," she added with a little shrug, dismissing the entire subject, "I do not pay much attention to such stories any more. At first – yes. They used to upset me. But now I do not even bother to deny most of them. Only one really upset me…"

She had risen now and was moving about her dressing room. She found a cigarette tray for me and placed it at my elbow. She did it almost subconsciously – a hint of the Dietrich thoughtfulness as a hostess.

"That very absurd story that I dress little Maria in copies of all my own clothes – that the child postured and behaved like a sophisticated grown person! I cannot imagine how anything so silly ever started. I did copy one dress of mine for my little girl. It was of such sweet, flowery chiffon material that I thought it would be nice for her. But suits like this" – indicating the Spring garment – "and lounging pajamas and evening gowns – no, I do not dress Maria like that."

As usual, the subject of Maria released a spring in Marlene.

"I try to be so careful of her – that she shall enjoy her little girlhood like a normal, happy child – as though she were not the daughter of a movie star. But this is sometimes difficult. Just this morning I wanted to make a walk with her." (She quickly corrected herself to "take a walk.") "So I quickly put on an old coat and without a hat or any make-up. I started out with Maria for a walk toward the hills. But we had not reached the sidewalk when some people who must have been waiting nearby caught up with us and asked if I were not Marlene Dietrich. We walked on a little further and they followed us. I tried to be nice: I thought if I smiled and talked to them a little while they would go away – but soon I found they intended to walk with us. So I brought Maria home.

"Soon I am taking her back to Germany to be entered in school. I want her to be brought up in the schools of my country. They are still a great deal more conservative over there. Children do not learn the things of the grown-up world so quickly. Here – I am a little frightened.

"The other day Maria had a birthday. I had invited several of her little neighborhood playmates, nice children of nice families, to share her birthday cake. There were some candles on the cake and the children suggested that Maria try to blow them out. In Germany we do not know this – but she seemed eager to try. She blew them all out but two – and one little child, even younger than Maria, spoke up and said, 'That means you will be married and divorced twice!' My poor baby – she looked at me, not knowing what the other child meant.

"Later on, the children suggested to Maria that they play Marriage and Divorce. You do not know how this frightened me – like something sticking in my heart. I forbade them to play such a game – and Maria was cross with me. She wanted to play what the American children play. That is why I say I am anxious to take her back to Germany for her schooling. I very much want to keep her a little girl for those happy years allotted to her...

"I do not know how soon we will be able to make the trip. I hope after my next picture – but perhaps the time will be extended for two productions.

"There is another story that surprised me when I read it in print – the story that I am returning to Germany immediately to make a German version of *Cleopatra*. This is most interesting – I did not know it until I read the paper.

"Yes, I want very much to return to my country to make a picture in my native language. But I have no definite plans for it. I should want plenty of time from my American contract to do the production justice. None of my pictures have been made in a German version – Mr. von Sternberg will not have slipshod methods used and there is not enough money involved to cover the cost of an entire film remade from the English. When I do appear before my own people, speaking my own language, I want it to be the best I have to offer.

"But we grow so serious," she said a little reprovingly, "and it is such a frivolous day! I feel so goot!"

"Cheasley Predicts *Domestic Changes* for Dietrich," by Clifford W. Cheasley. *Motion Picture*, July, 1932

Maurice Chevalier, Marlene, and Gary Cooper, 1932.

Before the end of the summer, Marlene's entire life – both off and on the screen – will undergo changes, according to Numerology. Her Numberscope also indicates that she will be an actress until 1941, when her life will change again.

Marlene Dietrich – who was born Magdalene von Losch – has an interesting personality and an interesting life, and her name and birth date are of the kind that the Numerologist likes to interpret for the indications of character.

The vowels of her original name total "7." This indicates that her viewpoint on life is a little above the ordinary, her tastes are individual, her likes and dislikes pronounced. This number "7" also shows a passion for dramatic art, which has grown steadily from childhood days, when her favorite game, it is suspected, was play-acting.

To the usual associations and experiences of everyday life, Marlene Dietrich is partly oblivious and partly indifferent, aloof, definitely disinterested. To be happy, she likes to take plenty of time before thinking and acting; to have the freedom to be alone whenever she feels like it (which is often); and to follow her "hunches." She is often out of patience with the interests and ambitions of other people; she cannot follow them mentally and so cannot truly sympathize with them or share emotionally in them.

The Numberscope of Garbo, which I analyzed in the May issue of *Motion Picture*, showed the same number "7" as the "Ideality" or Motive number of her character. The two stars therefore have a similar viewpoint on life. Dietrich, however, with the same indifference, has an ability to hide her opinions under an outer expression of tact, patience and diplomacy. In conversing with her, unless she happens to know you very well, it is not easy to discover what she really believes.

The combination of this inner "Motive" number of "7" and her outer "Expression" number of "2" proves that the stronger note of mystery, characteristic of all "7's," is outwardly subordinated in Marlene's case to a sincere effort to mix easily with everyone, to adapt herself to the immediate circumstances with very little show of temperament.

The real Dietrich, the dreamer, who is creative in idea, individual in intention, self-sufficient and in love with the esoteric, Oriental and the unusual, is not fully shown in the broader versatility which is characteristic of her on the screen. Here we have an artist, who is capable of being surprised at her own ability and who has that quality rarely found in a public favorite – obedience. This last is true despite her recent difficulties with her studio.

The number "2" as her "Expression" number reveals that Marlene Dietrich is not only a dramatic artist, but has such a degree of sensitiveness and impressionability, and is so anxious to cooperate and to avoid discord and resistance, that her success in her career will depend largely upon the vision and character of her directors. She is screen material that could be easily cheapened, confused or spoiled by the wrong direction.

The birthday of Marlene Dietrich was December 27, 1904, and the total derived from the numerals of this date is "8." To Numerology, this is the key to her destiny, the pattern of her life, with its past, present and potential opportunities.

Dietrich was born into a current of experience leading to positions of prominence socially and financially, as well as to the establishment of a condition of good health, which as a child was not well assured. The numbers of her birth date show that this wealth and health should be gained through her artistic expression before the public, from her early childhood years until she is thirty-seven. In that year of 1941, an end to her public career will give her the opportunity to contact the artistic field from the entirely new angle of production and management. This calculation says that there is a trend in her affairs that will carry her from the professional to the business side of the theater or screen, where the public will get the influence of her training and experience, but will seldom see or hear of her personality.

The years of 1930, 1931, and 1932 mark the peak of a cycle of effort in the direction of the screen, which Marlene Dietrich commenced somewhat accidentally in 1924. A series of unlooked-for events and contacts in that year changed the whole course of her career, although she was already headed for a personal success in another artistic field – music.

For the present year of 1932, the Numbers indicate that Marlene Dietrich is once more on the brink of extremely important changes, which the movie public will read of during the late summer. She will not be missed from the screen this year, but in the fall of the year and during 1933, an effort to tackle entirely different roles, under different direction, seems to be before her.

It will be difficult, until the influences of 1932 are past, to do more than present Marlene Dietrich as an unusual personality. Her wonderfully versatile dramatic talent will have to wait for its fuller development in 1933 and the few years following. She will be found capable of much greater dramatic freedom than she has been allowed.

Marlene Dietrich has reached the end of the first phase of her screen success, and soon will be a different personality, just as she is reaching the end of many phases of her personal life in 1932. She will find much to change, adjust and discard in this year that will affect her domestic life and her public career. When these adjustments and settlements are completed in the next few months, her work in 1933 will prove to the movie public what Numerology interprets from her name and birth date.

"Will Garbo and Dietrich Be Deported?" by Dorothy Calhoun. Motion Picture, July, 1932

Greta and Marlene "undesirable aliens"? That's hard to believe. But there is a bill before Congress now, asking the deportation and exclusion of foreign-born players! If it becomes a law, will America be a heavy loser?

Garbo has just renewed her U.S. immigration permit for another six months – but will it be renewed again? Does she, or doesn't she, face deportation – whether she wants to stay or not? And are Marlene Dietrich and Charlie Chaplin and Ronald Colman and Ramon Navarro "undesirable aliens"? Does America want to chase the foreign stars out of the country?

"There are one thousand movie actors and actresses in Hollywood who don't belong here!" shouted Congressman Samuel Dickstein of New York on the floor of the House of Representatives a few weeks ago. "There is discrimination against American beauty and talent which doesn't seem to get the same break as imported stars!"

Then, while the eagle flapped its wings, the patriotic Mr. Dickstein introduced a bill which, if passed, might ban Garbo, Dietrich and Chaplin and all the other foreign stars from Hollywood! It would ban *all new* foreign talent!

Perhaps the drive against foreign-born film workers has already started. Sergei Eisenstein –the greatest director of the world, according to many authorities – was ushered out of the United States a few months ago. He went to Mexico to make a picture, planning to re-enter the country later. But he was allowed only a four-week permit to travel from the Mexican border to New York, where he could sail for Russia. Duncan Renaldo has been arrested by immigration authorities, and charged with being a Romanian when he said he was an American in getting his passport to go to Africa to make *Trader Horn*. John Farrow, Australian scenario writer and former fiancé of actress Lila Lee, has been deported, charged with entering the United States illegally.

And all the foreign-born players are shaking in their expensive American-made shoes, wondering if the Dickstein Bill will separate them from what a titled English lady, brought over to teach our crude actors the manners of British aristocracy for a Lonsdale picture, referred to sweetly as "your darling, delightful American dollars."

England already has such a law as Congressman Dickstein proposes – limiting the number of foreign players who may appear in English films. It does not ban American players altogether, but limits them to a few outstanding stars – such as Corinne Griffith and Adolphe Menjou – who cannot be replaced by any English player. So far, there has been no retaliation by Hollywood, but if the Dickstein Bill becomes law, only alien actors "of distinguished merit" or hired for parts requiring "superior talent" may play in American movies.

Such a law would have prevented the unknown and then unwanted Garbo from entering the country; it would have deprived the world of that miserably poor immigrant boy, Rodolpho Guglielmi, who later became the world-famous Valentino; it would have denied fame to Ramon Samaniego (Ramon Novarro), who came into the country ragged and unknown; and to Ronald Colman, who starved in New York for years before he won recognition. Indeed, Maurice Chevalier and George Arliss are almost the only foreign stars in Hollywood who were already known to be "distinguished" when they arrived for their American debut.

"It has never been a secret to alert producers that it's the moviegoers, not themselves, who create stars," says B. P. Schulberg, Paramount executive. "The fact that some foreign players are popular today is wholly because the nation wants them so. While the Dickstein Bill specifies that the rank and file of European actors, not recognized as artists, should be excluded, it is from the rank and file that we have a great opportunity for developing talent.

"Any legislative measure to exclude the acting talent of foreign countries would be unfair to that privilege of selecting its own international favorites which the American public has always held inviolate. Besides, the condition is far less alarming than painted. The percentage of foreign players in films, compared with Americans, is astonishingly low."

Although the indignant Congressman certainly erred when he placed the number of non-American actors and actresses who are making their fame and fortune in Hollywood at a "thousand," it is undeniable that there are many foreigners among the most important stars. What would American motion picture history have been without a Mary Pickford, a Charlie Chaplin, and a Rudolph Valentino? Would we have reached our present leadership in the film industry throughout the world without our Garbos, Colmans, Shearers, Dietrichs, Del Rios, and Novarros? And among the stars of future American pictures will undoubtedly appear other foreign names – Tala Birell, Sari Maritza, Nils Asther, Anna Sten, Gwili Andre…

If immigration laws had been stricter so that they had excluded from our shores a certain Dutch merchant called Van Goebel a couple of generations ago, we would not have had his virile descendant, Clark Gable, to set the hearts of five million feminine moviegoers fluttering today!

The Academy of Motion Picture Arts and Sciences has been in existence four years. In that time the prizes for the most distinguished performances have gone to *five foreign-born players* – Emil Jannings, Mary Pickford, Norma Shearer, George Arliss and Marie Dressler; and the *three native-born Americans* – Janet Gaynor, Warner Baxter, and Lionel Barrymore. Would the reputation of American pictures have been as great without the gorgeously human Dressler, the sophisticated Shearer, the polished Arliss, the poignant Jannings, and America's Sweetheart, Mary Pickford?

"Hollywood needs more stars than the United States can supply," says George Arliss bluntly, in commenting on the possibility of a ban on foreign actors. "Possibly without new blood from abroad we might sink into a rut that would result in stagnation. Hollywood makes pictures for the whole world – it should *draw from* the whole world for talent."

Does Hollywood need its imported stars? It would seem that America is large enough and cosmopolitan enough to supply every possible picture need for its hundred and twenty-five million citizens, and yet – it took Sweden to produce a truly great siren for the screen, it took Paris to furnish us an utterly satisfactory man-of-the-world, it took Italy to give us a real romantic lover, and the London slums to send us the greatest comedian of them all.

Our screen needs strange women – exotic and mysterious. And America, though it produces beautiful, even gorgeous women, has not given the screen any true sirens since the days of glamorous Barbara La Marr, Myrna Loy's beauty is the exotic type, but Myrna Loy's personality is that of Myrna Williams from Montana. All of Theda Bara's writhings and leopard skins could not make Theodosia Goodman of Rochester exotic. Gloria Swanson and Constance Bennett are seductive women, but hardly mysterious. When Greta Garbo showed the world what it wanted of a woman, the motion picture industry began a feverish hunt for "other Garbos" – other women with the same appeal. They found them – but not in Philadelphia or Terra Haute or Kansas City. They brought the heavy-eyed Dietrich from Germany, the haughty Landi from England, the impassive and smoldering Birell from Vienna. They sent for Pola Negri to return. They tried one American Garbo, but Carman Barnes is now playing minor roles on the stage.

Our screen needs romantic lovers – subtle and skilled in the game of sex. And American men may be dominant, virile and handsome, but they are seldom subtle. Richard Dix, Fredric March, Gary Cooper, Charles Farrell, Robert Montgomery, Warner Baxter, Douglas Fairbanks, Jr., are all red-blooded, chivalrous and strong, but their appeal is through deeds, not kisses. The finesse of Chevalier, the leashed passion of a Valentino, the gay tenderness of a Novarro, the suave courtliness of a Lukas are all needed to complete the pattern of the American motion picture. John Gilbert, alone of the native screen heroes, fulfilled that need, until Clark Gable brought virile brutality to the women moviegoers and made them like it.

If Congress should shut the door to any but recognized European talent, it would be a death blow to the hopes of hundreds of aspiring English, French, Swedish, German and Spanish players, to whom Hollywood is the Promised Land. The undoubted fact that they want to work in American pictures because that is where they will make the most money should not prejudice Americans against them. After all, most of them give us our money's worth – or they wouldn't be stars.

"The reason I am going back to America without accepting offers in British pictures," Clive Brook frankly told London reporters recently, "is very simple. I have to consider my bank balance. I suffered like everyone else in the Wall Street panic and there aren't enough pennies in the bank to allow me to play just how and when I would like. I'd love to make pictures in England, but an actor who has made a certain name for himself in Hollywood should be very careful in approaching British pictures."

Maurice Chavalier, answering angry comments of his native Paris that he had deserted them for American gold, is quoted as saying frankly that that was the only reason an actor would want to work in Hollywood – where the one thought was hurry, hurry, hurry in order to make money.

A recent editorial stated bitterly that Greta Garbo's American earnings have been invested in Swedish match company stock and other foreign bonds – but this is not true. What if it were? And what if many of the highest-paid stars included in Conrad Nagel's list of "only twenty-three headline salaries" are aliens? What if Congressman Dickstein's "thousand" foreign players are really to be numbered among the 25,000 registered "extra" men and women players?

"The American motion picture industry," argues C. C. Pettijohn, counsel for the Hays organization, before the House Immigration Committee, "has gained a position of pre-eminence throughout the world through the free flow of talent from one country to another, and the fact that Hollywood has become the center of film production for a greater part of the civilized world now gives employment to a third of a million people in the United States yearly."

Victor McLaglen, English star, has another view of the situation. "I feel," says Victor, with the directness that made him a Major in the British Army, "that if a man earns his living in a country it's only right and fair that he should become a citizen of that country. America has always had a reputation for being hospitable and kind to visiting artists and on that account I hate to see her ban foreign actors. Yet, if England has made it difficult for American actors to get work in British pictures, I suppose such an action of retaliation is justified. However that may be, I have already taken out my first papers toward citizenship and I expect to become a full American citizen before very long."

Millard Webb, well-known Hollywood director who has just returned from England, where he directed two pictures, says, "The most important reason for the dearth of American screen players in British pictures is purely financial; they haven't the money to pay American salaries. Even so, they occasionally take a flier, so to speak; and the officials co-operate with them in every way to stimulate production.

"I am sure that if we make things tougher here for the British actor, many English producers will work the right wires and we'll have even more unemployment in our ranks that we have today. After all, retaliatory methods are like Kentucky feuds – each side goes the other one better each time, until they're both exterminated.

"American pictures can use all the talent they can find, whether it's from England, Germany, France, Russia or Czechco-Slovakia, or the Orient. Our pictures go all over the world and it must certainly be an effective factor in international harmony that some of our stars come from abroad."

And what says the greatest foreign player of them all, the Sphinx-like Garbo? Nothing at all! Congressman Dickstein and the other deportation agitators aren't worrying Garbo half so much as *she* is worrying Hollywood! Her present silence is more ominous to Hollywood than all the rumbling of legislative thunder. The question: "Will Garbo be deported?" may arise if Garbo stays – but what if she doesn't stay?

The fact that she has renewed her immigration permit makes it appear that she plans to stay – at least six months longer – but she would have had to renew it even to stay until her present contract runs out. Both she and M.G.M. refuse to talk about the possibility of her signing with them again. She has been receiving $7,500 a week – and is said to be asking $15,000, while the studio is trying to arrange a compromise salary more than half-way between the two. Her business manager, Harry Eddington, is reported to have resigned from M.G.M. to be better able to "talk business."

When *Grand Hotel* was previewed, many reviewers thought that Joan Crawford stole the picture – yet in the version released, it is Garbo's picture. Hollywood rumors have it that it took ten days' extra shooting, after the preview, to build up Garbo's part so that it overshadowed Joan's. The rumors add that if Garbo doesn't sign again, the "original" version will be substituted. This sounds preposterous, however, since the picture has now been released many weeks.

Friends close to Garbo say that she has been heard to say, "I can hardly wait to get away from this place." She is anxious to travel, to visit all the big cities and famous pleasure spots of Europe, they say. She has a great deal of money. Some also say that she is considering a world tour, lasting a year or two, making personal appearances along the way. Such a project should bring her a million or more.

Hollywood would not be surprised to see her go back to Sweden for a few months' vacation, still keeping Hollywood guessing. But if she does leave, Hollywood expects her back. For no star has ever abandoned her career at the height of her success, and stayed "retired." Maude Adams tried it on the stage, but came back. So did Geraldine Farrar.

Garbo today is a star "of distinguished merit" and "superior talent" – which would undoubtedly permit her to stay if the Dickstein Bill should become a law. But what of the future stars who are bound to come from Europe? Garbo, herself, once would have been excluded. Is America going to exclude or deport other foreign players who might become stars?

Dorothy (Donnell) Calhoun became the Hollywood editor of *Movie Classic* magazine in 1933 and remained at the helm of the "sensationalistic" publication until 1935. She wrote frequently for *Motion Picture Magazine*.

"Marlene Dietrich's Husband Rushes to Her Rescue Like One of Her Heroes" by Nancy Pryor. *Movie Classic*, August, 1932

Twice, Rudolph Sieber has arrived at her side in the nick of time – Chevalier's wife dashed over from Paris to save Maurice from gossip – and Miriam Hopkins could even depend on her estranged husband to be there when needed. It's a habit with Hollywood husbands, wives and ex's!

At the Hollywood opening of *Grand Hotel*, Marlene Dietrich, introducing her husband, Rudolph Sieber, to one of her friends, said, "It is too bad that every time my husband visits me he arrives just in time for *trouble*."

She referred, of course, to her studio difficulties that were, at the time, occupying considerable space in the newspapers under the headline, "*Dietrich and Von Sternberg Walk Out on Contracts. Star Refuses to Report for Work with Another Director. Paramount to Sue.*"

Herr Sieber's only other visit to Hollywood took place at the time the former Mrs. Josef von Sternberg was suing Marlene for alienation of the director's affections, basing her suit on an interview Marlene had allegedly given on her vacation abroad.

On the latter occasion, Herr Sieber, blond, young, smiling, and affable, lent considerable strength to Marlene's side of the story by casually scoffing at the "alienation" charges. In time, the American public came to the conclusion that if Marlene's husband saw no particular reason to get excited about Marlene's friendship with von Sternberg – why should anybody else?

Without really doing anything about it at all, Herr Sieber turned the tide of public sympathy back to Marlene at a time when it was highly important that she retain that sympathy. The flurry died down, the embers of gossip turned to ashes, and in time, Herr Sieber took his leave. Soon afterward, Marlene got a retraction from her foreign interviewer, and Mrs. von Sternberg withdrew her suit.

There were no reporters or photographers on hand to record the departure of Rudy Sieber from Hollywood. (There had been many of them to witness his affectionate reunion with Marlene and Josef von Sternberg upon his arrival.) He merely went back quietly to his directorial work in France and there was little more heard of him until –

Trouble once more reared its head upon Marlene's career.

This time the difficulty lay not in the realm of affection, but in the cold, cold world of business. Marlene and von Sternberg had written a "beautiful" (Sternberg's own description) story of a lady of the evening. Paramount, slightly alarmed at the censorable features of the story, had set to work on what von Sternberg later referred to as "operations" – with the result that both Marlene and Josef did their now famous "walkout."

The strained relations lasted just long enough for Rudy Seiber to make a flying trip from Paris to his beautiful and distressed wife's side. While von Sternberg traveled off to New York in what looked like a huff, Rudy and Marlene remained in Hollywood and gained innumerable allies to Marlene's cause.

The picture of the happy young couple sun-tanning themselves on the beach at Marlene's home, romping with their young daughter, and entertaining at informal Sunday afternoon parties created a new version of Marlene in the Hollywood mind. Hardened gossip-writers, many of whom had never been privileged to glimpse this softer side of the inscrutable German girl, took to their typewriters in glowing defense of her stand.

Rudy Sieber, as affable as before, did more than contribute his bit to the new impression. The disinterested onlooker got the idea that it just wasn't fair to pick on a girl as swell as Marlene, with such a nice guy for a husband as Rudy. We're not offering the version that this picture of devotion and domestic happiness had anything to do with the thawing of the hearts of the studio executives – but the upshot of the rebellion was that Marlene, von Sternberg and Paramount called off their battalions of lawyers and everything is as bright again as one of those nice beach days down at

Marlene in Shanghai Express, *1932.*

Marlene's. Once more, Rudy Sieber had arrived to see his wife safely and happily conclude one of her Hollywood worries. And he has stayed on to ease her mind about those kidnap threats, and to see that both she and her little girl are protected.

A very modern version, you might say, of the old-fashioned nick-of-time hero who always arrived on the scene just in time to protect the heroine's honor or save her scalp from where it had been strapped to the railroad tracks by the dastardly villain. Only the 1932 Hollywood version of the same story has the hero and heroine married, and the troubles are no longer confined to the railroad tracks. Also, in place of dashing up on the proverbial pony from a mile or so away, Hollywood's nick-of-time mates have been known to make dashes (by steamer or plane) from such far-off places as New York, London or Paris.

When rumor began to kick up dust that the Maurice Chevaliers were on the verge of divorce, Yvonne Vallee Chevalier came all the way from Paris to be caught by the news camera, affectionately kissing Maurice from the train steps. You see, the Chevaliers had been so enthusiastically publicized as one of those "happy, happy Hollywood couples" that mean old divorce rumors might have had a bad effect on Maurice's hold on the public.

We don't know why it is that a news picture of a man and wife holding hands, or kissing, or smiling at each other is supposed to allay the suspicions of the public so quickly – but it is a very popular legend in Hollywood. (Ann Harding and Harry Bannister were photographed at their own fireside just one week before the divorce story broke.)

Mrs. Chevalier arrived just as the rumors were kicking up the most dust. It was being said that Maurice was interested in first "this" actress, and then "that" one. Because he was once dining at the Cocoanut Grove with Marlene Dietrich, both guests at a large dinner party, it was supposed that Marlene was the object of Maurice's affections. But Marlene had been absolved of snatching Josef von Sternberg's affections too recently to make the Chevalier rumors anything but just that – rumors. Even the most suspicious-minded couldn't go for the story that Marlene was going around snatching everybody's affections at the same time.

Jeanette MacDonald's name crept into the surmises when Marlene's didn't hold up. But then Jeanette was hardly plausible, either, because the folks were already sold on the idea that Jeanette and her business manager, Robert Ritchie, were secretly married.

Before Mrs. Chevalier departed, most of the talk had gone up in smoke, and while some of the folks aren't exactly satisfied that all is well between the fascinating Frenchman and his wife, they have at least stopped trying to pin the difficulty on anybody in particular. With her nick-of-time appearance as Maurice's devoted wife accomplished, Mrs. Chevalier sailed back to France, where she will probably remain until something else happens.

Miriam Hopkins and Austin Parker, though separated, maintained for several months a delightfully interesting study in the general "handiness" of matrimony. Every time Miriam was on the verge of being announced "engaged" to any one of several Hollywood gentlemen, she would be seen dining with her husband just long enough to quell the gossip. For more than a year Hollywood was in considerable hot water about Miriam and Austin. They were alternately supposed to be madly in love with, first, each other – and then a couple of other people.

Nancy Pryor was a frequent contributor to entertainment publications.

"Marlene Dietrich Gets Kidnap Threats – Child Under Constant Guard." By Janet Burden. *Movie Classic,* August, 1932

"Most Famous Mother in Hollywood Receives Demands for Twenty Thousand Dollars from Kidnap Ring – Ruse to Trap Them Fails"

Last March, when the Lindbergh atrocity stirred the country, Marlene Dietrich's neighbors noticed that the bedroom windows of her house were being covered with a heavy iron grille, and that whenever her little girl, Maria, went out to play, she was followed closely by a guard, as well as a nurse. Marlene was in terror of having her own child kidnapped.

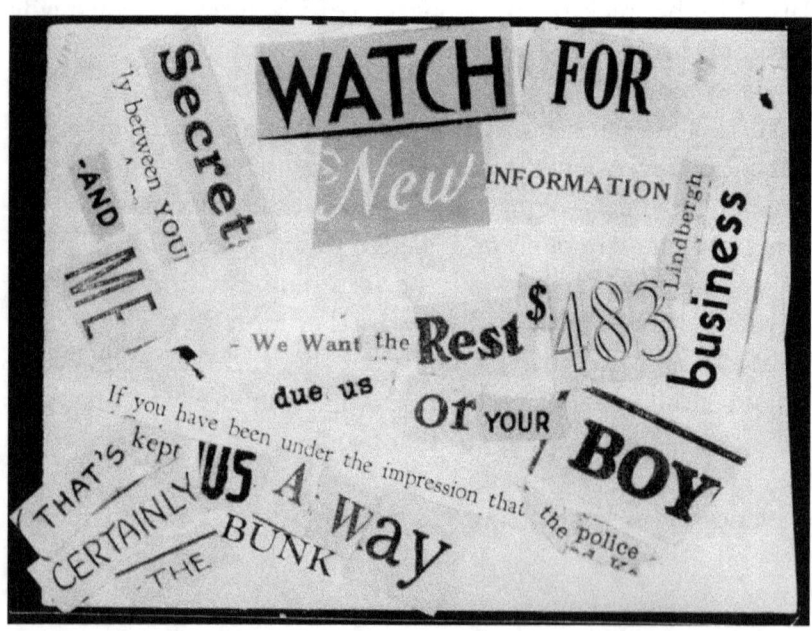

Kidnap note.

A newspaper printed a photograph of the house (actually owned by Charles Mack of the "Two Black Crows"), with a white arrow pointing to the barred window of the nursery. The next day, Marlene moved secretly to a cottage at well-guarded Malibu Beach, while bars were put on all the windows of the Beverly Hills house. Soon afterward, Marlene's director-husband, Rudolph Sieber, arrived from abroad. There were rumors that he would take the little girl back with him to Europe, where she would be safer.

Marlene's fears about her child's safety have not been baseless. She has received five notes of threat and warning, filled with such sentences as "If you want to save Maria to be a screen star, pay, and if you don't she'll be but a loving memory." The first demand was for ten-thousand dollars. Marlene turned each note over to the police, but the news of their receipt was kept from the newspapers – until the would-be kidnappers' letters crossed, sending one intended for Marlene to another woman, and the other to Marlene.

The kidnap ring expressed resentment at Marlene's ignoring their demands. They sent her this message, "Say, what's the big idea? Attention! Is the future of your girl worth it? Marlene,

Kidnap note.

Marlene, you'll be sorry!" They told her that now she would have to pay them double.

There were no handwriting clues to work on, as in the Lindbergh case. Each word in each note had been cut from a magazine or newspaper, and pasted together to form the message.

Marlene, advised by the police, placed a dummy package where the kidnapping notes told her to leave the money, but it was not touched. A more threatening note followed. Marlene is taking small Maria to the studio with her these days. The Dietrich set at the studio is locked. An armed guard accompanies Marlene wherever she goes.

Janet Burden was an entertainment reporter, and frequent movie magazine contributor.

"Keeping Slim *on Her Own Cooking.*" *The New Movie Magazine,* August, 1932

Marlene Dietrich worries about her figure only now and then – and in between times she eats all the foods banned to less lucky stars, and cooks some of these dishes herself!

Melba toast and black tea may find their places on the menu of Marlene Dietrich, Paramount importation from Germany, but several of her native and not so calorie-proof dishes are included on it as well. She may have orange juice and toast for breakfast, but she'll follow through with paprika chicken or baked ham and sweet potatoes later. Dutch apple cake, or snow pudding.

Sunday starts off with a late breakfast and bacon as a special treat.
Breakfast: Orange juice, Melba toast, crisp bacon, coffee.
Dinner: Tomato juice cocktail, paprika chicken, lima beans, celery curls, lettuce, Russian dressing, demi-tasse.
For Monday, honeydew melon, Melba toast and coffee is the breakfast menu.
Luncheon: Tomato salad, French dressing, rye bread toast, black tea, stewed apricots.
Dinner: Baked liver, baked potatoes, creamed celery, cucumber salad, cream dressing, cracked wheat rolls, Dutch apple cake, lemon sauce.
The favored Hollywood lamb chops gain a place on Tuesday's menu.
Breakfast: Baked apple, bran muffins, coffee.
Luncheon: Pear and cream cheese salad, rye bread, frosted coffee.
Dinner: Tomato juice, broiled lamb chops, string beans, fruit gelatin, demi-tasse.
Wednesday's meals start off with sliced peaches, whole wheat toast, marmalade and coffee; with fruit salad, black tea and toasted rye bread for luncheon.

Dinner: Tomato soup, roast beef – rare, escalloped potatoes, combination salad with French dressing.

For Thursday breakfast: Grapefruit, cracked wheat rolls, coffee.

Luncheon: Baked eggplant, asparagus salad, iced tea.

Dinner: Fruit cocktail, baked ham, baked sweet potatoes, beets, orange sherbet.

Popovers are the inducement for Friday's breakfast which includes grapes and coffee. For luncheon a bacon and tomato sandwich, and tea.

Dinner: Celery curls, roast lamb, browned potatoes, peas, snow pudding, coffee.

Saturday's breakfast includes melon, cornbread, honey and coffee, with a tomato-cheese soufflé for luncheon.

Dinner: Bouillon, broiled chicken, Waldorf salad, broccoli, fruit cup.

Here's a recipe for Dutch apple cake, which Marlene bakes herself:

1 cake yeast
¼ cup lukewarm milk
¾ cup scalding hot milk
¼ cup sugar
2 ½ cups flour
¼ cup shortening
1 teaspoon salt
1 egg yolk beaten

Soak yeast in lukewarm milk. Add to scalded milk. Add half the sugar and flour. Let rise until double in bulk. Then beat in the rest of the flour and other ingredients. Spread thinly in greased baking pan. Let rise in warm place until doubled again. Press thinly sliced apples into the dough in even rows, covering the dough. Sprinkle with ½ teaspoon cinnamon mixed with a half cup of brown sugar and dot with currants. Bake in 375 degree oven.

"Is Marlene Dietrich Being *Frightened* Away from America?" by Franc Dillon. *Movie Classic*, September, 1932

Marlene in Blonde Venus, *1932.*

The German star has found sensational success in Hollywood, but little happiness. And now, to cap the climax, she cannot go anywhere without armed guards – and the life of her little girl, who means far more to her than fame or money, has been threatened. When she returns to Germany in December (her contract expires then), will she ever come back?

When Marlene Dietrich's contract is completed in December, she will have been in America for two and a half years. Those close to the glamorous German star whisper that these brief, tumultuous years have so frightened Marlene that she wants to go "home" – to Berlin – for good and all, in December.

In America she has been annoyed by stares, persecuted by the press, faced with lawsuits, subjected to gossip, and threatened by criminals. She has seen friends lose their fortunes in American banks, she has been bored by Hollywood social life, involved in studio arguments and forced into hiding, by fear of danger to her little girl, Maria.

At the moment, she lives in a state of armed terror, going nowhere without guards. Detectives guard the closed sets on which Marlene works, follow her wherever she goes, and watch her home day and night. Even when she goes to the movies – which is recreation, not a risk to most people – drastic measures are taken for her protection. Two limousines speed down the boulevard. The first draws up at the curb in front of the theater and four armed detectives leap out. They start pushing the crowd back, and by the time the second car has arrived they have made a pathway to the entrance. Down this protected path Marlene, Maria, the governess and Josef von Sternberg rush. The four burly guards close in behind them and sit one on each side of the party, one in front, and one behind during the performance.

"Nonsense," said Marlene and von Sternberg in unison when I asked them if it were true that she will not return to America after her trip to Germany in December. Yet there are disturbing signs that the slow enigmatic smile, the gorgeous figure and exotic beauty that have made Dietrich an American idol may be lost to us. As long as six months ago, according to one of her close friends, Marlene was anxious to leave.

"If I could get out of my contract, I'd go home right now," Marlene is quoted as saying angrily at that time. "I have plenty of money now and there is a play I would like to do in Germany." But Marlene denies that she is considering the stage. "My only plans now are for a holiday," she says. "When my contract with Paramount expires in December, I am going to Europe for a vacation."

This sounds mild enough, but at the time of her outburst to her friend, it appears that Marlene consulted the immigration authorities and discovered that under new rules it would be difficult for her to return to America, once she had left for the second time. She sent for her mother and sister, who are even now said to be on their way to Hollywood to visit her. Knowing the immigration difficulties, if Marlene plans to leave America next winter, she is only too likely to remain abroad.

Two years of American life, so different from life in Germany, have worn her resistance, tried her patience and tortured her nerves until it is easy to understand the fear that may drive her away from a country where she has found success, but not happiness.

She arrived in Hollywood frank, honest and with no inhibitions, determined to like us. She greeted the first interviews like friends. Then came her first experience with American customs. Someone in the studio publicity department, remembering a press-agent's ABC's, hinted that Marlene was just eighteen years old.

"Ridiculous!" exclaimed Marlene, when she heard of it. "I'm not a girl. I'm a woman – I have a child. I'm twenty-five! And I do not see why I should pretend otherwise, or have anyone pretend for me."

And then she was told that she must not mention her child, must not wear the locket with Maria's picture, which she showed proudly to everyone. She was bewildered. Why shouldn't she tell she had a child? A beautiful little girl whom she adored? Why would Americans not like her so well on the screen if they knew she was a mother? What strange people! She did not – could not – forebear talking about her child.

By this time the press began to print many things that Marlene did not understand. Often she was deeply hurt. Once, in a burst of tears, she fled from an interviewer when the writer compared her to Greta Garbo.

Her recent quarrel with Paramount, when she declined to make a picture with another director than von Sternberg, added to her unhappiness. Marlene has been very lonely in Hollywood and von Sternberg has proved a staunch friend as well as a careful, sensationally successful director. At first she tried going to parties, but she stood at one side, gazing wonderingly at the strange ways in which Americans amused themselves, listening with growing boredom to the continual talk of pictures and contracts which is Hollywood's social chatter. Now Marlene does not go to many parties. Her men friends can be counted on the fingers of one hand – von Sternberg, Hans von Twardowski, Maurice Chevalier. Her close women friends would leave several fingers to spare – Joan Crawford, Tallulah Bankhead, Bebe Daniels, and a Viennese princess married to an American business man.

A foreigner's confidence in the safety of our institutions must have been badly shaken by the huge losses of Nils Asther, and other foreign stars in the Hollywood bank failure. "I had not a penny in that bank," Marlene declares, "but many of my friends had."

However, it was when her secretary, opening the morning mail, came on a kidnapping letter, a demand for money, a threat to steal little Maria, that terror of what could happen in this country must have struck Marlene's heart. Bewildered and frightened by a series of unpleasant events, it is easy to believe that when Marlene goes to Europe soon, she may not return.

She has formed no permanent ties. Her life here has been lived in temporary fashion. Unlike a majority of stars, who first sign a motion picture contract and then rush out and buy a house, Marlene has chosen to live in rented homes.

"Why should I buy a home in Hollywood?" she asks. "I rent a very nice house. It is suitable for Maria and me and I have no responsibilities, like taxes and other bothersome things. I do not intend to buy any real estate here. I don't want to be tied down."

Marlene is very frank in her determination that Maria shall be raised in Europe. She does not attend an American school but has her lessons at home with a German governess.

"I want her to have a fine education, an education that she can get only in Europe," Marlene says, frankly. "I want her to be surrounded by European culture. After all, she is German and it is better for her to be brought up in her own country."

Inasmuch as Maria is now nearly eight years old, her "bringing up" must necessarily start soon, which lends weight to the rumor that Berlin will soon be Marlene's permanent address. Little

Maria told me that she does not want to go back to Germany. Just now she is very much enamored with her swimming pool, the beach, going to the studio to have lunch with her mother and playing around the sound stage with little Dickie Moore, who is working in *The Blonde Venus* with Marlene.

But the child's play has been considerably hampered since the kidnapping threats were received. She is no longer allowed to run on the beach. She must always be within sight of her governess and two heavily armed guards. When she goes to the studio to meet her mother, she is accompanied by the governess, the chauffeur and a guard.

When Marlene received the first threat note, she immediately turned to Mr. von Sternberg. Before he even notified the police, he sent one of his most trusted employees to Marlene's house to protect her. *Later it was discovered that this man, sent to guard Marlene's own house, had been convicted of a federal offense.* Isn't that enough to destroy her confidence in anyone?

A succession of threats followed. Iron bars were placed over every window in the house making it look like a high-class private jail. A double lock was placed on every door; the iron gate padlocked; an elaborate electric alarm system installed.

No one can walk down the quiet street on which Marlene lives without being watched by two guards. If anyone hesitates even for a moment, he is immediately suspected, questioned.

Inside the house a German police dog, powerful and intelligent, guards his youthful mistress. During the first few weeks after the threats were received, the dog became ill.

"He's a sick dog. You'll have to leave him in the hospital for a few days," the veterinary said.

"Sick or well, he must be home tonight," Marlene replied. She had faith in her dog. He is German!

Alone in a strange country, not understanding our little kidnapping habits, can she be blamed for being afraid? And Marlene has been afraid. It is whispered that she is on the verge of a nervous breakdown. When an enterprising news service photographer recently dodged the watchers on the lot and caught a snapshot of her walking with a burly detective, which was printed in the next morning's papers, Marlene was so overwrought that she had to leave the studio for the day.

When her husband, Rudolph Sieber, returned to Europe after his recent visit, underworld threats forced him to cross Chicago and New York under a heavy guard of private detectives. Even her friend, director and discoverer, Josef von Sternberg, has been advised to take precautions to protect himself. Iron workers spent a month installing artistic, but effective grille work over the windows of his Hollywood apartment. The back door, while an ordinary door to the casual observer, is lined with bullet-proof steel. He also keeps two German shepherd dogs, one wire-haired terrier and one Scottie in the apartment. When he drives out in his shining limousine, he is accompanied by his chauffeur and two armed men.

Chief Blair, of the Beverly Hills Police force, and District Attorney Buron Fitts are enthusiastic in their praise of Miss Dietrich.

"We immediately branded the kidnapping threats as the work of an amateur, either a crank or a disgruntled servant, but we had to take the same precautions that we would have, if we had thought the threats came from an organized band of racketeers. For an amateur can be just as dangerous," Chief Blair says. "The night we set the trap for the would-be kidnappers, who did not appear, Miss Dietrich refused to go to bed at all. She wanted to be in on everything. At the dinner table she kept jumping up from the table to wait on us, although she had adequate help. And all night, she kept rushing to the kitchen every hour or so to make coffee for the men. It seemed to give her great satisfaction to do things, personally. She felt that she was helping."

It was during this time that Marlene's husband, Rudolph Sieber, had to leave for his work in France. Can you imagine his emotions at leaving his wife and baby under such circumstances alone in a strange country? "I'm satisfied that you're doing everything possible to protect my family," he told Chief Blair before leaving. "But, for God's sake, catch those men and shake them down."

"How do you shake men down, Chief Blair?" asked Maria, enthralled at the interesting prospect.

But it is Marlene who has been shaken, shaken out of her sense of security, shaken out of that Teutonic calm that has masked her emotions so effectively since she came to Hollywood. Who could blame her if she prefers to return to Europe to stay? Her husband, her family, her friends are there. She is financially able to retire from active work this minute if she wishes. If she doesn't wish, she will surely have no trouble in getting all the work she wants in Europe.

Will *Deep Night*, the picture scheduled to follow *Blonde Venus*, end Marlene's American career? Have we frightened away our best-loved German star?

Franc Dillon was a frequent contributor to entertainment publications.

"Dietrich – The Lady and the Tigress! by William E. Benton. *Screenland,* October, 1932

Marlene, 1932.

Tawny hair, slanting eyes, smooth, feline grace – she's the Blonde Tigress! Get this new and revealing angle on Marlene from Character Analyst Benton and compare it with your own qualities.

All human beings are alike, yet each is distinctive – unique. Your features, if properly analyzed, can furnish the key to your real character and possibilities. William E. Benton, *Screenland*'s "Faceologist," can perform this vital service for you through these three modern branches of human analysis:

FACEOLOGY. The study of the features. Send your photograph – a small snapshot which can be sent in an ordinary-sized envelope.

GRAPHOLOGY. Send sample of your handwriting. A dozen words are sufficient.

NUMEROLOGY. Send your full name – including given name – and your birth date.

Send these indexes of your character with 25cents and stamped self-addressed envelope to William E. Benton, Screenland Magazine, 43 West 45th Street, New York City, and you will receive a comparative analysis of yourself that will entertain as well as help you.

You have noticed that all unusual personalities resemble or suggest some bird or animal – yes, sometimes there are even those who suggest certain fish. For instance, von Hindenburg has been compared to a great bulldog; certainly he has been a dog of war for Germany. Friedrich Nietzsche, the great German philosopher, wrote of "the superman" and likened him to a great blond beast.

The Royal Bengal Tiger has been worshipped even more than it was feared all through India for countless centuries. The whole "cat" tribe, even tabby, the house cat, was worshipped and had temples built to her glory all along the Nile. The Egyptians saw something marvelous in her "nine lives" or tenacity to this life, coupled with her fecundity and wonderful care of her young.

The heroes and heroines of the motion picture world can but expect to be likened to the creatures they suggest, if that has been the fate of the world's best-known personalities down the corridors of time.

Marlene Dietrich may not believe in the transmigration of souls or that she was ever a Royal Bengal Tigress. But I can see much of the likeness to that royal animal in her face today. Her mass of tawny gold hair, and greenish-blue eyes tipped up at the outer corners, are most feline in appearance. There is something in her smooth controlled movements suggestive of quiet, cool efficiency. You have never seen her in a position that she did not seem as graceful as a tigress, be it in repose or quick but quiet action.

Think of all the people you know with the almond-shaped eyes of Dietrich – do you know of any who are dull and stupid with such eyes? You do not. The chances are that, those who come to mind with such eyes are clever, alert, controlled, and can do a great deal with the least apparent effort.

You might do worse than take a look into the mirror at the windows of your own soul. If your eyes are as widespread as Marlene Dietrich's – that is, so wide between the eyes that there would be room for an eye and a third, put yourself down for a most unusual person, for the great majority of the world's population have just the space of the width of an eye between the eyes or a fraction less. She is literally and figuratively broadminded, but very level-headed and balanced about it.

"Cats," you know, have a marvelous sense of taste, touch and balance. No matter how they are mauled or manhandled they always land on their feet. If you, too, have this width between the eyes and a head as wide at the temples as Marlene Dietrich's, you too will have this sense of balance, rhythm and harmony.

Did you ever note in the pictures and busts of great musicians this tendency to breadth to the head? Had Dietrich chosen music, especially musical composition as a career, she might have had equal or greater fame and fortune than she has won as an actress.

Now I suppose you wonder what connection there can be between the cat tribe and music. Well, cats may not be far enough evolved to sing, but they are the world's best and most earnest midnight serenaders! Charles Darwin, the father of the theory of Evolution, could show us most interesting things about the aeon-long efforts creatures make to do the thing that they eventually master. Dogs bark, lions roar, for all the world to hear and know their feelings. Cats and tigers use their vocal ability to show their personal feelings toward one another.

Some people, like dogs, make a great show of their loves, hates, fears; their barking shows their momentary feelings. The whole cat family can wait quietly, patiently, until the proper moment; then, achieving the object of their stalk, one may hear nothing more than a most contented purr. Rub a cat's fur the right way and you can hear her try to sing a song of happiness; do the reverse and she has quite efficient ways of showing her displeasure. They say dogs worship men, but cats do not; certainly the Royal Bengal Tiger seems to reserve all feelings of love for the mate.

Marlene Dietrich is a harmonious though somewhat inscrutable personality who would have made an ideal Priestess in the Temples of the Cat Goddess of the Nile.

In this mechanistic, bombastic age of noise, confusion, haste, one with her feline personality awakens a response in the breast of millions because of the subconscious feelings of harmony, softness, and a perfect adaptation to place and time.

To best understand personalities sometimes it is best to compare them with their direct opposites. Let us consider persons with the round eye and bland stare of a gazelle or deer – they are often guileless, staring in open-eyed wonder at a world full of things they cannot master or understand.

Try this interesting experiment: open your eyes as wide as you can, if you are all alone; go before the mirror and let your mouth drop open, too; then, while holding this admittedly stupid expression, try to think, plan, decide, and you'll find the minute you are doing so your expression has slipped or changed to a more cunning or cat-like one.

Perhaps you think I am a cat lover or a Dietrich "fan," but I am neither. As a character analyst I find this study of animal traits and physical comparison to people is extremely useful. It's fun for anyone interested in personality and it's unconscious or conscious betrayal in words and actions.

Dogs have evolved from the ancient wolf ancestor into man's best friend and protector. Methinks tabby, though, was in the house and by the hearth long before her shaggy enemy was allowed past the kitchen door. For she has the most cunning and ingratiating personality.

How did the cat ingratiate herself into the hearts of men? By a thousand graceful feminine wiles. Watch a cat who has decided to adopt your hearth and home. Graceful posing, pretty purring, and an uncanny capacity to appear and disappear at the most opportune times!

Marlene Dietrich suggests the beautiful blonde Royal Tigress, not the ruthless hater of mankind. Don't forget the man-stalking tiger is the outcast like the rogue elephant.

Marlene Dietrich has a splendid, somewhat pointed chin, so she has the courage to fight for what she believes to be right for herself and loved ones. If you have a chin like this, you too have the courage to pioneer.

The live, tawny hair tells a story of a somewhat happy-go-lucky independent inner nature. There is an institute, in fact, there are many of them in Germany, where if you sent one hair of your head they would put it under a most powerful microscope and tell your racial type, about your health, probable occupation, and a world of interesting and most intimate things about your personality.

Your nose tells more about you than any feature, however, and shows the most constant impressions of desires of your nature. If yours is wide-winged and somewhat retroussé, like our subject's, you too will be one of strong but controlled emotions. Some of the world's greatest coquettes have such noses.

If you have ever watched a pussy cat rub up against someone whose favorable attention she wanted you were amazed at tabby's ability to gain favor tactfully. There are a great many things to be learned from every feature of every creature. You never saw graceful swimming water fowl without webbed feet.

Human Engineering is a most fascinating study and if Marlene Dietrich's parents had taken her to a character analyst as a little child the potential, musical and dramatic traits of great promise would have revealed themselves most surely.

Marlene Dietrich is only one of the earth's millions of interesting personalities. You may be her opposite in everything, yet achieve a life as interesting through knowing and being yourself just as she has. You may have an inferiority complex or the reverse, but in either case it should be understood and harnessed for your success and happiness here and now. You could do far worse than get the truth about yourself if only on suspicion that you too have the potentialities of a great personality.

William E. Benton was a popular "Faceologist," and profiled many film stars for various entertainment publications.

"Is Dietrich Through?" by Ruth Biery. *Photoplay*, January, 1933

Hollywood is eagerly discussing Marlene Dietrich and her problems.

Her contract with Paramount is finished in February. Will she re-sign? Will she make pictures with other directors than von Sternberg? Will she remain in this country or return to Europe as has been rumored? That Maurice Chevalier gossip? What was behind the seeming unfriendliness between herself and von Sternberg?

What was all that fuss about the kidnapping of her daughter? Was this just another publicity racket?

Literally hundreds of curious, anxious questions.

Marlene has not granted an interview for seven months. She has remained isolated behind her forbidden guard of nine detectives. Yes, I said, "nine." Neither Marlene nor her daughter has moved without the protection of armed guards for many, many weeks. She had added what threatened to be an indefinite silence to her well-managed defense.

But now she has broken that silence. "It is right that the American people who have been kind enough to see my pictures should know and understand. It is right that I, myself, should tell them"

She paced the floor of her simple, yet luxurious dressing-room suite while she was talking. Dressed in a white flannel suit with perfectly tailored trousers, coat, shirt and tie (the extra-wide brim of her white hat was the only concession to her femininity), she paced the floor with rapid, well-balanced and concretely graceful strides. She smoked one cigarette after another. She was nervous. Breaking a protective silence is not easy for a woman as intelligent and, at the same time, as sensitive as Marlene Dietrich.

I tried to find proper words to describe her even as I sat watching her, but it was difficult. Dressed like a man, she was so obviously a high-strung woman. Her nervousness, her great grace, her rapid, high-tensioned speech made her so supremely feminine that one forgot the trousers.

She was curious about all that had been said about her. She had me repeat the rumors. When I hesitated at something which seemed to me too cruel, too absurd, she urged me on. She laughed merrily as the gossip mounted. When I had finished, she sobered.

"I didn't see anyone for more than half a year. I am stepping out from that silence because I have wanted to tell the truth.

"The fact is Mr. von Sternberg has wanted me to work with someone else. It's *me* that always asks him to make my pictures. There are letters which Mr. Schulberg has from me saying, 'Please make Mr. von Sternberg do it.

"Both of our contracts are up after the next picture. I will not remain in Hollywood. I am sure. I will go to Paris and Berlin and London and sing. I have some stage offers. Mr. von Sternberg is tired of pictures. He wants to go to Japan. And I will never make pictures in America with anyone but Mr. von Sternberg."

Although Marlene did not know it, she was merely verifying what Josef von Sternberg, himself, had told me when those two were at war with Paramount over the making of *Blonde Venus*.

"I am going to retire. I had just so many stories in me. I wouldn't be surprised if I have to make *Blonde Venus* and one more (the terms of his contract – also Marlene's) and then never make another."

Hollywood cannot, of course, understand such an arrangement. A star of Marlene Dietrich's potentialities to retire from the screen because she will allow only one man to direct her! A woman who would reject all that money!

I wonder if America can understand her. Marlene Dietrich is so all-inclusively European. And despite the efficiency of communication in this modern era – Europe is still Europe and America still America. Marlene's viewpoint is wholly theirs. One must bridge the Atlantic to even begin to understand her.

She tried to make me see it.

"My contract could have gone longer. I wanted to be free when he was free. I, myself, don't like making pictures. I can live without making them. I am not the movie actress.

"I haven't *got to act* to be happy. I can be quite happy without acting. I know so many actresses with their terrible desire to act. They cannot be happy unless the desire comes out of them in acting.

"I don't have it at all. I have other duties. And money. Money doesn't mean a thing to me."

I asked her if this wasn't because her family has money. She shrugged. And a shrug from Marlene Dietrich can be more expressive than an entire volume of words from another woman.

"Yes. We have money. But I could not draw from my family's money what I can draw from this."

The sweep or her arm included the entire Paramount studio.

"But money is not important. To be happy is what is important."

Ah, Europe, could you but teach this to your neighbor!

"I do not know as I can make you understand. My vocabulary is still so limited. If I am not happy when I work, I am not satisfied. I am happy with Mr. von Sternberg because I trust him. How do I know what another director could do with me?

"I was not the big sensation in Europe that publicity stories have stated. Europe knows that. I had made a picture. I was not very good in pictures. When I met him in Europe and he asked me to make *The Blue Angel*, I said, 'You had better not take me, I am terrible in pictures. No!'

"The studio did not want me, too. They told him I was terrible.

"He said, 'I will have to take a test to show *you* that you are not terrible and to show UFA, too. You are all stupid!'

"And I was not a great actress on the stage, either. Not a star, as has been said. In Europe no young girl is a star. I had played leads, but that is far from being a star. It is impossible for a young woman to be a star in Europe. It takes a very long time before Europe makes one a star.

"He took a test. He made *The Blue Angel* with me."

She did not need to tell that *The Blue Angel* was the sensation of Europe and that she became a sensation in it. She did not need to paint the picture of how she proved the exception to that rule that no *young woman* can become a star on the Continent. She was one by popular acclamation.

And she did not need to tell me – although she did – that Josef von Sternberg, through his direction, had done it. What no other director has been able to accomplish, he had done. He had transmitted her natural beauty and ability across the film chasm.

And now that she was a sensation in her own land where she had formally been only a modest beseecher, they wanted her to go to America. She said, "No." Why should she desert glory and success in the hand for possibilities in the bush? No one in America knew her. It would be beginning all over again. It would mean a new language, even. Why should she leave her family for something uncertain when she had a certain Europe at her feet?

But when von Sternberg asked her again and said, "Come over and make pictures for *me*. Not for Paramount, but with me -."

There was no uncertainty there. She knew what he could do with her and for her. He had done it in Europe. He could do it in America. Whether any other man could bridge that film chasm (no other *had*) was a huge question mark. He was the bird in the hand. She came to America to make pictures *with him*.

She is leaving America because she will make pictures with no one except him. The only possible chance of her returning is for the same reason that she came to us originally.

"This is not because of any *Svengali* and *Trilby* influence, but because he is the best friend I ever had in the world. People have said he casts a spell over me. That is ridiculous. I am devoted, but I made the devotion myself because my brain told me to. It is only common sense to me.

"Can you think of any one casting a spell over me? I hate anyone wanting to clamp a hand down on me. I would never make a contract for longer than six months because I hate the idea of being nailed down. I resent it terribly.

"But when I *devote myself* to someone, no one can undo it.

"People should be able to understand that. If you meet a great person, you become devoted. If they knew him – he has no way of talking with stupid people. He has no patience with me while I am stupid. Which I understand. Why should he waste his time!"

But to change! To work with anyone else! It is actually beyond her comprehension. She gave an example which she is afraid our people will not understand. I am going to risk it.

"Before I had my child, I stopped and looked at every child in the street. I was so crazy about all children. But now – when I have my own. That is perfection. Why should I look at others? I have the best, all children for me – right at home. I feel that way about directors. I have the best. Why should I look at others?"

I am a bit afraid, even as is Marlene herself, that America will not understand her. She is leaving us in February, for always – unless von Sternberg, who is definitely "sick and tired of pictures," (his own expression), should change his mind. She will have made only five pictures in her three and a half years among us, but with those five she has chiseled a niche on the portals of fame, comparable only to the one of Garbo.

It is comprehensible why she should wish to be understood "just once" before her departure.

Her American life has not been happy. Her first year – Mrs. von Sternberg's suit for alienation of affections. The suit was understandable from a wholly American viewpoint – it was completely

Marlene and Dickie Moore in Blonde Venus, *1932.*

a puzzle from Marlene's European one. She had a husband. He understood. Why should not Mr. von Sternberg's wife do the same, she reasoned. Incidentally, I have known both Marlene and von Sternberg since she first came and I have always said both in print and in person that Marlene's devotion has always been as she now explains it.

A mental and, to her, common sense one.

Then – the fight on *Blonde Venus*. Von Sternberg did not want to direct it. The studio wished to make the story saccharine. He bolted. Richard Wallace was assigned as director. *She* bolted. You now know why. Von Sternberg really went back and directed that picture for the sake of Marlene. He hated it then – he hates it now. And no man can do a truly great picture with a story which he hates.

And then – the kidnapping threats for her baby. Any description of her suffering would sound like an exaggeration. That Marlene Dietrich has a mother complex, no American would question. To her, the extent of her love is only as natural as her refusal to be directed by any man other than the one who bridged the screen chasm for her. The letters she received were made up of words clipped from newspapers to avoid any trace of handwriting. People said it was a joke.

They continued for six weeks. Each new letter showed a new knowledge of her movements. Why had she hired detectives? Why had she taken her child to such and such a place the day before? Marlene Dietrich was close to a mad woman. Neither she nor her child even now stir in the open today without armed guards.

The bars on the windows of her home are inches thick.

During the thick of the daily threats, she received word from the department of immigration that her two German maids should return home. She wrote a letter that she was employing eleven Americans – nine of whom were made necessary by the dangers of this country.

Must she send away the two Germans, the only ones whom she could truly trust with her child? – The American government let them remain.

Then – the Chevalier gossip. Marlene and Maurice are friends. But – she laughs. "They forget I am married and I am not divorcing my husband. He is coming for Christmas and then we shall be really happy and gay."

Her husband has had many clothes made for Marlene at her tailors in Paris. He sent these clothes back to Marlene with Maurice Chevalier! Again, perhaps only Europeans could fully understand friendships like these.

I do not believe Marlene will cry when she sails to sing in the theaters of Paris and Berlin.

"My child will be safe over there." A throb in her voice when she says it. "Not no more troubles. We all have them. But less troubles and not so much silly talk.

"But I am happy I am able to give so many Americans work in protecting me from these strange customs. Some good has come."

Her eyes twinkle.

I think they will twinkle when she waves goodbye to the Statue of Liberty which has not meant all liberty for her.

Impossible, perhaps, for an American to vision happiness at waving goodbye to that statue!

Impossible, perhaps, also, for a European like Marlene, to vision happiness at waving it a second time!

"Has America Declared War on ALL Foreign Players?" by Frank Cates. *Movie Classic*, March, 1933

Marlene with Max Reinhardt and Ernst Lubitsch, Hollywood, 1933.

Murray W. Garsson, Special Assistant Secretary of Labor, has been investigating every foreign player in Hollywood – and several are about to leave. But how does the government determine which players are to be deported? He tells you in this story – and prophesies a law to ban all alien players except those of the first rank, like Arliss and Chevalier, whose places could not be filled by Americans!

Garsson, who has been investigating Hollywood's aliens, says, "I would not even venture a guess as to the number of foreign players illegally in Hollywood – there are so many of them. These people will have to get out and go back where they belong. We are doing this to protect American actors and actresses. We do not object to the bringing of a player like Chevalier here to do a part no one else can do. But we do object to hordes of players coming here and settling, many of them illegally and, while claiming allegiance to another flag, taking the work that is so badly needed by our own players."

The panic is on in Hollywood's foreign colony. And it is not Old Man Depression that is causing it, either. The cause of said panic is a gentleman named Murray W. Garsson, Special Assistant Secretary of Labor, who journeyed from Washington to see what foreign stars, and would-be stars, are in America illegally – and to see that these players hasten back to their native lands as rapidly as they can arrange their affairs and secure transportation.

The result is that scores of foreign players are digging up immigration papers, long since dusty, and are attempting either to set themselves right with the American government, or depart as gracefully as possible. It was probably only a coincidence that the Marquis de la Falaise and his wife, Constance Bennett, started for Europe three days after the immigration authorities sent for Henri. But, within a couple of months the Hollywood foreign group will be much – very much – smaller than it is now.

According to Mr. Garsson, every foreign player, writer, director and technician in Hollywood will be investigated; and if any are here without the proper permits from the Immigration Department, they will be asked to leave immediately.

"I would not even venture a guess as to the number of foreign players illegally in Hollywood," Mr. Garsson told me. "There are so many of them that any man's guess is as good as mine. And these people will have to get out and go back where they belong. We are now *requesting* them to leave. If they do not do so, we will arrest them and deport them. We will stand for no foolishness. We mean business."

Among the foreign players now in this country whose status is being investigated are: George Arliss, Charles Chaplin, Elissa Landi, Marlene Dietrich, Lupe Velez, Lili Damita, Maurice Chevalier, Gregory Ratoff, Maureen O'Sullivan, Nils Asther, Tala Birell, Anna Sten, George Brent, Diana Wynyard, Clive Brook, Ronald Colman, Frank Lawton, Mona Maris, John Warburton, Leslie Howard, David Manners, Colin Clive, Herbert Mundin,

Ursula Jeans, Lyda Roberti, Paul Cavanagh, Benita Hume, Ivan Lebedeff, Lilian Bond, Gwili Andre, Ralph Forbes, Wera Engels, Boris Karloff, Bela Lugosi, Sari Maritza, Paul Lukas, the Marquis de la Falaise, and a horde of lesser acting lights, together with writers, directors and technicians. In short, the papers of all the foreigners are being checked – particularly those who do not have long-term contracts with any studio, for studios usually take pains to make sure that their foreign stars' papers are in order.

This drive against the foreign players has been prompted, Mr. Garsson says, by protests on the part of the Actors' Equity Association and the Lambs Club of New York.

"These two organizations have been hot after the Department of Labor in Washington for a long time," said Mr. Garsson. "They have been protesting against the influx of foreign players who, they declared, were taking the jobs that belong to Americans.

"We have been very kind to the foreign players," said Mr. Garsson. "We have tried to show every courtesy possible. We would grant a player a six-months permit. In scores of cases, these players took advantage of us and stayed on and on without even thinking of renewing the permit. They just took things into their own hands. We are stopping this now. We are doing this to protect American actors and actresses. It would have been done long ago if native-born players had dared to voice their protests. I have asked American actors why they have kept silent. They explain that they have been afraid to speak because they feared reprisals from those *higher up* and from the studios. They need not fear that any longer, for the studios are cooperating with us fully."

Studios are gladly supplying records of when their foreign workers entered this country, so that the investigators can check with the files of entry permits in their possession.

"It is shameful," Mr. Garsson adds, "the way some of these foreign players have abused their privileges here. Scores of them with no jobs in sight have come to Hollywood and free-lanced, taking the work that otherwise would have gone to Americans and gradually building up reputations at the expense of our own people. A lot of them would act for less money than the Americans have been accustomed to; naturally, the assumption is that the work would go their way."

And to show that the government and Mr. Garsson mean business, John Farrow, writer, born in Australia, was arrested the first week that Mr. Garsson was in Hollywood. He was a surprised young man when the blow fell. He was dancing at an exclusive night club. In his arms was the bewitching Mona Maris. A dreamy waltz was playing. They were gliding over the floor, murmuring the usual nothings, when an immigration officer tapped Farrow on the shoulder. He stepped outside and was under arrest on charges of illegal entry.

That is what will happen to all of the foreign players and others in the film business who are here illegally and who do not depart willingly. That is why the panic is on.

Already, more than twenty players, some of them prominent, have promised Mr. Garsson that they will leave. They are being given sufficient time in which to straighten up their personal affairs. If they overstay that time, the heavy hand of the law will fall, and they will be given transportation they do not expect or like.

The Dickstein Bill, now before Congress and admittedly about to be made into a law, will solve the foreign player problem, Mr. Garsson says, and will make changes that will greatly affect the foreign colony in Hollywood.

"The Dickstein Bill," says Mr. Garsson, with conviction, "will be a blessing to those American men and women who are making their livelihood by working on the stage or in pictures. This bill will prohibit the bringing of foreign players, directors, writers or technicians, *unless they are of proven worth and have genius in their line*. Similar legislation against American players is already in force in most other countries.

"No actor, actress, director, writer or technician will be permitted to come to America to *seek* work. There will be no more actresses spending a year and a half here to learn the language before they can make a picture. Film companies will not be permitted to bring in any of these people without a special permit, and then they will not be allowed to stay on indefinitely. This rule will apply to such players as Marlene Dietrich, Maurice Chevalier, George Arliss and Greta Garbo, the same as to any others.

"If a studio wishes to import a player from a foreign country for a picture, the officials of that company will have to present a sworn affidavit to the Immigration Department, stating that they *cannot find any player in America who is capable of playing that part*. Or if it is a writer, that *there is no writer in America who is able to write said story*. And then a permit will be granted only for the duration of time needed for making the picture or for writing or directing the story. Then the player, writer or director will have to go back home. He will not be permitted to stay here and shop around for another job, as has been the case in the past. And if a picture company cannot prove that there is no one in American ranks who could do the job, that company will find itself in a lot of trouble with the government.

"We will not attempt, ourselves, to say who is a genius. We will not have an underpaid clerk pass judgement on anyone who claims to be a genius. We will not meet the boats and test foreign actors for genius. We will take the word of the picture company – *but the company had better be sure it is telling the truth about it.*

"With the passage of the Dickstein Bill, the American actor will be assured of an opportunity to make a living. And this assurance is surely needed. You would be amazed if you could hear the stories of some of these American players. Why, only yesterday, an American actor who is known wherever pictures have been shown – a man who was a featured player – sat across from my desk and told me his story. He has worked but seven days in the past two years, because foreign players of his type, who have come here and made their homes, have taken the work and parts he used to do. And he did them well. He pulled ninety cents out of his pocket and said, 'Mr. Garsson, this is all the money I have in the world. And I borrowed this to come down here to see you and tell you how badly we need the work the foreign actors are taking.'

"That," declared Mr. Garsson, "is a condition we must remedy. We do not object to the bringing of a player like Chevalier here to do a part no one else can do. We love George Arliss, who is in a class by himself and takes no work away from anyone; and we have room for a Ronald Colman or a Clive Brook. But we do object to hordes of players coming here and settling, many of them illegally and, while claiming allegiance to another flag, taking the work that is so badly needed by our own players.

"With the passage of the Dickstein Bill there won't be such a thing as a lot of 'extras' over here who are foreigners. That is where the Dickstein Bill will be of benefit. Those people will not be allowed here. There are thousands of 'extras' of our own who can do all the 'extra' work we need done. Why not let them have the work and get money enough to eat on?"

And then Mr. Garsson pointed out something else – the matter of behavior. He said that even if a player has a legal permit to be here, he or she must behave or that permit will be revoked. He declared that while misbehavior has not been of more than average prevalence, there has been a certain number of offenses. Complaints of alleged offenses all have to be investigated, putting the Immigration Department to considerate trouble and expense.

Mr. Garsson also revealed that there are several supposed "foreign aristocrats" in the film business who are proving to be native Americans, posing as foreigners in the hope that they will get a better chance in pictures. "There are not many of them," he explained, "but there are a considerable number. They are coming to light now." On the other hand, there are several members of the film colony, born abroad, who are now naturalized American citizens like Norma Shearer, Edward G. Robinson, Victor McLaglen, Fifi Dorsay, and producer Mack Sennett.

Another condition that has existed in Hollywood for some time will take the count when the Dickstein Bill is passed and the new order of things is in effect. This is the little matter of renewing permits simply by spending a pleasant weekend in nearby Mexico.

For a long time, it has been the custom among foreign players to go to Aqua Caliente, famous racing and gambling resort of Mexico, just as their six-month permits expired. After a pleasant little holiday in Mexico, the players would re-enter the United States under the immigration quotas allowed from their respective countries and would be all set for another six months. This has "burned up" a number of American players who do not get enough work to afford trips to Caliente, but it will be ended with the new law. "We are curbing it right now," said Mr. Garsson. "It would have been curbed sooner, had we been told about it."

And so, that is the situation in the Hollywood foreign circle at this writing. No one except Mr. Garsson and his assistants knows just who will depart; but it is certain that there will be a general egress of foreign players – some of them prominent – very shortly. Of course, many of them will no doubt be going "just for a visit to the old home," but the Immigration Department knows what prompts the visit – which, in many cases, will be permanent. And in the very near future, it will be American players, playing the roles in American pictures.

It will take more than a good-looking pair of legs to swing a permit for a foreign picture actress to get by the authorities at New York harbor: it will take acting ability so unusual that no one else in America can take the part she is scheduled to play. And those close to the picture business say that it will help the picture companies, for it will stop them from bringing possible future stars from abroad and futilely trying to make box-office hits of them. Studios won't waste time and money, searching for "discoveries." They will get the best talent from the start.

Frank Cates was a frequent contributor to entertainment publications.

"Dietrich Dodges Lawsuit by Ending Revolt – Future Films To Be German-Made," by Dorothy Manners. *Movie Classic*, March, 1933

When Marlene declines to make *Song of Songs* without guidance of von Sternberg, studio promptly sues her for $185,000, and she changes mind – but end of contract will find star and director reunited in Germany.

Marlene Dietrich has decided to save $185,000 of the good iron men she has earned in America, simply by returning to work at Paramount, instead of "sitting out" the remainder of her contract. In other words, the second Dietrich vs. Paramount war had ended almost as peacefully as the first, when Marlene did a walk-out because she would not make a picture unless directed by Josef von Sternberg (and walked back within a week.)

Marlene will make *Song of Songs* under the direction of Rouben Mamoulian – the first picture she will have made in this country without the guiding hand of von Sternberg. But she is in the same frame of mind as a child who has been promised that she may attend the circus as soon as she gets her tedious homework done. In this case, *Song of Songs* is the homework, and the promised circus is her new agreement with von Sternberg, which will take her back to her beloved Germany to make Dietrich-von Sternberg pictures for UFA release.

There can be little doubt that Marlene is through, most definitely through, with Hollywood. Almost from the start of her Paramount contract to its financially lucrative completion (with Marlene drawing $4,000 weekly), she has been in almost constant turmoil with her producing company. Quarrels over stories, bickerings over leading men, and long drawn out disputes over her being directed by someone besides von Sternberg have made Marlene's stardom one of the most tumultuous tie-ups in Hollywood history. One gets the impression that both star and studio will be glad when it's all over.

The new difficulty was far more serious than the walk-out of a few months ago, both in its inception and in its threatened lawsuit. Marlene wanted to make *Song of Songs* (written by Herman Sudemann, famous German novelist and playwright), but she did not want to do it with any director other than her discoverer. To add to the complications, von Sternberg's contract had expired and he had not re-signed with Paramount. Marlene's own contract had but a few weeks to run, where upon Marlene conceived the idea of merely "sitting it out," apparently.

But she reckoned without her producing company, which had already spent more than $185,000 on preparatory work for the picture. An entire battery of lawyers was engaged to bring Marlene into court for "breach of contract" – nearly $200,000 worth of "breach." For a day, it looked as though Marlene was planning to fight the thing out in court. But suddenly, her attorney, Ralph Blum (husband of actress Carmel Myers, close friend of Marlene and von Sternberg), went into conference with the Paramount attorneys, and it was just as suddenly announced that the threatened difficulties had been successfully ironed out and Marlene was returning to work.

No mention was made of a cablegram, said to have been sent by von Sternberg in Berlin to Marlene in Hollywood, which may or may not have advised his protégé to call off her war – because of the adverse publicity that might accrue from it. For, after all, Marlene and von Sternberg still hope to release their pictures in America, after they team up again in Germany, where Marlene and her husband (Rudolph Sieber) want their little girl to be educated and where she and von Sternberg made their first picture, *The Blue Angel*.

Besides objecting to having any director besides von Sternberg, Marlene objected to the selection of Fredric March to play opposite her. But, she surrendered on both objections. The picture started "harmoniously!"

"Marlene Dietrich Tells Why She Wears Men's Clothes!" by Rosalind Shaffer. *Motion Picture,* April, 1933

No, she says, she doesn't wear them to be sensational. And she isn't trying to start a revolution in feminine attire – though she says that if other women tried them, they'd never go back to skirts. Marlene says she just followed the pajama-and-slacks idea to its logical conclusion – and adds that she has never been more comfortable or felt better-dressed in her life!

Marlene Dietrich says, "The public is always getting excited over something, anyway. First, I uncovered my legs, and people were excited over that. Now I cover my legs, and that excites them, too…I am sincere in my preference for men's clothes – I do not wear them to be sensational…I think I am much more alluring in these clothes. Wearing such clothes, too, there is a sense of perfect freedom and comfort. I never was comfortable in one single dress that I have worn in all my life. Women's clothes take too much time – it is exhausting, shopping for them. Men's clothes do not change; I can wear them as long as I like. I only hope other women try them and find the comfort I enjoy in them, free from all the constrictions of the conventional women's wear."

These are a few of the highlights gleamed from the first interview given to a screen magazine by Marlene Dietrich since she first startled Hollywood, and the world, with pictures of herself in men's clothes, with appearances at places about town in men's clothing, appearing nonchalant and looking comfortable.

Marlene caused something of a sensation when she did her first American-made film, *Morocco,* by appearing as an entertainer in a café, in a full-dress suit and top hat. People gasped, said, "How continental!" And let it pass. Then came her latest film, *Blonde Venus,* and again Dietrich was in a dress suit – a white one, however, trimmed with stripes of brilliants. Now she's wearing

Marlene in Paris, 1933.

mannish attire off the screen, and onto the very streets of Los Angeles. Since Marlene is fortunate enough to have a limousine and a chauffeur, she is spared the mobs that would greet an ordinary woman in such extraordinary garb – but even so, she causes a furor at every appearance.

Are the struggling women of the world to have a Joan of Arc come out of Hollywood in the person of Marlene Dietrich? Are the fashion-creators of Paris to be defeated by the lovely Marlene in her one-woman Battle of the Century? Is Marlene's fashion ultimatum going to be the "shot heard 'round the world," and are Marlene's breeches a new banner of freedom for the women who spend their lives and their money, trying to keep abreast of the styles, which change every three months?

These are some of the questions that thinking people in Hollywood have been asking themselves of recent weeks, since Marlene Dietrich has gone Garbo one better by appearing at shops, cafes, and even premieres, clad in men's garments – daintily tailored to show the provocative Dietrich curves, but men's garments, nevertheless.

Marlene has a wardrobe of ten tailored suits, with trousers, in her very modernistic cedar closets. She has street suits, tuxedos, as well, and a dinner coat for special occasions. These suits are no cheap jersey or flannel slacks, no flannel sport coats made to look mannish. They are expensively tailored, padded-shouldered, men's wear suits, with only this difference – the coats are fitted to Marlene's feminine curves, and the trousers are closed to one side, as a tailored skirt would close. Otherwise, in every detail, they are men's suits.

The most astonishing thing about this one-woman dress reform movement is that it should have originated with a beautiful film star, famous for her femininity, and especially for her beautiful legs, which she now conceals with the wide, long trousers of the male mode. If it had been launched by some homely or aging freak, some reformer, some feminist seeking to claim all men's rights, or some girl-athlete long on muscle but short of sex appeal, it would not have been so unexpected.

But for such a movement to be started by the lovely, languishing Dietrich – the old-fashioned mother Dietrich, who had to have her little girl with her before she could begin to be happy in Hollywood – the wife Dietrich, who loves to cook for Herr Sieber those delectable German dishes, the concocting of which is the pride of the German *hausfrau* – the Dietrich who can take a yard of feathers and look like the most ravishing *Lorelei* ever put on the jumping celluloid – well, it's just too much.

There has been a storm of gossip, not all of it nice, that has surged about those trousers of Marlene's. When Marlene appeared at the premiere of *The Sign of the Cross* in regulation tuxedo suit, with a man's felt hat with a wide brim pulled over one eye, and a long, black topcoat, gloves in hand, also mannish, and accompanied by Maurice Chevalier, Hollywood's breath stopped entirely for a few seconds.

As the couple went to their seats, there was some discussion between them as to whether Marlene would occupy the seat on the aisle, the man's side. Chevalier insisted that she take the inside seat. At intermission, Marlene, nothing abashed, went into the foyer, and graciously posed for the photographers even doing a few high, wide and handsome kicks in the spirit of fun, to demonstrate the freedom of the knees bestowed by the trousers she was wearing.

It was most feminine and disconcertingly charming Dietrich that greeted me the following day in her dressing room at the studio, where she was preparing for *Song of Songs*, her first venture in films without the direction of her mentor, Josef von Sternberg. The large, beautifully formed eyes were accented by long sweeping lashes, plentifully mascara-laden, and shadowed. The mobile lips were carefully rouged. Long fingernails, carefully kept, were carmined, accenting the graceful droop of the soft white hands. Blonde hair, carefully waved, snug to the head, disappeared under a neat black tam worn over one eye.

All utterly feminine – and then, for contrast, the square, padded-shouldered masculine suit, the white wool sox, worn like a man's, with high tops, and soft kid, square-toed oxfords, with a small flat heel and entirely bereft of feminine embellishments. A man's shirt, four-in-hand tie – and that was Dietrich.

"Are you aware of the gossip going around, concerning your wearing of men's clothes?" I popped, waiting for the Olympic frown and the lightning bolt, with what stoicism I could summon.

"I do not hear gossip, so you see it is easy for me to ignore it. I go about very little – always with a few friends, who are used to my clothes. I have been to four parties in the last three years. Yes, I know there have been some articles in the papers. The public is always excited over something, anyway.

"It has been said and printed that Mr. von Sternberg, your director, has quarreled with you because of your wearing trousers. Is this true? Does he disapprove of them?"

"This is very silly. It is not true. Mr. von Sternberg adores them. He thinks them more feminine on me than dresses. Von knows I am sincere in my preference for men's clothes, that I do no wear them to be sensational."

"And Herr Sieber – how does he feel with two pairs of trousers in the family?"

"Of course, he likes my clothes. After all, we have been married for nine years, and he knows that I have always preferred such clothes. In Europe this is not unusual – there are many tailors there who specialize in such clothes for women. I have worn full-dress suits to parties before now."

"You are such a feminine type of woman – so soft, rich fabrics, and furs, have no lure for you?"

"No. I never liked such things. I must wear them on the screen – but even my negligees have always been tailored, for my own use."

"Do you – er, if we may be so personal – don't you ever wear fussy underthings – you know, with lace and things on them?"

"With these suits, I wear no underwear but tailored, mannish silk shorts. That is one of the wonderful things about wearing such clothes, too – there is a sense of perfect freedom and comfort. I never was comfortable in one single dress that I have worn all my life. If you should ever wear these clothes, you would always prefer them for the comfort they give. Your movements are freer in them, you are fully clothed in any posture, without fear of having to pull down your skirts, or of having a 'run' start in your stockings. It bestows a feeling of poise, of well-being. You are not conscious of clothing."

"In your life, do you feel that there is any time or place for feminine garments?'

"No. Except on the screen."

"Don't you feel the urge to be alluring, to dress up sometimes in fluffy ruffles?"

"I think I am much more alluring in these clothes." Here Miss Dietrich pulled out a snapshot of herself in her mannish garb. "I never can look like that in women's clothes," she said, eyeing the snap fondly. "Here is another one – they tell me this is I, but I am sure I can never look like that," she said, laughing, as she held out a most unflattering newsprint purporting to be of herself, in men's clothes.

"Women's clothes take too much time – it is exhausting shopping for them. Then there are hats, there are shoes to match, there are handbags, gloves, scarves, coats, all those accessories." She shrugged her dainty, but padded shoulders. "I could never find the time nor the interest for all of that. Those things require so much study, such discriminating selection, with all that matching that is required – no, for me it is impossible.

"Then the styles change – and it must all be done over again, every few months. It is very extravagant to dress as most women do. Men's clothes do not change; I can wear them as long as I like. People say that it is because I am economical that I buy these things. That is not exactly true. I like to be extravagant sometimes. If I want something, I have it. But I do not like to have so much of my time and energy taken up with something in which I have so little interest, as clothes. These clothes that I wear just suit me.

I have a fanatical love for modern things. I will only live among modern things in my home.

"Yes, it is true that I have similar suits made for Maria, my daughter. I find that at the beach, and in fact anywhere that she is playing outdoors, she is so much better protected in trousers than in skirts. With dresses, there is a worry of sweaters, and coats and all the rest of it. Her bare legs are likely to chill. In trousers, she is free and protected. Of course, she enjoys them – and she has a child's delight in dressing like mama. She also has other clothes – conventional little-girl clothes – when she wishes them.

"I had no idea when I started wearing my tailored trousers that I was starting anything for other people. Many women have been wearing slacks, and before that, pajamas, so it seems to me that my clothes are a logical conclusion to these. I started wearing these clothes for my own satisfaction. I do not believe that they suit every woman. I think that a woman must be the feminine type, and she must be tall, preferably with square shoulders and narrow hips, to wear men's clothes well."

Whether Frau Sieber thought she was starting something or not, the fact remains that she has. The smartest women's shops are now featuring just such suits for Spring wear. The suits come with both trousers and tailored skirts; sometimes with a mannish topcoat as well. Mannish skirts and ties are worn with these suits; also, sweaters.

Dietrich's own wardrobe includes a tailored skirt for every trouser suit, just in case. Some of them are divided skirts, some simply the conventional tailored skirt. Her preferences lean to grays in hard-finished serges and herringbone weaves.

"I started wearing these men's suits in public places last summer," said Marlene. "It was purely a matter of convenience. I live at the beach and would be in them for the day. After dinner, often my husband and Mr. von Sternberg would wish to go up to the Boulevard to see a show or a picture. I would be tired, and plead that I did not wish to go, because I would have to change all my clothes and dress and be uncomfortable. They urged me to come as I was – and so it began. Well, the public is always excited about something, always seeking something new to discuss. I don't mind. I only hope other women try them and find the comfort I enjoy in them, free from all the constrictions of the conventional women's wear. I know they'll never go back to skirts."

Rosalind Shaffer (1896-1990) was a scenarist, publicist, and writer. In 1928, she helped found the Hollywood Women's Press Club with Louella Parsons. Shaffer worked as an entertainment columnist and feature writer for newspapers, and the Associated Press. She also worked in the publicity departments of Columbia, RKO, Paramount and 20th Century Fox studios. Her novel, *The Finger Man*, was made into the 1933 film, *Lady Killer*.

"Why Dietrich Wears Trousers…
Marlene's reasons as to why she has been appearing in public in trousers tailored in regular masculine style" by Jean Cummings. *Modern Screen*, April, 1933

"Seen at the opening of *The Sign of the Cross* in a man's tuxedo, Marlene Dietrich topped the entire evening! Maurice Chevalier, who spent the intermission with the German star, seemed positively envious of the perfect cut of Marlene's mannish coat."

The above item, in a Hollywood paper, brings Marlene Dietrich's "trouser season" to a climax. Besides Chevalier, most of the men at the theater cast longing glances at the beautiful, blond gal who stood, hands in pockets of the most perfectly fitting tuxedo in town!

True, trousers are nothing new to Dietrich! She has been wearing them for months around Hollywood. Worn them so *often*, in fact, that there is grave doubt in the minds of many onlookers that she even *owns* a dress now! Worn them in spite of the fact that almost every writer in Hollywood has twitted her. Hollywood doesn't like it! Says so – and means it! Still, Dietrich goes on wearing her trousers.

Why?

Almost everyone in the colony has put forth at least one answer to the question…but until now, no one has thought to ask the lady herself! Here is Marlene's own answer – told quite matter-of-factly and without pose.

"I wear trousers for the reason that they are more comfortable!" smiled Dietrich (who at the moment was wearing gray flannels). "One can slip into a pair of trousers in two minutes, even without the aid of a mirror, and lounge around in perfect ease. The men's shirts and coats that I wear are also more comfortable than most any dress I have ever worn. I wouldn't advise *every* woman to wear trousers, however, because they don't fit every figure…my shoulders are wide like a pair of masculine shoulders!"

Before Marlene continued, I noticed that while she was wearing a suit, she wore no vest! A striped shirt with a broad, black four-in-hand tie. Silk sox and low-heeled shoes! A small beret, worn over one eye, completed the ensemble.

"Trousers and masculine clothes make me appear *more* feminine than dresses do!" Marlene went on, crossing her feet as she leaned against the door of her dressing room while lighting a cigarette. "I think you will agree, that certain types of women look well in masculine clothes…even better than they do in frills and laces! I always wear plenty of flowing gowns in my pictures, but in real life a man's suit makes me feel (and, I hope *look*) more feminine than the most beautiful dress in the world!

"Also, it takes too much time, trouble and *money* to be a well-dressed woman in Hollywood. Motion picture stars are always buying some terrifically expensive gown, wearing it once or twice and then discarding it because they *can't afford* to be seen in the same dress more often! As for me, wearing a dress more than twice is easy. If it weren't for the fact that the style changes before one has the opportunity to get the gown on the third or fourth time! Isn't it silly to spend all that money…just for a whim? It really isn't worth it!

"In my present wardrobe, though, I have ten suits – a few pairs of extra trousers – a sweater or two – some shirts and a polo coat! That is all I need – the style will be good two years from now! I tried to figure out, the other night, what it would cost me to wear dresses during those two years…I quit before I reached the astounding total!"

The other day, we overheard several women talking about Dietrich's costume at a recent party. They seemed unanimous in their shocking reaction. The group of *men* at the party had eyes for no other woman! Are women jealous of Dietrich in pants? Or do they hold the idea in contempt? What do you think?

Jean Cummings was a frequent contributor to numerous movie magazines.

"Intimate Facts About Marlene's Wardrobe," by Franc Dillon. *The New Movie Magazine*, May, 1933

Half the women in the United States are eager to step into Marlene Dietrich's trousers! Oh, some just like them. Five thousand pairs of slacks were sold to women in one Hollywood shop alone. But this season the customer says, "I want a pair of trousers just like Marlene Dietrich's."

All of which has left Marlene completely bewildered.

"Why all this fuss about my trousers?" she asked, with just a suggestion of a frown on her smooth forehead. "I've always worn them. I wore them for years in Europe before I came here. I wore them in my first picture here. No one made any comment. Now, suddenly, everyone starts talking about them and all the women are wearing them. Why?"

For Marlene, who has adopted pants for nearly all off-screen appearances, feels that they are her own property; that no one has the right to interfere with her individuality, as it were.

"I love these little pants," she said, patting the leg of her gray trousers. "I like them for several reasons. They are comfortable; they are economical because the styles in men's clothes do not change often; and I think they suit my type.

"Only the most feminine-looking women should wear trousers," Marlene continued, and she practices what she preaches, for she always looks feminine in spite of her mannish clothes. She usually wears a small beret or a soft tailored hat, and her hair is always arranged in soft waves about her face. Her nails are always manicured in feminine fashion and usually painted a brilliant red.

She resented being criticized for allowing her eight-year-old daughter, Maria, to wear trousers. "I bought pants for Maria because they are warm," she explained. "Even in California the nights are cool and I think it is wise to keep her legs warm."

It was when she appeared at the premiere of *The Sign of the Cross* dressed in a man's evening costume, complete in every detail, that she almost stopped traffic. And at night clubs, wearing a tuxedo; shopping on the boulevard wearing one of her many business suits, or wherever she went, dressed in the height of men's fashion, she aroused *ohs* and *ahs* of envy, admiration and criticism. The girls followed her lead like sheep and Hollywood suddenly looked as though it had been entirely deserted by the feminine sex.

An enterprising manufacturer rushed a "Marlean" suit into the market, a tailored one boasting a pair of trousers as well as a skirt; and the Paramount studio officials decided it was time to act. They remonstrated with Marlene and wearing her trousers in public. And Marlene replied in her quiet, but nonetheless effective manner, that what she wore off the screen was her own business.

"If this be publicity, then let's make the most of it," said the Paramount publicity department, and blithely turned the full glare of the spotlight on Marlene's pants.

"I'm sorry I ever posed for pictures in them," Marlene said ruefully, and now refuses to talk about them to anyone. Six months ago she spoke of them naturally. Today the subject is just one more grievance she holds against America. And perhaps part of her annoyance is due to the fact that although the women imitate her, they do it, for the most part, badly.

For though half the women in the United States want to wear pants like Dietrich's not one out of a hundred can look as she does in her well-cut tailored trousers.

But Marlene's figure isn't the only secret of her success in wearing trousers. She knows how to underdress them. She wears no frilly, bungle-some underwear. A net brassiere and a pair of tailored silk shorts (men's shorts) are the foundation for her costume. Her shirts are made to order by a shirt maker who also makes her shorts of the same material. Her men's shorts cross over in front like a wrap-around garment with two small buttons on each side. Four tiny pleats in front and back give the fullness necessary for a woman's figure.

No corset or girdle, not even a garter belt, are worn to take away from the mannish effect. Long stockings would break the line of the trousers leg, so she wears men's socks and garters.

Watson and Son, tailors to many of the smartest dressed men in Hollywood have had to forswear allegiance to the male sex. Numbering among their patrons Dietrich, Garbo, Bankhead, Hepburn, Joan Crawford, Sally Eilers, Barbara Stanwyck, and many other stars, it is only natural that all feminine Hollywood is rushing to them.

"Miss Dietrich, Miss Garbo, Miss Hepburn and Miss Bankhead are the only girls who wear men's trousers," said Mr. Watson, "and theirs' are identical.

"Tailoring for women is quite different from making men's clothes," Mr. Watson said. "We don't make exaggerated clothes for men but I think a mannish suit for a woman should be exaggerated. For instance, if the shoulders of a woman's coat are made very wide, it tends to make her hips look slimmer, adds height and grace.

"Most of the girls still prefer the more feminine version of trousers. We make Miss Dietrich's trousers 22 ½ inches at the knee, 18 ½ inches at the cuff, which is 2 inches deep. But most of the girls prefer a 24-inch knee and 22 inches at the bottom."

Marlene does not usually wear men's shoes, although she has several pairs. She wears a heavy walking shoe which resembles a man's oxford. She sometimes wears ghillies with her suits. "I wear walking shoes with low heels because they look better with tailored clothes, and they are more comfortable," she told me.

"Most American women look so charming in feminine clothes. I think they should wear skirts," she said tactfully. "I wear the kind of clothes I like and the clothes that are most becoming to me and I expect other women to do the same. I think it would be a pity if all women suddenly appeared in trousers."

Marlene in Blonde Venus, *1932.*

"The Mystery of Marlene," by Elsie Janis. *The New Movie Magazine*, May, 1933

In nineteen and twenty-nine at Paramount studios I was discussing some scenes for the Revue we were planning with Albert Kaufman, one of the few executives who has remained with the organization. (For the last three years the heads of departments have been riding the rapidly revolving door of power as if it were a merry-go-round. I don't know now who has caught the brass ring!)

Halting our discussion, Al tossed a half-dozen photographs across the desk saying, "There's a girl we have just signed up. She looks like a great bet for pictures." I gazed for the first time into the eyelash-draped eyes of Marlene Dietrich. All the photographs were in men's clothes.

"Is she a male impersonator?" I asked.

Al laughed. "I should say not. She has more 'it' and 'that' than anyone we've got. Sings, dances, and a fine actress! But she usually does a number in men's clothes. She's a big stage favorite in Germany!"

Having specialized in male impersonations myself, my appraisal was slightly tinted with criticism. "She is very attractive, and wears the clothes well!" I said. "But she doesn't look anything like a man with all that fluffy hair sticking out under the top hat!"

"Well! She's not a bit masculine." Al was looking at a gay, laughing picture. "It's funny; she's very feminine – has a baby and a husband," Al added.

"That's good!" I said, referring to the afterthought of propriety.

"I guess she just likes to wear pants," Al concluded.

The pictures were laid aside and we returned to our own affairs, little dreaming that in less than four years Marlene Dietrich's trousers would be everybody's affair. Al Kaufman's explanation still is the correct one. Hollywood with all its demoralizing magic has not altered the fair German's ideas, but its small-town attitude and her success have, I think, given her the courage to express them

Marlene in Blonde Venus, *1932.*

and stick to them even if she gets stuck with them.

She is still feminine, she still has the same husband, and her child, though no longer a baby, receives more maternal devotion than any I have ever seen, with perhaps the exception of myself when I was her age.

Half the women in the world have fallen for or risen to (according to one's point of view) pyjamas. From the country girl in her homemade gingham to the *demimondaine* in her French-made velvet and ermine. There must be something to them. I know there's too much in many of them.

The answer is comfort and freedom. Certainly the desire is not to be like the men, but modern women can't be blamed for trying to "snitch" a little of the ease men enjoy; to be able to cross the legs without staging a tug-of-war with a dress, or to walk beside the male companion without the usual and now *passe,* "What's the matter? Are you walking with me or just following my trail?"

I'll admit that Dietrich in complete masculine attire is a little ahead of the procession, but I also predict that it will soon catch up and pass her, because she needs that mass of spun gold sometimes called hair for her screen work and when the Eton bob comes bob, bob, bobbing along dressed in brother's Sunday suit, Dietrich will look like a "weak sister" by comparison.

I can't help thinking of how gay and mischievous she looked in those pre-American pictures and remarking that a film success in our Land of the Free is an expensive business. The income tax collector holds the first mortgage on your achievements, the press the second, the public the third, the studios have the right to turn a young girl's laughter into a deserted wife's tears, the camera and

Father Time both have options on your face, while the masseuse has a lien on your fat. Foreigners may take what's left back to their respective homelands at will, but if by chance they want more punishment, the emigration laws make them sit up, beg for, and then wait for it! The speed with which it can dim its luster, when a smoke screen of criticism is thrown out! The star may still be there, possessing all the brilliancy that established it in the firmament of fame, but smoked glasses are reserved for the sun.

In Marlene Dietrich's case, the screen of smoke is just starting really to rise and she is doing nothing drastic to soar above it. I think she must feel that the form of suffocation doesn't much matter, and if she must wear a mask, to satisfy the public which two years ago was at her feet (not to mention what they are attached to), then why not a gas mask? The German ones were far superior to ours in the War!

In France, England, Germany, and other countries, the public judges an artist by what he or she does in the theater. I don't believe the things which have happened to Dietrich would be possible in Europe.

For instance, Josef von Sternberg, an astute, brilliant, and far-seeing young Hebrew, made a picture before he ever directed the dazzling Darling of the Deutch. It was called, *The Salvation Hunters*, and he made it on a shoe-string or maybe just a plain string. But it was so good that I sat one night and listened to Mary Pickford, Douglas Fairbanks and Charles Chaplin rave about it for an hour. They said, "This man is a genius; he will revolutionize pictures!"

Mr. von Sternberg was not ready for the revolution at the time, so he went to Germany, and when he returned he brought it with him in the perfect form of Marlene Dietrich. They had worked together over there, and here, great things were expected; no one was disappointed.

Morocco was a sensational film and it introduced new camera angles, sequences without driveling dialogue. It gave us a new and better Gary Cooper and, above all, Dietrich.

What happened? The country became Dietrich delirious. Garbo was not to be given time to say, "I tank I go home." She was to be replaced.

Film fans wrote more notes to the magazines than the late President Wilson wrote during the International Havoc. People raved so much about Dietrich's legs that I was tempted to round up a group of Follies girls and picket the theaters, carrying signs reading, "Give the home legs a chance!" "Buy American!" was then an unborn slogan.

Paramount preened the feathers in its cap and crowed lustily over its find – and then the "gossip garglers" burst into activity. Dietrich and von Sternberg were inseparable! She ate every meal with him at the studio restaurant! Well, whom would she eat with? The gateman?

Gargle! Gargle! Gargle! "What can that beautiful creature see in that funny little man?" The fact that the little man turned her slender feet from the path of mediocre marks to the high-road of dreams and dollars couldn't explain her devotion and gratitude.

Mrs. von Sternberg probably had to read in the papers that her husband's affections had been alienated, but with the arrival of Miss Dietrich's husband and small daughter the alienation suit was swept off the front pages. For a while the star was permitted to do a little work, which, after all, was what she had come over to do.

Being a good actress and a fascinating personality is not enough to interest the public, according to the press agents. A campaign of mother-and-child publicity was launched for Dietrich; pictures of the two doing everything but taking a bath flooded the magazines. Our local gangsters took time off from hold-ups to read about the private life of the film favorite and forthwith laid a plan to kidnap the apple of the lady's beautiful eye.

They let her know of their plan in no uncertain manner. Fan mail was tossed aside while threatening letters from the pseudo-kidnappers were read with terror. The result was bars to throw depressing shadows from the sunlit windows of her Beverly Hills home and an armed guard that would do credit to Al Capone to mar the intimate picture of mother and daughter who were inseparable.

In every studio stars are balking at bad stories, and directors are refusing to direct films unless changes are made to meet with their approval, but the von Sternberg-Dietrich rumpus over *Blonde*

Venus had to be kicked around by the press until it finally got lost. After seeing *Blonde Venus*, I regret that it could not have shared the same fate, for though the delightful Dietrich made Gulliver look like a statue by comparison with her travels while trying to keep her "cheeild," and did everything but a back flip to make the public forget the floundering plot, *Blonde Venus* was pretty bad.

We are used to seeing Venus without arms, but one without a leg to stand on – Ah, No! Mr. von Sternberg and "Messrs" Paramount, you ain't done right by our Marl!

Several months ago Ye Editor asked me if I could write a story about Marlene Dietrich and I had to decline with regrets, and real ones, because I had never met her. I had watched her eat at the studio, which she does very daintily, but I didn't consider that the basis of the sort of article I like to write.

So the subject was dropped, but being one of her ardent fans (which you may have gleaned), I still hoped that one day our paths would cross. Last week they met and we stopped to talk somewhere between El Mirador Hotel and the pool at Palm Springs.

Perhaps I dreamed it? Ah, no! It all comes back to me now. I had gone down there to shake off old demon Flu. Devastating D. arrived, complete with husband, child, bodyguard, and Maurice Chevalier. They walked into the pool-side restaurant as we were finishing lunch, which was a bit of luck; if they had arrived earlier no one would have eaten any lunch!

I say they walked in, but on that first entrance *she* might as well have been walking alone, so concentrated was the attention she paid to her well-tailored gray suit, with its padded shoulders above which perched the small, well-shaped head in its halo of gold and topped by what was a cross between a beret and any modern woman's chic hat.

I spoke to Maurice, who was charming as usual, but had a sort of a "Don't ask me" expression in his eyes. I thought it meant, "Don't ask me why she wears them," but the next day I learned the truth.

He was standing gazing at the mountains which surround our favorite weekend resort. As he stood leaning against a pillar in front of his bungalow, he looked so at peace with the world it seemed a shame to wake him, but I did, by yelling, "Camera!"

He greeted me and we talked about the weather. After dragging the climate around for a few moments I got up courage enough to say, "I'd like to write a story about Dietrich, but I've never met her and…" I got no further.

"You would like her, Elsie," he said, "and she would like you, if she got to know you. But I couldn't introduce anyone to her down here. She is worn out and very nervous, and she is just here to rest, and…"

Maurice was saved the embarrassment of tangling himself in a web of more explanation, by the arrival of dashing D. herself, followed by her pleasant, and very easy-to-look-at husband.

Far from appearing worn out, she seemed to be literally walking on the desert air, which though famed for its buoyancy, is not *that* powerful. Hatless, her golden crown waving in the breeze, she approached. Dressed in faultless white flannels, a lemon-colored turtle neck sweater covered her very feminine chest. She was also wearing a broad smile. In fact, she was the girl whose picture I had seen in 1929.

Noting that she was not going to make a detour, which would have been simple, Maurice said, "I will introduce you to her right now!" He did, and then started to explain me – "Miss Janis was the first beeg star I…"

Diplomatic D. made me quite proud when she interrupted him, saying in that unforgettable cello voice, "I know, I know…" She smiled at me through a curtain of half-inch lashes and turned to her husband. "It is quite cold, I think we should have coats," she said. "You too, Maurice!"

The two men excused themselves and left us. We also dallied with the climate for a moment, then I said, "I want to write an article about you and your trousers. I think I understand just how you feel about them. I used to wear them a great deal on the stage."

"I know," she said. My chest expanded; she really had heard of me, then?

"It's funny," she continued, "the excitement about them, but I think people are getting used to them now." Obviously she has no idea of hiding behind anybody's shirt.

"It's silly to say that my trousers caused any trouble between Joe von Sternberg and me. He always liked me in them, and he knew

I always like them. They are more comfortable; one may walk better. When I first came here, we would be going to see a picture or something – I would say I suppose I must change to a dress and Joe it was who said, 'No, you can go as you are.' So I went."

"And why not?" said I, going right into my pro-pants speech. "At least, you are not flaunting the much-advertised legs. I think that's what they're complaining about!"

She laughed and glanced down at the beautifully creased offenders. Her lashes lay like small black feather fans upon her rougeless cheeks. She raised them again and I thought she must be pretty strong to do that!

"They save a lot of money – trousers," she said.

Maurice and friend husband returned. The car was waiting. "I shall see you again, I hope," she said, punctuating the phrase with a firm hand-clasp. I hope she hopes so for she is one of the most attractive people I've ever met. What does it matter what she wears? It isn't so long ago that a lady couldn't smoke, drink or go on the streets alone. In fact, being a lady was about the hardest life a gal could choose! Which brings us to the vital question – When is a lady not a lady? And I say – When she has to remind people that she is one…

Elsie Janis (1889-1956) was an accomplished actress, songwriter, and author. She was a headliner on Broadway and on the London stage, and entertained troops during WWI. She starred in a half dozen silent films between 1915 and 1919. Her numerous musical compositions include, "Love, Your Magic Spell is Everywhere," and "Oh, Give Me Time for Tenderness." She wrote the screenplay for the 1931 feature film, *The Squaw Man*. In 1934, Janis became the first female announcer on NBC radio. Janis was lesbian. In 1932, she entered into a "lavender marriage" with Gilbert Wilson, who was sixteen years her junior. For a short time, the couple lived in Sleepy Hollow, New York, but when the short-lived marriage ended, Janis moved to Beverly Hills, where she lived the remainder of her life.

"Is Marlene Dietrich in *Love* for the Second Time?" by Sonia Lee. Motion Picture, June, 1933

Marlene Dietrich has changed. She has changed in the last few weeks from an emotionally inert person to an eager, laughing, enchantingly vital and young girl. Can it be, as it is whispered around the studio, that Brian Aherne – her leading man in *Song of Songs* – has given Marlene an interest in life, the first dominating and absorbing interest that has touched her since girlhood?

Marlene Dietrich's mystery has been cumulative. Unlike Garbo, whose elusiveness has a well-defined basis in her unhappy first experiences in Hollywood, Marlene has had a placidity, an inscrutable, trance-like quality which has baffled Cinema town with greater intensity as the days have gone by. She made real the *Trilby* tale of a woman living in a dream – so complete was the seeming abstraction. Garbo hid within her home. Dietrich hid within herself!

Marlene and Brian Aherne, 1933.

Her face – a lovely Benda mask – revealed nothing of the woman. Her experiences, her reactions, her attitudes toward life and people were sealed within an impenetrable wall. Marlene, until recently, has given the impression of a colossal, majestic indifference, which has set her apart from the clamoring, ambitious, fame-ridden cinema populace.

No one has ever known the reason for that manifest detachment. To no one has she confided the secret that explains it. But we believe that, at last, we have the key to the Enigma of Dietrich.

Only when a woman's heart is dead can she face the world with an inflexible calm. Has Marlene's heart been comatose since she was seventeen?

Some months ago, a man who knew Marlene Dietrich well, when she was a young, aspiring violinist – eager, vibrant, hopeful, and trusting – saw the Marlene Dietrich that Hollywood has known for three years. He made a revealing comment about Marlene, the star.

"I couldn't believe it was the same girl – she's a different person entirely," he said. "When I first knew Marlene, her beauty transcended that of any woman I have ever seen. She was breath-taking, glorious, with an elemental quality that made men gasp and bow in homage. She was electricity personified. The current of her vitality reached out to everyone who came in contact with her.

"She was gay, audacious – always laughing. Her musical career seemed assured. She was something of a prodigy with the violin – and great things were prophesied for her. And she was in love. We all knew it.

"Her idol was the conductor of a symphony orchestra – and his genius had a terrifying appeal for her. And to him she gave her fresh, young worship. She gathered her beauty and her glory and her promise – her idealism and her dreams – into one concentrated cup and gave it unstintingly to this man, who stood in her mind for every worthwhile thing in life.

"Then, suddenly, she changed. Her vivacity departed. That appealing softness disappeared. Later we learned why.

"It seems that this man no longer found the ingenuousness of this girl engaging – her naïve love worried him. And so one day he staged a cruel scene. He called Marlene to come to his home – and when she came, she saw this man she adored through the window and very evidently making impassioned love to a woman there with him. The lights were on and the drapes undrawn. The act was well-planned for the disenchantment of an eager girl.

"She stood there – in the cold drizzle. And couldn't tear her eyes away from that window. Beauty was shattered before her very eyes. Something in her must have died then. A different Dietrich must have gone away from that sight. When we learned the details, we could well understand the cool, impassive indifference that had replaced her questing, warming, vivacious nature."

The time came when an injury to her hand closed the door to a musical career. Acting claimed her. Life was no longer terrifying – it had little power to hurt her. She met it with a figurative shrug of the shoulders.

Marriage came to her. There is no question that she has given a fine, loyal, abiding affection to her husband Rudolph Sieber, young German director. Certainly, no child is blessed with a more absorbing love than Marlene showers on her daughter, Maria. No service is too small – no effort is too great. In a town where many mothers leave the details of their children's lives to servants, Marlene has refused to recognize that need. Maria's food is frequently prepared by her mother. She is brought to the studio to lunch so that Marlene may have an extra hour with her youngster.

We aren't drawing wrong deductions when we say that the love that Marlene has given her husband has been of a different variety from that first flaming passion which had such a signal effect on her life.

Certainly, she has remained the impassive Dietrich through the years of marriage and success. Certainly, nothing has happened – until recently – which might awaken her to the exuberance, and awareness, and humanness, that were hers at seventeen.

Myths have arisen to explain that dead calm of hers. Josef von Sternberg was the *Svengali* to her *Trilby*. Her stolidity was only an expression of her nationality. She was homesick for her native land. She hated pictures. But not one of these reasons – in the light of the revelations of this man who had known her well – now hold.

It was this disillusioned Dietrich whom von Sternberg discovered. She was, nevertheless, an arresting personality and brought a vivid stimulant to the American screen.

But an enigma she remained. Nothing bothered her very much. Interviewers found themselves perplexed by her indifference.

Even silly gossip, threats of kidnapping, troublous conflicts with her studio, and the extremes of fortune – all of which have come to her in Hollywood – have been met by that characteristic shrug of hers.

She displayed that same apathetic unconcern to public opinion during the time when she was rating yards of newspaper space with her adoption of masculine attire. She appeared at premieres, in shops, and at the studio in men's tailored suits. Where another woman would have made her famous legs a public menace, she chose to hide them in un-intriguing trousers.

Marlene in Song of Songs, *1933.*

Hollywood's more impressionable denizens catapulted their legs into trousers, and the war was on. To be, or not to be, feminine? Marlene's tailored shoulders expressed complete indifference. She was indifferent even to Maurice Chevalier's reaction. It is said on good authority that he had protested her adoption of the trouser regalia for public appearances.

"I hate being conspicuous," said this shy man. "Your pants make me so." And so a hiatus in their friendship resulted.

It may well be recorded there that the pants fad is a monument to the ingenuity and brilliance of Tom Baily, the head of the Paramount publicity department. Outside of Garbo's silence, nothing has rated the furor that the Dietrich pants have. He advantageously capitalized her personal preference to the point where it became a subject of national discussion.

Meanwhile, Paramount and von Sternberg, Dietrich's mentor parted company. And in excessive loyalty Marlene balked at making a picture under other direction than his. Finally, *Song of Songs* was chosen – with Rouben Mamoulian at the directorial helm. Marlene was pacified.

Brian Aherne, a strikingly handsome chap and Katharine Cornell's leading man in the celebrated stage play, *The Barretts of Wimpole Street* – after withstanding flattering contract offers from every studio – capitulated to Paramount's offer to play opposite Marlene in this picture. Six feet two and a half inches tall, slender, athletic with azure blue eyes and brown hair, with an ascetic, typically British face – he is the perfect foil for Marlene.

From the first, their evident interest in each other excited comment. They lunched together, sat together on the set. And the remarkable thing was that Marlene – for the first time in months – wore skirts. Tweedy, tailored affairs. But still skirts. She sacrificed, in part, her splendid gesture of defiance to the world. Here, evidently, was someone whose opinion counted.

Suddenly, we are conscious of a new Marlene Dietrich – no longer weary and restrained, but an ardent, young, voluble, vital girl. Her face is alight with interest. The outbursts of temperament that were expected on this picture failed to materialize. She had definite ideas of what she should, or should not do. But her attitude is uncomplicated by the hysterical tantrums that actresses employ to carry their point.

In the studio commissary – when Brian Aherne and Marlene are lunching together – their enjoyment of each other's society is manifest. Marlene chatters with the excitement of a child. She curls her legs under her, or swings one restless foot. She might be a girl of sixteen out for a holiday.

There is no question but that the Marlene Dietrich of other days is gone. The change in her personality is evident. With the melting of her aloofness, she exhibits the vibrancy of elastic youth. Her face is softer, sweeter. Her eyes are believing again. And this transformation shows in her work in *Song of Songs*.

And it is a role which a placid Dietrich could never have played. In it are scenes that are daring in the extreme. The scenario writer has not minimized the passion that flames through the original story by Herman Sudermann. Witness the stage directions in one section of the script – a scene in which Marlene presumably poses in the nude for the sculptor (Aherne) in the drama. It reads, "Show as much of Dietrich's shoulders as the Hays office will permit."

In yet another scene, Marlene is shown thrilling at the imagined touch of the artist who is molding the torso of the statue.

What has caused this extraordinary alteration? A rather unhappy woman one month – and a human, pulsing personality the next? A nature like Dietrich's loses scars slowly. Perhaps that first experience of hers had hurt so deeply that only a similar, vital situation could arouse her from her lethargy.

Today, Hollywood is asking – Is this NEW Dietrich the result of recaptured youthful illusions through a new emotional awakening?

Sonia Lee was a prolific writer for numerous movie magazines.

"Marlene *Is Free at Last,*" by Ruth Biery. *Photoplay,* July, 1933

Marlene onboard the SS Europa, *1933.*

When you read this Marlene Dietrich will be in France.

When is she returning to the country that gave her international fame and to which she has, in turn, added a certain prestige?

I went to ask her this question a couple of days before she was to depart. And I was really a bit sorry I had sought her. She was so like a young girl beckoned by spring; so like the adventurer off to his first uncharted cruise of exploration.

"I am free! Free! Do you know what that means? I do not want plans. I do not want to know exactly what I will do. I am going to France and spend the summer with my husband. Is that not enough?"

She stretched her arms toward the great beyond which lay, not in the luxurious little dressing room in which we were talking, but in the great world into which she was going after nearly three years in American studio activity.

"This is the day I have waited for! Now, I can sit back and wait. I do not have to plan. If a beautiful story should come, I can do it. This is my new arrangement with Paramount. I have signed for only two pictures. Now, no one can say, 'We must have a Dietrich story. It must be finished by a certain date.'

"A company cannot be expected to let a star sit back and wait a year if she wishes. It cannot afford to let her wait until the right story comes. It has an investment. But, now, there is a new idea contract. Freedom means happiness. I have it! Why must I say what I will do when I do not want to even think about it?"

Marlene's fight culminated in her new freedom, after she had shown her dissatisfaction.

"I telephoned Mr. von Sternberg in Berlin and he advised me to make *Song of Songs*. Now I do my own way about *everything*. No. I'll not sign another long contract. Never."

It is well known that Paramount offered her the proverbial world with a fence. Price was no consideration. As for directions, they welcomed von Sternberg with a home week celebration. He is to do a Crawford-Gable picture while Marlene is away.

Whenever Marlene speaks of "we" and "our" she is referring to the team of Dietrich and von Sternberg. "We can produce our own, if we desire. When they make a picture in America, they have a hundred thousand dollars of costs before they start. We would have no such burden if we should ever operate on our own."

Marlene paused. Her eyes were on the trees in the Paramount yard beyond the open door. I wondered if she were picturing them as trees of France or Italy or perhaps some tiny island in the Mediterranean.

"Do I understand that you will make pictures only with Mr. von Sternberg?" I asked.

"Of course. Why must people forget that I came to the United States only because he asked me. I was pushed into being a *film* actress. I am not one in the usual sense, you know. I will act in his pictures or I will be his cutter or his assistant director. When he wants me to work with him, I will do so. And it does not make any difference whether it is in Hollywood or Australia.

"They have said we have separated. That is ridiculous. On the contrary, this last month has made me more certain than ever that

I have always been right. If he wants me to, I will make pictures only with Mr. Sternberg! No, I will not make personal appearances in Europe. I will not make films for foreign companies."

Mr. von Sternberg has not announced his entire plans. Contrary to reports from Europe, he did not confer with European producers about work for himself or Marlene. He refused to grant interviews and all reports of his activities over there were hearsay.

He did make an agreement with the editor of a Netherlands magazine that he would talk to him about American pictures but *not* for publication. The day following the two-hour conference, this editor wrote requesting Mr. von Sternberg to release him from his promise because as an editor, he felt he owed the people of Holland the von Sternberg view of American pictures. The director replied, "You must not be angry with me if I prefer to continue to remain silent. It's a matter of absolute indifference to me whether I am praised or censured. Nothing I can say would ever be important. My screen work alone might be of consequence and I am not too certain about that."

Despite this international silence, Josef von Sternberg will have his office in Hollywood. And the business of that office will be the making of pictures.

He needs little financing from even himself. I haven't a doubt that he will be able to repeat with his fair partner helping to edit, direct and cut – in addition to acting. For she spoke the truth when she said, "I am not a film actress in the usual sense, you know."

Marlene Dietrich is the most interesting and the most baffling of them all. I knew her better than many; I understand her less. Even Garbo is easier of interpretation.

I did not believe at one time that Marlene was sincere in what may seem to us an almost fanatical devotion to von Sternberg's work. I questioned whether she would refuse the huge sums which I knew American companies would offer. But I believe now. Fact proves that she has been constant to her statement, "I only came to this country to make pictures for him; I will return for the same reason." German conditions have made only one change.

She will vacation in France.

As I sat watching her on this afternoon so soon before she would leave us, my mind reverted to the first time I had seen her. She was the honor-guest at a luncheon. She had just arrived; this was her initiation.

No woman could have looked more feminine. A blue chiffon gown trailed about the toes of her slippers; a large floppy hat of the old garden variety hid everything except that translucent complexion and those intense eyes. Yet she appeared stolid, even Frau-ish, as Americans interpret the term. She looked more matron than actress. The betting odds among writers were six to one against her!

She was there to be bet upon; to be viewed and written about as a prospective celebrity.

But when we left I had an odd feeling. I had the unprecedented sensation that I was not just one of an audience watching the monkey in its cage, but that I was, indeed, the monkey. I wondered what her description of us would be, even as I was leaving to describe her. She still does that to me. I retreat from an interview with her feeling the exhaustion which rightfully belongs to the one-being-interviewed.

I reminded her of that first personal appearance. I told her she had looked stolid. "It was the *dress* that day," she explained. "But I had on this suit, this same suit I am wearing today, when I *came* to America."

That suit is a perfectly-padded and tailored man's gray, smooth serge. She was wearing a reddish-tinged, strictly masculine shirt and red tie with it. Man's shoes. Even the shirt was the one she had planned to wear when she landed in New York.

She had come onto deck in it, ready for her first step on American soil. A Paramount official took one glance and said, "But you can't. You can't see the reporters in that!"

When she finally saw them, she was in dainty gown, elaborate fur coat. The same official had pinned coquettish orchids upon her shoulder.

The next day she prepared to call upon New York friends. Another male suit, shirt, tie, hat. "But you can't! You can't! They wouldn't let you walk through the streets of New York! In Hollywood…maybe…"

So she looked to Hollywood with the same longing of freedom with which she is now looking to Europe.

But when she appeared here in the attire which had been her customary garb in Europe (except for teas and evenings), the world claimed she was imitating Garbo.

"You *can't* be said to be imitating Garbo," they protested.

It was then that she became the best-dressed woman in Hollywood. Her ultra-feminine costumes out-styled those of either Lilyan Tashman or Kay Francis. And there was always a corsage on her shoulder. Flowers had become synonymous with feminine apparel to her!

She was miserable. "I was *so* fed up. I could not *stand* them!"

There were other "you can'ts and you mustn'ts." She had come to the land of *freedom* to find less freedom that at any moment since she left school.

Only one understood her. His understanding had induced her to come to this country; it kept her here. She and von Sternberg became partners, co-workers fighting for freedom – freedom to express themselves through pictures. It was the American public that gave her the initial courage to return to the clothes to which she was accustomed. She wore a dress suit in *Morocco*. The public adored it. The white male suit in *Blonde Venus* reiterated this approval.

But it was during her first return to Europe that she recaptured almost complete independence. She returned with Maria, the seven-year-old daughter who is more important to her than countries or careers. She brought trunks filled with newly tailored male suits. She wore them. She took a home. She refused to talk to the press and refused to read what they had written about her. She led her own life according to her innate desires.

There was only one restraint. Her contract. She could insist upon freedom in her work to only a certain point. "They blamed Mr. von Sternberg for me. In fact, I hid behind him. He was blamed for what I thought and I let him be blamed."

She once told me, "I forget everything that is unpleasant so easily. I remember only the happiness and there has been much happiness, too. Maria adores it here."

And today she added, "I have become used to my home. There is a little sadness in taking the dear things from their regular resting places. But in a week, I will forget. I will be free…"

And she will return free. She will return to work again with the man who discovered her exactly as she came to work with him in the first place.

Marlene Dietrich is the only woman I know who has spent nearly three years in this country without having some stamp of our "melting pot" branded upon her. Including Garbo. Garbo has received, at least our bureau-of-engraving-greenback impression. She has learned the American value of money. Dietrich still considers it completely unimportant in relation to happiness. And has proved this by refusing heretofore the most astonishing offers ever tendered an actress.

She wants only the European freedom to do as she pleases.

And, at last, she has it! Until October, when she will return.

"Is Dietrich *Indifferent* to Her Public?" by Elza Schallert. *Motion Picture,* September, 1933

When Marlene Dietrich made her cross-country train trip to New York, to embark for a three months' vacation in Europe, press dispatches carried reports of her refusal to leave her compartment to greet the crowds that had gathered at various stops en route to catch a glimpse of the exotic German star. Reports indicated that the enthusiastic cheers and cries of the crowds for Marlene apparently fell upon deaf ears.

Was Marlene being unfriendly or aloof? Perhaps; perhaps not. She was traveling with her little girl and, in view of kidnap threats she had received, she wanted privacy, no doubt. This is understandable. But crowds do not stop to seek the more subtle reasons why stars sometimes try to dodge them. Crowds judge by appearances. And appearances made Marlene seem cool to their interest in her.

It is on old unwritten law that anyone who has sought fame, especially in the movies, and has been fortunate enough to achieve it, has no right to demand what is conventionally known as privacy. Nothing – not even a great emotional crisis – exempts him. Garbo, alone, has been allowed to be an exception; and, of late, observers have detected a drift of resentment toward even her; the prophets are saying that she might soon come out of her monastic solitude or suffer at the box-office. Which brings us around to the question: Was Marlene misguided in being deaf to the crowd's cheers, no matter what her reasons were?

The Barrymores, America's First Family of the stage and screen, never think of crying for privacy. They always manage to have it when they choose, because they are highly intelligent, dignified persons who know how and when and where to seek seclusion, isolation or the so-called privacy. Lionel Barrymore could enjoy absolute privacy right in a crowded drawing-room and never appear boorish about it.

And where is even the Inquiring Reporter who would attempt to interrupt the privacy, so to speak, of Ethel Barrymore or John? It simply couldn't be done. Yet the Barrymores never forget their obligation to the public, which has made them what they are and has paid them handsomely. They have too high a social sense for that and, besides, they are entirely too grateful to reveal openly to anyone what their true emotions might be on any subject or occurrence.

Contrast Marlene's seeming aloofness with the attitude of our great show-women, who, despite their individual high gifts of talent and ability, never forget that there is such a thing as the public. I refer to Geraldine Farrar and Mary Garden of the operatic and concert worlds and Marie Dressler and Mae West of the stage and films. The ravages of nature would, indeed, have to be visited upon a train carrying them to interfere with tossing kisses to an admiring group.

Marie Dressler has been known to shout recipes for cough medicine from a moving train to a mother with a croupy child at her apron-strings, and Geraldine Farrar has been known to sing from her taxicab to a crowd awaiting her exit from the theater after a matinee performance.

Those little acts might smack of the theatrical, yet in the final analysis, when the measuring rod is applied to fame, and the devotion of the public – the only real fuel which keeps the fires of celebrity burning – is reckoned with, they are found to be very smart business, a small investment of charm carrying big returns.

Marlene, of course, may have had several perfectly legitimate reasons for "ducking the crowds" at various stops before reaching her destination, especially the typical "jerk-water" towns through the Middle West. For one thing, she wore men's attire on the entire trip, according to reports.

Now, it seems perfectly in character to spring real man-tailored pants, vests, coats, shirts, hats and camel hair ulsters in Hollywood at the different popular restaurants, where most of the film colony lunch or dine. Anything and everything unusual or "different" goes to the colony. The more unusual and startling the better (so far as publicity is concerned.) Hollywood is ever a showcase, with the weird, the bizarre and the impractical in sartorial effects constantly being exploited by star and "extra" girl alike for one – and only one – reason: publicity.

But it is difficult, and slightly out of key, to try to get away with style irrationalities, such as strict men's attire, in the conservative centers of the United States and, especially, in the "sticks." Maybe Marlene's feminine intuition guided her in her refusal to greet the crowds. For even broadminded Paris later booed her male attire.

However, one wonders just what she had in mind when she lunched with the wife of a rich New York realtor and theatrical promoter in male garb at the popular and smart restaurant, Sardi's. New York wasn't at all startled or thrilled by Marlene's appearance in pants, coat, vest, shirt and tie and slouch hat, but was surprised that she should go to all the trouble of "putting on an act" of which they had already been apprised through countless publicity notices, news pictures and Western press dispatches.

New York was also considerably abashed by her walkout on the musical comedy hit, *Take a Chance*, right in the middle of the biggest song hit of the first act. Since Marlene apparently engaged seats for herself and a woman friend in the very front row of the middle section of the theater downstairs, her walk-out attracted no end of attention and appeared designed for that purpose. Needless to say, she wore male attire that day, also. New York seemed to feel that her exit, ill-timed or well-timed, according to opinion, smacked of a very time-worn and once-honored "gag," and its very antiquity had a saddening effect.

A teacher of psychology who has never seen Marlene on the screen brought up her name, as well as others that capture front-page stories, in conversation with me recently to illustrate to what excesses the human impulses of unhappiness and dissatisfaction will go to find expression.

"In the case of Marlene Dietrich," he observed, "merely to suggest a concrete example, it would appear that she might be very unhappy for some personal reason in the environment of her work, or her domestic or social life. Otherwise, she would not rush to the extreme that she has in the matter of completely reversing woman's mode of dress. If my understanding of Miss Dietrich is correct, she abhors publicity, yet by dressing as she does in conspicuous places, she achieves the very end she decries. Such procedure usually shows an unhappy or distraught mental state.

"Of course, underneath everything, Miss Dietrich may not be sympathetic toward American customs, American people. She may regard the country physically as very beautiful or very stimulating, but she may dislike the people and their customs intensely. Her bitter experiences with threats from kidnappers may have logically produced such a reaction in her.

"If she felt any emotion of resentment or intense dislike or hatred, the reasonable way for her to express those feelings would be exactly as she has done – to throw down the gauntlet to American women by defying their conventional mode of dress, namely, by donning men's clothes – to show dispassion toward the devotion of her admirers – and to treat her co-workers charmingly and graciously one day and ignore them completely the next. All of such conduct clearly follows the line of rebellion and dislike, and is the direct result of hurt or misunderstanding, either real or fancied. Incidentally, only a very sensitive and exceedingly feminine mind works in the manner described and produces results such as these we have discussed."

The professor, of course, was talking purely in the abstract, but his reasoning, if applied directly to Marlene in some respects, would certainly show method.

There is no question that Marlene Dietrich has completely changed since Paramount first brought her to Hollywood on the suggestion of Josef von Sternberg three years ago.

A clear picture of her being introduced at a huge luncheon to the press in a fashionable hotel immediately following her arrival from Germany floods the memory. It was Spring, and the blue-eyed, flaxen-haired Marlene, in a flowered, billowy, chiffon dress and large, drooping hat, was a picture of loveable loveliness.

She seemed totally unsophisticated, very bright, charmingly natural – and yet those qualities did not pall with any obvious insistence upon sweetness. One expected her to have a certain wise, metropolitan flair because, after all, she was the product of one of the most cosmopolitan cities in the world – Berlin.

Within a few months after her arrival in Hollywood, I met her socially a number of times in the home of Ernst Lubitsch and elsewhere in the foreign colony. She was always engaging, but withal aloof and reserved, the qualities which distinguish many foreign-born women.

At that period, she hadn't found or determined upon her screen character. She was an indefinite personality – not the positive type of today. She was the chrysalis that was to develop quickly into the exotic bloom that first shed its tuberose perfume in *Morocco*. Undoubtedly, the von Sternberg influence was largely responsible for the dramatic metamorphosis.

Just what the next cycle in the evolution of Dietrich will be is beyond conjecture, for the reason that whatever is real in her personality has not as yet irradiated through the artificial guises which she has assumed in her screen portrayals.

Rouben Mamoulian, Garbo's personally selected director for her forthcoming production of *Queen Christina*, recently finished guiding Marlene in *Song of Songs*, which is reputed to reveal an entirely new facet of her personality. She objected strenuously to making the story and having Mamoulian (rather than von Sternberg) as her director and threatened to stage a walk-out on Paramount, but after a lawsuit by the studio was mentioned, she changed her mind. And, according to all reports, was happy while working on the picture.

There is a depth to the feelings of Marlene Dietrich that has not as yet been revealed on the screen. Perhaps Mamoulian succeeded in extracting it from her. This is her profound mother love. She may be as cold and technically accurate as a modern skyscraper in her work, but in the hallowed sphere of motherhood there are few women in any walks of life her equal.

In the early Fall she will return to Hollywood, and this despite the fact that at one time she asserted she would never come back to America, once her contract was ended. Von Sternberg will again direct her for two pictures.

Maybe on the forthcoming cross-country trip – if there should happen to be devoted crowds waiting at different stops along the line – Marlene will see fit to blow a kiss in their direction. Or again, she may tip her hat.

Hollywood, however, gives her credit for too much originality to repeat on the male attire "gag" in the future. Hollywood gives her credit for knowing a good publicity idea when she sees one – and being clever enough not to overwork it.

After all, trousers of any cut are still pants – and isn't the American public infinitely more interested in human, sincere and artistic performances of its stars, both on and off the screen, than in any sartorial stunts?

Elza Baumgarten Schallert (1892-1967) worked as a publicist for legendary theater owners Sid Grauman and Thomas L. Tally. In 1921, she married Edwin Schallert (1890-1968), the music and drama editor of the *Los Angeles Times* from 1919 until his retirement in 1958. Elza and Edwin wrote a monthly column, "Hollywood High Lights," for *Picture Play* magazine. Elza became a proficient magazine writer, and hosted a popular radio program on the NBC Blue Network during the 1930s. The Schallert's spoke fluent German, and Elza interviewed many German refugees in Hollywood. Actor William Schallert (1922-2016) was the couple's only child.

Marlene in Song of Songs, *1933.*

"Dietrich Declares Herself!" by Herbert Cruikshank. *Screenland,* October, 1933

Extra! Extra! The only magazine interview granted by Marlene in Europe! Read about her plans, her startling frank opinions! "Yes, I like trousers, and I shall continue to wear them!"

At fair Versailles, basking peacefully a few leagues from Paris, there is a very swank, very smart, very exclusive hotel called the Trianon Palace. It is named for the nearby historic piles where once the ill-fated Marie Antoinette spent gay moments pretending to be a farmer's daughter. But the hotel has two distinct advantages over the palaces from which it takes its title. The plumbing is strictly modern. And it shelters a real, live Queen, instead of being shrouded in drowsy, sun-webbed memories of one long dead.

For at Versailles, in the Trianon Palace Hotel, surrounded by husband Rudy Sieber and a cordon of guards, Marlene Dietrich, Queen of the Screen, holds her Court. And the beauty and the chivalry of Paris clamors for admission to the charmed circle of her presence. Presentation at a Buckingham levee, invitation to a White House soiree, a season pass (tax exempt) to the Paramount theatres, these are simple to attain in comparison to an interview with Mar-lay-na. Here, in *Screenland,* she speaks for the first and only time during her stay in Europe. And from her own seductive lips here is the reason for her silence.

"It is not easy for me to meet people. I am always embarrassed and ill at ease. I do not carry my heart on the tip of my tongue. So it is difficult for me to know what to say. And many of the questions that one is asked are either quite terrible or quite silly."

She speaks sincerely. And when one considers that she is on a holiday, there can be no great criticism of her decision to barricade herself against a host of inquiring reporters that would reach from the Arc de Triomphe to Napoleon's Tomb. But despite her reticence, where Marlene goes the press follows. At a Parisian premiere, an unostentatious Dietrich was spotted in the audience by a lens man camouflaged in a box for the purpose. She attempted to out-maneuver him by veiling her face in a handkerchief. But the picture-snatcher finally won the day by pretending to abandon the chase, and then, suddenly, like a Jack-in-the-Box, hopping out upon the stage. Boom! Flash! And he got his gal. Wherever she goes, it's the same story. And it gets a bit tedious.

Reminded that the Press has been kind to her, Marlene bows a gracious acquiescence.

"That is true. But it is my idea that an actor is entitled to rise or fall by the quality of his art and his pictures. I cannot get accustomed to the idea that there is any public interest in the fact that such-and-such an artist has tea at such-and-such a place. And with whom. I do not see that this is legitimate news.

"You say the press has been friendly, and I agree. That is why I was simply amazed at the unkind attitude of the New York papers during my last short stop there. Perhaps there was a misunderstanding. But I feel that I was cruelly and unjustly criticized.

"As you know, I had only a few hours before sailing, and as it was impossible for me to see all the plays, I hurried from theater to theater trying to see the best bits of several. With such a schedule I had to leave each during the progress of some scene. And to my amazement I was accused of discourtesy toward the players. That was not fair. Nor was it fair for reporters to attack me without investigating."

I recalled that there has also been criticism of the star for concealing those famous legs of hers in the voluminous folds of trousers. Now to ask a girl about her pants, whether she wears 'em, whether she doesn't, if she will or if she won't, well, there are other questions easier to ask, and equally to the point. However, here's what Marlene has to say about it.

"I fail to see that there is anything unusual about wearing trousers. Many other women have worn them. In Hollywood they are quite common. In my pictures I am costumed in all sorts of frills and feathers, and away from the studio it is a relief to get into sensible clothes. Yes, I like trousers, and I shall continue to wear them."

In Paris, however, the star sticks to skirts. It seems there is a law. And no matter what a gal's inclinations may be, her boyish spirit must be curbed when it comes to donning the lower half of a masculine outfit. All this, it is said, was gently intimated to Marlene by Monsieur the Prefect of Police shortly after her trousered arrival. And Marlene took the tip. But the topper to the tale, as they tell it along the Rue de Castiglione, is that Madame, the wife of Monsieur the Prefect of Police, besieged Marlene to attend her fete as guest of honor, and please, oh please, to wear ze pants! Marlene accepted. But Marlene left her pants behind. That is to say, she wore skirts.

But in tweeds or chiffons, this changeling star is the idol of the Continent. Whether she appears in trim, mannish, tailored grey, with masculinely cuffed and linked flannel shirt, a loosely knotted cravat at her throat, appropriately shod, and with the famous soft chapeau slouched boyishly over one smoldering, come-hither eye, or whether she affects pure feminine fascinations, with daintily slippered feet hidden in soft, clinging skirts, with flowers at her shoulder, and her shapely head carefully coiffed, Marlene is utterly fascinating. Paris knows, admits, and admires.

No woman deserves the description "orchidaceous" as does Marlay-na. She defines the word perfectly. Like an orchid there is nothing "natural" about her beauty. She is no rosy-cheeked milk-maid type. Nor is she a bounding, Sunkist, hundred-percent American product of the great out-doors. She is a carefully cultivated, exotic, almost too perfect product. Her haunting pallor, fairly slashed by carmined lips, the sweep of sooty lashes that fringe her hypnotic eyes, the marvelously penciled brows, the blood-dipped beauty of her finger tips, the careful carelessness of her hair, all combine in a triumph of artistry.

Yet the languor that should accompany this ensemble is not part of Marlene's personality. She moves briskly, decisively. She clicks her heels in true Prussian precision upon introduction, and extends a cool, firm, strong hand that returns the pressure of a solid grip. Her eyes meet yours, direct, unwavering, soft, yet with a green glint of cynicism lurking in their grey depths. Her voice is utterly lyrical. The words it utters reflect a mentality masculine in its incisiveness. Like a boy she crosses one long leg over its mate. But those legs are divinely feminine! Which set of characteristics make the true Dietrich? My guess is neither – and both. In any event they form a combination that is irresistible.

At present she is having fun in Paris. And on the Riviera. And, indeed, wherever she goes. Long, low motors sweep her and her entourage through the adorable, leafy boulevards of the French capital to tea at the Ritz or at Laurent, to the theater, to Les Ambassadeurs, or a dozen different night-spots such as keep Paris gay twenty-four hours a day – or, at least, at night.

As Marlene, in person, is a Parisian sensation, so are her pictures. It is not a question of "have-you-seen-her-latest," but of "how-many-times-have-you-seen-it." And if the answer doesn't admit a half-dozen visits to the theater, you don't belong in our set. This goes for the mondaines, the demi-mondaines, the semi-demi mondaines, and the women who sell white orchids and cabbages amid the mingled fragrance of flowers and onion soup that pervades the great, dawn market called Les Halles.

Upon the authority of Messrs. Ike Blumenthal and Frank Farley, the astute and erudite gentlemen who keep the Continent safe for Paramount, and *vice versa*, you many have it that the socially elect of the beautiful, brilliant city plead for projection-room previews of Marlene's new ones.

Nor is this hysteria confined to Paris. In visiting Vienna, Marlene was as the mercy of enthusiastic crowds that actually threatened her safety by thronging around and seizing for souvenirs like fans the world over. In Berlin of course, she is "kolossal" with a capital "K." And so through Europe. But it is these besieging crowds of idolators that have helped make the star shy of contacts with the multitudes.

She misses Hollywood. And she seems a little surprised that she does.

"When I am there, I long for New York. In New York, I am hungry for a glimpse of Paris. When I reach Paris, it seems that I simply must visit Vienna. But when I reach Vienna, Berlin looks more alluring. And then – and now – I am homesick for Hollywood again! You know, Hollywood gets you after all!"

Information about the picture that is to be first on the schedule when she returns this Fall is scantily supplied with, "I do not know. There are two stories, with a possible third. I really do not know which will be first. Mr. von Sternberg is working on one of them now. He will direct me, too. I leave all that to him."

So it seems that the really curious must ask Joe. He knows.

In addition to her personal success, her social triumph, the victory of each Dietrich production, Marlene is having a very definite effect on French fashions. And that means that her influence extends to all the feminine world, and the masculine world that pays the bills.

Not trusting the ocular proof of the Marlene vogue apparent in the Parisian fashion parade gowns at the Grand Prix, the Drag, Chateau Madrid, all the spots where style is paramount, I consulted an American girl who has made good in Paris, Mlle. Lillian Fischer, probably one of the world's authorities on dress, and presently Fashion Editor of *Harper's Bazaar*. She gave confirmation of the Dietrich vogue.

"There is no denying the fact that Hollywood is having a great influence on fashion. The wide, floppy hats you've seen at the races are directly traceable to Mae West. Joan Crawford has served as inspiration for the puffs and bustle effects. But Miss Dietrich is responsible for a style that is even more revolutionary, and that is the return of feathers to fashion. All kinds of feathers. But especially Birds of Paradise.

"There is a story that is both romantic and dramatic about this returning vogue, and it has served to make Miss Dietrich even more of a heroine to a certain class. That class is the guild of feather-workers. This is a highly specialized industry, and with no demand for its skill, the workers have been drifting into other lines of endeavor. Very shortly, I think, the guild would have been extinct. But Miss Dietrich's picture penchant for feathers has actually resuscitated an industry."

So, you see, a Hollywood star can save an industry, can restore prosperity, while princes, professors, presidents struggle with economic problems. The sphere of influence dominated by Hollywood and its satellites is world-wide. The stars are persons of vast and vital importance after all. And of them, lo, Marlene Dietrich's name looms large.

And so, until Fall, we'll leave her in the murmuring sun-flecked shadows of Versailles, where the spectral Court of a far French Queen smiles approval on this new royalty. Leave her to Herr Sieber, her husband; little Maria, her daughter; Frau von Losch, her mother, and the citizens of Paris. Among them all she should find companionship to suit her mood.

Herbert Cruikshank was a popular Hollywood columnist.

"War Clouds *in the West*?" by Kenneth Baker. *Photoplay*, December, 1933

Is another civil war brewing in Hollywood?

Will Mae West and Marlene Dietrich square off for a bitter battle of the "sexies" to determine just who is queen at Paramount? Will one of Hollywood's lots again prove too small to house two outstanding stars – this time the curvaceous Mae and the Orchidaceous Marlene? Will the classic conflict of Gloria Swanson and Pola Negri, Hollywood's most famous intramural struggle, which rocked Paramount to its very foundation a decade ago, be re-enacted with Mae and Marlene opposed in the up-to-date warrior roles?

Questions, questions, questions! Conjecture, speculation, consternation! How the tongues do wag as the instinct for gossip, in the world's most gossipy town, scents as thrilling a topic as this!

What started all the buzz-buzz excitement? Just six little words, that's all.

But what pithy words, in a statement attributed to Marlene – and maintained by her to be a misquotation – which were printed in New York newspapers and flashed all over the world, when the exotic Dietrich arrived back in the United States from her vacation in Europe.

Probably you read them.

"I never heard of Mae West!"

She denied saying it. But, of course, it was too much of a "natural" for a gossip to overlook. Who else had threatened, and indeed usurped, Dietrich's supremacy at Paramount but Mae West? Who had more reason to be cattily jealous of Mae than Marlene Dietrich?

"I never heard of Mae West!" – in those six little words Hollywood was sure it heard the tocsins of a coming Hollywood war, started, as many wars are started, by a loosened pebble gaining speed until it becomes an inexorable avalanche!

The pebble Hollywood identified as the natural rivalry of Marlene and Mae for the queen star's throne at Paramount. And the avalanche –

Here's the situation, as Hollywood adds it up, at this writing: Marlene denied the quotation in New York, but she waited until her arrival in Hollywood to explain it fully. During that touchy time, Mae scoffed at the whole matter. Said she, "Miss Dietrich is too intelligent to show any jealousy toward me, even if she felt it – and I know she doesn't. We aren't at all alike on the screen.

"She used to come into my dressing room and tell me how she and her daughter, Maria, played my songs at home. She said it for publicity? Nonsense – to show jealousy of an actress on the same lot would not be good publicity." Mae dismissed the thought.

Then came the corrected version of the Manhattan reportorial confusion. It seems that Marlene, slim, in trim curveless feminine attire, was queried regarding the effect of Mae West fashions in Paris.

"I never heard of Mae West *fashions*," quoth Dietrich blandly, according to the later version – and Marlene must have swallowed the last word, because none of the reporters caught it.

Did that explanation please Mae? Well – not exactly, to judge from La West's somewhat testy printed rejoinder. Where the first report had failed to get a "rise" out of her, the second drew return fire.

"What, she never heard of Mae West fashions? Why, she wore them herself in her last picture, *Song of Songs*! I even heard that she wore my corset so she could show the Mae West curves. But, of course, you'd have to verify that from the wardrobe department."

So the newspaper gossip ran, dragging the issue into the "retort courteous" stage, which as everyone knows, just precedes the "quip quarrelsome" – and that's right next door to open hostility!

Paramount's wardrobe department scoffs at the far-fetched idea of Dietrich's making use of one of West's binders, explaining that Marlene did wear a corset in peasant scenes of *Song of Songs*, but that it was especially made for her slim figure.

The studio itself has taken a "much ado about nothing" attitude toward the whole rumpus, but Hollywood is sitting back, wondering if there might not be just a little fire behind those tiny puffs of smoke, just a little fire which might eventually warm up the

Marlene with Brian Aherne in Song of Songs, *1933.*

Paramount lot as it has not been heated since those torrid days some ten or so years ago when Gloria Swanson, then the undisputed queen of the studio, found her throne challenged by a foreign invader, known as Pola Negri.

You see, Hollywood still vividly recalls the battle of the titans which plunged Paramount into almost factional warfare for three years, which practically divided it into two armed camps, which provided Hollywood history with some of its most amazing and amusing anecdotes of big time star struggles, jealousies and counter jealousies – all within the walls of the same Paramount Studio which Mae West and Marlene Dietrich now call their professional home.

It all was built up from just as inconsequential a source, and in many other ways it paralleled the present West-Dietrich set-up. Pola Negri came from Germany, as did Dietrich, although she followed Swanson, where Mae West, the present domestic star, has followed Marlene, to Hollywood.

Both were then queenly and self-determined persons, as indeed are both Dietrich and West. Both represented different types of sex-appeal; both possessed different and clashing temperaments.

It was in the hey-day of Swanson, when she was the undisputed feminine dictatress of the Paramount lot – when, believe it or not, she was more in the news than is Garbo today, because she did more.

Into the Swanson domain, with an unprecedented fanfare of cinema trumpets, came Pola, queen of foreign films, after her German-made *Passion* had swept this nation as well as Europe. From then on things began to happen and kept happening – how they kept happening!

Gloria Swanson dressed in an elaborate bungalow at the far north end of the studio lot; so Pola Negri must have one equally as ornate at the south end.

From each bungalow a clear view down wide "Peacock Alley" was afforded of the other, and this very fact resulted in a dramatic incident.

The studio, entertaining a convention of its salesmen and representatives with a mammoth banquet on one of the stages, had requested the presence of both its queens to top the ultra-Hollywood program of orchestra, dancing girls, and endless coursed dinner. Both had agreed to come.

Eight o'clock, the appointed hour, passed; neither has shown up. Nine o'clock. Ten. The guests fidgeted; messengers were dispatched but to no avail. Neither was "quite ready." Eleven o'clock; still no Swanson, no Negri.

Finally, in walked Gloria. Then, and only then, did Pola regally make the Grand Entrance!

Old timers at Paramount still chuckle about the famous "skirmish of the cats." The old Paramount lot, which had grown out of a barn, was at one time infested with mice which threatened to eat up the wardrobe, the commissary and even the stars; so a horde of alley cats had been assembled to rat the place. For years, these cats had gathered daily for food near the commissary in an e-e-yowling mob, and often Gloria, who was fond of them, had paused in her regal rounds to pet them. The cats were a time-honored tradition.

Pola arrived, glimpsed the cats, shuddered. She couldn't stand cats! She wouldn't work with cats on the lot! But the cats remained.

Gloria returned to Hollywood from her triumphant tour of Europe sporting a brand new husband, the Marquis de la Falaise de la Coudray, and a brand new title (when titles in Hollywood were very, very scarce) of "Marquise."

By a curious coincidence Pola went out and married Serge Mdivani, and garnered the impressive title of "Princess."

Paramount itself inadvertently fanned the flame of rivalry when, by one of those inexplicable production plans, it placed Pola in a picture with almost identically the same plot and character as that of Swanson's *The Humming Bird*. Both stars portrayed apaches in a Parisian setting, and the pictures were released not too far apart and at a time when Gloria was becoming dissatisfied with her Paramount status, and anxious to produce her own pictures.

Such were the incidents that peppered the history of the Swanson-Negri episode for three feverish years – and it is just such a "battle of the queens" that gossip insists is in the making now.

If there actually exists an undercurrent of hostility engendered by the West-Dietrich complications, and it develops into something of the sort, it could easily be "colossal."

Admittedly "no angel," Mae's caustic wit if directed at Marlene could certainly "do her wrong." On the other hand, that stubborn Teutonic will of Marlene's, revealed more than once during the recent criticism of her masculine attire, would prove a formidable defense.

What a clash of temperaments could be stirred up – what a battle royal!

And what a Roman holiday it would make for Hollywood!

But what a headache for poor Paramount – to face another civil war, another exhausting battle of stars with Mae and Marlene – its two queens – going to it!

Yes, yes, Hollywood gossip has promised itself a merry winter!

Kenneth Baker was a Hollywood columnist, and movie magazine contributor.

"The Strange Case of HITLER and DIETRICH" by Princess Catherine Radziwill. *Modern Screen, December, 1933*

Twice last summer, the world of the motion picture touched the realm of international diplomacy and intrigue. Twice, Marlene Dietrich was visited secretly by soft-spoken, swiftly-moving men. Each of them gave her a message from Adolph Hitler, Germany's dynamic Chancellor, a message that offered her a place as unbelievable as it was magnificent in Hitler's Reich. Each time, she vouchsafed no answer and the messenger fled from her chagrined and baffled.

Not long ago, she returned to America.

Her return brings to a pause as amazing a chain of international events as current history can offer. Positively, it represents the one test to which the mercurial Herr Hitler has set himself and failed utterly.

Herr Hitler and Dietrich, these are not names to be linked lightly. It is of Hitler's doing, not Marlene's. Here are the facts.

When Miss Dietrich went abroad last spring, she went to rest. With mind unclouded by worries, she took a lovely white house in sunny southern France. The town was small and cozy and Marlene was a distinguished visitor. For a while, she lived contentedly and quietly, rebuilding her health after the harsh siege of Hollywood picture-making.

The first messenger from Hitler came like a bombshell, rousing the sleepy townsmen to garrulous gossip. He was blond with a mustache like his master's, and his square-set shoulders sloped awkwardly under a coat of obviously unfamiliar cut. He was a man made for a uniform with ribbons across its chest, and his eyes burned with a fire that Marlene did not understand.

This first emissary told her a story that stunned and thrilled her; that must have left her mind a welter of fancies and thoughts.

Before this visit, Marlene's foretaste of it all, the now-famous statement in Germany's official motion picture organ, the Film Kurier, that warned all German-Aryan actors appearing in foreign countries that the Chancellor expected them to return to the Fatherland or be forever excluded from any possibility of obtaining work in the motion picture business in Germany. There were whispered intimations of reprisals against the families and loved ones of any who dared to rebel. All these things had been brought to Marlene's attention.

Shortly afterwards, Hitler's first ambassador arrived with his cleverly planned message. Its first purpose was to banish any resentment Dietrich may have felt at being ordered about; its second was to summon her, not as a subject or slave, but as Napoleon might have summoned Josephine; as a Czar, almost, summoning his Czarina. That is how Hitler summoned Dietrich.

In effect, this message was: "You are not to regard the warning in the Film Kurier as pertaining to you. It was meant only for the others. Whenever you wish to return, you will be welcomed with open arms. For you, Adolph Hitler has a special regard and a special place."

Before I tell you of that regard and that place, you should know Adolph Hitler's intentions. He sees before him a triumphant Germany to the glory of which all Germans must labor. During the stay I made in Germany last Spring, when people could still talk about things they are forbidden to mention at present, I talked with many men and women connected with the German movies. They all and each one declared that the present Chancellor had the intention to suppress on the screen any production not filmed in Germany by a German concern.

In accord with this program, he had made up his mind to rally to his colors the famous German stars working abroad. Already, he was projecting measures which would compel these stars to give up their work abroad or renounce their native land.

And now – he had selected Marlene Dietrich to be the banner-bearer of Nazi Germany. It remained only to lure her back.

So, when his first ambassador appeared abruptly to throw her quiet and contented existence in that tiny French town into utter confusion, he was polite and formal, no doubt, but his offer came like a bolt from the blue. I think that offer would have turned the head of almost any woman in the world – except Marlene Dietrich.

The Chancellor would accord Dietrich the power to direct the destinies of German picture production according to her best rights and judgments; her decisions to go unquestioned and her job of so-called Czar, or rather Czarina, to be handled solely by her, without any outside interference. Her rights would include absolute control of production, with ability to accept or to reject everything from story idea to director, to okay or veto the choice of cast, billing, film cutting and the hundred and one other details attendant upon picture-making.

That ambassador went back to his master baffled and chagrined, I have said. Presently, such is the determination of this man Hitler, another took his place and returned to the quiet, white house in France. The newcomer interviewed the lovely lady most skillfully. When he might have blustered, he cajoled; when he might have flung his fury against her calm, he pleaded. Never a trace of fiery Hitler's dictatorship found expression in that French parlor, nor an echo of brow-beating tactics.

In Berlin, where Nazi boot heels rattle endlessly over clean cobbled roads, this officer's report produced a minor sensation in Hitler's inner circle. Probably, sundry hothead would have wreaked their vengeance on Miss Dietrich if they could have reached her. But not the iron-willed man who is now Germany's dictator.

The very few people who know of this story have asked why he has acted in this matter in a way so foreign to his nature. Rebellion he has invariably crushed; but now he entreats. Why?

Strange to say, Marlene Dietrich is the only being on earth who has succeeded in touching a warm chord in his heart. In his opinion, she is the greatest German woman in existence at the present day, the one unsullied glory on the honor roll of German citizenry. He never misses seeing any of the productions in which she appears, and his one unfulfilled ambition is to bring her back to Germany.

The fact of the matter is that Hitler, although he might become furious if anyone hinted to him that such was the case, *is in a sense in love with Marlene Dietrich!* Not with the woman herself, whom he has never met, but with the glamorous figure of her screen self.

Her entire life appeals to him. In a certain sense, they have much in common, for each is a self-made person and Marlene has known much of the drudgery and despair he must have felt before he gained his place in the sun. She is the only woman who has escaped the ostracism in which he holds all others. In his mind, women are relegated to their homes.

And what of Marlene, now that she has returned to America? When one has been offered the world, what is there left? Well, there is the sunshine of California and a gay coterie of dear friends, all of which she would have been forced to sacrifice if she had accepted Hitler's offer to head his revived movie industry. There is a delightful climate, and there is a warm spot in the hearts of millions of Americans who have accorded her far more recognition than she ever gained in her native land. And there is a free country called America in which her tiny daughter can grow and bloom.

These things Marlene values. To hold them for herself, she has offered Hitler's scheme no encouragement.

But Hitler is not easily deterred. If you wonder at his leniency and self-control in a case where he might have been expected to resort to more violent methods, just remember that Hitler, the strong man, has also his weak spots.

As he dreams, in those rare moments that he is idle, he thinks not of the woman herself but of the lovely creature he has seen on the screen before his tired eyes. She has become a symbol of the greatness that is to be Germany's in every field of endeavor as well as the movies. Desperately, he wants her back for Germany. He grudges, I'm sure, the American public the sight of her and her deep, blue eyes.

Two significant things happened recently when Marlene Dietrich returned to America.

Questioned by reporters about Germany and Chancellor Hitler, Marlene was the epitome of diplomacy.

"I am an actress," Marlene evaded, "it is foolish to question me about political matters."

However, misquoted by one reporter as saying, "I may go back to Germany when Hitler is not there," Miss Dietrich was horribly agitated.

Her mother lives in Germany, you see. It is a matter of record that where it has not been possible for the New Germany to punish those who have talked against it, their relatives have suffered.

The second significant thing occurred when Marlene was questioned about her future plans.

"After I make *Queen Catherine*, I hope to have another holiday in France," she said. "Then I shall return to Hollywood for one more picture. After that – well, perhaps I shall work in France. Who knows – so far in advance?"

Princess Catherine Radziwill (1858-1941) was born in Russia to Polish aristocracy. In 1873, she married a Polish Prince Wilhelm Radziwill. She was prominent in the Imperial courts of Germany and Russia, and was involved in many scandals. During her lifetime, she authored two dozen books about European royalty and the Russian royal family. She traveled the world and spent two years in prison in South Africa for forgery. During her time incarcerated, she wrote her autobiography, *My Recollections* (1904). In 1918, after the death of her second husband, she settled in New York City. She spent the rest of her life publishing books including *Russia's Decline and Fall: The Secret History of a Great Debacle* (1918), *Rasputin and the Russian Revolution* (1918), *Confessions of the Czarina* (1918), *The Firebrand of Bolshevism; The True Story of the Bolsheviki and the Forces That Directed Them* (1919), *Secrets of Dethroned Royalty* (1920), *The Intimate Life of the Last Tsarina* (1929), *Nicholas II: The Last of the Tsars* (1931), and *The Taint of the Romanovs* (1931). Radziwill also wrote for numerous, international magazines.

"Marlene In A Rage!" by Edna Perry. *Movie Classic,* January, 1934

Marlene in The Scarlet Empress, *1934.*

Picture Marlene Dietrich in a rage, with gold hair ruffled and deep blue eyes ablaze, running, stumbling, across the studio lot, screaming at astonished executives, who could hardly recognize their most impassive star! For three years, Marlene had met rumors, lawsuits, criticism, misunderstandings and production troubles with a shrug, a lift of the eyebrow, a low-voiced, "Who cares?" But this was not the exquisite, bored, impassive Dietrich, screen star, who faced them like a blonde fury; this was the mother of small, eight-year old Maria Sieber, who has that day become a motion picture actress, playing Marlene as a child in *Catherine, the Great*. I asked Marlene to tell me the story, and here it is.

My question was so simple, "How did you happen to let Maria play in *Catherine, the Great* with you? Is she going to be an actress?" Yet it magically served to open the door to a reserve that is more disconcerting because it is so gracious. Marlene's eyes suddenly glowed. Her smile became something to remember.

"She is going to be what she desires," Marlene told me. "Who am I to say what she is going to be? She is not the kind of child who says, 'I am going to be this or that.' She has said that she does not want to be an actress. 'You have so many troubles that I would not want to act,' she has said again and again. She sees the long hours, the difficulty in getting stories, the worries – she lives the life of an actress with me, you see. And she does not want to be one. But, then, Maria lives from day to day – as I did as a child. I wanted only one thing – to become a mother. I always wanted a baby."

"And does Maria?"

Marlene smiled. "No. She says, again, 'I am too much trouble to you.' She sees how I worry when she is sick or something does not go right for her. Maria has no complexes. She just lives. I have heard her say, 'I want to be – anything!'"

"I understand that you lost your temper on the set yesterday, Marlene, when they attempted to make Maria study. Is that right?"

Marlene's eyes flashed. She leaned forward. "Yes, I lost my temper. For the first time on this lot, I raised my voice. You see, it is very unusual. I allowed Maria to work only because Mr. von Sternberg wanted her. He is directing. He wanted her because he had to have a child who looks like me." She shrugged. "I would not have done it for anyone else. But Maria would look like me."

And Maria did. The rushes of the child's work are really startling. Even that fascinating little droop at the mouth, so like her mother's, is there.

"The nurse and the guards took her down to the city at seven-thirty in the morning to get her certificate to work," Marlene went on to explain. "I had to come to the studio so that if anything delayed her, I could fill in and we could take scenes with me. It was very hard on her because she does not like to ride in automobiles. When she got back, I got her ready. Then she was lying in a big bed for the scene three hours. The lines were in English. She talks English, but she *thinks* in German. I was afraid of them. When she had finished with the bed scenes, I wanted her to rest for the dialogue scene. Then, to my amazement, a teacher walked on the set and took her by the hand. 'I have come to take you to the schoolroom.'"

"What! Take my child to the schoolroom?" Marlene asked the teacher.

Maria has never been in a schoolroom in her life. Her teachers are private tutors.

"If you wish, I will teach her on the set," the teacher replied.

"But how can you teach her anything when she does not read or write English? It's perfectly ridiculous!"

The teacher insisted and pointed out a capital "A" to Maria. "Now, what is that, my dear?"

"Ah," answered Maria, with perfect German pronunciation.

"Not 'ah,' but 'aye,'" answered the American teacher.

"Nein. *Ah*," insisted Maria.

And then Marlene Dietrich screamed and rushed to the front office. "I did," she admitted. "I screamed, I tell you. I wouldn't scream for myself, but for my *child*!"

Of course, the newspaper reports that the permit to work had been taken from the child were ridiculous. The child had a permit for two days only and she worked those two days.

"It was not the teacher's fault," Marlene added. "If the child were going to work in pictures, she would go to school on the lot, of course. Only she is *not* going to make more pictures."

I told Marlene that people seemed to think that she had a complex on the subject of Maria.

"But this is ridiculous. When people have asked me to talk before, I have said, 'But why? I could only say what every mother would say. Mothers will read it and perhaps remark, 'She is right' – but they will not be amazed. Each mother feels that way about her child."

Other actresses have stormed. But Marlene's deadly quiet – her amazing ability to keep silent and let the other fellow wrangle himself in words – is the true secret of how she has handled each situation until the teaching-of-Maria. When Paramount wants her to sign a new contract that she does not desire, she says, "No." She does not argue or threaten or talk about her great box-office value. She simply says "No" until a contract is suggested that pleases her – and then she says "Yes" in the same, quiet manner. I can imagine the surprise of the Front Office when Marlene Dietrich, *the mother*, whirled in upon them.

The dressing-room in which we were talking about Maria was packed with white flowers – Marlene's favorite. One of the largest baskets of white chrysanthemums that I have ever seen centered the table.

"I sent those to Maria, yesterday, upon her first day of work," Marlene said. "And she sent me these," pointing to a dainty, smaller basket. "She insists upon paying for them, herself, from her salary. Her father sends her some money. They have a secret arrangement between them. I urge her to save it. But she *must* buy me presents.

"And when her father comes! Even the swimming pool was filled with flowers for his last arrival. She had them in every corner – white roses and white camellias."

"You have never sent her to school, Marlene?"

"No. That is because I am not settled anywhere. She would only get started…" Another shrug. "That is the problem, of course. She has no children with whom to play. I invited some in and I found them playing house. I heard them saying, 'Now, my brother is in love with your sister. When she comes in, he must kiss her.' Talking about love-making and playing love-making before they were eight! I could not have that, of course. I did not know what to do.

"Of course, when her father is here or when we are in Europe with him, everything is all right. He plays with her. They are like children together. They adore one another. If you think I have love for my child, you should see my husband! And when I am not working, I play with her here, too. I am with her so much because she has no children to play with…"

"And are you raising her according to German or American custom?"

"German. Not exactly as I was raised, but with the same idea back of it. I never had one moment to myself. I went to a state school from eight until one o'clock. Then, after lunch came a piano lesson, followed by a gymnastic one. Then French and my English lessons. Then we took walks in the park. That was in Berlin, you see. And I was in bed at seven o'clock each night until I was confirmed at sixteen. Yes, Lutheran. But my husband is Catholic and Maria likes the Catholic Church.

"Maria has a German teacher in the morning. She teaches her everything in German. Maria *thinks*, as I said, in German. Then she walks with her nurse. At twelve she takes her piano lesson. In the afternoon, a teacher *talks* to her in English and reads her stories in English. She is not learning grammar and lessons yet. I want her to get well-started in spelling and things like that in German first, so that she does not confuse the two. Then, three times a week, she has her dancing lessons. She plays in the garden and studies her lessons for the next day. She loves to be outdoors. And she likes Palm Springs. I send her down there once in a while. Yes, I will tell you who accompanies her: there are the chauffeur and the teachers and the guards."

"How many guards have you now?"

"I have eight. I always had seven before, but since this NRA – I employ one extra."

My mind flashed to remarks that I had heard certain *American* citizens make about adding extra help to aid the NRA! I asked, "And is Maria's diet German, too?"

"Yes. First, there is no white bread and her vegetables must be cooked in their own juice, not in water. She has meat three times a week and fish one day. The meat is boiled, always. And twice a week she has the insides – what do you call it? – of the animals. The livers and kidneys and sweetbreads and brains. I try to keep her from highly-seasoned foods. She loves them. And she adores your American pies! I keep her away from them as much as I can.

"Maria adores America. In Europe, when she saw an American flag, she stopped and threw out her arms and said, 'My home!' And she tells everyone in Europe about America!"

"Marlene, do you know the latest rumor is that you are going to divorce your husband?"

She laughed. Marlene Dietrich laughs aloud seldom. She smiles, but does not laugh. But now – genuine, infectious laughter. "The only reason that my husband is not coming over here now is because I want to go back to Europe as soon as this picture is finished. I do not have to stay here between pictures. It is difficult for us all. But divorce? No! I would not separate Maria and her father, and I would not separate myself from my husband, either. Certainly, you can quote me! Oh, it is funny!"

I changed the subject quickly. Somehow, her laughter had been convincing.

"And do you allow Maria to go to motion pictures?"

"But of course. She loves them."

"All pictures?"

"No, not all pictures. It is difficult. She wants to see them all. But you cannot let a child see a picture you cannot even explain; because, to explain, you must tell her things that you don't wish her to know so young."

It was Maria Sieber's mother speaking, and not Marlene Dietrich, the glamorous screen star.

Edna Perry was a frequent contributor to movie magazines and entertainment publications.

"Dietrich Isn't Afraid of Mae West!" by Sonia Lee. *Motion Picture,* January, 1934

"Why do all these unkind rumors pursue me – how do they start?" asks Marlene Dietrich, back from Europe to play Catherine, the Great. "Like this latest rumor that I am jealous of Mae West. That's utterly ridiculous! I am not jealous of anyone. Oh, yes, I know the stories – that I fear Miss West's rivalry, that I am envious of her sensational and sudden popularity, that I have refused to meet her. They are all lies.

"This is the truth. When I saw the preview of *She Done Him Wrong*, I was thrilled by this new, arresting, dynamic personality. Miss West was in New York, making personal appearances. I had never met her before – but I wanted to congratulate her on her magnificent performance. So, I sent her a telegram." (As a matter of fact, Marlene wired bushels of flowers to Mae.) "I recognized Miss West as a star before anyone else did. I met her before I left for Europe, and we became friends.

"When I returned from abroad – after five months – a dozen reporters met me at Quarantine, outside New York harbor. They fired a barrage of questions at me – and one of them asked what I thought of the new Mae West styles. I answered honestly that I didn't know that a new style had been inspired by Miss West. I was stupidly misquoted – quoted as having said that I had never heard of Miss West!

"And the next thing I knew, I was reading such stories as 'Dietrich Asks: Who is Mae West?', 'Does Dietrich Fear Mae West?', 'Does Mae West Threaten Dietrich's Supremacy?', and other equally implausible tales.

"Why should there be rivalry between us – between any stars? Every star brings something different, something vital, something extraordinary to the screen. It is by virtue of that that stardom is awarded them. Stars must stand or fall alone. Qualities, achievements, abilities cannot be compared. They are too individual.

"There is a place on the screen for every personality. This country is vast. The motion picture industry is large. There are thousands of theaters that must be supplied with pictures. Why, then, should there be jealousies? Why, then, should there be this ridiculous discussion of rivalries and envies? One star can do one type of picture – another, an entirely different one. Comparison is not only unfair, but unnecessary.

"I have never envied anyone. Envy is not in my character. What someone else does cannot interfere with my progress or my success.

"Success doesn't mean enough to me to motivate petty emotions. It has never absorbed me to the exclusion of every other thought. It has neither formed nor modified my attitudes, my reactions, my beliefs. This thing called 'Fame' has been unimportant in my life.

"I left Germany on the very day I knew that there I would be famous. *The Blue Angel* opened in Berlin. I was at the premiere, and from the theater I went directly to the boat that was to take me to America, where I was to bid again for fame, in a strange land – in a strange tongue. If fame had been of vast importance to me, I would have remained in Europe, where my place was assured. But I came here, six thousand miles away.

"And I am glad. No other place in the world produces the finely-balanced, progressive, artistic pictures that Hollywood does. As long as I remain on the screen, I shall remain in America." (And this would seem to dispose of the report that she will heel Hitler's demand that all German stars return now to the Fatherland, or stay away forever.)

"If my career should end in Hollywood, I would undoubtedly go back to Europe to live. My husband is there. I have been raised there. I belong there. However, no one knows what time will bring. Whatever I might say would be only a guess."

Marlene sat with one pantalooned leg casually draped over the arm of her chair, her inscrutable face vitalized by a mutinous mouth. And she was intangible beauty come to life. There was a luminous quality to her face – electrifying, breath-taking. Yet she finds no joy in her beauty. For, sitting there, she said, "The task of a movie actress is to be beautiful all day long. I would prefer not to be. I am not feminine enough to want to stand in front of a mirror for hours on end. I get tired of looking at myself." She stuffed her competent, sensitive hands into her jacket pockets, and in all sincerity declared, "I resent the necessity of looking at myself – of looking at myself constantly. That is the hardest part of being in pictures – of being a star in pictures.

"No, I am not an actress before all else," she continued with cool detachment – the individual, not the star. "If I were, I would have some of the reactions that everyone tells me an actress must have. I am not absorbed in myself. I am not driven by the necessity, the urgent desire to do one particular role. I don't take acting seriously. I act because Mr. von Sternberg tells me that I must."

Acting, to Dietrich, is not a great passion. Surprisingly enough, it is the technical end of the motion picture industry that intrigues her.

"I would much prefer to work behind the camera," – and her eyes are alive with enthusiasm – "rather than in front of it. I am fascinated by the mechanical end of picture-making. Even now I help cut my pictures, and sit in conference on every question from the inception of the story, until the completed film is ready for delivery to the theaters.

"Someday, perhaps, I shall work with Mr. von Sternberg behind the camera – not for it. But in the meanwhile, he tells me that I must act – and so I do. I don't want to wait until I am old before I abandon acting. I would be happy to do it now – tomorrow, if I were permitted. I want to do other things before age has closed its doors on me and on my enthusiasms.

"For the moment, acting must be enough. I make no plans. I do not look to the tomorrows. I live for today. I have neither hopes, nor ambitions – nor desires. I have never wanted anything very much. I asked of life only one thing – a child. And that I have.

"Ever since I could consciously realize it, I have lived in the present. A day has spanned my every emotion. You might call me a fatalist. Certainly, I believe that a star marks our course from birth, that our destiny is unchanging and unchangeable. Whatever has been written, when we first open our eyes on life, will happen. We can do nothing about it.

"What we become – what happens to us – is in the lap of the gods. I am less happy at the year's increase, but that is natural. When we are young, life has a thrilling tempo. We have illusions and delusions. Everything is beautiful. The sun shines. The days are cadenced with joy. There is a zest to every breath we take. As we grow older, problems increase, become more complicated. Life is more difficult. I am not unhappy – only less happy than when I was younger, when I was my Maria's age or just a little older."

Marlene Dietrich has found herself in situations that would mar the philosophies of almost any other woman. She has kept her philosophy intact – that philosophy of hers that includes grace and calmness and stoicism and patience with events. Neither studio maladjustments nor distasteful personal publicity has jarred her sense of values. Her balance is the product of a clear and concise mind, mystically inclined. She has found peace in faith. But that peace has not subtracted from the flame that is Dietrich. This woman is neither fame-ridden nor driven by ambitions. She designs no plan for living. Behind the wall of her philosophies she remains immune to criticisms and applause alike, going her own serene way.

Dietrich – the riddle. Dietrich – the impassive. Dietrich – the unconcerned, the colossally indifferent. They are only myths, born of this belief of hers that every mortal is wax in the hands of a definite Fate. Without words, she is expressing herself.

She is baffling both as a woman and as an actress. As a woman – because she knows the meaning of steadfast loyalties, of basic virtues. As an actress – because she does not know the meaning of ego, of envy, of plot and studio counter-plot, of the tantalizing and brutal urge to be important, to be dominating.

Rather, she is a shy, sensitive person, who truly finds no compensations in the clamor and symbols of stardom. Fame and glory, and glamour and money she would willingly exchange – if she could – for anonymity. For the peace of being an individual, without the insistencies of a career, and the tumultuous pace of stardom.

"An actress," says Dietrich, "sounds silly when she declares that she would exchange places with an unknown. But it must be marvelous to belong to yourself. Nothing in my life is mine – nothing but my thoughts."

"The Loveliest Star," by Elizabeth Wilson. *Silver Screen*, February, 1934

I've got to write a Dietrich story. And I hate to write a Dietrich story. But I've got to write a Dietrich story because I like two lumps of sugar in my coffee, fancy sports shoes, and a quarter occasionally for those fascinating slot machines at the Clover Club – and because it's going to be a long hard winter with plenty of huffing and puffing. Writing about Dietrich, with a two cent vocabulary and a pocket dictionary, is like scratching initials on the Mona Lisa with a rusty nail. Like giggling at the thrilling awe and exquisite pageantry of a New England sunset. Like spilling blackberry jam on an old and rare piece of lace. I have never understood why the benches along Riverside Drive face the street, and the occupants blandly watch taxis colliding with Chevrolets all unmindful of the serene beauty and mystery of the Hudson River behind them. And I have never understood why dumb clucks write about Marlene Dietrich. There is so little beauty in this world, it should not be defamed by clumsy pens – or rattling typewriters. Dietrich – beautiful, mysterious, exotic as a white orchid and as disturbing as the sensuous rhythms of the "Bolero" – a subject only for poets like Edna St. Vincent Millay.

Marlene in The Scarlet Empress, *1934.*

But I've got to write a Dietrich story. I'd much rather write about Jimmy Durante and string out a lot of "hat-cha-chas" and "Am I moitified" or about Alice in Wonderland and get all tweet-tweet and Gaynorish. But the boss said Dietrich – and just because three years ago, come what may, Consolidated Gay went down instead of up it's got to be Dietrich.

As the whole world knows, Roosevelt is president and there's an NRA and Josef von Sternberg is whipping up a little something at the Paramount studios called *Catherine of Russia* as Dietrich's next starring picture. Of course you realize that unless you're queening it in Hollywood these days, you can't belong to the club, and what with Catherine and Christina and Bess and Marie Antoinette romping around in whalebones and ruffles, the place is beginning to look like a hand of poker. But we like it. Briefly now, for the benefit of those who came in late, we'll skip lightly over a few of the episodes in the life of the Great Catherine, which von Sternberg has chosen to depict in this dramatic historical opus.

As a child the Princess Sophia Frederica (Marlene Dietrich's little Maria) of Anhalt-Zerbat, Germany, is denied dolls and toys and sternly prepared for marriage to royalty by her mother, the Princess Johanna (Olive Tell). One day, after the little Princess Sophia now played by Marlene, has reached her teens, the household is thrown into a fever of excitement, for communications arrive from King Frederick of Prussia confirming arrangements for her marriage to Grand Duke Peter (Sam Jaffe), grandson of Peter the Great. And that is something.

Fifteen years old, frightened but impressed at the same time, Sophia hides an old rag doll, which her mother knows nothing about, in her trunk, puts on the best clothes and her bravest smile and sets out by carriage for Russia. And it was quite a buggy ride in those days of boggy roads. But ah – the dashing Count Alexie (John Lodge) has been sent from Moscow to escort the little German princess to her future husband, and the Count has a neat figure, besides a lot of unruly hair. Quite delighted, oh, yes, indeed, quite. Sophia repulses the Count's ardent love making by expressing devoted loyalty to the Grand Duke, who has been described by the Russian envoy as the handsomest man in all Europe. Sophia's years of Prussian training stand by her now – she can't help feeling all aglow when that fascinating Count flirts with her, but what's a Count when a handsome Grand Duke awaits her in Russia.

The princess is given a royal welcome at the Kremlin in Moscow, where such blonde loveliness has never been seen before. Her Imperial Highness, the Empress (Louise Dresser) loses no time in warning her that it is her duty to become a dutiful wife and the mother of a son, so that there may be an heir to the throne. Immediately, she changes the princess' name to Catherine and the shy little German girl from Anhalt-Zerbat becomes a Grand Duchess.

But the first bitter disappointment comes when she meets the Grand Duke Peter, for instead of being the handsome youth described by the Russians, the heir to the throne is obviously imbecilic and quite revolting in appearance – in fact, we may even call him a degenerate. He has only two passions in his life, his mistress (Ruthelma Stevens) and his regiment of toy soldiers. But just the same he is male enough to be extremely piqued when he notices that his young wife abhors him. Count Alexie slyly informs Catherine that her marriage with Peter need not become too tedious because he will make it his business to be always near her. Good old Alexie.

Following the magnificently barbaric wedding and feast, the Empress spies upon the newlyweds in the bridal chamber and is infuriated when she learns that Catherine is determined to repulse Peter – and poor Peter, on his wedding night, has to find solace in his wooden soldiers. After that there's "in-law trouble." Well, about a year later Catherine gives birth to a son and all Russia rejoices and rings bells and shoots cannons – all except the Grand Duke Peter and the Empress who've got a pretty good idea about the legitimacy of the youngest heir to the throne of Russia. Catherine then revives the old Russian custom of receiving loyal subjects in her boudoir – and takes a keen personal interest in the young officers of her regiments. But you've read your history books and I don't have to tell you about Katy's whimsies.

Oh, indeed. Russia was in an awful state the day I arrived on the Paramount lot bent upon getting a Dietrich story or something. I arrived in time to see a queer spectacle, so queer in fact that I began to wonder if the worst suspicions of my family were about to come true. *Not Dietrich the Glamorous in a truck!* At first I thought that it was Marie Antoinette on her way to the guillotine, and that silly old Paramount, with childish simplicity, had gotten its queens and history all mixed. But it seems the costumes (twenty of them and each more grand and heavy than the others) Marlene wears in this picture are so delicate and expensive that the studio won't allow her to sweep up the sidewalks with them. Which is all right with Dietrich, for it is quite a job carrying forty pounds of something around on your back when you're used to the freedom of pants. So every day, when she gets ready to go on the set, a low-geared cub truck, or "Minnie" as it's called by the workmen, backs up to the curb and the exotic Marlene becomes a truck-load. But what a pretty sight it is when the seventy-five yards of ruffles begin to ruffle in the breeze.

Stage Nine on the Paramount lot, where the Empress is throwing a party for the express purpose of humiliating the young Grand Duchess Catherine, is as silent as the tombs. Wan figures in satin and muffs and jewels and green boots sit around on the Kremlin stairs or the uncomfortable pews of the Cathedral – strange gaunt apostolic figures – never making a sound, hardly breathing it seemed. I immediately decided I had walked past a red light and onto a stage where a scene was being taken – but no – it was only a rehearsal. But so quiet you could hear the proverbial pin drop way over there behind Marlene's dressing table. This is the only place in Hollywood where you can find such a startling phenomenon. Usually on sets, when scenes are not actually being taken, the workmen are hammering away, the prop boys running here and there, the phone ringing, soundmen shouting, maids and valets giggling and drinking coca-colas, and extras playing cards or visiting each other. But not on von Sternberg sets. His rehearsal is as quiet as his "take." He wants to keep the atmosphere of his picture and, believe me, he certainly keeps it. Huddled up in a studio chair I felt all the barbaric splendor, religious fervor and drafts of old Russia. And was quite sure that if I so much as sneezed or coughed I'd be banished at once to darkest Siberia. But that's the way von Sternberg works – and it is a very effective way, for no director in Hollywood gets atmosphere and perfect timing into his pictures so well as von Sternberg. Those gaunt and grieving apostles who decorate the chairs and pews of the Kremlin and the Cathedral, are symbolic of eighteenth century Russia, and they give the same feeling of Fate and Destiny to *Catherine of Russia* that the drums give to *Emperor Jones*. These figures – there are two hundred of them – are von Sternberg's conception executed by Peter Ballbusch sculptor.

But with all its deathlike quietness, it seems that a lot of fun and kidding goes on on that set. Someone painted a neat little dog-house sign, and every time anyone meets with the Master's disfavor, he has to wear, "I'm in the dog-house" around his neck. Bert Glennon, the cameraman, wound his wrist watch during a take one day – though you or I would never have heard it – but it brought the ire of von Sternberg down upon his head. He was upset about it, and went around grieving for several days until someone noticed that he looked just like the grieving apostles; so now they call the apostolic chairs the Glennons. Monty Westmore was the next to incur the von Sternberg wrath by changing wigs when wigs shouldn't be changed. So now Monty is in the dog-house.

The minute Marlene comes on the set bleak Russia becomes warm with beauty. The hair-dressers and make-up girls simply adore her and Bert Glennon, the cameraman, worships the ground she walks on. Only last week Dietrich gave Nellie, the hair-dresser, a fur coat – the first fur coat Nellie ever had – and if you so much as let one little belittling word against Marlene slip from your lips when Nellie is around, you'll find her curling irons at your throat. Marlene talks very little to the extras and featured players on the set – but she smiles – and when Marlene smiles at you that's all that's necessary. It takes hours for that marvelous tingling sensation to wear off.

In fact, I hear that Marlene, even in the privacy of her home, talks very little. She listens – beautifully. And when she is pleased with you she gives you a smile and a firm warm hand shake which mean more than a dictionary of words.

There is none of the "great star" business about Marlene at the studio. Though most of the featured players have their maids and valets with them on the set, Marlene never has a personal maid. She waits on herself – assisted by the studio hair-dresser and makeup girls. Rarely using a stand-in, she stands for hours in those horribly uncomfortable regal gowns, with their pounds of whalebone and iron hoops – and even when she is given a chance to rest she can't sit down and relax – not in those dresses. The day of the marriage ceremony she wore a crown that would not stay on unless it was clamped tightly to her temples, and from nine until one she endured that metal pressing against her nerves until she nearly went crazy. When von Sternberg called "lunch" she broke down and cried – she had suffered so long. Perhaps you think it is rather silly of Marlene to suffer without a murmur when it isn't entirely necessary, but remember that Marlene, like the little Princess Sophia, came from Germany where the old Prussian idea of enduring pain is still dominant. And then, too, Marlene has great respect for von Sternberg and will never do anything to hold up a scene or upset his famous "tempo." Which is rather nice, don't you think? Certainly such thoughtfulness isn't found much in Hollywood these days.

Indeed, no one has ever seen Marlene explode or become temperamental or sarcastic on a set. She is always the quietest member of the cast. No matter how many times a player blows up in his lines and the scene has to be retaken, Marlene never shows the least impatience or annoyance. The scene where she meets Count Alexie on the Kremlin stairs had to be taken forty times – and forty times Marlene had to run up and down those steps. But not once did she complain. Only once has she ever been known to become the least bit impatient on a set. It was the day that little Maria worked at the studio with her mother, and according to state law, had to study for a while between scenes. Although she speaks English, little Maria reads only in German, so when the school teacher insisted that she read from an English text book, Marlene became rather annoyed. 'You cannot hope to teach my child English in one day,' she coldly informed the teacher. "And besides, she is tired now and needs to rest." There was a scene – a terrific scene. Dietrich won.

I was on the set on one of those unfortunate days when the same scene had to be taken over and over again. A grand actress and trouper, Louise Dresser just couldn't keep from blowing up in her lines. Actresses have "bad" days just as we do, when nothing seems to go right. Von Sternberg will be furious, I thought, and sort of winced to think about the deluge of sarcasm on its way. But no. He turned out to be the sweetest, most thoughtful director I have ever seen in such a trying situation. With Louise nearly in tears because the words just wouldn't come right. Herr Jo simply pranced up like a pixie, gaily chuckled her under the chin, and laughed away, just as if that nasty old scene was really the most unimportant thing in the world. And Marlene never batted a famous eyelash. When I got a little bit nervous because the "takes" were running up into the forties and decided I'd better go home, Marlene lightly said, "It is nothing. It happens to all of us." Well, if I had been standing up there for three hours in a forty-pound dress and supporting a Russian bayonet and spear, I'm not at all sure I could say, "Tut, tut, it's nothing." Why I was worn out just sitting there trying to play dead.

Elizabeth Wilson was a prolific writer for movie magazines, and wrote dozens of articles for *Silver Screen* and *Screenland* magazines during the 1920s through the early 1940s. She was a frequent contributor to *Liberty* magazine from 1944 until 1949.

"The NEW Marlene," by Della Mason.
The New Movie Magazine, April 1934

With the exception of Joan Crawford, no front-line star of Hollywood has changed her off-screen personality with such unsettling abruptness as Marlene Dietrich.

In the comparatively short time the glamorous German has been with us we have been treated to the off-stage character of the pining girl who longed for her native country and her own little Maria; who loved to cook meals with her own hands and complained there was nothing interesting to do in Hollywood except listen to the radio.

It was something of a shock to the local press when this girl who they had set down as a beautiful blond *hausfrau*, suddenly did a complete right-about-face and developed into the sensationalist of the von Sternberg-Dietrich studio walk-out, the trouser fad, and the four burly bodyguards.

It was not at all unusual for one of Marlene's antics – either her appearance with Chevalier or von Sternberg at a premiere in tuxedo, the bars she had placed on every upstairs window of her Beverly Hills home to protect Maria from kidnappers, or the supposed Paris ruling against her trousers – to reach you via the front page along with your orange juice and

Marlene in, 1934.

fried eggs. Interviewers came away from Marlene, no longer with excellent German recipes, but with bulging notebooks filled with fashion tips for men, how to dodge kidnappers and tips on exotic temperament.

For a while she became as aloof as Garbo. Interviews were refused. Visitors were banned from her sets and even the camera crew and technicians were invited outside while Marlene rehearsed.

That Josef von Sternberg had a great deal to do with this radical change in Marlene cannot be denied. An intensely effective showman himself, there can be little doubt but that he molded Marlene's off-screen personality with as deft a touch as he created her screen portrayals.

It was he who first objected to the fraternizing of his exotic star with the studio co-workers. It was von Sternberg who created the unapproachable aura about her. He is too keenly in tune with public reaction not to realize that too much down-to-earth normality was out of line in the character of the fascinating woman he shadowed with his camera lens.

But the story that Marlene was a dazed *Trilby* to von Sternberg's *Svengali* was as silly and mistaken a rumor as ever came from the Hollywood Hills.

As the new off-screen personality of Dietrich begins to be as freely circulated as her two other private life transitions, I think this particular fact will become increasingly clear.

For there *is* a new Dietrich, a Marlene who is a strange composite of her two former selves, plus a new independence that is created solely by her own thinking and her own moods.

So far as their studio work is concerned she is still perfectly willing to let von Sternberg write the gospel. If he works better on closed sets, in isolated privacy – that is something which will not be disputed by Marlene. She has implicit faith in his ability to guide her professional destiny. But Marlene, herself, is at present a creation solely of her own moods and temperament.

There are no rules for this new Dietrich. You cannot say "She is so sweet and lovely and unassuming just like she used to be" any more truthfully than you can say "She is pulling a Garbo with her new temperament and isolation."

No longer is Dietrich definitely etched as a *hausfrau* or a trousered sensationalist. Marlene is doing exactly as she wants to do about everything as it comes along. There is no definite mood… or pose. She is being decidedly, and excitingly, *herself*.

I have known Marlene ever since she first arrived in Hollywood and I rather think she likes me. Yet I have never interviewed her except in the formality of the publicity department or in her studio dressing-room.

Recently, I requested an appointment at her luxurious home in Beverly Hills so that I might get a more vivid picture of her intimate background. Her answer was typical, "Perhaps sometime you will come to my home as a guest. That would make me very happy.

"But interviews are part of my professional life. I do not take the studio work home with me…to Maria!" And that, bluntly or not, was that. It meant, that as a guest my lips would be bound by all the laws of good taste and social decency not to gossip about her intimate home life.

For Marlene does not tolerate tattling. Her two German maids, the negress cook and her chauffeur would cut off a right arm before they would reveal Marlene's home life.

Just recently, Dietrich's studio "stand-in" was abruptly dismissed because of an interview she granted about how it felt to double for the great Marlene. "I feel," she told me the last time we talked together, "that I should have the privilege of revealing what I wished revealed about my private life. It is too easy for others to distort my actions for publicity *color*."

In spite of this decided yen for privacy the new Dietrich is in no sense a recluse. She attends movie premieres and the opening of local stage plays. The other evening, she stood in line at her favorite café waiting for a table. She is frequently to be seen darting in and out of the smart shops. Strangely enough, she does not mind people staring at her, or pointing her out so long as they do not ask her silly questions or hound her for autographs.

There was a time when Marlene was accused of "ritzing" everyone on the Paramount lot. But if those accusations were true… they belong back in Marlene's second Hollywood personality, her days of being The Great Star.

Now if she feels like crawling through one of the office building windows to chat with the girls in the publicity department, "Because I do not feel like walking around to the door," she does it.

But lest you think by these telling examples that Dietrich has slipped back to the personality of her first months in Hollywood, let me hasten to assure you that such is not wholly the case. She can be as imperious and imperial as "Catherine," the great queen she portrays. Yesterday's intimacy and yesterday's jokes do not mean tomorrow will find her in the same mood. She walks moodily and unspeaking past the same windows she crawled through with surprising lack of dignity the week before.

Last week's gay "Hello" may be today's frigid "How do you do?" On one of her gay days she may give her confidence freely and actually enjoy granting interviews. The next day she will see no one.

But it is quite obvious the new Marlene has gone feminine with a vengeance. She is no longer a striding, swaggering masculine figure among her four bodyguards. The strong-arm boys have completely disappeared from the studio, and only one remains at her home to protect Maria.

Dietrich's new "suits" have skirts and luxurious furs to trim them. She wears a great deal of jewelry with everything…even in the day time. Her studio dressing table is burdened with exotic perfume bottles and the most expensive blossoms the florist's shops have to offer. By the way, she has a unique and different method of applying perfume to her person. She sprays scent on her long, ruby-red finger tips; and toilet waters more expensive than your treasured bottle of imported stuff are used to curl up the ends of her blonde hair. In place of the beach slacks, and heavy tweed suits she used to wear to the studio, she has lately been seen in trailing velvet hostess gowns.

When a friend recently accused her of going in for an ultra-luxurious mode of life, she merely shrugged.

"I surround myself with beautiful things for one reason…Maria. I want my little girl to grow up with the love of beautiful things in her heart. Everything I have, and everything I do, is for her alone."

For, through every phase of Marlene's changing Hollywood personality that one thing, her consuming maternity and her idolatry of her little blond daughter, has not changed. Maria is the one definite, set influence in her whole life.

Many people were surprised, in view of her consuming protection of the child, that Dietrich permitted her to play a small part in *Catherine, the Great*. And no matter what reason Marlene may eventually give for this, the truth is simply that Maria begged her to…and Dietrich cannot say "No" to her little girl's pleadings.

Of course she would not permit her to continue to work in pictures if she could not be present to supervise every gesture she made. She has no intention of launching Maria on the career of a "child actress." But Maria's heart would have broken if some other child had been selected to portray her glamorous and beautiful mother as a little girl.

And so Maria it was! The pros and cons of what people might think about Maria's advent into the movies were not considered by this new Marlene who is doing just exactly what she wants to do for the first time since she has been in Hollywood!

Della Mason was a contributor to numerous movie magazines.

"You Have Sex Appeal!" by Marlene Dietrich. *Hollywood Magazine*, May, 1934

Marlene with Douglas Fairbanks, Jr.

What is Sex Appeal?

Is it the excitement of amorous passion in men?

Is it the unconscious charm exercised by every beautiful woman?

Is it dangerous to those who possess it as to those who come under its fatal influence?

Can a woman exert this extraordinary power over men without being labelled "a bad lot," "no better than she ought to be," "a scarlet sister," "a loose woman," "a lady of no reputation," and all the other time-worn tags which the more circumspect of her sex have thought fit to hurl at her through the centuries?

My screen past should certainly qualify me to express an opinion on this much debated question. For invariably I have been cast either as a callous little "gold-digger," a woman of the streets living by my wits, a "lady of the town" beguiling and hoodwinking good men and true from the straight and narrow path, a notorious night club queen, or the vamp deluxe exulting in her feminine fascination.

Yet so fraught with misunderstanding is the subject of sex that it is almost impossible to disentangle it from the substratum of half-truths and stupid mis-statement that surrounds it.

Sex is essentially neither wicked nor dangerous. It is only the evil-minded who see in it a hideous and horrible menace. Their viewpoint is probably clouded and distorted by some of these subconscious repressions and hidden complexes we hear so much about.

Rightly used, sex can be a great constructive force, and if in the films in which I have appeared it is shown in a discreditable light, that is an indictment of the civilization that has misused it, not of sex itself.

After all, sex is the dominating factor of our lives. It brought us into the world. It underlies most of our actions, and certainly all our emotions, such as the love of parents for their children and their astounding indifference towards them when they have ceased to care for one another; it is the motive force of awakening adolescence with its blissful dreams.

In a sublimated form it is responsible for the promptings of our pity and sympathy for dumb animals, for little children, for the hurt, the maimed, the crippled; for the blind hero-worship the young girl feels for the adventurous athlete; for the protective male instinct for the damsel in distress and the glow of satisfaction he experiences when he discerns the adoration in her eyes.

All these things are purely physical – as physical as the love that Othello felt for Desdemona, and she for him. Shakespeare summed up their fundamental attraction for each other in the words, "She loved me for the things that I have done: I loved her that she did pity me."

It is only when the little green god of jealousy steps in that ugly passions are aroused and stark tragedy rears its head, as in the case of the unhappy, half-crazed Moor.

But sex appeal is not confined to these great figures of the drama. It is rampant among all sorts of unimportant people, not least among the boys and girls of today. And, believe me, sex appeal can be most devastating of all when wielded by the very young!

For incredible as it may seem sex appeal is not confined to hard-boiled men and women of the world. It can be detected even from the earliest years. You either have it or not, as the case may be. Only very occasionally can it be acquired, and then – like most other hothouse growths – it is never as strong and forceful as the native variety.

A person born with sex appeal is noticeable for his or her self-assurance, self-confidence, self-respect, if you like. One feels right with one's self, in tune with the universe, at one with God.

Yes, the vitality that fairly oozes out from these highly temperamental people, and stirs a corresponding excitement in all those who come in contact with them, is spiritual in essence. It has something to do with innocence – the sort of passionate innocence that betrayed me as the hapless "Lili" in *Song of Songs* into giving my heart into the keeping of the worthless young sculptor.

How often is this magnanimous gesture mistaken for a baser motive?

When this natural impulsiveness is combined with beauty and charm, it is irresistible. It is so powerful, so magnetic, that it can make old age and middle age feel young again. It can make youth itself aware that it is alive, and that life, above all else, is worth living.

Can you blame youth for wanting to experience these delightful sensations? Can you deny the boys and girls of today their desire to experience all that life has to offer? Would you withhold from them the rapture and joy of their new-found freedom?

The hunger for romance is a very real phenomenon, and the moving picture seems to assuage, in some degree, this universal craving. It is really rather pathetic when one comes to think about it. I suppose it is because the cinema has come to symbolize for most of us all that is young and vital, charming and romantic. Its constellation of stars scintillate across the screen heavens, and represent romance in a remote yet tangible form.

Because of its commercial possibilities, film producers have exploited sex-appeal to the *nth* degree.

Soft-focus bathroom scenes and indiscreet bedroom episodes are a common feature of the movies. There is no end to the suspicious circumstances in which the heroine is persuaded to part with her virtue and her modesty. The fertility of the film fraternity in inventing variations on this theme presents an intricate problem for solution by the star who is wholeheartedly sincere about her work. For only the scissors of the film censors can save the reputation of an actress who has once consented to enact these celluloid Delilahs, or to appear in roles of questionable taste.

I am not exactly prudish. I believe that sex is the biggest thing in life. Without it the world would come to an end. But I realize that it is artistic suicide for an actress to become a slave to one type of characterization.

No actress worthy of the name wants to be cast as a beautiful "clothes-horse" – a peg on which to hang a hackneyed love-tale and some sentimental "close-ups."

Incidentally, if you ask a cameraman, or "close-up" expert, to define sex appeal, he will probably tell you that it is "a face with good camera angles."

Conscious as I am of the enormous debt I owe to my cameraman I beg to differ from that definition.

Sex appeal is, I think, an infinite capacity for living, a *joie de vivre*, an enthusiasm, an eagerness for the chase, of the hunter for the hunted.

In a single word, "Sincerity."

"Why Garbo and Dietrich Lead Solitary Lives," by Gladys Hall. *Motion Picture*, June, 1934

Garbo is in love! Dietrich is in love!

No, not with Rouben Mamoulian or Josef von Sternberg or Rudolf Sieber or John Gilbert or any of the gentlemen, transitory and otherwise, who have figured in the headlines concerning these two most famous and isolated foreigners. They are in love with – themselves!

Garbo's Great Love is *Garbo*. Dietrich's Great Love is – *Dietrich*. Other fancies may come and go, other attractions may attract for a brief time, but none ever takes Greta or Marlene out of herself. Each continues on her solitary way. And solitude is sometimes the cause of a self-centered attitude toward life – and sometimes the result of such an attitude. In *their* solitude, Garbo and Dietrich are seemingly lost, Narcissus-like in their own reflections; other images are no more than shadows that touch the surface of their lives lightly and non-essentially. Their mirrors tell them all that the other images might like to tell them.

Consult M. Sigmund Freud, the father of modern psychology and he would tell you, I am sure, that when an individual becomes an eccentric, deviating from the herd and the habits and manners and customs of the herd, it is because the individual is an exhibitionist; it is because that individual profoundly and passionately believes his own individualism to be superior to and set apart from that of others.

Anyone has to be an exhibitionist to be an actor. But to be an eccentric is to be an exhibitionist of the first string. It is to cry aloud, "Look at me! Watch me! I am different! I am in the spotlight! I am separate from the rest of you. I do not do things as others do. I do not think as others think. I am curiouser and curioser! I have detached myself from my fellow-men the better for you to see me, hear me, notice me!"

So much for the eccentric. The intrinsically modest and conservative individual, on the other hand, makes himself as inconspicuous as possible. And he does this by conforming to the herd in every way possible. He knows that if he adopts and wears the protective coloration of his fellow-men, he will go unremarked.

Dietrich and Garbo have, consistently, even passionately deviated from the herd. They have both been in Hollywood several years now, but never, self-consciously, of it. They do not do as Norma Shearer, Mary Pickford, Joan Crawford, Miriam Hopkins do. They remain away from all social contacts with their fellow-players.

No premiere ever is graced by Garbo; seldom by Dietrich. No social function is blessed by either great presence. Few persons have ever been vouchsafed a glimpse of Garbo, even on the MGM lot. When Dietrich is seen on the Paramount lot, she is attired so fantastically or so sumptuously that to say she is the cynosure of all eyes is to understate the matter pitiably. They entertain no one except a small, almost unknown group of friends who are, really, nothing but extensions of their own personalities.

They wear, in but slightly differing ways, the provocative mantle of mystery and elusiveness – the most provocative, the most publicity-stimulating garment in the world.

Garbo lives in her well-known and widely-publicized isolation. And by so doing she seats herself in the very center of the spotlight. If the curious happen to find out where she is living, what high walls and massive shrubbery surround the Swedish jewel – and they *do* find out, of course, as small children have a way of finding hidden Christmas gifts – she immediately moves to another hideaway and the hunters are again in pursuit.

Garbo will not grant interviews to the Garbo-starved members of the press. The result is that she is besieged as she would never be if she courteously accorded stories in the normal run of things. As it is, she has evolved the greatest publicity value of any star in pictures. She attracts more attention, more reporters and photographers, more hopeful snoopers and would-be scoopers that she could ever manage to achieve if she stood on a high hill and delivered a valedictory.

Photographers crawl under bushes in attempts to record her at her sun-bathing. When she is in New York, reporters trap her in elevators, try to bribe chambermaids to admit them to her suite, pursue her in taxicabs, and weigh down the gang-planks of outgoing ships – playing a game with her, seeing if they can make her talk. This frenzied avoidance of contact with intermediaries between herself and her public – this is exhibitionism in a mask, any psychologist would tell you. The reverse of it would be the mild amusement of one who finds that people want to talk to her and casually gives out such stories as are reasonable.

Off the screen, Garbo dresses, as everyone knows, with such marked dishabille and disregard of all feminine fripperies and modes as to be instantly, constantly *marked*. She wears a mannish overcoat and an old beret or slouch hat. She uses no makeup. She goes about with limply uncurled hair. And these, friends – and foes, if any – these, too, are signs and portents of a great self-love. Psychology says so.

It used to be thought that women who spend hours in front of their mirrors, beautifying their faces, fussing with their hair, trying on one gown and then another, laboring with permanent waves and marcels and all the what nots of women – it used to be thought that these were the vain ones, the conceited sisters. Psychology has disproved that.

The ones who titillate and primp are, actually, the modest ones, the ones who suffer from inferiority. They are not satisfied with themselves; they are doing all in their pathetic power to improve on what doesn't please them; what they fear will please no one else. It is those of us who clap on an old hat, eschew the beauty shops, and boycott the dressmaker who are supremely self-pleased, blandly unconscious of the fact that we may not be pleasing to others. Or so deeply entrenched in our own egotism that we don't even *care* whether we please or not.

Garbo does not need companionship; she does not need the commonplace and comfortable rubbing of elbows with her fellow-mortals. She knows of no one she enjoys being with any more than she enjoys being with herself. She is self-sufficient.

Garbo reads all of the screen magazines, reads every word printed about herself. This much has been pretty well ascertained. And how intoxicating must be the knowledge that her neighbors, her discharged servants, her remotest acquaintances out of the past are waylaid and urged to speak of the Hermit of Hollywood.

There have been stories written about Garbo, the Goddess; about My Neighbor, Greta Garbo; about the possibility of her nursing a broken heart; about the possibility of Garbo's being dead – dozens and dozens of stories, some sensational, some silly, all of them unnecessary if Garbo ever gave authenticated stories to the press at reasonable intervals about reasonable matters. But no! To give casual stories in the normal way would be to kill dozens of other stories, not normal at all. Subtle and devious are the ways of ego!

Marlene Dietrich modifies some of the Garbo ways to a certain extent. She came here after Garbo. It would not be clever of the individualist to copy a predecessor. Dietrich will, sparingly and reluctantly, grant interviews to those of the press she can manage to tolerate. But the interviews must, when written, be submitted to her for reading and approval or, as often happens, disapproval.

She will not say, as Norma Shearer might, "I have thought over the idea you want me to talk about very carefully. Here is what I think. Do the best you can with it and for me" – and let it go at that. No, the Dietrich words are pearls that drop from the Dietrich lips and as such they must be polished and protected as the gems of great price they are. Not very long ago Dietrich tore a perfectly well-intentioned story into shreds before a writer's eyes and deposited the pieces in the nearest waste-basket.

She will not talk about this; she will not discuss that. She is scornful of the public's interest in the love-life, the home-life, or the political opinions of the stars. Not a syllable, then, must escape into print that does not perfectly accord with this particular brand of self-obsession. No man, no woman at the helm of a nation could be more choosey, more cautious about his or her publicity.

Self-obsession, you see, can never say, or think, "What does it matter?" To the self-obsessed, everything that touches the "Self" matters poignantly, passionately and absorbingly.

Dietrich's masculine attire is another manifestation of exhibitionism. Nothing but. Let no one tell us that she wears men's clothing because it is more comfortable. It might be at the North or South Pole or in a frigid climate. Not in sunny, sub-tropical California. Anyone who has to wear heavy trousers, shirts, coats here, knows better. The woman who chooses to wear male attire does so because it is one of the short-cuts to the center of the spotlight! It proves itself. Reams of copy, tons of photographs, pages and pages of discussion *pro* and *con* have gone over the presses because of the curvaceous Marlene's exotic deviation from the heard.

Marlene loves her small daughter, Maria, with, I am certain, even more than the usual maternal passion. Yet the child's face and form also mirror Narcissa. Marlene dresses the little girl in mannish attire, as she dresses herself. Marlene is willing for the child to follow in her screen footsteps. Marlene is encouraging the child to copy her own mannerisms, points of view and attitudes toward life.

A little bird tells me that Marlene's dressing-room is crammed with photographs of Marlene. With each new sitting she orders hundreds of pictures. Not to mail out to admirers. All photographs to fans are sent out by the studio. The stacks of pictures ordered by Marlene are for her personal use only. What she does with them is just one of the minor mysteries of Marlene. This same dressing-room is wall-lined with mirrors, so that no matter in what direction Marlene turns her beautiful head a reflection will be seen. She does not need to kneel, like Narcissus, on the slippery edge of a pool.

Unlike Garbo, Marlene graces the studio commissary frequently. Observers have noted that the only time she does not lunch there, beholden of all eyes, are the times when her costume is not particularly striking or during sequences of her pictures when she is not at her most sumptuous. Usually, Marlene waits until one o'clock or after to enter the lunchroom, waits until everyone is sure to be seated. And then, wearing mannish attire or one of her more magnificent costumes, she strolls in, accompanied invariably by director von Sternberg and certain, very certain, that every eye is riveted upon her. Garbo strikes the imagination a left-handed blow by not being visible at all. Dietrich strikes more directly by being visible only when she must evoke startled admiration. Both methods stimulate the imagination to fever pitch.

It has been said that Marlene's friendship for and with director von Sternberg is but another manifestation of self-consciousness (with the accent of the "self"). Her director and discoverer admires Marlene inordinately; he believes in her as one believes in a divinity. In his eyes, Narcissa sees her image reflected in its most delicious aspects.

Perhaps Garbo and Dietrich are right – who knows? There are plenty of human beings in the world; plenty of grubs who paint their faces and rub elbows and love their neighbors as themselves and go to parties and are self-deprecatory. Maybe the world needs two rebels in high places.

These two great women of Hollywood, Garbo and Dietrich, have deviated from the herd. Abnormality is always more interesting than normality. A veiled lady is infinitely more provocative than a nude. If you have to pay ten cents extra and walk through a couple of curtains at a side-show, you are proportionately more eager and more curious. Suppressed editions are always more sought after than ordinary best-sellers obtainable at any book stall. This is exhibitionism – and of all show-women now alive Garbo and Dietrich must make Barnum shiver in his grave to think that he died too soon…

Gladys Hall was a frequent contributor to movie magazines and other entertainment publications.

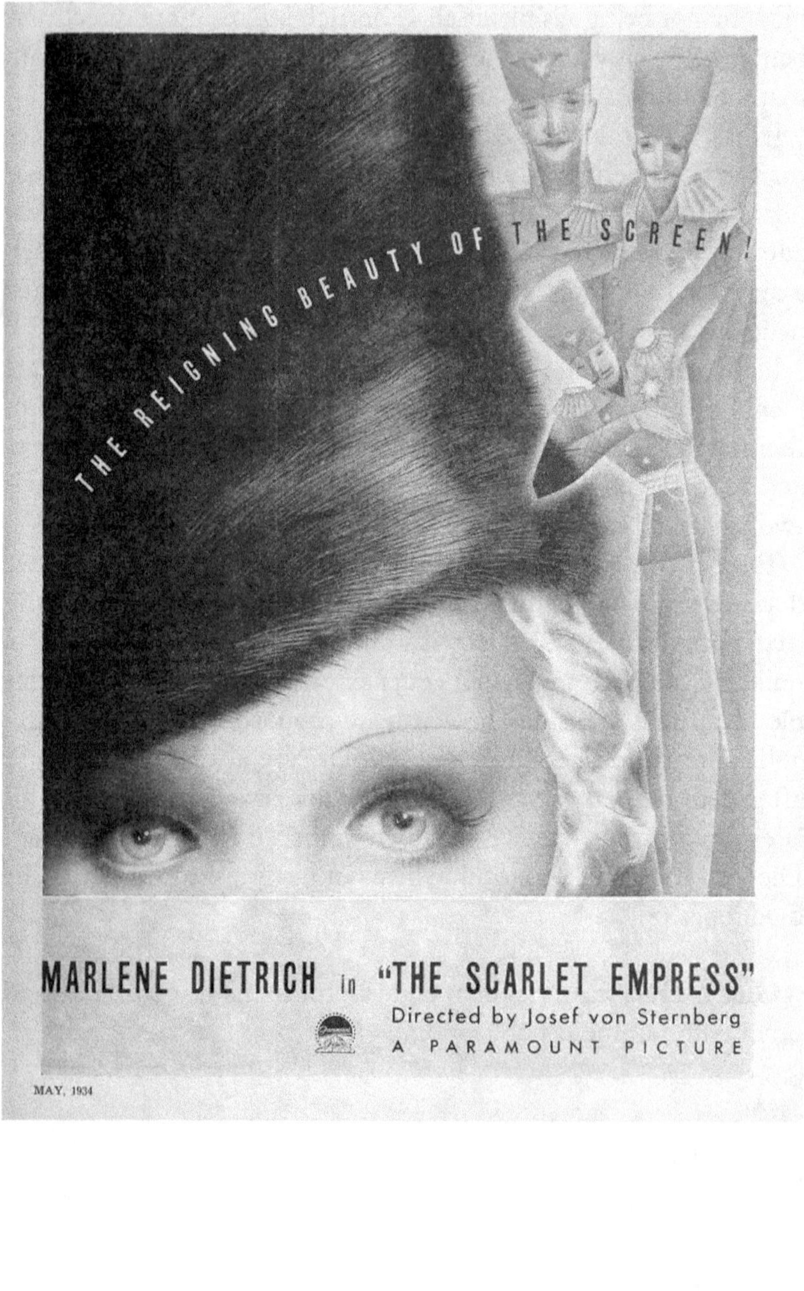
THE REIGNING BEAUTY OF THE SCREEN!
MARLENE DIETRICH in "THE SCARLET EMPRESS"
Directed by Josef von Sternberg
A PARAMOUNT PICTURE
MAY, 1934

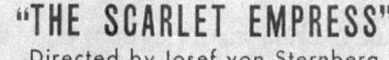

"Let Me Tell You About Marlene Dietrich," by John Lodge. *Modern Screen*, June, 1934

Don't take it to heart so. Mr. von Sternberg always uses more takes than any other director. He does the same thing with me, you know.

I looked into Marlene Dietrich's smiling, understanding eyes, heard the warm sympathy in her voice and thought that I might be a motion picture actor after all. It was my first day on the set of *The Scarlet Empress*. That day, when I said one line over and over again from morning to night, making innumerable takes had about swept my self-assurance away. And I had had a lot of it. After all, I had been a practicing lawyer in New York City and a New York lawyer doesn't get rattled at anything. I had played small roles in *The Woman Accused* and *Murders in the Zoo* and a larger one in *Little Women*, but here was my big chance.

To work opposite Miss Dietrich under Mr. von Sternberg's direction had seemed the thing that would definitely set me as an actor. But that afternoon, I felt myself slowly going to pieces, definitely doubting my ability. I thought to myself, "If you have to take a day to say one line, you must be a pretty bad actor."

It was then that Miss Dietrich came over and gave me the reassurance I needed, at the moment I needed it most. That doesn't sound like the "high hat Marlene," does it? But then I found that there is no "high hat Marlene."

She is herself always and that self is a warm-hearted, understanding woman. I don't care what she's worn in the past, or what she wears in the future, she comes through as "mature femininity." That was my first impression of her and I think a man senses these things instinctively. When I say she is a mature woman. I mean she could never be a cutie. You could not confuse her with the numberless blondes with shapely bodies who overrun Hollywood.

Marlene and John Lodge in The Scarlet Empress, *1934.*

She's a wife, a mother, an artist. She has lived deeply and she gives out, to those who contact her, the richness of her living. She gives it out in a wise and quiet way that is typically her own.

As time went on, I not only got used to Mr. von Sternberg's methods, I grew enthusiastic about them. I think they are the only ones by which a great picture can be made. He lives and breathes the production he is making. He thinks in terms of spectacles, but concentrates on his human beings. He oversees every detail, no matter how small.

An instance of this is the wig I wore. The hair was five inches long and he insisted that it must follow my own hair-line. In spite of wig-makers and costumes, he himself looked at the wig to see that his instructions were carried out. To prove how right he was, everyone kept asking me whether I had let my hair grow. It would have taken two years for it to grow to that length, but people didn't think of that — they only knew that it seemed like my own hair.

Contrary to public belief. Mr. von Sternberg does not make puppets of his players. He chooses his people for an inner quality they possess that will make them express the characters he has to work with. So what he really did with us was to make us express our own selves more clearly through the characters we played. Miss Dietrich, used to working with him and having an enormous power of concentration, did this excellently in *The Scarlet Empress*, I believe. In fact, she gave so much of herself to her role that when the picture was finished she was absolutely lost for a few days. She played the violin for relaxation. I understand she always does this after a picture.

Her child, Maria, is a born actress, and so it seemed most fitting for her to portray her mother in childhood. And even this little girl got the intensity and concentration of acting that is Miss Dietrich's, because her mother coached the child in every movement.

But don't imagine from this that Marlene Dietrich is an intense automaton with no thought but work. You should see her romping with Maria. That child has been pitied because she has bars on her window and a bodyguard hovering about her, but she also has a mother who adores her and Marlene still had the greatest fun cooking for Maria on the days when she did not have to work at the studio.

You should have seen her playing with my little girl, too. Lily is four years old now and, although Maria is about twice her age, Miss Dietrich knew exactly what to do to keep them both happy.

On Mr. von Sternberg's sets, behind locked doors, the actors say each line many times. Each time a particular word is emphasized until the right "take" is found. So, you see, if Marlene Dietrich is a Trilby to von Sternberg's Svengali, as is generally thought, all I can say is, we are all Trilbys, for Mr. von Sternberg works the same with everyone while doing dialogue. He is striving for perfection and he gets it.

Strange as it may sound, in view of the deep dramatic roles she has been playing, I believe Miss Dietrich is really a fine comedienne and that comedy is her forte. Her humor is quiet. It consists mostly of pantomime. Her eyes, her mouth, even her eyebrows, express everything. She didn't ever have to say, "I don't like this," for one to know she didn't. A fleeting tilt of her head, the merest fraction of an upturned nose, a curve of her lips would suffice. Mr. von Sternberg, in comparison, is voluble, yet his terseness always wanted to make me roar. Once when he was having trouble up on the sound boom, he looked down at me and said seriously, "I hope all my enemies become directors!" At the same time, it seemed the most delightful curse in the world.

I have spoken of Miss Dietrich's womanly sympathy and I think I ought to tell you how she meets an emergency. I had an accident on the set, which everyone outside seemed to think was a publicity yarn, for the press department gave out that I had fallen off a horse. I resented this because I am a fairly skillful horseman. This is what happened.

During the picture. I rode three Arabian five-gait horses, two stallions and one mare. It was with the last that I had my accident. I was supposed to ride through three huge gates to the castle, with about eighty horsemen behind me. Because I had my back to the camera in this shot, and because five-gait horses, like the mare, are not used to picture work where they have to break suddenly into a gallop, Mr. von Sternberg wanted me to use a double.

However, I had gotten his own idea about the perfection of detail and so I couldn't hear of it. I knew the cowpuncher who would have doubled for me may have ridden better than I, but he would ride loosely and not erectly as a soldier would ride. In other words, I wanted to maintain my character all through the picture. Well, in making this scene, I started the mare through the gates, but because she wasn't used to going into a gallop immediately, her hind legs got twisted and she went down, bringing me with her and pinning me underneath her so I couldn't get free. Behind me dashed the other horses and I tell you that it is a miracle I am here. Some of the horses jumped over my horse and me, and others were reined off to the side before they could be stopped. Only my leg was injured.

Marlene Dietrich did nothing to cause any excitement. She didn't grow hysterical or rush about as many another woman would have done. When she made her way slowly to my side, I noticed how white she looked. She was biting her lip, too, but otherwise she seemed perfectly collected as she inquired about me. Her solicitude showed only in her voice and her pallor. When I thought I had convinced Mr. von Sternberg that no bones were broken, he nevertheless insisted that I have my leg X-rayed. Although I was merely bruised, he wouldn't let me ride again if it wasn't necessary.

Upon seeing the rushes with the cowpuncher in my place, I insisted he wasn't riding "in character" and Miss Dietrich, with her little smile and her expressive eyebrows, used to tease me about this. "You don't take your work seriously, do you?" she'd say.

The experience of working with Marlene Dietrich has not only given me a new insight into picture-making, but an insight into a woman about whom so much is conjured. I can't think of two women as different as Dietrich and Garbo, or Dietrich and Hepburn. Greta Garbo seems to lack the warm human quality and to have the almost sexless appeal of a beautiful statue, while Miss Hepburn's personality seems a cold electric one, no matter how dynamic it may be.

I may be wrong about Miss Garbo and Miss Hepburn, but after *The Scarlet Empress*, I feel I do know Marlene Dietrich and I believe she is the most natural woman of the screen today. There was never any awe between us. She never tried to make me feel I was playing opposite a goddess, but on the contrary, opposite a very real, fun-loving, flesh-and-blood woman who was quite content to be just that.

John (Davis) Lodge (1903-1985) was born into a political family. He graduated from Harvard Law School in 1929, and practiced law in New York City, beginning in 1932, for several years. He was also a stage and film actor. Between 1931 and 1940, he made twenty-one feature films including *Little Women*, *The Scarlet Empress*, *The Little Colonel*, *Bulldog Drummond at Bay*, *Tonight at Eleven*, and *Just Like a Woman*. He served in the U.S. Navy during WWII, and was elected to represent the state of Connecticut in U.S. House of Representatives from 1947 until 1951. He served as Governor of Connecticut from 1951 until 1955. Lodge was then appointed to be the U.S. Ambassador to Spain (1955-1961), the U.S. Ambassador to Argentina (1969-1973), and the U.S. Ambassador to Switzerland (1983-1985).

"Dietrich and von Sternberg Rumored Rift; Ditto Mae West and James Timony," by Dorothy Donnell. *Movie Classic*, July, 1934

Hollywood breaks up other things besides marriages – such things as friendships, long business associations, director-and-star combinations. It may be that it has broken up two of the most famous teams of Hollywood – namely, Marlene Dietrich and Josef von Sternberg, and Mae West and James Timony.

Not long ago director von Sternberg and his star had an argument on the set of *The Scarlet Empress*, and as the German actress rushed away, von Sternberg raised his arms to heaven and made the now famous remark, "I have created a *Frankenstein*!"

That argument, gossip now hints, was nothing compared to the remarks made by Marlene in the studio cutting-room (an apt place for cutting remarks), as she watched herself as "Catherine the Great" almost lost among granite monsters, grotesque shadows and weird camera angles. In effect, her remarks ran as follows, "I shall not stay! I shall go home! Your gargoyles have more chance to act than young actors! I am tired of Art!"

It is said that the star and director each did their own cutting of the picture, producing two very different versions. Which of these versions will reach the public remains to be seen. If it is von Sternberg's, say Marlene's intimates, she may up and accept the offer that Hitler made her last year and return to Germany to head the new, struggling all-Aryan film industry there. Husband Rudolph Sieber has rushed to her side.

Mae West and her trusted friend and manager, James Timony, are another twosome who may not be able to stand the strain of Hollywood, although their association has existed for nearly fifteen years. For some time, rumor says, Mae has been restless under the direction of the big, burly Tammany lawyer who has handled her business for so long. A short time ago her set was barred to him, as well as to all others. And residents of the exclusive apartment house where Timony had an apartment in order to be near Mae say that he has moved away.

"Heretofore, all interviews were referred to her manager for appointment; now, Timony shakes his head. 'You'll have to ask Miss West," he says glumly; "I'm not handling her interviews now."

"Mr. Timony is getting his check as usual," Mae says, curtly. "He is still my *business manager*." (Is there a slight stress on the word "business"?)

Not so long ago, Mae and her manager were insistently denying rumors that they were married. Now, simultaneously with the reports that have rifted as business partners, come romance rumors about the Queen of Sex Appeal – rumors that a prize-fighter is attentive to her, that a writer is "that way" about her.

Dorothy Donnell was a playwright, and longtime Hollywood gossip columnist. She was a frequent contributor to *Motion Picture* and *Movie Classic* magazines.

"The Real Marlene Dietrich Exposed," by Hilary Lynn. *Hollywood*, August, 1934

When I walked into Marlene Dietrich's dressing-room all I knew about her was what you know about her – what we've read in the newspapers and magazines – and those rather confusing and contradictory impressions which her screen personality reveals.

When I walked out, two hours later, I had a "talkie picture" of Marlene Dietrich – an honest, soul-reaching photograph of her feelings and beliefs that has never been presented in print before.

This was my first meeting with Marlene – yet in those two hours of monologue (after the first five minutes it stopped being an interview) I realized I was privileged as probably no Hollywood journalist had been privileged before.

As Marlene herself said, "I don't know why I talked so freely this afternoon; I suppose I just felt like expressing myself." Whatever the reason, I'm eternally grateful that she did!

The simple, straightforward, charming personality she revealed to me in her un-glossed, unretouched self-portrait was so utterly unlike the erratic, capricious and somewhat self-conscious. Marlene Dietrich whom we thought we knew, so completely refuted what has heretofore been written about her, that I'm going to give you a literal transcription of our conversation so that you can judge for yourself.

It started with a bombshell.

"In Hollywood I am, what you might say, protected from life. It is a kind of monastery."

I came to – blinking. Hollywood – that jig-saw puzzled town of freaks, continual combustions, front-page newspaper rows, and a medley of odds and ends of everybody and everything from all corners of the earth – this existing habitat of lunacies and miracles, a *monastery*!

"Really, I mean this," Marlene continued. "What is my life out here? Driving from my house to the studio – working on a picture all day – driving home again. Never seeing anyone except those people who work with me on the set. Never even having to grant an interview unless it is arranged by special appointment through the studio's publicity department. I am alone most of the time. I have quiet. I have peace. Yes, one could say – I live within the serene, sheltering walls of a haven. Something has happened to me since I've been here."

She was silent for a moment, apparently struggling for the right word. Like most foreigners, not quite at home in the language, she spoke slowly, cautiously, selecting every word with painful accuracy.

"Perhaps other foreign actors have not been affected in the same way. For I am actually afraid now to leave Hollywood. I do not want to go anywhere else; I'm not used to the people – not used to the crowds. I'm frightened to death of the reporters who jump out at me when I get off a train, of the cameramen who run after me down the street, of the strange people who hound me for my autograph. I have been isolated too long to be comfortable in the world any more.

"At first, you are quite right, I did not like it. When I came out here from Europe, three years ago, I actually hated it. I was lonely, unhappy, I could not speak the language – I was an alien. Because of this I couldn't bring myself to see people. With the exception of a few German friends whom I had known abroad, the only people I saw were my little girl, my director, Josef von Sternberg, and my servants. Because there was nothing else to do, my life resolved itself into the simplest, quietest kind of routine.

"As you may well imagine, the monotony of this existence almost drove me insane. I missed the stimulation of the interesting personalities I had known abroad – I missed the exciting arguments late into the night at Berlin or Paris cafes. I missed meeting people who are doing something outside of my own profession. Like practically everyone else who comes here, I started to criticize Hollywood sharply and loudly during those first few months. It was insufferably dull.

"Naturally, I could hardly wait to take my first trip back to Europe. But a funny thing happened. When I returned to Germany, I discovered that I had 'gone Hollywood.' No, no, not the way you people out here mean," she said, smiling at the look on my face. "I mean I found myself saying nice things about Hollywood – praising everything to the skies until my friends and relatives actually grew angry. To my own surprise I realized that a great change had come over me in those few months I'd lived in California. I felt uncomfortable in Europe.

"For instance, I was annoyed at their inefficiency. This will amuse you, probably – but I couldn't bear it when I went to the department stores in Paris, asked for something, and had to wait hours until they brought it to me. I was irritated at the old ladies who waited on me over there, instead of the brisk young girls you have here.

"When I asked to look at a pair of shoes, they would bring me one shoe, and then take two hours to find the mate. Then they must go to their lunch on the stroke of twelve – it made no difference whether they were waiting on a customer or not. If you've been abroad, you know how they like to eat. And yet, I found myself saying, 'Why should they eat so much and so long?' I who used to think eating so tremendously important.

"In that brief vacation abroad, I had learned that for me, the conditions of my life here in California were really so much better. I was so much freer in America, I discovered, than I had ever been abroad. There were not all the old restrictions and conventions to bind me down. These things now disturbed me. So I could hardly wait to come back here."

The blue-eyed, fair-haired Teutonic goddess in the powder-blue linen trouser suit curled up on the couch opposite, eyed me quizzically. Her perky visor cap – cross between a jockey's and a sailor's bonnet – gave her an even more seductive appearance than she usually has.

"Why must they write all that nonsense," and the graceful sweep of her hand seemed to include an invisible army of critics and enemies, "about my hostile attitude toward Hollywood, when I am actually so content here?"

I was peculiarly conscious of an irony in this last question – an irony of which Marlene was innocent.

Before visiting her dressing-room, I had lunched with a little American hotcha actress, a girl who has had to make a fierce fight for recognition, and who only now is coming into her own. Jokingly, I mentioned that I was meeting Marlene Dietrich for the first time that afternoon and was wondering what I'd talk to her about. "Why don't you suggest a topic for a story?" I asked.

"Okay – that's just what I'd like to do," said Miss Hotcha, and her eyes flashed. "Ask her what foreign stars do with all the money they make over here. Do they spend it in this country, or do they hoard it? And then send it abroad to invest there? Some of them were only ham actors over there, getting about fifty bucks a week. Then they come over here and make a fortune. I tell you it isn't fair to us Americans. They're taking what rightfully belongs to us."

A discriminating person would discount most of what this envious girl had said. Still, her questions were loaded with a certain amount of dynamite. Marlene seemed to welcome this opportunity to clear up a misunderstanding that so many Americans have – a misunderstanding that has to do with a legendary favoritism shown by producers to foreign stars – and foreign actresses especially.

"Perhaps my critics don't realize," remarked Marlene, "that I've been in this country not for ten, fifteen or twenty years – but exactly for three years. Perhaps they do not know that I only recently started my present big salary. Previous to that, I was still on trial for American producers and American audiences, and was receiving a fraction of what most important stars were then drawing.

"Then consider the parts I play! In this type of role, and I've been cast in them ever since I arrived here, I can expect a screen life of from five to ten years at the most. After that, I am through! Pouf – out like a light, and probably forgotten. For, you see, I am not clever like those American actors and actresses who, after their screen careers are over, open dress shops, beauty salons, garages and interior decorating firms. They can do this because, having lived here always, they understand the desires of the American public. I cannot, because I am a foreigner, and I do not understand. Perhaps then, when you consider this, and what my present expenses are, you'll not think I am being so enormously overpaid.

"First of all, before the studio gives me my salary check, eight percent of it is deducted as a government tax, because I am an alien. Then before I can consider any of it as my own, I must think of the fifty percent which goes to the government for income. Does it astonish you when I tell you that I wrote out a check for $85,000 for the United States government last year?

"Also, as you know, I have eight guards continually on duty to protect my child from kidnapping. I pay them each $55 a week. Which makes $440 a week for protection, doesn't it? And these charges I cannot deduct from my income tax because the government says – 'you don't *have* to pay the guards.'

"Now, perhaps what people might blame me for is that I *do* spend a lot of money. But I do not understand the value of money. I never *have*, because I have no brain for such things.

"My money goes – not for investments abroad – but to keep up the standard of living I feel is necessary for Maria and me. We are so alone that I try to make our surroundings as beautiful as possible to make up for any other lack."

The young German director, Rudolph Sieber, her husband, who bears such a startling resemblance to Marlene that he could easily be mistaken for her brother, can spend only two months a year with his family in Hollywood.

"For instance, last year I looked for a house on the beach, because it was healthier for Maria to be by the seaside. I searched for weeks, but could find nothing that suited our purposes, except Marion Davies' house. True, it was far too large for us, but I was willing – foolishly maybe – to pay the $1,200 a month asked for the rent, so that Maria could be in an environment which I believed she needed." She sighed.

"I suppose if I returned to Europe, I could right now demand at least half the salary I am getting here. With the small income tax, and my living expenses cut in half, perhaps it would be wiser…yet I prefer Hollywood now!

"I am foolish – not?" In her earnestness to justify what she termed her foolishness, Frau Rudolph Sieber had dropped into the German idiom. Charming – and pathetic!

Marlene with Maria at a polo match in Los Angeles, 1934.

"Is Von Sternberg Ruining Marlene?" by Katherine Albert. Modern Screen, September, 1934

You have only to look at Marlene Dietrich's face, only to hear her talk, to know that she is an unhappy woman, but it occurred to me, as I sat watching her latest picture, *The Scarlet Empress*, that she would be less unhappy if she fired her director, Josef von Sternberg.

To Marlene the idea is incredible. She does not – or will not – realize that now she is much greater than he, in spite of the fact that her studio has told her that in almost those words. Anyone who witnesses *The Scarlet Empress* must realize it.

Just listen to these truths. While working on *The Scarlet Empress*, von Sternberg rehearsed John Lodge in one particular scene at least fifteen times as is his custom. At the end of rehearsal Lodge turned to Dietrich and said, "I've got the jitters. I must be a rotten actor to require so much rehearsing."

Dietrich answered, "It doesn't prove that at all. He rehearses me just as much."

Once – and only once – Dietrich had the temerity to change *one* word of dialogue and the assembled actors and actresses were treated to a tirade of abuse which is still remembered. Von Sternberg stopped shooting, began to tear his hair, marched up and down the set and, pointing at Dietrich, shouted, "Have I created a Frankenstein?" All because she changed a single word of dialogue!

Only once has Dietrich been directed by another man. But Mamoulian – who wielded the megaphone on *Song of Songs* – has the Continental viewpoint so thoroughly and is so schooled in a tradition similar to von Sternberg's that it is not a fair test for Dietrich's acting ability.

While *Song of Songs* was being filmed, they say that von Sternberg remarked, "I don't think it is a good story and I doubt if Miss Dietrich will make the picture." When asked what Dietrich's reaction to the story was, he thundered, "Miss Dietrich will think as I think – *naturally!*"

When Dietrich is away from von Sternberg, she can be gay and carefree. With him, she is silent and morose and her manner changes when he enters the room. Someone asked her if she were afraid of him. This, they say, was her reply, "No, not exactly afraid – but he is always correcting me and I'll do almost anything to keep away from his continual nagging."

And yet she has autographed a picture of herself to him like this: "To Joe from Marlene. Without you *nothing*, with you *everything*."

Von Sternberg chooses all Dietrich's stories and, being essentially a cameraman, he is looking for scenic effects rather than great acting scenes.

He okays all her publicity and even – or so the story goes – once ordered an interview "killed," an interview that Dietrich had liked, because it did not make her glamorous enough. Naturally, Dietrich allowed him to kill the story.

When *Twentieth Century* was being filmed, Dietrich visited the set one day. As she walked on she discovered John Barrymore doing an imitation of von Sternberg which had everyone in stitches. At first Dietrich seemed shocked. She glanced around quickly to see if von Sternberg were nearby. When she discovered he was not – she laughed.

All of these incidents will show you how completely dominated Dietrich is by von Sternberg at the studio. There are some stories too sinister even to be rumored, but those close to Dietrich – and there are very few – feel sure that von Sternberg would be delighted if Marlene's daughter, Maria, were shipped back to Germany. One rumor about how he tried to accomplish this is going the rounds of Hollywood, but I should not care to repeat it here.

Now, Marlene does, on the set, exactly as von Sternberg orders. Never, at her home, does she rehearse her part or try to create it to her own liking. She studies her lines and rehearses before von Sternberg because he does not want her to come to the studio with any preconceived notions about how the role should be played.

It has also been talked around that von Sternberg used a very unusual trick in one of the last pictures to enforce his domination over not only Dietrich, but also over the other actors and actresses on the set. They say he ordered that the individual scripts of dialogue be printed without punctuations for all the actors – for the following reason: He did not want any of the actors or actresses in this picture to so familiarize themselves with the dialogue that he would not be able to tell them how to speak it.

Perhaps you think Marlene is one of those easily molded women. Not at all. Away from her director she has opinions of her own. She has strong likes and dislikes.

Not so long ago she, who so often fights shy of interviews, broke down and talked at length to a *Modern Screen* reporter. Usually so silent, Marlene spoke with utmost frankness. And these are some of the things she said.

"This is life. Right now. Today. This hour. This minute. You cannot always be waiting to do and to be what you honestly want to do and be. What you don't take, you miss.

"In Hollywood, I cannot do as some do – work, work, work – and save my money for the manner of life I want later on. I must have a nice house, a sunny garden for Maria, my servants from Germany with me.

"That is why I think about making pictures in France. In France I can live pleasantly for less money. In France actresses are not taxed so heavily. There I would not have to pay sixty percent of my income to the government. So even if I did not make as much I would have more."

Speaking of her husband, Rudolph Seiber, she said, "When two people love each other, no outside thing should interfere. They should know how it is between them. I haven't a strong sense of possession toward a man. Maybe that's because I am not particularly feminine in my reactions. I have never been. I have never wanted feminine attractions. Even when I was younger I did not want to attract boys. In fact, I very much wanted not to attract them. I had no beaus, no crushes, until I met my husband."

Now all this constitutes the attitude of an intense individualist, a woman not cut from any pattern. In her private life she has strong opinions of her own and, when she is in the mood to talk, she is not afraid to express them.

Why, then I ask you, is she under the complete dominance of Josef von Sternberg when she comes on the set? She considers him a great man, a genius, a god. Opposing von Sternberg on any issue, Paramount has discovered that it opposes Marlene, too. If Marlene cannot make the picture von Sternberg has chosen for her and make it as he feels it should be made, she prefers, infinitely, to make no picture at all. Even though this forces her into open, nerve-wracking, exhausting rebellion – even though this means money out of her pocket.

Yes, sir – Josef von Sternberg has the Indian sign on Marlene Dietrich. It is curious to see what he is doing with that power.

Marlene in The Scarlet Empress, *1934.*

I want you to see *The Scarlet Empress.* I honestly want you to watch this beautiful, fascinating Marlene Dietrich ploughing her way through that cumbersome, massive film. And then, if you're as great a Dietrich fan as I am, if you have a belief in her very real acting ability – maybe you'll sit down and write her, begging her to try another man at the megaphone.

I think that von Sternberg has failed in his duty toward Marlene's public, in the duty he imposed upon himself when he discovered her in Germany. I want to know what you think about it.

It has taken a long time but from picture to picture von Sternberg has been slowly and surely devitalizing Dietrich. Now comes the grand climax of that process in *The Scarlet Empress.* The film is a dreadful hodge-podge of sets. Full of gargoyles, confused episodes, and action so vague and fleeting (as if von Sternberg were afraid of action) that you hardly know what is happening. Through this maze walks the beautiful, exciting Dietrich – a woman who could be such a splendid actress if properly guided, but who is slowly being ruined because she leaves her strong personal questions at home and because she is an individual only when away from her master. She is putty – beautiful putty, it is true – when she is in his hands on the set.

I'm sure that it would delight Paramount if Dietrich would walk in and say, "In my next picture I shall have another director." The studio knows, surely, that if left alone von Sternberg will ruin their valuable property – Dietrich. Can't something be done to save her?

Von Sternberg is a fine director. He has proven that, but it is not good for one man to direct one star forever.

Let von Sternberg take other actresses who would profit by the low key in which he has emotional scenes played, who could learn something of fine restraint from him.

But Dietrich needs to step out and become the real, the vibrant, the great actress she can be if she will shake loose the von Sternberg dominance.

And remember this. I'm speaking of von Sternberg's dominance in a purely professional way. It is only when Marlene comes on the set that she accedes to his every whim.

I cite as an example the time when her beloved little daughter, Maria, was threatened by kidnappers. Marlene has refused to mention this for a long time but she did break her silence recently.

"Never," she said, "will I forget the night I came home from the studios and my maid handed me that first special delivery letter. It was filled with horrible words, spelled with letters cut from newspapers. It warned me that if I did not give the writer $10,000 as a first payment against demands that Maria would be kidnapped.

"The house we lived in at that time was set far back from the street at the intersection of a boulevard. I was instructed to leave the money in five and ten dollar bills, in a package on the floor of a car parked ten inches from the curb.

"Their diabolical cunning only added to my fears.

"They could secure money left in this way easily, under cover of the traffic, when their car was held up with all the others at this particular crossroad.

"We put the money in the car. And all day and all night we sat in the house, our eyes glued on Maria. I notified the police in spite of their warnings not to. We hired guards. It was like nothing real.

"The next day the second of what was to be a chain of letters arrived. They had seen the car and the package of money. They also had known the police were watching. They demanded $20,000.

"It kept up for months. We lived in constant terror. We put bars at our windows until we were living in a prison. Guards were with us constantly and yet there was that never ceasing fear that maybe there would be one moment when the vigilance would not be great enough.

"The only good thing about it is that my husband was with me. Always when I am in difficulties it is the same – not that he comes because of the difficulties. Always he comes for a happy visit. And then he is with me when I need him."

You see? It is Rudolph Seiber, her husband, who is with her in times of personal stress. It is to him she turns for aid in her private life.

She gives her screen life to Josef von Sternberg. And that is bad, bad for her career.

For I think that all loyal Dietrich fans deserve the privilege of seeing her act under another's direction. After you've seen *The Scarlet Empress* you'll know what I mean. Let's try to convince Dietrich that she needs someone else on the set. Write to her. Tell her so. I truly believe that Paramount Studios – whether they will admit it or not – would thank us.

And you – Marlene – you're greater than von Sternberg. He has done all he can for you. He brought you to America. He discovered you. You want to be loyal to him, I know, but you really should show some loyalty to the fans who believe in you.

Listen, Marlene – just between you and me – why don't you just *try* another director!

Marlene Dietrich in "THE DEVIL IS A WOMAN" with Lionel Atwill, Cesar Romero, Edward Everett Horton, Alison Skipworth and Don Alvarado
A Paramount Picture

"Marlene Dietrich Answers All Your Questions," by Ben Maddox. *Modern Screen*, February, 1935

I have just had twenty minutes with Marlene Dietrich.

It took me three months to get them. But when I finally got to La Dietrich she talked as she has never talked before. So this, really, will have to be an unusual sort of story. Because the woman herself is so extraordinarily different.

An appointment with Marlene can only be made after her greatest maneuvering. Her agent sorts the sheep. So few are chosen that half a year has elapsed since she was last interviewed. I felt complimented when her agent telephoned me that he would be glad to have me interview her.

Then came one broken date after another, for three months. Finally, I was told to appear at the studio. I was walked out to her dressing-room. She hadn't yet come off the set. In two minutes, a large gray Rolls-Royce drew up and out stepped a maid who expressed disappointment at her mistress' absence. A few more minutes and Marlene came walking around the corner from the sound stage.

We were left alone in her dressing-room.

She was attired in a striking black satin Spanish gown of elaborate design and over one ear she wore a red flower. But I didn't pay much attention to her costuming. I came to see Dietrich.

Sitting on a small straight chair beside her desk, she turned toward me. She was gorgeous. She has the biggest blue eyes, in which lurk a constant twinkle. There was a slight curve of merriment on her wide, lovely mouth. I suspected that she classes interviews as amusing.

Marlene isn't a terribly curious person herself. She is polite and kind. But she distinctly has enough in her own life to keep her occupied.

"You have been subjected to such a lot of criticism," I began, "that I thought you might like to give me a story on what your four years in Hollywood have meant to you. We've had everyone's opinion but yours."

She smiled a little. Just as she does on the screen. To myself I stated that they can protest all they wish about beauty being no longer a woman's major asset. See Dietrich and succumb!

Perhaps her remarkable charm is due in part to her serenity. She is still, not silent. And friendly, though not fluttery. Her voice is slow, caressingly rich in tone.

"I should not like to do the story in the first person, as if I were writing it. Somehow, that sounds conceited to me," she said.

The phone rang. Excusing herself, she answered it. It was a good old-fashioned instrument, not a coy French hand-piece. She uttered one word – "No." With no attempt to explain something which didn't concern me, she faced me again, waiting for me to speak.

"In what ways do you feel that you have been changed by Hollywood?"

"I do not believe I have changed, except to grow older, of course. And I have more responsibilities. There is a realization that a whole production rests on one's shoulders. But Hollywood? It doesn't do anything drastic to people. Certainly not to those who have strong personalities and firm minds of their own."

"They say that you were dowdy when you arrived. And the Trilby legend has hung on."

Marlene smiled anew. A smile of hers can reveal so much. It makes questions suddenly seem trivial banter.

"That theory that I was dowdy, a dumb German housewife-kind-of-actress is absurd. I came from metropolitan Berlin. And I brought trunks full of Parisian gowns. If you will compare photographs of me then and today, I do look better, now. But that isn't any Hollywood polish. That is the effect of time. You examine old photographs of yourself. They, too, will be quaint."

That was a long speech for Marlene. She hesitated, then continued, "As for this von Sternberg-Trilby chatter, it is humorous to me. Anyone with intelligence can see that I'm not hypnotized.

Obviously I have something of my own behind this face. You can't put a brain into a woman's head if it isn't there already."

I wondered about her approaching split with von Sternberg. He has announced that she will not do her next film under his direction. Apparently, she will switch to Ernst Lubitsch. This report crops up every once in a while. It has come up again at this writing. Marlene stated, "People will make much of nothing. This is the situation: I do only one picture a year. Sometimes it has taken Mr. von Sternberg nearly a year to find a proper vehicle. He will be a long time cutting and completing this one we are finishing now. He thinks I should not wait around when he hasn't a story for me. I did the one picture away from him, with Mamoulian, only because he telephoned me from abroad and advised me to. We are not separating now. If, until he is ready for me, I find something I like I will do it for another director."

All of which blasts beforehand the mystery that is apt to arise when she works in 1935 with a different man at the helm.

"How has Hollywood changed your mode of living?" I queried.

"Not at all. My parents had money. I live as I did in Germany, except that I have to have guards here."

She has been residing in the pretentious Colleen Moore place in Bel Air, and I had heard that she had leased it for two years, indicating permanency. So I inquired about it.

"But I just rent it from month to month," she retorted. "I never tie myself down. How do I know what will happen? Where I shall want to go?"

"But you do like Hollywood?"

"Oh, yes indeed. And this is strange. I am not bothered here as so many stars claim to be. Why, I am not even recognized on the streets.

"There are too many stars for one to be a novelty. Nor do they try to disturb my home life. No one ever attempts to climb over my walls, to break into my house. A few children come and ask for autographs, but that is not nuisance. I think all this talk of lack of privacy is odd. I notice it only when I am *away* from Hollywood. Then everyone stares and I am scared. I am eager to get back here where it is quiet and peaceful."

Rudolph Sieber, Marlene's director husband, has decided to stay in Hollywood permanently. That is, as long as his wife is fated to remain. Their four-year separation, which was punctuated by twice-a-year visits, is thus over.

"I was only away from my little girl for the first six months I was here. I didn't bring her from Germany because I was very uncertain. I didn't know whether I was to succeed here. It was for her own good that she stayed at home until I learned. Now she is growing up to be very American. I think that personality is determined when one is very young. I was never allowed to express any emotion in my face, to show dislike for anything. That is why I couldn't act all over the set. I would be ashamed to be unrestrained. But Maria is being raised to have freedom."

Hollywood plays such jokes on ambitious women. Marlene has escaped the town's capricious whims. She has had no terrific disillusionment because she never was lured into a worship for fame.

"I always had an admiration for the screen. But I never dreamed of becoming a star," she said. "Even when I first came to Hollywood it was not the fame and the money which attracted me. I came to work with Mr. von Sternberg."

"But doesn't the money mean a lot to you?" I probed.

"No. Half of what I earn goes for income tax. I could accumulate more in Europe. Or I could go on the radio here and make enough in a year so I should never need to work again."

"The applause, the flattery, do they please you?"

"No," she replied. "I am not proud of being a film star! I see no reason to be. Compared to important professions this, that I am doing, is so unimportant. Even in comparison to the stage this work of mine falls far short. On the stage you must struggle for years before you can advance to a lead. In pictures, stars are made overnight because of their beauty. There is a haste and a lack of dignity to film stardom. I do not mean to criticize. There are many stars here who have great talent. I merely say that from my own standpoint I am not at all proud because I have become a film star."

Such modesty had never come my way from a Hollywood lady. So I asked, "But what makes all this worthwhile to you, then?"

"The sheer joy of acting, of creating a characterization, of being associated with Mr. von Sternberg."

"And," I reiterated, "have you no desire to stand on your own feet, to work with another director? A fine actress should be as fine under any guidance, shouldn't she?"

"Certainly she should. But I do not understand why I must prove I am not an automaton. As I said, if I find an interesting story I will do it with someone else. Then I shall return to Mr. von Sternberg's direction."

"And the stage…?"

"No. I haven't command enough of English to act on the stage in his country. Perhaps someday again in Europe. As for the screen, when there are no more plots which are appealing, then I will stop.

"I have never been the kind who could mix with many people, so I have few close acquaintances in Hollywood. In Berlin I had three or four friends. Does anyone really have more? Here I go straight home from the studio. I am perfectly content to have just a few friends. I do not want any more. There isn't time. Between my home and my work, I am kept busy."

"But how can you develop your personality if you don't notice what others are doing and adapt yourself in various ways to suit those others?"

"I said I thought one's personality was determined when young. I don't believe in making one's self over. I have never tried to please everyone. If it is someone I respect highly I pay attention. But I don't want to make other people over, either. And as for developing, I have never endeavored to consciously improve myself. That is confusing. I mean, of course, that I do my best to be my best. But I simply trust to life to mold my personality."

I was becoming more and more intrigued with this amazing woman. So feminine is she, and yet so thoroughly brave in her convictions. Every article about her has been an attempt to reveal how she has been changed by Hollywood. They've missed the point. Marlene has been perfectly poised. It's the rest who have been doing the flustering.

But if her replies to my pertinent questions have astonished you, wait until you hear her sum up these four film years in America. I asked her what she considers her accomplishments to date.

"I have a child," she said, without a second's pause. There was no mention of Hollywood peaks! I must have looked startled for she then added, "And I have made a few people happy. That is all."

"But your career!" I exclaimed, so used to listening to the cinema stars' chatter on and on endlessly, egotistically.

"Ah," she declared, "there is so much more in life for me. Earning the respect of the people I love, carrying out my duties to them, bringing up my child…"

You have read numberless tales about Marlene. No one had ever gone to her and frankly asked for her own explanations. I'm glad I did because now she seems not a high-hat mystery, but a normal, eager, and loyal woman. Four years have brought overwhelming changes to Hollywood. But none to the tranquil, tantalizing Dietrich.

Even if she hadn't behaved so intelligently during my twenty minutes with her, I'd have approved of her. She is so marvelously beautiful.

Do you suppose she has ever delved into Lord Chesterfield's tomes? Remember, he advised, "address yourself to the senses if you would please; dazzle the eyes, sooth and flatter the ears of mankind, engage their hearts and let their reason do its worst against you."

I am sure of few things in this perplexing world, but one of my certainties now is that none of the slams on Marlene could have been written by a man who has met her!

Ben Maddox was a Hollywood journalist. He was gay, and became infamous for "outing" actors Cary Grant and Randolph Scott in print. He wrote several articles about the actors' close friendship, living arrangements, and the several homes they shared during the 1930s.

"Marlene Dietrich."
Silver Screen, May, 1935

She is the "Trilby of Hollywood." Joseph von Sternberg, the Svengali of this combination, has made pictures that everyone raved over – *Underworld* for example. He is unquestionably an artist. But there are some people who feel that there is too much director in Marlene's recent pictures and, undoubtedly, her latest, *The Devil Is a Woman*, will prove that this team of director/star is either a happy one or a union which is not giving the screen the results which lie within the power of Dietrich, our loveliest star.

Sometimes an artist, when he becomes expert in his technique, will paint a still life which is meaningless, while a lesser painter will produce a canvas of distinctly lower standard which tells a story. A connoisseur will rave about the first painting, but the public will take the second to its heart. Perhaps the screen is not yet ready for the sort of picture that is created to glorify the artistry of direction and photography.

Anyway, Marlene Dietrich has a new contract, and the Hollywoods are full of directors.

Marlene in The Devil is a Woman, *1935.*

"Marlene Looks Ahead!" by Leonard Hall. *Screenland*, June, 1935

Marlene and Claudette Colbert (another high profile bisexual actress) at a celebrity party hosted by Carole Lombard at the Venice amusement pier in Los Angeles, June 20, 1935.

Marlene Dietrich stands at the fateful crossroads of her film career today and raises those glorious eyes aloft to two sign-boards. One says, "To new heights in better pictures." The other reads, simply, "This way out!"

The issue is now squarely up on Unser Marlene. Will she be a good sport and a hard worker? Or will she be a moping cry-baby? For the long-famous team of von Sternberg and Dietrich has been rudely torn apart. Hollywood's most famous artist-director firm has gone out of business. From now on, von Sternberg goes his way, and Marlene goes Paramount's.

Her producers have tossed a fresh deck on the green table, and called for a new deal all around. No longer will the hypnotic maestro with the handle-bar moustache wave his magic wand over the symphonic Marlene. She has signed a new contract and will make her next film with another stick-waver. Von packs up his genius and seeks new fields to conquer.

Thus ends one of the most remarkable associations Hollywood has ever seen – and the artistic life of one of the most fascinating and baffling figures of the day reaches another thumping climax! What will this gorgeous critter do now? Will she start afresh, willingly and hopefully, with another boss? Or will she sit about mourning the loss of her discoverer, teacher and guide – thus going, very quietly but quickly, to hell in a barouche? Don't we wish we knew? And doesn't Mr. Paramount?

The old team had to go. Its act had finally reached the stature of one of the most dazzling and break-taking flops the film world has ever known. *The Scarlet Empress* had left woe in its wake, and the new one, *The Devil Is a Woman*, had given its producers a ghastly case of head-scratching and moustache-gnawing. Something had to go bust – and it did.

Now Marlene is on her own – and so is von Sternberg. I rise in meeting, clear my throat and say it is the best thing that could have happened – for their sakes, for the company's sake, and for ours.

Dietrich was no longer an actress, but a puppet. Von Sternberg was no longer a first-rate movie director, but a *Svengali*, casting his spell about a beautiful woman who had come to depend upon him for every eyelid-flutter before the camera. It is no exaggeration to say that she has leaned on his direction as some souls do on drink or drugs.

This "Pygmalion and Galatea" monkey-business has been going on so long that many of us have wondered whether she can really act – whether old von Sternberg can actually direct a lick! Then we remember her in *The Blue Angel* and *Morocco*, those first films of hers that knocked us headlong from our pews. Then we recall that von Sternberg, before he turned ego-driven Master, directed *Underworld*, one of the finest movies that ever blew up in our faces. But now they've got to prove their worth all over again!

I've made it my business to investigate this affair for you, and the other day I witnessed Dietrich under the new deal. I found a Dietrich nobody knew existed, but had always hoped for. It wasn't the Marlene who once told a *Screenland* reporter, "It is not easy for me to meet people. I am always embarrassed and ill at ease." It was no orchidaceous baby-doll doing a second-hand Garbo. Nor was it a defiant Dietrich in pants, tailored for publicity and getting horse-laughs from the peanut gallery where we film fans sit and watch for sincerity.

No, indeedy – the Dietrich I saw the other day was a new one, and a pip. A beauteous and bewitching woman-Dietrich – gracious, friendly and poised. An A-number-1 vision in a long black velvet tea-gown, high-necked and long-sleeved, with a bunch of purple violets at her waist and an honest smile on that superb pan!

I sat and talked with this New Deal Dietrich. Around us gabbled and gobbled a hundred and fifty charter members of the New York Motion Picture Free-Loaders Association, guests at a mighty cocktail party and sandwich-grab tossed in her honor. Three years ago you couldn't have dragged Dietrich to one of these rackets with a span of tractors – yet here she was, big as life and twice as beautiful, taking it like a major, meeting the mob one by one, with a smile and a word for everybody. After the dizzy ducking of the past, it was a fair treat to see this queenly cutie take her hair down and go regular! As an old-time omen-taker, I take it as a good omen for the future.

I dared to sit right down beside her on a golden chair – as close as I am to you this minute! – and ask her how she felt about the "Great Break-Up."

"I am very unhappy about it," she said, and she looked unhappy. "But it was von Sternberg's wish, and that is the way it will be."

"Have you any idea what director Paramount has in mind for you?"

"Not the slightest," she said, "and no story has been chosen for my next picture. As soon as I get back to Hollywood these things will be settled." She said it with more resignation than good cheer.

She had arrived in New York in a blaze of Page One publicity. She stifled idle talk of a Garbo-Dietrich feud by remarking that she had never even met Miss Garbo. And when one brash Broadway cameraman suggested that she raise her skirts and display several inches of the beautiful legs that helped make her famous,

Marlene caught our fancy by saying, "I see no reason for it. They are very well known!" And she has trouped nobly, no matter how unhappy she may be.

Dietrich says that the "Fatal Parting" with von Sternberg was his wish. At this I lower one eye-lid. Her company may have had some notion about it, too. There is no doubt that she mourns his loss.

The "Princess Paley," who went to Hollywood to appear in the French version of *Folies Bergere*, and is a warm friend of the German girl, says that Marlene not only feels deep gratitude to the director, and reverences him as an artist, but is really fond of him, too. The "Paley" also offers an interesting but ominous sidelight on the strange partnership that is no more.

Marlene in The Devil is a Woman, *1935.*

"I'm No Trilby, Says Marlene Dietrich," by Herbert Cruikshank. *Motion Picture*, June, 1935

More than any other star, the description "orchidaceous" fits Marlene Dietrich. She's no sunflower nor hollyhock, no beauty of the hedgerows, but a pale, exotic blossom of the night. She is hot-house perfection, synthetic loveliness, with every fault of feature minimized by skillful artistry, and every virtue of face and form brought to fullest flower.

I knew she was terrified by crowds and by reporters. Already newspaper headlines had screamed such silly trivialities as that Marlene didn't snub Garbo the night they met in that Hollywood café. How could either of the girls "cut" the other, when they never met? She dreads misquotations and the misinterpretations of her remarks. Yet there were questions to be asked. After all, this was an interview.

"Of course, I'll answer any question," said Marlene. So I began.

"You are traveling with twelve trunks, I hear. Apparently you approve Hollywood styles."

"Twelve trunks!" she exclaimed, "Ah, no! Just sufficient changes for a week's stay in your city. You see, New York demands a variety of costume greater than in Hollywood. Here the days have so many different phases. There are breakfasts, the forenoons, luncheons, matinees, cocktails, dinners, theatres, suppers and the clubs after that. One dresses for each occasion. In Hollywood, things are simplified. The routine there is home, the studio, and home again – with an occasional night out.

"There is no playtime there. You'd be surprised what care, what thought, what work goes into the making of a motion picture; not only in the actual shooting, but in the preparation. There is no time for anything but work. Hollywood is a workshop. For us, New York, Paris, London, Rome, Budapest are the playgrounds.

"Of course I approve Hollywood styles, especially for Hollywood – which, you must understand is a place apart in all the world. Hollywood fashions have a definite influence on world fashions. They are reflected throughout Europe, especially at the sports resorts. Naturally, I may do some shopping here. It depends entirely upon whether I see anything I like well enough."

Hollywood a workshop, I thought. And we regard it as something of a merry-go-round.

I asked, "Do you mean to say there is no *life* in Hollywood – no excitement?"

"Rather that the life is very different. Surely there is no night life as it is understood here, or in the European capitals."

"Is it necessary to be well-dressed in Hollywood?"

"Very necessary. That is, when we are on parade – at premieres, for instance. It is mandatory that every star shall live up to the preconceived notion of the public. But when we are working in the studio, sweaters and slacks are more convenient to wear to and from the dressing-room."

Jean Harlow with Marlene at Café Trocadero nightclub in Hollywood, 1935.

This, I imagined, was as good a time as any to ask my most embarrassing questions. So, swallowing hard, I inquired, "Do you still – er –wear – er – pants?"

Marlene looked a little weary, as though to answer, "What, again?" But she smiled.

"When it is convenient, yes. There are occasions when trousers are more desirable, more comfortable than skirts. It is then not only I, but many players, wear them. I do not see why we should not share the comfort enjoyed by men."

"Do you still wear masculine evening clothes?" I hazarded.

Marlene shrugged her expressive shoulders.

"That was a vogue of the moment," she said.

And I didn't press the point.

"Do you go out much in Hollywood?"

"No, very little," she said. "I have explained that it is a place of work, primarily."

"Have you many friends there?"

"Very few friends. Sometimes it is very lonesome. One can be very lonesome, you know."

Yes, I knew. But how could she know? Gloriously young, gorgeously beautiful, happily married, at least passingly well to do, blessed with a daughter whom she adores, and in turn adored by millions. How could she be lonesome? Yet, looking at her, I knew that this was true. "One can be very lonesome." That "one" meant Marlene.

I snapped from this brief reverie as a velvet-footed maid approached.

"Pardon, Madame, the gentlemen of the press to see you."

Marlene turned to me.

"You will understand," she said.

Well, I can take a hint! Doing my best to manage a courtly bow over her flowerlike fingers, I made my exit as the reporters and cameramen trouped in. I paused at the door as flashes lit the room with lightening-like brilliance. Marlene was posing. One of the photographers said, "Lift the skirts, please; let the public get a gander at those million-dollar legs!"

Marlene's heavy-lidded eyes looked very weary. She withered the cameraman with a glance. Or, at least, she gave him such a glance as would wither any but a news-photographer. Then her soft voice came to me as she replied, "It is not necessary. They are well known!"

"What Is Dietrich's Destiny?" by Warren Reeve. *Photoplay*, July, 1935

Hollywood's greatest *Svengali-Trilby* alliance is ended – and Marlene Dietrich remains the screen's premier problem actress and its major mystery star.

The problem is what to do with her in pictures. The mystery is her destiny on the screen.

Josef von Sternberg spent five years trying to solve the first, and attain the second. In that time, he dedicated his entire art and energy to the task. But now the von Sternberg-Dietrich saga has been sung. It was the saga of an intelligent, artistic man's unbounded faith in the promise of a woman. It was the story of a woman's reverence for her *maestro*.

When von Sternberg recently said bluntly to a dazed Dietrich, "We have gone as far as we can together. I shall direct you in no more pictures," it was as if he had confessed, "I have failed to steer you to the fulfillment of the promise I saw in you when I found you in a Berlin musical show and dropped everything to guide you to greatness. I have failed to discover the jewel which I know hides somewhere within you. I don't know which way to go with you from here. Five years have proved that I am not your man of destiny. Let us forget these years and start over again – with someone else."

There are two sides to the pathos of the situation. There is the pathetic spectacle of an artist cheated of his masterpiece. There is the sad sight of a pupil repudiated by her teacher.

And then there is the tragic picture of a potentially great career wavering helpless on a precarious ledge in the shadow of the summit.

Stars are rare in Hollywood. You can count the great screen stars on your fingers. Marlene Dietrich from the start has been a potential great motion picture star. Von Sternberg recognized this when he first saw her in Berlin. After he had worked with her in *The Blue Angel* he was sure of her promise.

He brought to Hollywood a lovely, Dresden doll Dietrich as fresh and as exhilarating as the first breath of Spring. He knew what he had – the chance for a supreme creation – the opportunity to mold his screen masterpiece.

He has been sincere and untiring. She has been loyal with an unquestioning devotion. Circumstances made this teacher and his pupil closer than any such ordinary professional alliance. He was practically a countryman of hers, the only one whom she could depend on in a foreign and critical land. She leaned on him for help in her tiniest problems. He found houses for her, helped her adjust herself to the new life. He coached, tutored, advised and jealously guarded her. She was tucked under his wing completely. Dietrich has made but one picture without him. Rouben Mamoulian directed her in *Song of Songs*.

If von Sternberg, after being professionally wedded to Dietrich for five years, still does not know what to do with her, how to guide her toward the greatness she has always promised but never attained – if he, Svengali, must throw up his hands and admit defeat, how can anyone else confidently take up the task?

Hollywood knows no sure answer for that – yet. But it shares von Sternberg's sustained faith that Marlene Dietrich, while no longer fresh and new to the screen, has a destiny that is yet unfulfilled.

For the past year or so anyone whom you might ask would assure you that Marlene Dietrich was slipping. "One more picture like *The Scarlet Empress*," they said, "and she's through."

She made that one more picture, *The Devil Is a Woman*, which was exactly what they meant when they said, "Another like *The Scarlet Empress* – that is, Dietrich deadened against a heavily artistic von Sternberg background. Then her contract ran out.

Now, inevitably when a star is known to be "slipping" in Hollywood around contract time there is only one thing to expect. If she is re-signed at all, it is at a smaller salary, which is logical, because she's worth less at the all-important box-office.

But when Marlene Dietrich slipped she slipped into a sea of film offers from other studios and Paramount had to argue with her for weeks before she decided to stay. One of their major arguments, which undoubtedly helped keep her at Paramount, was a new term contract calling for $250,000 for two pictures a year – and under the terms of the agreement, she can make a good deal more than that.

Marlene in The Devil is a Woman, *1935.*

That's not bad for a star who is "one picture away from the ash heap." And it wasn't sentiment which made Paramount so generous, either.

The fact is that, good pictures or bad, Dietrich carries a prestige second only to that of Garbo. It's an international prestige. More visiting big guns from Europe, Asia or Timbuctoo seek to meet Marlene than any other actress. Not long ago when a radio-telephone service was inaugurated between Japan and America, the editor of a leading Tokyo newspaper wished to talk over it to a Hollywood actress, by way of adding a little touch to the occasion. The actress he requested and spoke to was Marlene Dietrich.

East, West, South or North means little to a favored few stars. Garbo, Chevalier, Jeanette MacDonald are others who can turn the foreign balance in their favor to make up for an occasional lightweight popularity in this country.

But the most important reason why Marlene Dietrich had to worry about too many good offers when the big break came was that Hollywood still feels she is a discovery not yet actually discovered!

And she's been right in Hollywood for the past five years!

It seems unfair to blame Josef von Sternberg wholly for this, or to indict him with the charge, often heard, of using Marlene Dietrich as a professional guinea pig for his artistic screen experiments. No one was more sincere than von Sternberg in his search for the right mirror to reflect her true brilliant beauty. He realized that Dietrich was potentially different from any other star and he was convinced that for her he must go off the beaten path – that he must find something new, completely different. In his efforts he leaned over backwards.

The result was the chain of pictures which were the real grounds for screen divorce: *The Scarlet Empress*, *The Devil Is a Woman*.

If you remember Dietrich in *The Blue Angel*, *Morocco*, or *Shanghai Express*, you remember her at the stage of greatest appeal.

What changed her? Perhaps the pictures themselves hold the answer, for Marlene Dietrich, although no longer the frightened, shy little foreign actress hiding in the folds of the *maestro's* cape, is just about the same today as she was in the days of her triumphs.

The Blue Angel was dramatic. *Morocco* and *Shanghai Express* were essentially melodramatic. They moved – they had action, drama, plot, suspense. Dietrich punctuated their spirited, contrived drama perfectly with her beauty and screen spell.

But the action and the drama were as necessary to Dietrich's effect as Dietrich's charm was to the picture's effect. All her best pictures indicate that Dietrich must be kept moving. She is not enough alone. She is too phlegmatic, her beauty and her personality both are too quiet to lend life to a heavy background.

Von Sternberg, however, was impatient with the lessons of those early successes. They made his star popular, they brought in the money, but they didn't lead beyond themselves to the destiny which he was convinced the future held for his *Trilby*.

He refused to make any more of that formula – and Dietrich has never been the same since.

Their professional divorce will justify von Sternberg's sudden honest decision, if only because it will give them both a clean slate and a fresh start.

Marlene, at last, has become reconciled to it, although at first she flatly refused to believe her director was in earnest. Her bewilderment was pathetic and touching. She kept repeating, "I shall never work with another director."

But that is over now. She has said that she would like to make a picture under Ernst Lubitsch. Recently she named Frank Borzage as another choice. There are several directors in Hollywood who would like a chance at her – each one with something new and fresh to bring to this star who has never fulfilled her promise.

Von Sternberg knew her, understood her and believed in her. But he wasn't the right man. And he was man enough to admit it, and man enough to do the only thing that could recreate Marlene Dietrich. She would never have deserted him.

What does this New Deal, dealt her against her will, promise Marlene Dietrich?

Pages from Hollywood's past records of *Svengali-Trilby* set-ups would indicate a gloomy, even fatal future.

D.W. Griffith and Lillian Gish were the first and most famous star-director inseparables. Gish was tops as long as she was with the pioneer, but when they split she made two or three indifferent pictures and then left the screen for good. Both Lillian and Dorothy "retired" to the stage after the Griffith era.

Carol Dempster, Griffith's second *Trilby*, on whose professional education he spent two million dollars, quit pictures the minute he ceased producing.

Mary Philbin, freed from the directorial tyranny of Erich von Stroheim, lingered on at Universal after her mentor had left. But she was never the same. Von Stroheim had discovered her in a beauty contest, taken her under his wing as von Sternberg took Dietrich, and built her into one of Universal's loveliest stars. She dwindled to eventual extinction when her *maestro* left her.

The only star in Hollywood's history who has survived the dissolution of a directorial dictatorship is Dolores Del Rio. But it cost her two year's absence from films. Edwin Carewe discovered the screen's most beautiful exotic at a ball in Mexico City and persuaded her high caste family to let her undertake a screen career. After the colossal failure of his epic effort, *Evangeline*, Dolores didn't face a camera for two years. Then *Bird of Paradise* launched her on a new and even greater screen career.

Incidentally, the man who directed Del Rio in *Bird of Paradise* was King Vidor. Vidor is now a Paramount director, and one of the several men mentioned to assume a role in Marlene Dietrich's rejuvenation.

History, however, does not necessarily repeat itself in Hollywood. New precedents are established every day. Certainly from the looks of things Marlene Dietrich has everything to give her unqualified backing in a fresh start. Lubitsch, himself, now the busy head man at Paramount studios, will drop everything and direct her personally if he finds the right story.

There is no reason for Marlene Dietrich to follow in the footsteps of the other *Trilbys* of which she is the greatest example. If she does not gain new life, new inspiration and revive the old enchanting Dietrich freshness, it will be her own fault. Von Sternberg has moved away from the Paramount lot. He plans to produce independently, and while everyone assumes that he and Dietrich will still see one another, he has stated flatly that he will have nothing even in the way of advice to offer her concerning her new career.

The road has never been more open to the destiny of Marlene Dietrich in which Hollywood has believed and continues to believe in.

Still no one can tell where that destiny lies, what it is, nor how to reach it – but from now on Marlene Dietrich and Hollywood will spend a lot of time trying to find out.

Warren Reeve was a frequent contributor to entertainment publications.

"Not the *Best-Dressed* – But the Most Important," by Katherine Hartley. *Movie Classic*, August, 1935

Haven't you wondered why Marlene Dietrich has never been suggested for the title of "best-dressed screen star?" Kay Francis, Carole Lombard, Norma Shearer, Joan Crawford, Grace Moore, Dolores Del Rio, Adrienne Ames, Genevieve Tobin, Veree Teasdale – all of these and many more have been "mentioned" for this coveted and much-disputed honor. But never Marlene Dietrich. Why? Because she holds a much more startling and vital title.

Marlene Dietrich is recognized as the most important fashion influence in the world today. More than any other actress, she starts trends that millions of women follow. It is her extravagant imagination, which swings from one daring extreme to another, that claims this ranking for her. And it is part of the explanation for the fact that, after three successive pictures that were only mildly popular, she has just signed a new and larger-than-ever film contract.

"The most important fashion influence in the world today!" That is a pretty broad statement, but there are some pretty precise facts to back it up.

Last May, for example, the socially elite of New York turned out in the grand ballroom of the Waldorf-Astoria to attend "The Lace Ball." The piece de resistance of the elaborate affair was the American Designers' Revue. All of the Hollywood designers and all of the important New York designers – Kiviette, Dorine Abrade, Lisbeth, Clarepotter, Helen Cookman, Elizabeth Hawes, Mabel Manning, Gladys Parker, and others too numerous to mention – had "showings." The gowns were applauded enthusiastically. But there were two presentations that climaxed the rest. Everyone went mad about them.

Marlene in The Devil is a Woman, *1935.*

One was a Spanish creation designed for Marlene Dietrich in *The Devil Is a Woman*. The other was a bridal party, dressed by Kiviette – and the bridal costume, probably for the first time in modern history, was Spanish in influence. The gown was made of lace, Spanish *peau d'ange*, and the bridal veil was draped, mantilla fashion, over a Spanish comb. Kiviette frankly gave credit for her inspiration to the gowns that Marlene Dietrich wore in *The Devil Is a Woman*. Likewise, Irene Hayes, who created the flower modes for the bridal party, credited the picture with the inspiration for the fan of carnations carried by the bride.

The clothes that Marlene Dietrich wore in that picture were designed especially for her by Travis Banton, famous Paramount stylist, who has fashioned all of her picture clothes and many of her personal ones, since she came to America.

And Mr. Banton told me, "Frankly, the gowns that Marlene wore in that picture could never be worn by anyone else. On the average woman, they would look ridiculous. They were to eccentric, too individual. But in modified versions, they will become the fashion of the season. Her fringe dress, for example, was the inspiration for Spanish shawl-like evening dresses that are already appearing in London, Paris, and New York. The lace stockings, the lace parasols, the lace mantillas, too… They have already become the vogue. Oh, yes, and the carnations! Because Marlene wore or carried carnations throughout the picture, this blossom has become the flower fashion of the year.

"The fact that I design for Marlene Dietrich," added Mr. Banton, smiling, "seems to be my greatest claim to fame. I made a trip to Europe recently, you know, and wherever I went, the name of Dietrich was on everyone's lips. Women haven't forgotten that it was Dietrich who brought coq feathers into the world of fashion – or that it was Dietrich, with her funny little peasant hat in *Song of Songs*, which she wore on the back of her head, that started women to pushing their hats backward. They haven't forgotten a thing… and I could almost go down the list of her every picture, and show you that in each she has started a new fashion ball rolling."

"Let's go down the list!" I begged him.

We did. And here are my gleanings.

It was in *Shanghai Express* that Marlene Dietrich first burst on the world as a fashion impetus. Mr. Banton dressed her in that picture, if you will remember, almost entirely in coq feathers. There were coq feather boas around her neck. ("Horribly out of style, and in atrocious taste," we would have said, if they had been worn by anyone less provocative than Dietrich.) There were coq feathers in her hair, on her gloves, and on her sleeves. Feathers, feathers, everywhere!

Travis Banton reviews costume sketches with Marlene, 1935.

It happens that, prior to the general release of that picture in France, one of the greatest fashion leaders in Paris gave a party. At that party, as part of the entertainment, she gave a private advance showing of *Shanghai Express*. Before twenty-four hours had passed, each and every one of those women had been in touch with her dressmaker, and had ordered coats, hats, dresses, evening capes, all simply smothered in coq feathers.

To this day, they remember that feather-avalanche in Paris. When Mr. Banton was there recently, the famous couturier, Lucien Lelong, mentioned it, and said, "So it's you we really have to thank for feathers!"

Then there was *Song of Songs*, in which, first of all, Marlene presented the coronet braid. It was widely copied, and was really responsible for those off-the-face hats that we began wearing at the same time – for, as Mr. Banton told me, "She had to wear that little saucer-shaped hat way back on her head to make room for the braid!"

Later in that same picture, when Marlene was the "Baroness," she wore a voluminous black velvet cape with a hood, which became the forerunner of our modern hooded evening capes.

And who dares to doubt that the Russian influence in clothes, did not definitely emanate from Marlene Dietrich's picture, *The Scarlet Empress*? Remember the Cossack hats and the Russian tunics that she wore, and the muffs that she carried? Well, how many of you had a little fur-trimmed Cossack hat last season? How many of you denied yourself a new dress in order to carry a muff? And if you *didn't* have any of these things, how many of you cast envious eyes on others who did? You know the answer!

It takes an extraordinary woman to sidestep the accepted conventional things, and dare to be different. Marlene not only dares to be different, but when she dares she changes the styles of the world! You and I don't rush out and buy coq feathers the minute we see Dietrich wearing them. The process of our enslavement is not such a direct one as that. We would feel foolish, appearing in our own little circles swathed in feathers. But the so-called fashion leaders of the world, with jaded clothes appetites, find inspiration in the sophisticated Marlene, and act on this inspiration at once. Gradually, the fashion filters through New York, Paris and London, in modified form, to us. And by that time there are enough people wearing feathers so that we don't feel too conspicuous in them.

Dietrich never dreads being conspicuous. Yet I feel certain that she does not dress as she does to create a sensation. If she creates a sensation when she appears, that is simply because she can't help it. There is that *something* about her that draws all eyes.

Mr. Banton explains it this way, "The reason why Marlene's costumes are always compelling is that she always acts, walks, and *looks* in tune with the mood of her costumes. When she wears an exotic costume, even an eccentric one, she is the exotic or eccentric person who goes with it. When she wears a girlish, flowing chiffon gown, she adjusts every detail of her personality to that particular creation. Yet, even in simplicity, she is never banal…and I do everything I can to keep her most simple gown from being that way, too.

"Not long ago, for example, I designed a simple-white chiffon for her to wear during her vacation in New York. But with that gown I had her wear a tremendous shoulder corsage of red carnations…and her gloves were of skin-tight black lace…so skin-tight that the pattern of the lace seemed tattooed on her arms.

"Even in simplicity we strive for the dramatic element, for Dietrich is a dramatic woman. And with it all, she has great chic… an innate intelligence about colors and fabrics and lines. When I show her a drawing of something I have in mind for her, she doesn't stop to think of its effect on other people. Quite the contrary…I have heard her say, often, while musing over the drawing, 'yes, I could feel like that. Yes, let's do it.' Marlene wears a thing only because it is what she *feels* like wearing. That's why her clothes are always such a success.

"Again the other day she came in to tell me that she had been invited to a formal dinner party for Thursday night. 'I know,' I said, 'you have nothing to wear.'

"'That's right,' said Marlene, 'and you know what I want this time? Something to wear with my new emeralds!'

"So, between now and Thursday I have to think up something that will provide a suitable background for emeralds. I don't know yet what that will be!"

But this much *we* know, Mr. Banton, few women may be able to afford emeralds, yet nothing will prevent the others from acquiring something similar to Marlene's Thursday gown. For it has been proved, time and again, that women the world over are Dietrich-clothes-conscious – and many thanks to you!

Katherine Hartley (Ketti Frings) (1909-1981) began her career as a copywriter, and worked as a feature writer for United Press International. She became a publicity agent, and was a frequent contributor to movie fan magazines – sometimes using the pen name "Anita Kigore." During a trip abroad, she met and married Kurt Frings (1908-1991), a German talent agent. Frings was denied an entrée visa, and it took the couple nearly two years to straighten out his immigration issues. Hartley wrote a story about their ordeal, titled "Memo to a Movie Producer." The story was adapted by Charles Brackett and Billy Wilder for the screen – titled *Hold Back the Dawn* (1941). Ketti became a screenwriter with impressive credits including *Jane Eyre* (1943), *Guest in the House* (1944), *The Accused* (1949), *The File on Thelma Jordon* (1950), *Come Back, Little Sheba* (1952), *About Mrs. Leslie* (1954), *The Shrike* (1955), *Foxfire* (1955), and *Mr. Sycamore* (1975). Her Broadway writing credits include *Mr. Sycamore* (1942), *Look Homeward, Angel* (1957-59) which earned her a Tony nomination, *The Long Dream* (1960), *Walking Happy* (1966-67) which earned her a second Tony nomination, and *Angel* (1978). She won the 1958 Pulitzer Prize for Drama for her play, *Look Homeward, Angel*. She wrote frequently for television, as well. Ketti and her husband – divorced in 1963 – had two children.

"For the First and Last Time – DIETRICH TALKS," by Chet Green. *Photoplay, December, 1935*

Marlene, 1935.

They have plans at Paramount to remake Marlene Dietrich.

But I wonder – do you remake someone like Marlene Dietrich?

You re-mold her masque on the screen – yes – and you pipe a new and spirited tune which may better carry an obbligato of tinkling silver in the box-office till.

But you don't drown out with the brighter tune of today the deep, haunting undertones of yesterday's symphony. You don't say, "switch your faith, alter your ideals" and behold the transformation

– just like that. You don't pour out the wine and expect the glass to sparkle more brightly.

She sat across from me in the exotically decorated drawing room of her home. Her white silk lounging pajamas were only a little more white and a little more soft than her complexion. While I munched a piece of her famous "bee's nest cake," telling myself once more that of all the beautiful women in Hollywood she was surely the most beautiful. I thought of those plans and wondered.

We had talked for possibly five minutes. Then I realized. The song is ended for Marlene Dietrich.

Her real song, which was her work with Josef von Sternberg, is ended now – but the melody lingers on.

It echoed with her words, "When you have been so devoted to the ideals of someone for so long and then change, it is not the same.

"I failed him," she stated simply. "I was never the ideal he sought. I tried to do what he wanted, but I didn't succeed. He was never quite satisfied with any of the pictures we made. He expected something great, something we never achieved."

She smiled slowly. Always, it seems, no matter what her words, her face wears a soft, composed smile.

"Perhaps that was his fault – expecting so much – but I don't think it was a fault. And I would rather be a failure hunting that goal than a success going along the average line.

"Just making pictures doesn't mean anything to me. It has never been enough. All my life I have had to have a higher interest."

After five years, I think it is time to try to understand Marlene Dietrich.

Now that there is no longer any theatrically occult Svengali-Trilby ogre to rise out of a bottle, like the Genie of "Arabian Nights" every time you mention her name, perhaps we hospitable Americans, we who have made her life miserable because we must have our intriguing legends, can settle down and relax into an open mind.

Marlene Dietrich happens to be, despite her unholy beauty, I think, something of an idealist.

If she had been the artificial, glamour-seeking poseur for which she has been wantonly denounced, I think she would have had for me, her first interviewer since the split, perhaps an artful explanation handy to toss off her professional divorce from von Sternberg. Furthermore, if she were playing to the grand stand, I think she would have had a glowing promise for the future handy.

She had neither. No guile nor gloss. Her words were simple and sincere, as simple and sincere as her beauty.

"It was I who insisted that he direct my last two pictures," she said. "Mr. von Sternberg did not want to direct them. He thought we should part long ago. He has always known what was right for me. He has always predicted what could happen.

"I remember when we made *Morocco*. It was the time when there was a great deal of talk in every picture. He cut down the dialogue so that when the rushes were shown at the studio everyone said, 'What's the matter? Why doesn't she talk?'

"'Wait and see,' he told them. It was something quite new and welcome, and, of course, it was successful.

"I had to beg him to direct my last two pictures. 'It will be bad for you,' he told me. He said the average public would not see the things in them that we worked so hard to get. He was right. He sensed the reaction of the public perfectly. But I would rather do them – I would rather do something different and daring than to be just a popular success. It is personal perhaps. I liked the pictures. I'm not influenced by public opinion, although I can understand. I do not resent it.

"I'm not sure, though, that the public knows what it does want."

Marlene Dietrich smiled again, that quiet, soft amused smile.

Marlene in The Devil is a Woman, *1935.*

She told of the steady stream of criticism because she was so "still and set" in her pictures. Yet, when the last one, *The Devil Is a Woman*, was released, protests poured in saying, "Where's the old Marlene? Why is she *jumping around?*"

She told of her recent trip to New York. She wanted badly to see *Point Valaine*, with Noel Coward, Alfred Lunt and Lynn Fontanne. But the time she had arrived in New York, the play was closed. That array of great talent was not enough to fill a theater in New York where tastes are pretty high and well delineated.

"Yet they ask us to please the audiences of every theater in the world," she smiled. "I don't think you can do that unless you keep right at the average line."

I wondered if that wasn't her job.

"That's a question, "she replied thoughtfully. "I don't know. It may be my job – but it isn't what I want to do."

"If I were a film actress at heart, if I could not live without making a picture – that would be different," she explained. "I have always made pictures because I wanted to work for Mr. von Sternberg – not because I wanted to be a film star.

"I only came to Hollywood to work with him. I only stayed to work with him. I have always admired him. I think he is a great artist. I had had offers to come to Hollywood before he called me, but I said no to them. I did not want to leave my family and my country just to be a screen star."

That is true. Both Fox and B.P Schulberg tried to talk Marlene Dietrich into a contract. She wouldn't listen. After von Sternberg had finished *The Blue Angel*, made in Germany, Dietrich gave him a book to read on the boat – *Morocco*.

"I think it will make a good film for you," she had said, but there was no idea of herself in the part.

"From the boat he cabled me to come to Hollywood," she told me. "When he told me to come, I came. I would have come to work with him if he were in Australia."

If that sounds as if Marlene Dietrich holds no particular love for Hollywood, then certainly she can't be blamed for that.

It is hard to feel sorry for anyone as beautiful as Marlene Dietrich. It is always hard to feel sorry for a motion picture star who apparently has everything in the world.

Yet there is no doubt that Dietrich has been treated shamefully here. She was greeted – few could explain just why – more like an intruder than a visitor when she arrived. Immediately the Svengali-Trilby legend was spun to invest her with an unholy aura. She was accused of imitating Garbo.

Of course, what no one knew or bothered to find out was that Marlene Dietrich was not a recluse by nature, nor was she interested in drawing herself into a shell to create a legend.

She was merely alone in a strange, aggressive, frightening country with but one friend. She was desperately lonely without her husband, her adored little girl, her family.

She heard preposterous stories about herself, but soon learned there was no use talking back. No one wanted to believe her. They could make up much better stories. So she said nothing.

Only recently on her trip to New York, she went down to the boat to see her husband, Rudolf Sieber, off. News cameramen were all over the place and snapped them from all angles. But not a picture was used in the newspapers.

With Sieber sailing for Europe, and Marlene returning to Hollywood, a separation story was much more intriguing, and pictures showing them together at the boat didn't help that out very much!

"I have been miserable often here in Hollywood," she told me. "During those first two years, when I was without my husband and Maria, I was terribly depressed. For the first two years, when I lived in Santa Monica, I saw no one. I had no friends to see. When I returned to Europe for my family the crowds actually frightened me. I became hysterical. I had been so alone in Hollywood."

Recently, of course, Marlene Dietrich has found a few friends in Hollywood. She pals around a lot with Carole Lombard and she advised me that the Richard Barthelmesses were steady customer's for the "bee's nest cake."

But few of her friends are close. She still feels as she has always felt – like an expatriate, and there are no interests of any importance outside her work with von Sternberg, of which she says reverently, "the experience of working all these years with his beautiful brain is something I would not have missed for all the world."

But now, of course, that is ended. Not because Marlene Dietrich wanted it to end and not because the studio wanted it to end.

When she knew it was ended, when she saw that to insist longer was to harm him, she said, "All right, I shall go back to Germany."

"You mustn't do that," von Sternberg told her. "They won't think you're sincere. They will call it a publicity gesture. No one will believe you. You should stay and make two pictures at least with someone else.

"It will be good for you," he went on, "and it will be easier for you. It is so easy, after what we have been doing on the screen to show emotions in the natural, average way. You must stay."

It was some time before Marlene Dietrich's new contract was signed. She wanted to go back to Europe, but she saw that if she did, it would make von Sternberg out as the bad man – the Svengali. They would blame it on him. They would say he told her to go.

One day she called him up from her dressing room. The contract was on her dressing room table.

"Shall I sign or not?" she asked him. "You are always right. Tell me – because I really don't want to sign."

"Sign," said von Sternberg.

"So, I signed," smiled Marlene Dietrich. "But I shall go home in the winter.

"My plans?" she repeated slowly. "Oh, yes, my plans are definite." Then in the next breath she said, "I never make plans."

It didn't sound as absurd as it reads. It wasn't even contradictory to me, for I knew she was talking about two different things – the plans which were to complete the new contract she had just signed – they were definite. Beyond that – who knows?

"Yes," she said, "everything is decided." Although her voice is always soft and her manner deliberate, there now seemed but little spirit in her voice. Like champagne that has kept its bouquet but lost its bubbles. Perhaps she was tired.

"I shall make two pictures here. The first is *Desire*, an original story written for me – one that Ernst Lubitsch was to direct me in before he became production head of the studio. I play a French adventuress. Gary Cooper plays with me and Frank Borzage directs it.

"The second is to be *Hotel Imperial* – you remember? – the picture Pola Negri made years ago with Maurice Stiller. Lewis Milestone will direct it.

"The first is light and adventurous. The second is dramatic and thrilling. They are regular film stories," she explained.

Her slow smile widened.

"But my contract will be up soon and then I shall go to Europe. I think I shall stay quite a long time. There are many places I want to go – England, Italy, Austria. I want to see my family, my sister and my mother in Berlin and my husband who is now in Paris. Maria is ten now. She adores America, but I want her to be educated in Europe. It is time she started in school there. I can't think of being separated from her.

"Pictures? I don't know. Perhaps I may make pictures in England or France or Germany – perhaps not. Perhaps Mr. von Sternberg will come to Europe. I hope he does.

"Miss Hollywood? Yes, I probably shall. I may want to come back. But I will not a sign a contract – any contract – just to be signing.

"It would have to be like the one I have now. You know," she smiled, "in my contract I have my choice of story, cameraman…"

"And director?" I asked.

"And director," she confirmed.

"Then you could have Mr. von Sternberg again?"

"Yes," she smiled, "if he would direct me."

I remembered the Paramount decree I had read in the newspaper. "We are going to remake Marlene Dietrich!"

But I don't think you ever remake someone like Marlene Dietrich. You don't remake an idealist without remaking the ideal.

Chet Green was an entertainment journalist, and frequent fan magazine contributor.

Marlene visits the set of Mae West's film, Klondike Annie, *at Paramount. The two actresses were leading sex symbols at the studio, but never rivals. They enjoyed a good friendship, and always tried to dispel rumors of a feud. 1935.*

"Behold *Dietrich*," by Hilary Lynn. *Modern Screen*, March, 1936

Marlene Dietrich is a vibrant personality, sparkling almost as brilliantly as the jewels she loves to wear. First and foremost, she has a grand sense of humor. She could live by her wit alone – without ever having to depend upon her beauty to fascinate. Too bad you can't meet her in person!

I'm not indulging in the favorite Hollywood pastime of telling you that "for the first time," the real Dietrich will be revealed. You *will* see Dietrich as she *really* is. In other words, through the eyes of those intimates who were allowed to share her life-apart-in-Hollywood. People who saw her day and night during that period when she built a wall about herself and pretended, in between pictures, that she actually was living that sophisticated, high-tension life she had left abroad.

The make-believe drama which Marlene played in that special salon of hers, made brilliant by her presence and her tantalizing wit, was helped by the fact that none of her friends spoke English. Only to those who understand Marlene Dietrich's mother tongue has been made known the power of her personality – something, I am sure, never mentioned in anything you've read about her.

This remote-from-Hollywood life was helped also by the constant interchange of cablegrams between her and her family and friends abroad. There were never less than twenty a day. And whenever the illusion began to grow thin, Marlene would telephone across the sea and have a long conversation about trivialities – the sort of talk that goes on between friends who are sure to see one another every day. On one of those occasions she even asked her friend to close the window of her apartment because the roar of the foreign city's street cars was too loud in Hollywood!

Those privileged ones, who were allowed to see her true personality, will rave by the hour of her keen brain and dazzling wit.

"If Marlene could write as well as she can talk, she would be considered one of the most important writers of this age" her closest friend told me. "The comments she makes are worthy of the best wags of the day. Unfortunately, most of them are untranslatable because she always employs her native slang and colloquial expressions, and these can never be transferred from one language to another. But if you speak her language, you have the desire to take down her conversations in shorthand. Her graphic epigrams are smarter than the wisecracks of the most sophisticated Broadway comedy.

"However, you have to suppress your desire and hide your pencil because Marlene would consider that impulse as foolish as the adjectives which writers used to describe her.

"For example, she remarked of a certain rather crude Hollywood director, who was putting on ridiculous airs because his sudden success had gone to his head; 'He looks like a hay-seed with a monocle in his eye!'

"And about a gaudy feminine star, who had just lost her husband, and wasn't being very convincing about her *great bereavement*. 'Here comes the Merry Widow again!'

"One of her grandest little jokes," he continued, "is to suddenly break off in the middle of a sentence when she has us all roaring, make her eyes go starry, arrange herself in one of her most languorous attitudes, and say, "Ach, ja. I am so glamorous, so exotic, so seductive – that it *hurts*!"

Being Marlene Dietrich's friend is a career in itself. Those who enjoy this privilege have time for little but this all-absorbing relationship. Haven't you known people who affected you so powerfully that all your own problems vanished into thin air? People who made you feel there was nothing so important as their whim of the moment, their interests, their desires, who made you their willing slave and constant shadow? Marlene Dietrich is one of these fabulous creatures.

But don't misunderstand. She doesn't mean to be commanding or imperious. On the contrary, Marlene is the soul of generosity and kindness. She seems to spend her waking hours thinking up ways to enrich the lives of her friends and to entertain them. When she isn't telling funny stories, she is plying them with savory dainties prepared by her own hands – all much too rich for a steady diet, but so delicious they can't be resisted. One of the favored few told me that during his six months as a member of the inner Dietrich circle he gained twenty pounds.

That's how the legend grew that Marlene, off-screen, becomes the domestic, retiring hausfrau whose chief delight is to stand over the oven in her perfectly appointed kitchen and bake a luscious cake. True, Marlene likes to cook and she does it expertly. But she does it, not because she is essentially domestic, but because she believes – to paraphrase Lord Byron that "man can do without poetry, music and books, but certainly man cannot do without cooks!"

This role of bountiful hostess, Marlene plays to perfection. She doesn't confine it to her few intimate friends. For instance, on the set, her generosity is outstanding. Every other week is gift week for her co-workers and the crew when Marlene's around.

The day she finished *Desire*, she distributed a few gifts on the set. Gary Cooper received an imported leather traveling case. The assistant directors and most of the technicians and crew each received wallets in which crackled crisp new fifty-dollar bills. The set hairdresser rated a pair of Italian marble lamps.

Recently she gave Jessmer Brown, her maid, a new coupe just because she thought Jessmer's car was growing shabby. And on an average of every ten days, Jessmer's mother, who happens to be the studio janitress, finds twenty-five dollars pinned to a note with her mane on it in "Miss Dietrich's" dressing-room.

Witty, brilliant Queen Dietrich – as capricious as a ruler with power of life and death.

A benefactress who sincerely wants to make life pleasanter for her devoted subjects! Yet – and here's the rub – every move she makes is motivated by sudden, unpredictable impulses. Not even a psychologist could chart her behavior or prophesy her next move. Which is one reason why she will always be fascinating.

Which is also the reason we label Marlene by such adjectives as sensational – exotic – erratic. She does whatever comes into her mind at the moment, without any thought of how people might interpret her actions. She never does anything for effect, having no desire to startle or shock. But if she happens to do so, it never troubles her.

When she decided to wear trousers and top hats, she did so only because she felt more comfortable in them. The ensuing publicity bewildered and irritated her. "Why should people be so interested in what I do?" she asked naively.

I tried to explain to her that she, more than any other screen actress, excepting Garbo, represented to these same people all the color, romance and mystery which they find lacking in their own lives. She laughed and shrugged her shoulders.

Most women can be catalogued. Some more easily than others. In each, there is usually a predominant quality which is obvious to the most casual observer.

But Marlene Dietrich falls into none of the usual categories. Sometimes she hovers on the verge of one, other times she's completely immersed in the opposite. Any one of a hundred alternate roles in real life seems to suit her as perfectly as either trousers and clinging feminine garments. She's as volatile as mercury and as changeable as a chameleon.

She's the dramatic, capricious, slightly terrifying allurement one hour – drooping hands and drooping eyes, mist far-away thoughts, with a general pervasive air of melancholy about her. The next, she's a romping child up to no end of mischief.

And when you finally settle down with a sigh of relief, all worn out trying to keep up with her sleight-of-hand character changes, she turns around and shows you a Madonna. The mother brooding over her child, Maria.

And now for the surprise which I've been saving up 'til last. It disproves all those ridiculous stories current about a year ago, concerning the harmful Svengali-Trilby influence von Sternberg exerted over Marlene. If there was anyone who wielded the influence it was Marlene. Was – and always will be!

Seeing her for the first time when he went to Germany to search for an actress who could play the starring role in *The Blue Angel*, von Sternberg said, "If that woman doesn't accept the role I am offering her, I shall never make a picture!"

And he meant it.

Hilary Lynn was a frequent contributor to movie fan magazines.

"The Real DIETRICH – *Unmasked*," by Ida Zeitlin. *Motion Picture*, May, 1936

"She's gay" – "she's sad" – "she's mysterious" – "she's frank" – "she's moody" – "she's equable" – "she's easy to get along with" – "she's hard to talk to" – "she's this and that" – and a dozen contradictory things at once.

Thus runs the legend of Marlene Dietrich. Ask ten people about her and you'll get ten different reactions. I saw her once in a New York hotel, en route from Europe to Hollywood. She was bubbling with spirits, flashing with fun, her high humor spilling over into impishness. I saw her again on the set, when von Sternberg was rehearsing the carnival scene for *The Devil Is a Woman*. Her white throat and shoulders rose from the soft folds of a black lace gown. Her bronze head was draped in a trailing black mantilla. Her face was so luminous that a gasp of spontaneous tribute rose from the crowd. She wasn't acting – she had just arrived to have her costume approved. But standing there, she was the symbol of all feminine loveliness.

I saw her eating in the Paramount café – with an apparently excellent appetite, even as you and I – talking earnestly meanwhile to a writer. Here was the easy, friendly atmosphere of any luncheon table. On another occasion, I saw her in her dressing room. There was no trace of the merriment of the New York hotel. No trace of moodiness either. She was quiet, serene, willing enough to answer questions, though by no stretch of the imagination, garrulous. There was a job to be done and she did her share.

The last time, I saw her – but that's another story. Before that time came, I'd developed what I can only hope was a pardonable curiosity about her. She seemed to glow and change like a jewel. Yet at the heart of every jewel of worth lies something unchangeable, giving it richness and depth. I felt that some such unchanging core must underlie her surface complexity, and for the life of me I couldn't help wondering what it was. It was something baffling.

One fact finally pierced my consciousness. However diverse opinions might be on other points, there was always one recurrent unanimous refrain. "Dietrich's the most generous person in Hollywood."

Wherever her name is mentioned, someone's sure to have a story to tell of Dietrich's giving – lavishly, unstintingly, with both hands.

"And that's not the point," one eager boy informed me, stumbling over his tongue in his loyal haste to tell me what the point was. "It's not enough for her to give with both hands. She gives with her thoughts, with her heart. Plenty of people give besides Miss Dietrich – cigars for the boys, candy or something for the girls – and let it go at that. But what does *she* do? She finds out what you *really* want – goes to all kinds of trouble to find out. Look at me, for instance – she gives me this swell suede jacket for Christmas. How in thunder did she know I wanted a jacket? One guy needed a camera and he got it. One guy needed an overcoat and *he* got it – fitted him, too. Can you figure all the energy that takes – and the interest and the kindness? Me – I call that *giving*!"

Convincing though it was, I hadn't needed this boy's fervor to convince me. The tales were legion. Of the check for overdue taxes found by a one man in his coat pocket – of the car ordered by her make-up girl, who was told when she asked for the bill that the bill had already been settled by Miss Dietrich – of her daily visits to an injured co-worker, with bottles of a special broth whose curative powers had been a tradition in her family. Another woman, less finely sympathetic, might have sent flowers. Might even have sent the broth by someone else. But Miss Dietrich starts where other people leave off. Day after day her car stopped at the door, day after day the slender figure emerged, bearing her own broth and her own good cheer till the invalid was well on the road to health.

Indeed, so honeycombed was Hollywood with these tales that one day the inevitable happened. A writer asked Miss Dietrich for a story about them. I was that writer. And I was shamed by the quiet scorn with which my request was received.

"You mean you want me to talk about these things?" she asked, her blue eyes darkening. "No." And the simple finality of the monosyllable was more effective than a volume of words could have been. "If I do anything that makes other people happy, then it makes me happy too. That's why I do it – not to make a silly cheap advertisement out of it.

"Forgive me if I seem abrupt," she added. "I was brought up not to talk about myself – that was considered poor taste. Also not to ask others personal questions. That was considered rude. I know it's the only way to get acquainted with people, but still it remains difficult for me. That is why, perhaps, I haven't many friends. Oh, yes," she over-rode my look of protest, "it's perfectly true. And not because I'm unfriendly. I am not. I am the greatest sucker in the world." She spoke with calm matter-of-factness, yet it was difficult not to smile at the droll charm of that homely Americanism on her lips. "I have no talent to see through people. I believe everything everybody tells me, and I *want* to believe it."

This trait, though called gullibility by some, seems to me only a rarer form of generosity. To those who have never been disillusioned, faith is a simple matter. But to face disillusion squarely – to know that you've been cheated by circumstances, by human nature, and may be again – and still to choose faith in preference to cynicism – argues, I think, a deeper strain of idealism than is found in most of us.

I'd begun to feel that all the Marlenes I'd heard about – Marlene the Sphinx, the Temperamental, the Trilby – were resolving themselves into one Marlene – a sensitive, warm-hearted woman, born with the temperament and imagination which instinctively seeks what is kind and sweet in life, and hurt, correspondingly by life's inevitable cruelties – hiding from those cruelties, perhaps, behind whatever mask the mood of the moment suggests.

John Gilbert had died only a few weeks before, and Marlene Dietrich had been a good friend to John Gilbert. They met last July. Gilbert's high-strung nervous system had been shattered by the disappointments of his private and professional life – by his futile attempts to find surcease from pain in one form of escape or another.

Marlene with John Gilbert, 1935. Gilbert was to appear in Marlene's film, Desire, *but he died suddenly before the film was made.*

It was to her understanding sympathy that he appealed. It was her understanding sympathy which she gave him. He poured out his heart to her. She didn't commiserate with him. She didn't say, "Poor boy, how sorry I am for you!" She did better that that. She showed him how unimportant were the phantoms of failure he'd been fighting against. She helped him turn his back on the past that was done, to face the future that might be anything he chose to make it. She restored to him the priceless gift of confidence in himself. People who had known him for years noticed the change – told each other that Jack Gilbert had never looked better.

"That's the heart-breaking part of it," said Miss Dietrich. "He was so full of plans – so eager to work, to live. 'I *must* work,' he told me again and again. He'd been asked to play in *The House of a Thousand Candles*, and was anxious to do it because his mother had once played in it.

"He was so gay – the gayest man I've ever met. He even made me gay, and that's something – because it's difficult to make *me* gay. They say he was moody – I don't know – I never saw him anything but kind. Not kind – how shall I say it? – as though he told himself, 'I *will* be kind,' but because it was the only way he knew how to be. He couldn't have been so hurt, if he hadn't been really good inside.

"That's why he needed friendship so badly – was so grateful for it. Some people take friendship very easily. They say, 'He is my friend if he is nice with me, if he does things for me.' The minute he does something they think he shouldn't, he is no longer their friend. To me, that's not friendship. You must take your friend as you find him. He's intense? – sensitive? Very well – that's part of his nature, part of what makes you like him. If it also makes him difficult at times, is that a reason to turn your back on him? He needs you all the more – and to earn the name of friend yourself, you must answer that need as best you can. It's the only thing that brings happiness – that, anyway, is my experience. I have never been happy from taking – only from giving."

Such is the philosophy of Marlene Dietrich's heart – the core of her being. On the screen, a *femme fatale* who takes men's devotion and rewards them with a mocking smile for their pains; in actuality, a woman who finds happiness in giving to people!

Ida Zeitlin was a popular entertainment writer for many fan magazines including *Modern Screen, Screenland, Photoplay, Motion Picture, Movie Classic,* and *Movie Mirror.*

"Unlucky Lady," Marlene Dietrich Has Beauty Unrivaled, and Talent Unlimited, but Not Luck at All," by Liza. *Silver Screen*, June, 1936

Marlene with Gary Cooper in Desire, *1936.*

Marlene Dietrich must have tossed her hat on the bed. And it must have been that little number she wore that was simply mad with aigrettes in the early sequences of *Desire*. As you probably know, as far as "we of the theatre" are concerned there is nothing you can do that will bring "bad luck" quite as quickly and as completely as tossing your hat on the bed. Walking under a ladder, spilling salt, having a black cat cross your path, and whistling in the dressing room – pooh! – mere child's play. Now of course you must not get me wrong, "we of the theatre" are not superstitious, not really, why only ignorant natives dancing the boola-boola in the Congo are superstitious – but just the same we don't take any chances, especially with hats – and, er – beds. (The "Lubitsch touch.")

The first time I met Marlene she shrieked so loudly I practically jumped out of my skin. It was at a small cocktail party at Tallulah Bankhead's and I hadn't been in Hollywood very long and I was awfully curious to find out if Marlene (who was quite a hermit in those days) was really as beautiful and glamorous off the screen as she was on, so naturally I found it a bit disconcerting to be screamed at before I was even introduced. First I thought perhaps it was anti-Press week and the very sight of a writer (flatterer) sickened her, but then I saw she was pointing dramatically at my hat, which was not made with aigrettes, and which I, quite flabbergasted by so much glamour, had tossed on the Bankhead bed. (Early Empire – William Haines.) "You must not do that," said Marlene in those fascinating guttural tones. "It is bad luck!" It certainly was – I continued as a fan magazine writer.

Marlene has been playing in bad luck ever since she came to Hollywood (Oh, I know she's been collecting thousands of dollars weekly – but money isn't everything, my child, though it's quite enough to force me to write this story.) Every movie star wants to be the Number One Glamour Girl of the screen, there's just no way getting around that. Personally, I'd be perfectly content to be an off-stage voice (the voice of Bugle Ann would be the climax of my career) and most likely you'd be quite willing to be the corpse in any murder mystery – but not so with those movie stars. They've got more pride and prejudice than Jane Austen ever thought of, and if they can't be Number One girls their little hearts are broken. That's the reason there can be no real friendships between screen idols of the same sex – they're all too busy being jealous of each, and how. You really can't love Katherine Hepburn if she grabs that cinema plum, *Mary of Scotland*, right from under your own nose, now can you? And when Claudette Colbert won the

Academy Award it brought out the Lucrezia Borgia in at least six other glamour girls who were quite certain that they should have had it. They all want to win, they all want the best pictures, they all want to be on top – it's the law of the jungle. And, dear reader, you've never seen such disappointment and misery in all your life as when somebody more glamorous, more popular at the box office, noses them out. Marlene Dietrich came to America with a sensational picture, *The Blue Angel*, to her credit, a pair of perfect legs and a simply beautiful face, and was immediately acclaimed by the Press, who had sort of been tipped off by the Paramount Publicity Department as the Number One Glamour Queen of the screen. Marlene liked her title. Who wouldn't? And she had every intention in the world of keeping it – Bennetts could come and Bennetts could go, and so could Del Rios, Crawfords, Lombards, and Francises, but Marlene was going to keep her title if it killed her. It practically did.

Of course I don't have to tell you, you old know-it-all, how important pictures are in a star's career. A movie star never envies another star's home, her husband, her car, or her clothes, but mercy, mercy, how she envies another star's pictures. A jolly little street brawl with baseball bats and garbage between the Gas House Boys and the Tenth Avenue Gang is nothing compared with the fight a star makes for a good picture. No matter how beautiful Bella is she knows only too well that beauty and personality alone aren't going to get her anywhere, but no, she's gotta have pictures.

Well, for a while there, Marlene was certainly sitting pretty for *Morocco* was a great success, *Dishonored* was a slight disappointment but Marlene was so devastating that it really didn't matter, and *Shanghai Express* continued the tradition of romance, glamour and adventure. Marlene rented inaccessible houses, put on a lot of mystery, and no one really saw her away from the studio. She still kept her title, other movie stars still hated her, and publicity people still salaamed three times before addressing her – but something was happening. A little meddling auditor discovered that the Dietrich pictures were not making money. Of course it couldn't be Marlene's fault (she certainly was the same as ever) so it must be Director Josef von Sternberg's fault. *Blonde Venus* was a definite failure so Paramount ordered Miss Dietrich to make her next picture *Song of Songs* without von Sternberg, but instead with that arty chap, Rouben Mamoulian, in the director's chair. Marlene complained bitterly, went home in a huff, and announced that she was leaving for Europe at once. (Garbo always tanks she'll go home, but Marlene always tanks she'll go to Europe.) Paramount started a million-dollar suit against her (all suits in Hollywood are a million or more) and Marlene tanked she'd do the picture. As a matter of fact, she and Mamoulian became very chummy, and she began to wonder if perhaps he wasn't a better director for her than "85-take" von Sternberg. But, alas, people laughed in the wrong places and the picture wasn't exactly what one would call a sensational success. Marlene demanded that von Sternberg be returned to her and he was – worse luck. In *The Scarlet Empress* he went mad for gargoyles and in *The Devil is a Woman* he went mad for masks, and the audience just went mad. Poor Marlene – all the glamour in the world at her fingertips and it wasn't doing her a bit of good. She and Mr. von Sternberg called it a day.

Well, Marlene was frantic. What to do! What to do! She could pick up a fan magazine and there wasn't a picture to be found of her all the way from the cooking department to the crossword puzzle. Crawford with gardenias – Mae West with curves – Del Rio with spangles – Hepburn with bangs – but no, no Dietrich. So Marlene changed her way of living, put on her most exotic clothes and lunched daily at the Vendome and danced nightly at the Trocadero, and of course if photographers were lurking around she really couldn't be rude to

Marlene in I loved a Soldier, *1936.*

them. She even made a "personal appearance" that rated her more space in magazines and newspapers the world over than she had ever had before in her life. The "personal appearance" was not on the stage of the Chinese Theater, but at Carole Lombard's party at the Fun House on the amusement pier. Marlene appeared in shorts. If I had a dime for every time I've seen that picture of her and Claudette Colbert on the slide taken that night, I could realize my life's ambition – I could own a race horse named "Wait for Baby."

So with portraits of herself all over several continents, and people getting all Dietrich-minded again, Marlene was all set to do a glamorous picture and once more be the big box-office star of America. Yes, things had changed, she was going to get the lucky breaks at last. She and Mr. Ernst Lubitsch – a Continental like herself – had become great pals, and Mr. Lubitsch of the famous "Lubitsch touch" had promised her if she would sign a new contract with Paramount he would direct her pictures, and what with her beauty and his "touch" – Mon Dieu! Mon Dieu!

Everything looked rosy, and Marlene was so gay she went out and bought the longest car in Hollywood. (That burned up Mae West all right). But poor gal, she just couldn't have any luck at all. Paramount began playing that little game we played when we were kiddies called "Fruit Basket Turn Over." When the excitement was over and everybody had rushed for a new chair, Mr. Lubitsch found himself in the great big expensive chair of production head of the Paramount Studio. Marlene had lost her director. But he promised to supervise the picture for her, so Marlene started *Desire*. "It can't miss," said Mr. Lubitsch. "You've got Frank Borzage for a director. You've got Gary Cooper for a leading man. There's nothing more glamorous than a beautiful woman thief. It's a natural!"

Well, some people liked *Desire* and some people didn't. Anyway, it was not the colossal success it was supposed to be. "Now, now, don't mind that," said Mr. Lubitsch to Marlene who was plenty worried. "I'll personally supervise *I Loved a Soldier* and you'll be simply terrific!" So poor Marlene put her trust once more in mere man and started to work on *I Loved a Soldier*. And then Paramount started playing games again – yes, good old "Fruit Basket

Turn Over" again – and this time, when the excitement died down and everybody had knocked everybody else down in a mad rush for a chair, imagine Mr. Lubitsch's surprise when he found that he was "it," as we used to say in the playroom – but "out," as they say at Paramount. Marlene, that lovely lady of no luck, not only lost her supervisor, but added to all that she discovered to her horror that she was supposed to go through most of the picture as a charwoman, and there's certainly no glamour about a charwoman. Marlene went home in a huff, packed her trunks, and announced that she would leave for Europe and a Korda picture at once. Then the studio said something like who are you to walk out on us, and Marlene told them simply by producing her contract, which very definitely stated that Lubitsch would direct her pictures. She had them where the hair was short. *I Loved a Soldier* was finally shelved after practically every glamour girl had refused to do it – and some $500,000 had been spent on it. But Marlene didn't leave for Europe. As we go to press, and right on the deadline, too, she has signed a contract with Selznick to co-star with Charles Boyer in *The Garden of Allah*. Well, the Garden is right down Marlene's alley. She can glam all over the place, and no mops and buckets of soapy water, thank you. As one of Marlene's most dyed-in-the-wool fans I'm keeping my fingers crossed (and my hat off the bed) for Marlene deserves a few breaks – and *The Garden of Allah* might just as well start them.

Liza was a pseudonym used by the editor of *Silver Screen* magazine.

"Drama in the Desert," by James Reid. *Movie Classic*, August, 1936

Marlene with Charles Boyer in The Garden of Allah, *1936.*

Marlene Dietrich felt slightly faint as she stood up and stepped out of the meagre shelter of the sun-umbrella. She started across the deep, hot, desert sand toward "the honeymoon tent," only a few yards distant. The short walk was an effort for her, but she struggled on, trying to smile, trying to let no one know how she felt. Everyone else probably felt the same way, in this blazing heat. Some of the men had been working under the direct rays of the sun for hours. And no one was complaining…

Walking in deep, shifting sand is not easy at any time. Her faltering unsteadiness, therefore, attracted no attention. The Technicolor make-up is very pale, all of one tone. Her own paleness escaped detection.

She reached the wide doorway of the large tent, resisted the temptation to grasp the canvas for support. Waves of heat, coming from the interior of the tent, struck her face. Powerful arc-lights, necessary for photographing this interior scene, were adding their torment to the sun's torture. Her old friend, Charles Boyer, with whom she was to make the scene, warned her, with a smile, that this "take" would be an endurance contest. She tried to smile in return, as she took her place before the camera. She had a flash of pity for Charles, in his heavy suit.

There were crazy black dots gyrating before her eyes; then, concentric circles of red, revolving dizzily. Unconsciously, she brushed the back of her left hand across her eyes, and forehead. Director Richard Boleslawski, quick in his perceptions, asked, "Do you feel all right, Marlainah?"

She nodded – and then, suddenly, limply, she dropped. Marlene, for all her will power, had fainted.

Five minutes later, the company doctor had revived her. She had had a slight sunstroke, he told her. She could not work anymore today. They must carry her to her car. She must go back to the hotel in Yuma, relax, rest. She tried to protest. She wanted to continue, didn't want to "spoil the whole day's work." They wouldn't listen to her.

When they arrived back at the location camp, a small, neat city of well-screened wooden "tents" on a level expanse of ground a mile away, one of the workers looked at a thermometer, 138 degrees! God only knows what it had been out on the dunes. One of the publicity men at the camp commandeered a company car, raced to nearby Sidewinder, teletyped the story to his boss in Hollywood. The next morning, a Sunday, every newspaper in the country carried the item that Marlene Dietrich had collapsed on the sand dunes near Yuma, while at work on the Technicolor picture, *The Garden of Allah*.

But not one newspaper carried the inside story of her determined effort to fight off faintness, her demonstration that she was a trouper.

I happened to be at *The Garden of Allah* location the next day. On every side, I heard the story. From Boleslawski, from Marlene's stand-in, from cameramen, from prop men. The story was no hoax. It had happened.

After I went out on the dunes, to the setting of the honeymoon tent and an imitation ruin of an old castle nearby, I wondered why they all had not collapsed; why Marlene was the only victim. As far as the eye could reach, there was nothing but sand, white sand, great wind-rippled hills and dales of sand. The sun, almost overhead, was merciless in its brightness, in its heat. The workers were commenting that it was even hotter than the previous day. And there was no shelter anywhere, except under one lone sun-umbrella. That was Dietrich's.

At a little after two, Marlene appeared, dressed in ankle-length gray chiffon, set off with a filmy orange scarf and a blue cape – her costume for the first scene of the afternoon. A beautiful woman, serenely poised. Her glamor is not something that the camera has given her; it is as natural as the candor of her blue eyes. You will see its reality for the first time in *The Garden of Allah*, filmed in natural color.

With Marlene was her daughter, Maria, dressed in a sports suit of light blue. She was almost as tall as Marlene, a young husky, exuberantly heathy girl. Rounder of face than Marlene, and freckled, but with the same blue eyes, the same light brown hair, the same lovely mouth.

All those on terms of any intimacy with Marlene – and they ranged from Boleslawski, the director, to Irving Sindler, chief prop man – asked her how she felt. "I'm not going to faint today," she told them.

The publicity man showed her the clipping from the Sunday paper, asked her if she had seen it. She had. "I don't know why they sent that one," she said. "It frightened everybody at home. Maria came down on the train last night, with her governess, just to make sure I was all right. She wouldn't take my word over the telephone."

Someone told her the sequel to her fainting spell, intending to amuse her. It seems that Joseph Schildkraut, also working in the picture, has a weak heart. To ease the physical strain from the brutal heat, he had been carrying an ice-bag around with him, keeping it pressed over his heart between scenes. When Marlene collapsed, he was the first one at her side – with his ice-bag, which he placed on her wrists. The company doctor rushed up, raised her to a sitting position, put a bottle of smelling salts under her nostrils. Suddenly, Schildkraut reached over, grasped the bottle and whiffed it himself.

Marlene did not laugh at the story, as others present did. She said, "He has a weak heart, you know. If I had been in his place, I probably would have done the same thing. I know I've often felt as if I, too, were fainting, seeing other people faint."

She had been expected to laugh; she had not even smiled. She had responded with sympathy, instead. That was, to me, a hint of Dietrich's humanity. I was to see much more of it during the course of the long, sun-baked afternoon. From two o'clock until ten minutes of five, the company waited for the sun to put the desired shadows on the dunes for the "confession scene" that Marlene and Boyer were about to make. For me, it was an afternoon of getting acquainted with Marlene Dietrich – actress, woman, and mother.

The Garden of Allah is being produced by David O. Selznick for Selznick International Pictures. It is the first picture that she has

made for any company other than Paramount since her arrival in America six years ago. She is also the first "glamour queen" to dare an appearance in a color picture. What impelled her to take the role of "Domini"?

"The color, principally. Color interests me. Naturalness interests me. And I enjoy experimenting – trying something new. I tried comedy in *Desire*, and liked it. Now I am trying color – and I like this, too."

Boleslawski told me that Marlene has a phenomenal sense of color and color harmonies. The night before, recovered from her fainting spell, she had stayed up until one o'clock, making today's costume, with the help of a wardrobe woman.

What new experiment will she try next? "As soon as I finish *The Garden of Allah*, I'm leaving for England to make a picture for Alexander Korda, perhaps with Robert Donat as my co-star, if he is available." To show the world that Dietrich still can be Dietrich without Hollywood? "No, there is no challenge in it. I simply feel that everyone should have a change of scenery, go away for a new perspective, every so often. I haven't been abroad for two years.

"And when I come back this time, in September," she added, with a wistful smile toward her daughter, "I won't have Maria" – she pronounces it *Mar*-ya – "with me. She will be going to school in England." Maria likes the prospect of school in England but dislikes the prospect of "being so far from mother."

The attachment of the two is eloquent in every glance, every gesture, every word. I wondered if the coming separation, which will be difficult for Marlene to endure for long, might be a signal that she has plans for returning to Europe permanently before long. Maria promptly interjected that she wants to go to college *here*. She likes America, its informality and freedom. It isn't old and stuffy.

Marlene smiled at her thoroughly Americanized daughter. "I have two more pictures to make for Paramount. The first will be a musical for Ernst Lubitsch. Something airy and gay, with a Viennese mood. I don't know what the second will be. Perhaps something else new for me. And after that – well, I'll let 'after that' take care of itself when the time comes."

Despite the heat, despite her collapse of the day before, she was enjoying the sand dunes, their beauty and fascination – enjoying them so much that she agreed that the setting cried for something new in trailers for the picture. Why not shots of the camp, of the crew at work, of Boleslawski in a directorial pose, of Boyer and herself preparing for scenes? (P.S. Selznick is making such a trailer!)

She has one worry about *The Garden of Allah*, "I wonder if I'm not in too many scenes? In *Shanghai Express* – everybody liked that – I was in very few scenes. Everything built up to them…I think I was in too many scenes in *Desire*, even though nobody else has said so yet. I don't want so much of the camera. I don't want them to become tired of seeing me."

As she had been talking, she had been watching the sky. "Where's the camera?" she asked suddenly. She was referring to her own small movie camera, ever-present with her. Maria handed it to her. Expertly, Marlene loaded it with film, set the aperture at the correct gauge, stood up, walked away a few feet, "shooting" some colorful extras, dressed as Arabs: Boleslawski with her orange scarf around his neck "to give him some color": Jedaan, once Valentino's favorite mount, which she and Boyer ride in the picture. Then she pointed the lens at Maria.

"Do your imitation of Joan Crawford, Maria."

The child, for a moment, was self-conscious before the strangers. Then she thought better of it. She tilted her head sideways at an exotic angle, raising a languid hand to her face, brushing away an imaginary lock of hair, slowly turning full-face toward the camera, with exaggerated intensity in her eyes. The mimicry, tellingly faithful, was Maria's own.

Maria has potential dramatic talent. But no acting ambitions. "Sometime," she told me, "I'd like to play Mother as a child in some picture, as I did in *Scarlet Empress*. But that's all. That would be fun. Even though I don't look awfully much as Mother did at my age. She was slighter."

Marlene denied that she was making any attempt to influence Maria's future. Maria will become what Maria wants to become.

"Right now," the child confided, "I think I want to write short stories. I've written some already. I see stories in everything, everybody I know. I wouldn't let anybody but Mother see them, though. They aren't good enough."

Marlene interrupted to protest, "They're very good, Maria. Especially the one about the lame princess and the four princes who wanted to marry her." Maria smiled, as if to say, "You don't have to believe her if you don't want to. She's my mother," and continued, "So far I've written in German. When I write in English, I have to stop to think how to spell words, and that spoils the flow of the story."

I asked Marlene how old Maria was. "Eleven. She looks at least fourteen, doesn't she – my great big girl? Sometimes I feel like the little red hen that hatched a little duckling, and kept wondering if it was hers, particularly when it ran into the brook and started swimming by itself," she smiled at the mental image.

Marlene has been on location for nearly three weeks. She had not seen Maria during that time. In the interim, Maria had tried a little experimenting on her hair – a rinse of some sort. She has missed some spots in back, which Marlene discovered. "I wonder what your father will say when he sees it?" Marlene teased, in mock severity. "I'll ask him to comb it more gently than you do," Maria teased back.

A reunion with husband-and-father Rudolph Sieber, a film director abroad, is another reason for ardent anticipation of the trip to Europe. Maria, one suspects, wishes that the three of them could be together in California for the rest of their lives. "I like it, all that I've seen of it."

"We *haven't* seen much of the world, or America, or even California, have we, darling?" Marlene asked her. "The only two cities we've seen in America are New York and Los Angeles. In between, we've seen only railroad stations. We've been to Palm Springs and Arrowhead. But we're going away again without seeing Yosemite, or Del Monte, or San Francisco. Though we *have* seen the sand dunes of Yuma."

Marlene was thirsty; Maria ran to bring her a drink. Marlene took a cigarette; before she could light it, Maria had a match ready for her. Marlene commented on the attentiveness; with amusement, asked the explanation, Maria, it developed, was supposed to learn eight pages of a lesson by heart over the weekend; if Marlene allowed her to remain one more day, Maria could postpone the memorizing a few more hours. (Marlene later acquiesced.) That, Maria thought, might be another reason why she had no acting ambitions; she didn't like to memorize. Except music. She is studying the piano with a teacher recommended to Marlene by a famous concert pianist. And Maria is enjoying it, particularly the playing of "some of Chopin's nocturnes." (As for Marlene, she confessed that she has given up playing.) Another interest of Maria's at the moment is Basil Rathbone, also in the cast of *The Garden of Allah*. She chided her mother with not getting a promised autographed photo from him yet.

The shadows on the dunes were lengthening. The company went into action. Marlene repaired her inconspicuous Technicolor make-up, which had dried in the heat of the afternoon, started again toward the honeymoon tent. This time Boyer was to rush out of the tent, followed by Marlene a few moments later, in search of him. She was to find him on a hillock of sand, gazing moodily toward the East. She was to make a confession to him, then walk away slowly, sorrowfully, through the sand – toward the camera. The scene went perfectly except for the walk toward the camera. The sand slithered underfoot, treacherously. Marlene felt that the walk could be more graceful, even though everyone else was satisfied with the scene. She went through it three times, until she herself was satisfied.

She played one more brief scene, greeting a French officer near the castle ruin, silhouetted against the setting sun. The light was fast fading from the sky as the scene was finished. Marlene went into the small, stuffy dressing-tent on the sand, changed into powder-blue slacks for the ride back to Yuma. Boleslawski decided that the cloud-effect in the sky was just right for one more "dusk" shot. Marlene, with make-up off and clothes changed and her day's work over, said instantly, "I'll be ready in a moment."

That – in desert country, or any other country – is called trouping.

Douglas Fairbanks, Jr., Marlene, Rudolf Sieber, at the Leicester Square Theatre in London for the premiere of Rembrant, *November 6, 1936.*

"Why Dietrich Waited for Donat," by Hettie Grimstead. *Screenland*, February, 1937

"Do you like Robert Donat without his moustache?"

That's the first question when film folks meet in London these days. Certainly Robert looks much younger now and his smile has gained an added frankness very charming, but on the other hand he seems to have lost something of that whimsical debonairness along with the adornment of his upper lip.

He shaved to play with Marlene Dietrich in *Knight Without Armor* because his glamorous fellow-star has a firm objection to acting in passionate love-scenes with a moustache – she says it scratches her face and spoils the proper dramatic effect of her kisses! And handsome, brown-eyed Robert is so intensely grateful to Marlene I'm sure he would promptly shave off all his hair as well if she told him she preferred her screen lovers to be bald.

For behind Robert's appearance in Korda's new film lies an amazing story of comedy and tragedy – never told until now – in which he has had a part far more poignant than any role he could mime before the cameras. Twelve months ago Donat was the first male name in British screenland, the thirty-year-old star on the crest of the wave with his fine portrayal in *The Ghost Goes West*, and producers in London and Hollywood alike bidding eagerly for his services. Irving Thalberg offered him three hundred thousand dollars to play "Romeo" to Norma Shearer's "Juliet" but Robert refused because he wanted to return to the stage again for a time.

So he put on a somber intellectual play with his own money and at the dress-rehearsal he dropped his little make-up mirror and smashed it to fragments. "Pooh! I'm not superstitious!" he laughed; but the piece proved a lamentable failure just the same and standing in the draughty wings one night, Robert caught a chill. He was ill for weeks, finally returning to the studios with a persistent cough. He arranged to film as "Hamlet" but after several postponements, production was shelved. He signed a contract to appear with Sylvia Sidney in her Gaumont-British picture, *Sabotage*, and then failed to appear on the set because his illness had developed into a painful throat trouble accompanied by asthma so that often he had literally to fight for breath. Thinking California sunshine would prove beneficial, he agreed to go to Hollywood and star for Paramount but the doctors warned him he might never survive the long journey – already he was so weak he passed most of his days in bed.

With the mild summer weather, Robert found some relief and thought he might summon sufficient strength to fulfill his long-standing promise to his old friend Alexander Korda, the man who gave him his first chance, to play with Marlene Dietrich in her British film. He attended Marlene's reception party with his throat specially treated with cocaine and sucking medicated lozenges, but his enemy struck again the day he should have enacted his first scene with the lovely star. He was once more lying helpless at his North London home unable to eat or sleep, gasping agonizingly for air.

Regretfully Korda suggested the story of *The Knight Without Armor* be altered for Dietrich to star alone without a leading man, but characteristically definite, Marlene refused to agree. "I know where are plenty of good-looking actors," she said, "but Donat has that necessary something that comes down from the screen to the audience. As soon as he enters a scene you are keenly conscious of him. I want him in my picture. Let us wait a while and see how he progresses."

While King Edward's own physician was attending the stricken Robert, Marlene worked on at the Denham studios making all those scenes of the old-time Russian drama in which the hero did not appear. Daily she telephoned the Donat home, giving sympathetic messages to Robert's gracious, auburn-haired wife Ella, sending him fruit and masses of flowers, sometimes driving over herself to see the actor even though it meant missing certain of the brilliant social entertainments admiring London has been constantly holding in her honor.

Four weeks passed and every scene in which Robert did not play was finished, while he himself was still too sick to leave his home. Again Korda pleaded anxiously with his star and this time she compromised. "He has just begun to try a new treatment and the doctors say it will be another three weeks before they can tell if it is a successful cure. So let us wait just that time and if Donat is not well again be then, we fill find another actor."

Marlene in A Knight Without Armor, *1937.*

Thus production was stopped and Marlene took a holiday, her salary suspended meantime since the pause was her own wish. She shopped and motored in the daytime and appeared at the cinema almost every night. (She adores Mickey Mouse and Popeye the Sailor and her favorite star is Carole Lombard.) Whilst Robert went to a hospital and spent sixteen hours every day shut up in a tiny room, with doors and windows sealed and a strange machine that is the latest wonder of medical science whirring beside his bed. It absorbs all the air and then passes it out again impregnated with secret chemicals so pungent even the nurse who operates it must be masked. But it proved a panacea at last.

When Marlene returned to the studio Robert was there to greet her – "Our Night Without Asthma" as Korda gaily declared. His gratitude to his fellow-star is deep and sincere for he knew how seriously his career would be affected if he had failed the public yet again. Commiserations he shook off with a smile. "Oh, we all have our bad patches in life. They help us to enjoy the good ones." He is glad to feel comparatively strong again, though he is forbidden to smoke and still has to sleep with the machine in his room every night, nor can he go out to parties for at least another three months.

Robert's doctor wouldn't even allow him to go to the dinner given when Mr. and Mrs. Lionel Atwill arrived or the big cocktail party which Basil Rathbone held at the stately Pinewood Club before he returned to New York. The list of his guests reads like the visitors' book at the Brown Derby – Douglas Fairbanks, Jr., Evelyn Laye and Frank Lawton, Frances Marion, Nigel Bruce, Charles Farrell, and Dietrich of course, wearing midnight blue velvet this time and a silver cap. Sally Eilers was there, telling everybody that her son is the most beautiful baby in the world and that she telephones him across the Atlantic three times a week. "I'm sure he recognizes my voice because he always gurgles back."

Also present was Wallace Ford, returned to his homeland because he was actually born here though he went to Canada aged seven. Our national attention to Tea-Time never fails to make him gasp and he nearly swallowed his cigar when he first saw tea being served in a cinema while the picture was in progress. Not to mention Constance Collier and genial Noah Beery and Roland Young, delighted with a new ivory addition for his famous collection of model penguins – he has over a thousand of them at his apartment in New York. The smallest will go inside a thimble while the largest is a ten-foot high effigy of a Polar King bird.

Hettie Grimstead was an English writer. She contributed to numerous Hollywood fan magazines. Beginning in 1950, she began a career as a romance/pulp fiction author. Her first of forty-four novels was *The Journey Home*. Some of her other titles include *Whisper to the Stars*, *The Captured Heart*, *Strangers May Kiss*, *Winds of Desire*, and *Song of Surrender*. *Susan in the Sun*, published in 1977, was her final novel.

"Projections: Marlene Dietrich," by Elizabeth Wilson. *Silver Screen,* September, 1937

Before the arrival of the beautiful Marlene Dietrich, simply dripping with silver fox and blue paradise, on our mundane shores some seven years ago, glamour in the American film industry had reached a new and most depressing low. Even the die-hards among the movie moguls had been forced to break down and admit that talking pictures were here to stay and God help you and Clara Bow. With the advent of the talking picture (remember when there were heated discussions in magazines and columns as to whether they should be called talking pictures or talkies? Oh boy, do I date!) the screen went in for much genteel lifting of teacups and eyebrows in English drawing rooms, in the Lonsdale manner. And it was all so frightfully "la-de-da."

Word got around that the allure girls who had been making an honest living by staring wide-eyed into the camera simply could not cope with a tea situation ("A Spode's a Spode, Clara, not a "Spade"), and, furthermore, could not begin to master the irritating sibilant and the broad "a." They were told to scram to the nearest diction teacher while the producers tore their hair and wildly wired contracts, quite indiscriminately, to the thespians of the New York stage who had been drinking tea and enunciating for years – too many years. The most unattractive people suddenly appeared on the screen. Fat divas from the Metropolitan Opera, scrawny leading ladies from the "Geeuld," and greasy earnest-workers from the Civic Repertory. The place reeked with talent, but not a whiff of glamour. The Escapists (and count me in) can't face life in the home, much less in the cinema, so they gave up movies and wondered whether they should try opium or Richard Halliburton.

And then into this dismal morass of too much Reality one day appeared something too breathlessly beautiful to be of this world, something startlingly arresting in scarlet and silver, with a shimmering scarf floating in the breeze, tuberoses in her hand, and aigrettes in her hat. Marlene Dietrich had arrived from Germany to co-star with Gary Cooper in *Morocco* for Paramount Pictures. And she had the glamour situation well in hand.

Though it has been a number of years now since Marlene in high heels (the Hollywood touch) followed Gary Cooper across the hot sands of the California desert – and fainted from exhaustion because von Sternberg failed to tell her that the scene was over – Marlene still reigns supreme as the most glamorous star in Hollywood. But, why be small about it, she is without a doubt the most glamorous woman in the world today! And Marlene loves it. A luxurious person, with more than her share of feminine vanity, she adores being called glamorous and beautiful. It's a lot of fun, and besides – it's very good business. Nice work, if you can get it.

From her friend, discoverer, and director, Josef von Sternberg, she has learned to look at herself as cold-bloodedly and professionally as if she were a share-holder in Dietrich, Inc. She knows that her acting isn't all it should be. As an actress she knows that she can never hope to compete on the screen with the Helen Hayes, the Claudette Colberts, the Sylvia Sidneys, the Barbara Stanwycks, the Bette Davises, and the Miriam Hopkinses. But as a glamorous personality she stands alone. No one can touch her. She can enter any nightclub or theater in the world and be the most stared at woman in the room. Dietrich, Inc. sells Glamour (preferred and *not* common) – and Dietrich, Inc. has never yet failed to pay juicy dividends.

Marlene goes about the business of being glamorous with charming Old World placidity. Her pictures take forever to finish, because the photography must be just so. She does not care how many "takes" she is asked to make – von Sternberg often made her take as many as thirty of very simple scenes – and she never storms and rages on a set when provoked by the harrowing details of making pictures. It takes nothing less than an earthquake to break up that magnificent poise. But don't get the idea that Marlene is the answer to every director's prayer, and that the line is forming on the left to direct her. Heavens, no. Marlene doesn't shriek, or throw hair brushes, or hurl expletives, but she has her own brand of temperament, which is far more deadly. Mr. Zukor's Glamour Girl Number One when crossed simply sits before her mirror and combs her hair. And there she will calmly sit until the director, the designer, the author, come around to seeing things eye to eye with her. She feels that she knows more about Dietrich, Inc., than they do – and I wouldn't be at all surprised if she didn't.

Marlene relaxes at her Hollywood home, 1937.

Sometimes, however, Marlene will become very feminine and pretend that she is humoring her tormentors. For instance, during the production of *Angel*, her latest Paramount picture, there was quite an argument over hats. At the beginning of every picture she has about forty hats sent out from Lily Dache in New York, and after posing, and more posing from every angle, she selects the ones she wants for the picture. But for a certain scene in *Angel* the director did not like Marlene's selection. "It's terrible," he shouted. "I won't shoot the scene with you in that hat." "What, you don't like my hat?" said Marlene calmly. "Very well. I will try on others for you." So she had Nellie, her faithful hairdresser and fellow conspirator of seven years, spread out all the gorgeous little Lily Daches in her dressing room. "Which one do you wish?" she asked the director, being oh so charmingly feminine and respectful. With great care the director selected one and handed it to her. It was a hat created in a moment of abandon to sit on the very tip of woman's crowning glory, but Marlene the minx, deliberately pulled it down over her forehead. "Please," she said, "you cannot like this hat. See, I look horrid in it. But if you wish, I will wear it."

"No, no," snapped the director hastily, wondering how he could ever have liked anything so impossible. "Here, try this one. It is just what you need for that scene." It was a Lily Dache that simply cried to be pulled down on the right side but sly Marlene casually pulled it down on the left side. "It is not becoming," she said, "but I will wear it if you wish." "Good God, no," shouted the director, "you can't wear that thing. Have you any suggestions? There must be something there." "Yes," said Marlene sweetly. "I like this one. She how well it fits?" I don't have to tell you, dear reader, that Marlene was trying on the very hat that she had decided upon in the first place.

Unlike all other little movie stars who avoid fittings almost as scrupulously as they do interviews and gallery sittings, Marlene simply adores wardrobe fittings. She will stand for hours without complaining while the studio dressmakers take in tucks here and put in pleats there and even after a hard day on the set she will think nothing of standing up half the night while a skirt is reaching perfection. They will tell you in the wardrobe department that Marlene likes fittings so well that she even fits dresses that have been discarded from the picture. That deep Parma violet velvet dress, with shirring down the front to give that soft draped line along the body, cannot possibly be used in the picture, and Dietrich knows it, but she will stand before the long mirror in her dressing room until each little shir is in place. Thanks to Marlene's passionate love for clothes and fittings Gail Patrick and other Paramount featured players, whose dress budgets for their pictures slightly resemble a cafeteria check, often fall heir to these expensive models and are seen whirling around in "B" pictures in "A" clothes. It's an ill wind…

Marlene loves layers and layers of floating chiffon and shimmering scarfs. She adores mad and extravagant hats of glycerined ostrich feathers mounted on tulle, or a riot of aigrettes, or a lovely sweeping paradise that fairly shrieks of Russia before the Revolution. Off the screen she prefers clinging white gowns because they make her feel very pure, very long, and very slim. Like Jean Harlow, whom she greatly admired, Marlene likes white, in clothes, in flowers, and in furnishings.

There is always a lull in Hollywood when the glamorous Marlene takes her annul trip to Europe, either to make a picture in London, or visit her husband in Paris. We who live in Hollywood and take pride in our town have nothing to show the tourist. "That," we say pointing out a $5,000 a week star stuffing her face with liver and onions at the Brown Derby, "that is Miss Cutie Pie." Cousin Lulu's face falls. "That girl with the dyed hair," she gasps loud enough for Miss Cutie Pie to hear, "why she has bad skin, and more ruffles under her eyes than I have on my dress. And look how stringy her hair is, and you would think, wouldn't you, that she'd know enough to wear a skirt when she lunches in a public restaurant instead of those old slacks. I *am* disappointed."

Marlene never lets us down. Other screen personalities may shrink to pygmy reality when seen in the flesh, but not la Dietrich. She appears at every opening night at every preview, at parties and at restaurants, even on shopping sprees, looking as if she had just stepped off the screen with all her glamour intact. When someone told her once that she was just asking for trouble by going to premieres and wading through thousands of fans, she said, "When I was a little girl I used to love seeing the film stars arrive at the theater. I would stand for hours watching for them. Why shouldn't the public have fun? And besides, I don't mind large crowds."

Marlene is five feet six inches and weighs one hundred and twenty-two pounds. She diets moderately and exercises moderately and has the most marvelous stamina of any actress in pictures. She usually rents a house in Beverly Hills while making a picture – this last year she had the Adrienne Ames house – and she revels in luxury. She never goes in for elaborate entertaining. Her home and her dressing room are always crammed with white flowers, especially tuberoses, and she once told an interviewer, "I could die smelling tuberoses." She loathes giving interviews, and never does except under pressure from the studio, because she claims she is always misquoted. She was horrified when she read in a New York newspaper that she had said, "Who is Mae West?"

Miss West never forgave her. She adores jewelry, is always being pursued by jewelry salesmen, and insists upon wearing her own jewelry on the screen. She has all the superstitious of the theater, will scream if you put your hat on the bed, and has the deplorable habit of jotting down telephone numbers on her white wall near the phone.

She, who was destined to become the most glamorous woman in the world was born on December 27, 1904, under the sign of Capricorn. Frau von Losch was living in Berlin at the time and Marlene was her second daughter. The child was christened Mary Magdalene, which in time she shortened to Marlene. Dietrich was adapted for stage purposes. Marlene was nine when war was declared and her father, captain von Losch of the 92nd Infantry Regiment was sent straight to the front. He was killed and buried near Kovno. One day when she was in her teens, she read a poem called "Death and the Fool," by the German poet, Hofmannstahl, and the words sounded so lovely and sad that she began reading them aloud. It was that day that she decided it would be a fine thing to become an actress and recite lovely, sad lines in public. She persuaded her mother to let her go to the Max Reinhardt school, which was connected with his theater, and while enrolled there she wrote two movie scenarios which were promptly rejected by all the movie companies in Berlin. She decided to devote her time entirely to acting in the future.

The first part she was given on the stage was that of the widow in *The Taming of the Shrew*, and that first night behind footlights was the most exciting in her life. Elisabeth Bergner was the star and Marlene at once became a worshipful admirer of hers. When she was eighteen years old she met Rudolf Sieber, a dialogue writer at one of the studios, and a romance followed. They were married in 1923 and two years later little Maria was born. Marlene believes that her mother is responsible for the famous poise she has today. "I was having a dancing lesson," she said, "when I was told by the teacher to dance with a certain boy I did not like. I made a face. My mother saw it and slapped me hard right on my cheek. 'You must not show your feelings, Marlene, it is bad manners,' she said.

The slap made a lasting impression – and I very rarely show my feelings."

Marlene was playing a small part in a Max Reinhardt production on the historic night when the celebrated director, Josef von Sternberg, sat in the audience. The next day she received a message from UFA Studios telling her to report there to discuss a part in *The Blue Angel*, which von Sternberg was to direct, with Emil Jannings as the star. She told von Sternberg at the interview, "I'm terribly sorry, but I am not good in films. I look horrid. I couldn't possibly play an important part in your picture."

"Learn a vulgar song for your test tomorrow," said von Sternberg who pretended not to hear a word she had said.

Marlene sang "You're the Cream in My Coffee" for her test, and nobody liked her or it – except Josef von Sternberg who informed Eric Pommer, the producer, that if Dietrich did not get the role he would go back to America at once. Marlene made the picture for $5,000. Today she gets $200,000 a picture. In 1930 she signed a contract with Paramount with a proviso that if she did not like Hollywood, she could return to Germany. But she liked Hollywood in time. In fact, she likes it so much now that she has decided to become an American citizen and has already taken out citizenship papers.

Of course Maria might have had something to do with this. Little blonde Maria, who one day may be a carbon copy of her famous mother, has gone American in a big way. She loves football and baseball and all American sports, she loves ice cream cones, and amusement parks and movies (her favorite screen hero at the present moment is Ray Milland). She is proud of being an American. Marlene likes to tell of the day in Paris on their last trip over when she and Maria and a friend were having tea at the Café de la Paix. Suddenly, Maria saw several Marines at a nearby table and such a nostalgia for America came over her that Marlene promised to catch the next boat. Maria is the great love of Marlene's life – she is the only one who can make Marlene forget her glamour. She may be a movie queen to the world, but to Maria she is only a fond mother who likes to fuss over her.

Whether or not Marlene has a sense of humor has often been discussed in Hollywood. There are those who will tell you that Marlene is a vain conceited woman who really believes in her glamour. And then there are those who tell you that she laughs at herself when no one is looking. A star not long ago told me that Marlene arrived at dinner one night with a whole batch of her newest photographs and calmly passed them around the dinner table asking everyone if they did not think them lovely. And there was the reporter who told me that he was asked to wait in Miss Dietrich's dressing room one day when she had promised him an interview. A sudden gust of wind blew the door of the adjoining room open and there was Marlene sitting at her dressing table, staring at herself in the mirror. It was quite some time before she remembered the reporter. But I happened to be on the set one day when Marlene was doing a terrific love scene with one of her screen lovers. "You love the woman," shouted the director, "you are mad about her. Give it everything you've got, be very passionate, but be sure and keep the shadow off Miss Dietrich's nose." If there was anyone who laughed longer and louder than I did – it was Marlene. I say the girl's got humor. But why should she be a campus cut-up when she can be the most glamorous woman in the world?

My favorite story on Marlene is the time that a very critical editorial on her appeared in one of the magazines. What the editor didn't call Marlene wasn't really worth calling. A studio employee showed it to her and asked her if she wished to answer it. "No," said Marlene carefully reading it through.

"But aren't you mad?" asked the girl in amazement, having expected to see Dietrich hit the ceiling. "No," said Marlene, "the first line says that I am beautiful and glamorous!"

"Marriage Is Enough!" by Marlene Dietrich. *Hollywood*, September, 1937

[Editor's note: This editorial, written by Dietrich, was in response to an article written by Melvyn Douglas titled "Wives Need Career!" which appeared in the same issue of *Hollywood* magazine.]

In view of my own employment, the fact that I urge marriage as the only career for wives may prove amazing.

My explanation is that my own work is keeping me from the establishment of a home, that I consider the loss a painful one. As one who has chosen a career, and who has followed it for more than ten years, I speak with a certain personal authority.

As it is impossible to roll back those years and make a fresh start, I cannot again select my course. If it were possible, perhaps I should not be Marlene Dietrich, film player.

Melvyn Douglas sets forth that a career gives a wife freedom of thought and of action – domestic and economic independence. He calls this an asset. I list it as one of the most harmful elements.

I have domestic and economic independence – and all that goes with it. So many handicaps! We will consider only one – the rumor that my husband and I are separating, divorcing, which has recurred again only recently, and which brings to my lips a fervent denial. My husband is a good, a fine husband. We are forced to be separated, however, by our diverse employments.

I think this very independence spells disaster. In marriage, small quarrels, if nurtured, become big problems. The woman who has a career on which to depend, whether right or wrong in the argument, says, "I'm going to leave my husband. I can make my own way."

The woman who has no career arbitrates with herself before she flies into trouble. Then she arbitrates with her husband and the little mole hill is smoothed over and marriage goes on its even and smooth course.

Wives who work are proud. "See how I contribute dollars and cents to the family purse," they say.

How wrong they are! How little dollars and cents mean when they are brought with such sacrifice! Perhaps a woman makes a few dollars and a few cents in a week and perhaps, at the same time, she keeps a miserable home, is of no comfort to her husband when he faces tribulations, ignores supplying him with little creature comforts. Once I heard a man say, "My wife boasts of making money, and we are saving it. Small money. But this very morning, after a poor breakfast, I lost my temper at business and I lost many times the amount in a single business deal."

The tactful wife, the wise wife, the self-improving wife has such a big career. American women talk of marriage belittlingly. The time is not consumed, they say. They must have something to do. There is plenty to do and the wife can give up making dollars and cents to stay at home, entertain her husband's business friends, interest them, and in this way make hundreds of dollars for her husband through improving his business chances.

I laugh when I hear the career wife say, "My husband and I, with our different interests, have so many new and refreshing things to talk about."

I laugh because I know men, and because I know they are egoists. I know that men like to have their wives think about them, and baby them, and encourage them, and sympathize with them when things go wrong.

There is no happiness for a husband to listen all through dinner and the evening to things about other men and then awake sleepily in the morning to find that his wife with other interests has forgotten to send out his laundry and he has no clean linen to put on.

In motion pictures, I think I find a certain wish-fulfillment. In such pictures as *Morocco, Desire, Shanghai Express*, and even in *Angel*, I am unemployed and the picture ends happily. In such pictures as *The Blue Angel*, in which I am employed, the picture ends unhappily. And these pictures are true to life.

In *Angel*, Mr. Douglas contends, there is a woman who is married and has no career who has nothing to occupy her hands and her mind so she gets into trouble. This is true. But Mr. Douglas overlooks one thing, and this is the husband, played by Herbert Marshall.

This husband is a very poor one. He is running around in diplomatic circles, to make a joke, and he has no time for his wife. He does not talk of love. He talks of big men and big things. And he is always going away places where he could very easily take his wife, who is a very devoted woman. This he does not do. So, you see, it is the man and not the woman and not the lack of career which is to blame for this painful domestic crisis.

Mr. Douglas says that today we have washing machines and house cleaning devices which give women much free time. But it is not a freedom of the hands a woman needs. It is a freedom of the mind. The thinking wife is always planning and scheming and mentally working to help her husband get ahead and it is here she is of service. One can employ menials to work with the hands. One cannot employ a mind inspired by love to do really helpful things.

Mr. Douglas says, too, that women who have careers are beautiful. I grant that many are. But surface beauty alone is not enough in a wife. What a man wants in a woman is poise, a feeling of restfulness. Beautiful women who work do not have this poise, this inside beauty which is so helpful to the husband.

From experience, I advise the woman of the early twenties to choose between marriage and career. If she chooses career, well and good. She should cling to it. If she chooses marriage, she should devote herself to this. The woman of the early twenties is not developed emotionally, she has no background of experience, what she does not know about life, love, homemaking, masculine psychology and other subjects is really remarkable.

From these years until the golden age of the thirties, she must study, improve, make a home, keep in step with the husband. All these things are a part of the marriage career and cannot be interrupted by these outside interests.

If there are children, she is to be doubly busy. She will find plenty to do, from advising her husband in his business deals, sizing up the people he brings home, making the home attractive to those who do come, properly training the children, to bring calm and be unruffled and consoling when he faces a crisis, which he will do often in his career.

Not only that, but the children need both parents for a balance. No mother is a mother who is away all day.

There are many things of interest to wives other than employment, including sports, such as tennis and golf, study of all kinds, from interior decoration to gardening, the making and developing of friendships. But I am not trying to preach. Each woman must turn to the things she likes best, to the things she feels she ought to do.

I am just saying that Mr. Douglas is wrong when he believes that good women can't make good wives unless they are out of the home most of the time, competing with the husbands, antagonizing them in offices, bossing them in factories, competing with them in professions, and trying to show how intelligent they are.

Men don't want competition – they want love.

"Dietrich Goes Light-Hearted?" by James Reid. *Modern Screen*, December, 1937

It's all very well to speak of Miss Dietrich's legs. They are very beautiful. And they haven't been a detriment to her. Maybe they've even helped her a little bit, but…

"So far, too many of Miss Dietrich's roles have been too much alike. Exotic manners, enchanting smiles, dreamy eyes, and – the legs.

"She has something else, something we are going to show in her next picture: a talent for comedy which the public knows little about."

So said Ernst Lubitsch, firing the first gun in the publicity campaign for *Angel*, starring Marlene Dietrich, directed by Mr. Lubitsch.

And his statement, which was much broader than it was long, started something. A rumor that Marlene was going light-hearted. A suspicion that she was weary of being an Exotic Enigma, sultry in a somber way, or, if you prefer, somber in a sultry way.

Marlene with Melvyn Douglas in Angel, *1937.*

If Marlene, who has gone to so much trouble to change her personality, is now going in for an unexpected change, it is news. News worthy of explanation. And if she isn't wearying of the Exotic Enigma business, that, perhaps, is news.

Whichever is true, she should be willing to answer a few questions to establish the truth. Even if she doesn't have much use for interviews any more.

It is difficult sometimes, but I still can remember when she was not always thus.

I can remember when she was a contradiction of practically everything that she seems to be today.

I can remember when she first arrived from Germany, the new-found discovery of Director Josef von Sternberg, and Paramount gave a huge party to introduce her to the Press.

The Press was more impressed with the party than by the guest of honor.

She was pretty, in a round-faced, wide-eyed way. But wasn't she a bit – er – plump? At least, the frills and ruffles that she wore gave that impression. If she had glamor, it was the glamor of youthful freshness, not of seductive sophistication and poise. She was nervously self-conscious. She was obviously awed by Hollywood. She was almost pathetically eager to be friendly.

The writers, that day, had a vague impression of a pretty German hausfrau, amazed to find herself in this strange new world.

Paramount publicized her as the last word in exoticism, and the writers wondered what Paramount was talking about. Until they saw *Morocco*. Then it was their turn to be amazed.

Here was no pretty hausfrau, self-conscious and timid. Here was a dazzling, daring creature, exotically mysterious, impelling seductive, such an "attractress" that it didn't much matter whether or not she was a great actress.

Writers clamored for interviews. And Marlene, flattered by the clamoring, eagerly granted them. Grateful for friendliness from these strangers who could do her so much good, she was friendly in return.

But the writers, who were willing to admit that their first impression had been wrong, and were prepared to be startled now, came away with amazing stories. Not stories about a woman with an exotic, mysterious past. Not stories about the secrets of attracting men. But stories that painted her as still a hausfrau at heart. Stories that revealed her loneliness in Hollywood, her longing for her husband and her little girl, back in Germany.

The press-agents shuddered. They tried to persuade Marlene not to talk about her Maria. She was supposed to be exotic, unusual, unconventional, unpredictable. Not a typical young mother.

Marlene, at first, did not get the point. Why should anyone expect her to be, off screen, what she was on the screen? She did not comprehend when they told her, "That's Hollywood." Off the screen, she was a mother. Surely, it was understandable that she should want to talk about her baby. She flatly refused to stop.

But the press-agents did not want her to be understandable. That was just the point. It was to her advantage, as far as publicity went, to be a baffling personality, a woman of mystery. To preserve the illusion that it was trying to create, the studio suddenly made it difficult for writers to interview Marlene.

The writers, not suspecting the studio, blared forth that Marlene was "trying to pull a Garbo." She couldn't have liked that. She probably resented it. But she finished what the studio started. She made herself inaccessible.

Soon, she began to acquire a reputation for being elusive off-screen. A reputation for being exotic, unconventional, unpredictable, difficult to understand.

With her husband far away, her constant companion was somber Josef von Sternberg, an association that gave Marlene a reputation for being somber, too. And when her husband, Rudolf Sieber, did visit her, taking time off from his own directorial work at the Paramount Studios in Paris, he and Marlene and von Sternberg made a bafflingly congenial threesome.

Again, for a time, Marlene was seen everywhere with Maurice Chevalier, who had just been divorced and was, supposedly, an eligible romantic. Yet Marlene still denied divorce rumors about herself. Hollywood was properly bewildered.

Then she did the most unexpected thing of all. She had been the one top-notch star who did not mind posing for leg art. Now, suddenly, she sheathed her famous legs, appearing everywhere in public in tailored trousered suits. A startled Press gave her a million dollars' worth of publicity. And she calmly denied that her trouser-wearing was a bit of shrewd showmanship.

"I never do anything to attract attention," she said, without once touching her tongue to her cheek. "I just happen to like the comfort of men's clothes. They are sensible. They never go out of style. They save time. And I like that, because I am lazy."

The spectacle of Hollywood's most feminine star preferring mannish clothes was the clinching proof that Marlene was an exotic.

In one respect, she made no compromise with her publicity. She brought her little girl over from Europe to be with her. She did not attempt to conceal the child, or her love for the child. They were inseparable. Marlene was patently proud of her motherhood.

That one exception to the general impression of Marlene's exoticism only made her the more baffling.

Then, last fall, Ernst Lubitsch, perhaps innocently, started the rumor and the suspicion that we were about to see a "new" Dietrich. A Dietrich less concerned with being exotic. A gayer, light-hearted Dietrich.

And events tended to confirm the rumor, the suspicion.

Marlene, in London, was going out to gay parties, and gay clubs, far more than she ever had in Hollywood. She was in the thick of the social whirl. And her constant escort was no somber sophisticate, but a gay young man named Douglas Fairbanks, Jr.

In America, she had always avoided crowds, remaining a woman withdrawn. In London, she was constantly going places where police reserves had to be called, to control the mobs.

Then, an incident happened during the filming of *Knight Without Armor* in England that indicated an amazing good humor on Marlene's part. In a bathtub scene, she slipped, sprawling naked before the camera crew. They were unspeakably flustered. Not so Marlene. She laughed, picked herself up, climbed back into the tub and went on with the scene.

The she returned to America, and one of the first things she did was to visit the Chief Naturalization Clerk in Los Angeles. All these years, America had had the impression that she was not particularly fond of America. Now, light-heartedly, she was declaring her intention of becoming an American, herself.

Soon afterward, for the first time within recent years, Hollywood was conscious of Marlene's going to parties – big, gay parties.

Then Douglas Fairbanks, Jr. arrived in town. And the London association continued in Hollywood. Once again, Marlene denied divorce rumors.

This time she said, "A woman approached me in London recently, asking what my husband could possibly mean to me when we were separated most of the time. I told her to consider the possibility that love might have something to do with it.

"I consider Mr. Sieber the perfect husband and father. After saying that, it's unnecessary to add that these persistent rumors are very, very wild."

Those who doubted Marlene's interest in comedy, even Lubitsch comedy, saw her start *Angel*, and saw her apparently enjoying it. They were able to see her because the "No Visitors" signs, once a fixture on Dietrich sets, had been taken down and put away. Apparently, the Dietrich temperament had been put away, too.

Hollywood remembered von Sternberg days, the violent disagreements between star and director about how a scene should be filmed, the countless delays while they went over to the side of the set and argued the point in German.

Hollywood remembered, and marveled at the change. For now, Hollywood saw a good-humored star who went through a scene an indefinite number of times, docilely, until the director was satisfied.

I can vouch for that personally. I was there during most of the picture.

Marlene intimated, when the picture started, that she didn't want any interviews. She didn't say, however, that she wouldn't give *one* – if someone waited long enough for her to be in the mood. So I waited. Hopefully, at the beginning; patiently, at the middle; doggedly, near the end. She gave the interview between the next-to-last shot and the last.

This picture is probably in the lightest mood of any that Marlene has ever made. Yet in it, oddly enough, she is not a light woman. She plays the respected wife of a British diplomat. As such, she has a new dignity, rather than a new light-heartedness. She is not an enchantress, but an enchanting woman. There is a difference.

As the diplomat's wife, she isn't supposed to be intentionally exotic. She has to be *un*intentionally so. But that doesn't mean that, between scenes, Marlene was joining the joking and laughter on the set, unconcerned with glamour. She was more concerned than ever before.

Constantly, between takes, she was in front of a mirror, studying herself, looking in her own eyes, smiling at herself, touching up her make-up or her hair, making sure of the effect. Whether she deserved it or not, her incessant mirror-gazing gave her a new nickname on the set: Narcissus Dietrich.

The mirror-gazing was so habitual, by the end of the picture, that even while we were talking, Marlene watched herself in a mirror. I saw her profile, mostly a very alluring profile, but disconcerting to talk to.

I asked her if there was any truth to the rumor that Marlene Dietrich had gone light-hearted.

Marlene patted a lock of hair, and smiled to herself. "Is there such a rumor?" she asked, in faint surprise.

I told her some of the grounds for the impression.

"So?" she asked, pursing her lips. "I do not think it is a rumor that will live long." She smiled. "I hope not, after these years of creating the opposite impression."

"You seriously mean that?"

She nodded, "Seriously, and frankly."

"The fact that you are making a comedy, and apparently enjoying it, indicates no new Dietrich?"

She patted another lock of hair. "I did not want to make a comedy, particularly."

"Don't you have story selection on your pictures?"

"Yes. But what I mean to say is, I wanted to do a picture with Lubitsch. He has genius. It merely happens that Lubitsch specializes in comedy."

She turned toward me, with a half-smile, and asked, "Why do people insist on thinking comedy is something new for me? I have made a comedy before, *Desire*, have they forgotten already?" She returned to mirror-gazing. "That was more comedy, really, than this is. That had no delicate problem of human relationships such as *Angel* has."

"The fact that you have done two comedies isn't a symptom that you want to do more?"

"Two are enough," she said with smiling certainty. "If I did any more, people might actually think I crave comedy, and expect me to do it. I don't want that."

"What do you want?"

"Drama. I feel more at home in it. It is what Mr. von Sternberg trained me to do, and what I have trained myself to do. It is what I like best. And it is more memorable than comedy."

"Do you have any definite plans about your screen future?"

"My next picture will be my last on my present Paramount contract. I don't know yet what it will be, but it will be a drama. There is a rumor that, after that I shall do three pictures for Mr. von Sternberg. The rumor is true. I don't know where they will be made. Perhaps here, perhaps in England. Wherever Mr. von Sternberg says. But that should dispose of all other rumors about what I am going to do on the screen for some time to come."

"*On* the screen, perhaps. But, *off* the screen, what of these rumors that you are going light-hearted? Were the English reporters all wrong? Isn't there anything to the impression of a new, party-going Dietrich?"

"Everyone is gay on vacation," she said, cryptically. "And I had an unexpected vacation in England. I had just finished a long, arduous, picture, *The Garden of Allah*. I had rushed over to England to start *Knight Without Armor*. Robert Donat was ill. The starting date was postponed. I relaxed, for the first time in months. I went out, for the first time in months. London was a great temptation, it was so gay, but the things we like on vacation are not necessarily the things we do when we are working."

She took a cigarette, and as I lighted it, she continued, "It baffles me, this Hollywood impression that I am developing into a demon partygoer. Actually, I have lived a quieter life since my return this time than ever before. I have gone out less. The few times I *have* gone out, the photographers have happened to be there. People have seen my picture in the paper, attending two or three parties. That is the only explanation I can find."

In the mirror, she watched the glowing end of her cigarette, and commented, "It is amusing that anyone should get this party-going impression of me. One thing I like about Hollywood is the quiet life I can live here. There are no distractions. It is possible to sleep eight hours a night. It is possible to concentrate on work.

"I haven't changed, going to England, and returning, and making a comedy with Lubitsch. I'm afraid it would take more than that to change me, at this stage of my career."

I asked, "Do rumors about yourself affect you in any way today?"

"I ignore most of them. What good would it do me to be annoyed? That would not stop them. They are part of the game. You have to put up with them. They go on and on, as long as you are worth mentioning. The only rumor that really annoys me is the one that I encourage the rumors."

A smile appeared in the mirror.

"Mae West and I were in her dressing-room one time, laughing at the story in a newspaper that she and I were having a feud. I said, 'How did such a story ever start?' And Mae said, 'Some poor press-agent was stuck for a story. He had to get something in print to show his boss. So he invented this one. That's how many a story starts.'

"And I know it is so. The publicity department comes out to the set and says, 'Please give us a story, Miss Dietrich.' When I have legitimate news, like word of Mr. Sieber's coming, I give it to them. Usually, I have nothing. They go back empty-handed. To get my name in print, they seem to think it is necessary, they make up some little story.

"I don't understand why they take the trouble. The important thing is what people think of me on the screen. What they read about me in newspapers is not important."

"You sincerely believe that?"

"If I didn't, I might make up the little stories myself."

Remembering the debt that Marlene owed to publicity in her development as a star, I made a mental note. Here is one thing, at least, that Marlene seems to have gone light-hearted about. Publicity.

Light-heartedly, too, she told me her squelching answer to the newest divorce rumors. "My husband is arriving next week. I am going to Europe with him for a holiday, and putting Maria in a school in Switzerland."

"Are you following through on your intention of becoming an American citizen?"

"The future will decide. If my future is here, yes."

"How do you reconcile your tentative plans to become an American, and your sending your daughter to school in Switzerland?"

"It is a French school. I want her to learn French while she is still young. It will be much easier for her. And she is old enough now so that she will not forget how to speak English."

"You are sending her, even though it means separation?"

For a moment, her face was shadowed. For a moment, I glimpsed Marlene Dietrich, the mother, not the glamorous star. "Yes," she answered, almost inaudibly. "I must think of Maria. Not myself."

Just then, Lubitsch called Marlene back to the set.

Her last words to me had not been light-hearted. Far from it. All through the short interview, in fact, she had tried to perish the thought that the rumor of a new Dietrich might be true. Yet, as I watched the "take," the thought would not perish.

One word in the dialogue was difficult for her. She struggled, first, to pronounce it in flawless English. Then she struggled to give the same word the nuance of intonation that Lubitsch wanted. They went through the scene once, twice, five times. Then they tried it again.

And Marlene did not "blow up." She did not become impatient with the English language, Lubitsch or herself. She was blithe about it all.

The picture had been shooting for weeks. Here it was at the very end, and they couldn't seem to get this last scene on film. Everyone's nerves were fraying. Everybody's but Marlene's. In this moment when no one else was light-hearted, Marlene was smiling.

But if she is light-hearted, if she is a new Dietrich, she is not the one to reveal it. Or explain why.

I think she still believes what she used to believe. Keep Them Guessing.

Marlene in Angel, *1937.*

"Oh, Give Me My Bandages and Crutches," by Duncan Underhill. *Hollywood*, December 1939

Marlene in Destry Rides Again, *1939.*

Miss Dietrich, with her celebrated symphonic legs at concert pitch and a new personality from which all the language and anger have departed, is the only legitimate reason the movies have ever thought up for their frequent assertion that the West was won in the saloons.

In *Destry Rides Again*, which is now galloping headlong through the badlands of Universal City, Man-Killer Marlene threatens to erase the memory of all the high-class cinematic torch-songs she has suffered through since she first swam into our national vision as the big gam-and-glamour girl in *The Blue Angel*.

Destry is an action picture, with a capital "A" standing for assault and battery. By its very nature it sets out to be the action picture to end all action pictures; either that or Number One in a cycle that will last from now until the last wad of gum is scraped off the last balcony seat in the last nickelodeon in the land. And Dietrich, formerly the queen of the close-up swoon and the high-class sacrificial scene beginning, "You are wounding me terribly, Nigel," is right down in the saloon sawdust punching and gouging and getting her head banged up against the spittoons.

The casting of Dietrich in a glorified Western is the most flaming stroke of genius since Babe Ruth was converted from a pitcher to a slugger, say many. The métier is such a distinct departure from the dying-swan roles of yesteryear that she is reveling up to her well delineated hips in it. Her maid complains that it is a very blurry three o'clock in the morning when Marlene leaps out of her silken couch and demands that the involved process of hairdressing begin; the gal is that eager.

The character Marlene portrays is one of a fine gallery of barroom cameos. As Frenchy, a gal with long stockings and a short conscience, she is required to mingle with a diveful of roguery and rectitude played by James Stewart, Charles Winninger and Sam Hinds, Brian Donlevy, Mischa Auer, Una Merkel, Billy Gilbert, Allen Jenkins, and Warren Hymer.

The casual mixture of any three of these worthies is enough to guarantee minor detonations within camera range. When the whole twelve, with Dietrich tossed in as the percussion cap, are in juxtaposition, the result is a barrage that echoes up and down the arroyos and canyons of Hollywood and sends an anticipatory shudder through the box-offices of America.

The *Destry* yarn, even after having been subjected to an overhaul job by the topnotch writing squad of Gertrude Purcell, Felix Jackson and Henry Myers, is still the tale about the crooked land baron who also runs a saloon and gambling hall to mask his nefarious deals. It is also, inevitably, the recurring fable about the tarnished vixen with the pliable heartstrings, the fighting fangs of a tigress and the lorelei figger that a wisp of thread imperfectly conceals. But, ah, the difference in 1940, and the difference is Dietrich!

Brian Donlevy, thus far the year's champion hiss-collector for his performance in *Beau Geste*, is plunked down in familiar territory as the big rye-and-roulette magnate who is also the headman of a villainous little band of real estate operators trying to entrap the poor but honest ranchers in the vicinity of Dietrich Gulch.

Donlevy, who is also mayor of the town, proposes to assess a head tax, or cover charge, for the passage of cattle over the lands he and his henchies are seeking to swipe.

Into this nicely fermented situation lopes James Stewart, complete with pallbearer suit, string tie, Princeton drawl and the disarming manner that seems to inquire, "Who hit me, dear?"

This casting coup is not so silly as it may sound, since the Destry of the scenario is a specialized type of ruffian who carries no hardware and depends on moral suasion, boyish charm and the poisonousness of his reputation to quell the desperadoes whom fortune strews in his path.

Jimmy is known throughout the length and breadth of the scenario as Deppity Destry, a self-looking dreamer whose boiling point is 500 degrees Fahrenheit. But the implication is always permitted to lurk in the underbrush that Destry has a spine made

Marlene in Destry Rides Again, *1939.*

by the Bethlehem Steel Company, and that he is a fire-spitting catamount when roused.

Some whimsical gems of dialogue that are permitted to issue from the dreamy-eyed deppity are, "Where are you goin' with that there Winchester, stranger?", "The West has found out that guns don't settle things, pardner. So don't use 'em'."

In another sequence where he is called upon to play pacificator, Jimmy warns a wild-eyed gunslinger, "Watch out, stranger. That ain't popcorn you're playin' with."

The catalogue of mayhem, both fistic and ballistic, that stretches from the first fade-in to the ultimate throbbing climax, calls for some of the gaudiest boffing that ever exposed itself to celluloid.

Mischa Auer, in the character of Boris Callahan, a Cossack cowboy of Irish sympathies, is the springboard of some of the savager slugfests. Auer hangs around Donlevy's clip-joint and has the bad judgement to get involved in a poker game with Frenchy Dietrich.

Dietrich, by devices known to dance-hall floozies through the ages, deprives him not only of his currency and nuggets, but also wins his pants. Boris demurs, in an expansively demure sequence, and Dietrich sets out to take possession of her winnings.

In this she is impeded momentarily by a pretty series of lefts and rights thrown by Una Merkel, playing Mischa's bride. When it came to shooting the fight scenes, Director George Marshall, in the interests of having enough leading ladies to finish the picture with, called in a couple of stunt gals to perform the fisticuffs; this despite the violent protests of Misses Dietrich and Merkel, who insisted they could fight their way out of any saloon ever built, however lacking in practical experience.

Nevertheless, two top-ranking stunt queens – Babe DeFreest and Helen Thurston – were substituted in the early takes, which called for a wrestling, biting, kicking and punching match over the entire 500-foot area of Donlevy's Bar & Grill.

The stunt kids came out of their corners in a low crouch and went flailing at each other as if the Golden Gloves depended on the outcome. Bloodthristy Thurston, impersonating Dietrich, had the reach on Dynamite DeFreest, but DeFreest was a more experienced infighter and mussed up the favorite when she got her head jammed between the brass rail and the mahogany bar.

When Director Marshall called, "Time," both battlers looked as if they had gone up against the business end of a mail train. At the end of the fight, when both contenders were prone on their pretty profiles, Marlene called, "Bring all the champagne from my dressing room and give it those kids!"

The champagne was brought, and the kids, when they had been picked up and pasted together, went for it just as devastatingly as they had gone for each other's throats a quarter of an hour earlier.

By that time the camera set-up was ready for the main bout, between Manslaughter Merkel and Dead End Dietrich. Inspired by the example of the stunt gals, and to add to the general rowdiness of the picnic, they pitched into each other with such gusto that it seemed impossible Marlene would emerge with her assets all in one piece. Nobody among the 500 spectators was enough of a spoil-sport to stop the battle and it ended in a double knockout.

Jimmy Stewart with Marlene in Destry Rides Again, *1939.*

A snapshot of the celebrated Dietrich legs as she staggered away from the carnage would be an item for any collector's book. Bruised, bleeding, dirty, and wrapped in the rags of her specially-made $25-a-pair stockings, they still somehow managed to achieve an air of nobility.

"Bloody," as Allen Jenkins remarked, "but still unbowed."

The Dietrich features, almost frantically animated under a thick layer of come-hither make-up and a superimposed stratum of dirt, sawdust and ingrained cigarette butts from the floor, had not escaped so lightly. A splinter the size of a toothpick was embedded in the celebrated right cheek.

The first words Marlene uttered after getting up after the double count of ten were, "I want a stunt check!"

And the demand stuck. She refused medical attention and the ministrations of her maid and hairdresser until the $35 for hazardous work before the camera was forthcoming. Una Merkel backed up the demand, loudly maintaining that she would picket the studio unless she too were paid for jeopardizing her neck.

As if by magic, the checks appeared. Everybody in the company agreed that the shakedown was justified. But as soon as Marlene and Una got their hands on the money they handed it over to Helen Thurston and Babe DeFreest, the two actual stunt girls who had whipped them up to their fighting frenzy and set the pace for the star bout.

Kid Merkel struck the most telling blow of the whole picture when she registered an uppercut on Warren Hymer's forehead with a bottle in her hand.

According to the plans of the humanitarian gentlemen who manufacture such weapons for the films, the bottle should have dissolved in harmless shreds upon contact with Hymer's formidable head. But the particular breakaway bottle that Una used evidently had not read the script, or else possibly it had become imbued with the spirit of atrocious assault that seemed to pervade the set.

At any rate, when Una let the blow go she put enough follow-through behind it to make it convincing. And the bottle, seeming to get the idea, also stayed in and punched, refusing to disintegrate harmlessly as per plan and inflicting a neat six-inch-stitch cut in Warren's brow.

As soon as he returned from the embroiderer's, the plucky victim of the assault when right back to work as a target for Una, who kept breaking bottles on his head for the rest of the afternoon, always taking careful aim so as to hit the stitches, which served as a bull's-eye.

That sort of thing epitomizes the spirit of Destry and Dietrich and their playmates. The delightful homicidal camaraderie of the thing is summed up in a stray line from the script.

"They slug each other happily."

Duncan Underhill contributed to numerous fan magazines. He wrote the 1928 "World Geography"-themed documentary short film titled, *Benares*. That same year he was the scenarist for the film, *Deliverance*.

"Dietrich Rides Again," by Dorothy Spensley. *Motion Picture*, January, 1940

If you read your daily film news you know that Marlene Dietrich is making her "come-back" to the tune of a reported $75,000 to $100,000 instead of the $250,000-$500,000 that it was rumored she received for her last film, made two years ago in England, and called *Knight Without Armor*. In it was good actor Robert Donat.

Marlene visits her friend, Mae West. on the set of West's film, My Little Chickadee, *1939. Both actresses were filming "come-back" comedic Westerns at Universal Studios.*

You have also read that La Dietrich's come-back piece is a rootin' tootin' Western, directed by that rootin' tootin' expert, George Marshall, whose last stint was conducting that able, but also wooden artist, Charlie McCarthy, through his paces. In this film, *Destry*

Rides Again, Miss Dietrich draws James Stewart, late of *Mr. Smith Goes to Washington*, as co-star.

The rumor around town and at the cocktail lounges is that a new day is dawning for Dietrich. *Prosit, fraulein*! That the glamour stuff which was her frozen asset is being thawed out, and that if Garbo Laughs, Dietrich Thaws. Too long have Dietrich's film appearances been nothing more than a series of plastic poses, beautiful tableaux. In *Destry*, everyone is yapping, you'll see a new Dietrich, a live Dietrich; a Dietrich across whose mobile face flit a hundred emotions.

Well, the rumors were right. I saw a smile, a grin, a grimace, a wink, all in quick succession, romp across that once immobile face. I saw La Dietrich, once the Glamour Girl Par Excellence of Paramount, the high-tide discovery of Director Josef von Sternberg's life, standing on the bar of Kent's "Last Chance" saloon at Universal Studios singing a torchy ballad about "See What the Boys in the Back Room Will Have," black suede skirt studded with rhinestone stars swirling about the famous Dietrich Knees. It looked like the good old days (for Dietrich) of 1931 and *The Blue Angel* which brought her – and von Sternberg – world-wide success. But the man in the director's chair was not the erstwhile Mr. von Sternberg.

Behind this omission is as powerful a story as Hollywood will ever know. Or tell. The saga of von Sternberg and Dietrich will probably be written down among the Great Love Stories of Cinemaland, if anyone ever gets around to writing it. Although they may both deny it, because their thinking is brightly lacquered and modern, and they pride themselves on being sophisticated, the story of the Dietrich –von Sternberg association was the reversal of the famous story of mythology, Pygmalion and Galatea, where a sculptor created a statue and fell in love with it, whereupon the gods gave her life.

Von Sternberg, a cinema sculptor, with a brilliant, experimental mind, fell in love with a woman and made a statue of her by his stylized, slow-tempered direction. It was a style that was splendidly adapted to tales of the underworld, those fine menacing films he made with George Bancroft, and the tragic depths of his first important film, *The Salvation Hunters*; but even the potent allure of Marlene, and she has plenty of it, didn't compensate for the living statue he made of her. Yet, strangely enough, it was von Sternberg who put her through the paces of *The Blue Angel*, the German film which sent her crashing to the front of the movie ranks.

It was this style, slow-making, ponderous as Wagner's *Flying Dutchman*, rococo and ornate, that was used in all Dietrich pictures, even after she left Paramount two-three years ago and walked slowly through Selznick's *Garden of Allah* and Mr. Korda's *Knight Without Armor*. Dietrich, herself, considered this somnambulistic style her medium of expression. It was the first thing that went overboard when La Dietrich met up with Director Marshall. "Make 'em natural. Kick out affectations," are Marlene's twin creeds. So Dietrich snapped out of it. The result on the screen is the kind of real life Dietrich who vows the crew and her co-workers – a lovable, friendly, cosy little woman. Universal wants the same sexy purr, the same cuddlesome quality, that Dietrich emanates on the air – over NBC with Charlie McCarthy, for instance. It is hoping it can capture the super-sex on celluloid.

To this end, and in the business of thawing out Miss Dietrich professionally, Joe Pasternak, production gentleman who is responsible for the long list of Deanna Durbin films, plus newcomer Gloria Jean and *The Underpup*, tossed the All-Time Glamor Girl, Marlene, into a role which made her a bad girl with a good heart, a café gal who died for her man, gave her a knock-down-drag-'em-out fight that took three days to film (both Dietrich and Una Merkel, the warring, refused doubles), doused her with buckets of water as part of the action, and handed her four torchy ballads to sing. It was the neatest antidote-to-stagnation trick of the week. Furthermore, Pasternak calls La Dietrich "Old Lady," the technicians "Cracker-pratt" and Marlene seems to love it.

Whether the last laugh is on the de-glamorizers, no one knows but Marlene. Deep down in her generous Teutonic heart she's probably darned glad to be given a chance to prove that she's not "poison at the box-office" as the Independent Theatre Owners Association once dubbed her in their memorable advertisement.

And, really, this Frenchie role is no departure in characterization for her.

"I have done several parts with action like this in them," she said to me. "Only people forget them. They remember only the older films." She nodded gravely, the rhinestone mist that glittered on her platinum curls shone in agreement when we said that *Destry Rides Again* completed the cycle and brought her once more to *The Blue Angel* and *Morocco*.

These two years of professional waiting have not been kind to Dietrich. They have been filled with the sort of artistic torpor that every actor knows. Because he has prestige to maintain, the unemployed, uncontracted actor cannot go out and rustle up a job for himself. He must let his agent make all the diplomatic gestures. He dies a hundred deaths waiting, day after day, for the right "break," the right role. It has doubtless been that way with Dietrich.

There were rumors about her "million-dollar" radio contract (February, 1938) which never materialized. When she docked from Europe the latter part of November of the same year, she was interviewed by ship reporters on the Capra film that she was to do. There was talk about the George Sand role she was to fill, even to the gents' pants that the famous Frenchwoman wore, and which Dietrich in her own private life had popularized. So far as can be now traced, there were no dotted line signatures, and the whole plan never passed the talking stage.

Dietrich – who has never been accused of being dumb, on the contrary – read Bromfield's *The Rains Came*, saw herself in the "Lady Esketh" role (and we do, too) and immediately suggested the novel to 20th-Fox's Darryl Zanuck, who bought it. It is said there was some talk that Dietrich would have the part. It would have been perfect casting if she had done it. But La Dietrich, sipping her breakfast coffee, read the next morning in a movie column that Myrna Loy has been signed for "Lady Esketh." In one of Hollywood's inexplicable studio moves, Dietrich was brushed aside. It was bad luck for Dietrich, of course. Or so it seemed. She had said "no" to other offers on the strength of what looked like the perfect role for her.

There is always one remedy for Dietrich when things go badly in Hollywood. It is to pack up and go to Europe. Once it was to Berlin that she fled but under the new regime she avoids it, whether because she is "persona non grata," I do not know. She was born Mary Magdalen von Losch, her father was a militarist of the Kaiser's day, and there is no racial stigma attached to a name like hers. With Germany on her "verboten" list, it was to Paris, Cannes, Antibes, that Marlene fled.

In Paris – on the Riviera – Dietrich could salve her wounds with her international café society friends. She could buy a dozen Lily Dache hats, and order Chanel's latest. It didn't matter if she did not make a film, as it did with some film stars. People have always remembered her. I can remember one night at dinner at Sig Rumann's when the first words a college professor asked me were about Marlene Dietrich. It is the same way up and down the professional scale – Dietrich is remembered.

Her popularity with male fans may be because of her femininity. She represents to them the Eternal Woman, all charm, seductiveness; as knowing as "Lilith" or one the "Venusberg" girls. Even actors, wise to all the feminine tricks of their colleagues, thrill to the prospect of working with La Dietrich. Mischa Auer, the comic of *Destry*, is no exception.

Dietrich's feminine following, of course, is probably formed by the fact that as a fashion-setter Marlene has no equal. Even if she makes but one film in three years, her femme fans can look at

Mischa Auer, Jimmy Stewart, and Marlene in Destry Rides Again, *1939.*

the nearest roto section and see a picture of Dietrich, dining with Erich Maria Remarque, or her husband, but wearing the latest fashion get-up. Dietrich – with Countess Dorothy di Frasso, or without her – in the Lady Mendl set or outside it – is always News to the boys with the flashlight bulbs.

Marlene's last sailing to Paris was not her most joyous, and on one score it should have been. She was leaving America for the first time as a full-fledged American citizen, her final citizenship papers having then been granted. What made her less joyous than a Hartz Mountain canary was the government's parting gesture. They deprived her of her jewels, and beautiful and valuable they are, too, until they had her income tax affairs settled to their satisfaction. It was rough going for little Miss New American of 1939.

If I know the Dietrich type, she probably took it very philosophically and didn't lock herself up in the deluxe suite to cry. She must have a good sense of balance and she could see that her lucky star was having temporary astral trouble, and her present predicament was not half bad when it was compared to the post-World War days in Germany where she was an extra girl, a violin student, young wife of an assistant director Rudolph Sieber (she's still married to him, too), young mother of Maria Sieber who is now fourteen.

It was only nine years ago that the Hollywood director Josef von Sternberg went to Berlin to make a film for UFA, signed a well-known actress to play opposite Emil Jannings in *The Blue Angel*. Then, one day, von Sternberg looked through a stack of photographs to select small part players. One face looked up at him and all others were forgotten. "Who is this girl?" von Sternberg asked. "Bring her in." So it was that Rudy Sieber's wife met von Sternberg. The woman who was signed for the lead opposite Jannings never played it. Her salary was paid, but Marlene acted the role. It was the beginning of Dache hats and Chanel gowns for the girl who was born Mary Magdalene, contracted to Mar-lene, in Saxe-Weimar.

If von Sternberg was the master and she the student, the sculptor to her statue, if he was Dietrich's "Svengali," re-shaping her to the fabulous creature she became, she has not forgotten what he has done for her, now that she is out of his orbit. They remain friends, and share an affectionate regard for each other. There is no more conclusive proof of their cordial relations than the fact the Joe has loaned Marlene his Rolls-Royce to ride back and forth from her Beverly Hills Hotel suite to Universal Studios. Her own high-powered chariot was commandeered by the French for war duty when she was in Paris.

Marlene also uses Joe's car for sundry domestic duties, like sending Maria, her buxom daughter whose face is a rounded duplicate of her mother's, and whose hair has the same strawberry brightness, to the dentist. And then shopping. Maria, like the tutored "fraulein" she is, has enormous fun in shopping. Gets ecstatically excited at the idea. Although Maria is listed in a film book as an actress, "1934 *The Scarlet Empress*, Paramount," she has no definite plans about carrying on the Dietrich tradition. Or perhaps – the Sieber tradition, for Marlene's husband is a film producer, who divides his time between Paris, New York, Hollywood.

Although Hollywood may chant about the "new Dietrich" the German actress is still pretty much the same sort that she was back in her Paramount heyday. At least as far as the set worker's reactions are concerned. Her generosities, her good fellowship, melt their hearts and heads to a February slush. However, Dietrich may have disagreed with people with Paramount, it was the front-office, the higher-ups, and not the gaffers, electricians, camera crew, prop men, who felt her wrath. Even now, with her Paramount contract long embalmed, I think she misses that frictional association. Maybe she likes to suffer. I wouldn't know.

She impresses one, in regard to Paramount, as very much like the divorcee who still loves her former husband and says so. She shows it in her actions, her first thoughts. After sitting about on the *Destry* set for three hours, waiting for a few priceless moments with La Dietrich – for she seems to have a distinct aversion to the press – and talking to the crew, I found nothing but praise for the actress. Not one sour note. Finally, I turned to Dietrich and asked her if she couldn't confess to one outstanding flaw in her apparently prefect nature. But even Marlene couldn't. "I even love Paramount," she said, which was, in her mind, the height of magnanimity.

It is easy to see how the set boys and girls could love her. She is so proletarian it hurts. She remembers that they get thirsty, like she does, and orders up a round of coffee for them. Five gallons it was, this day. During the heat wave she sent for several dozen neck ice bags and distributed them to the technical crew. Someone saw the bill. It was $25.00. The publicity department is won to her by her gift of a dozen bottles of champagne, and the fact that she let them toss three buckets of cold water over her to make some extra stills. They sent her a big bouquet of flowers. The whole set reeks of Mutual Admiration and Love.

An important Universal executive has a prop man (Props' wife buys the posey) put a fresh rose-bud in a vase on La Dietrich's dressing-table every morning. The assistant director, Vernon Keays, wears a silver watch-whistle in his lapel. Gift of La Dietrich. It says, "I come – Marlene" and is a smashing victor for the democratic spirit. When Marlene first arrived on the set, Mr. Keays would summon her to the camera by knocking politely on her dressing-room door.

"Why don't you just whistle, Vernon?" suggested the lady of the rose-bud. It developed he couldn't summon up a good whistle, so Dietrich had her jeweler fix that up. The whistle was on hand the next morning. Her sound recorder sports a handsome new watch, gift of the actress. There are those who prophecy that Miss Dietrich, like all of her warm-hearted type, will die poor. If she does, she's had a swell time spending what she earned.

But the adulation gets a little sickening. An extra girl gushes, nasally, when we ask Miss Dietrich for a confession of human error, "I love you, Miss Dietrich!" At that moment, through the loud speaker, a *Rollo* voice announces, "Miss Dietrich, all of us boys up here want to thank you for the coffee." Dietrich lifts her hands like "Brunhilde" at the second act curtain and thanks *them*. Sure, she means it. She loves to give things to people. The announcement swells into applause and the whiskered cowboys on the set, also debtors to Miss Dietrich, cheer. Then the loud speaker breaks in again. There's no mistaking the source of the gratitude. "Miss Dietrich, it's the boys up in the catwalk who are thanking you!"

The scene is impressive. Any minute the Marine Band may march in, playing the "Stars and Stripes Forever."

We wonder what Dietrich – and Helen of Troy – has that millions of women and us don't have. Inspired by the cozy mood of the moment, we drew near enough to ask her. "How do you know that you haven't got it?" answered Dietrich, huskily. "Maybe you just haven't had a chance to show it!"

Between camera set-ups, La Dietrich granted us a few more questions. She was surrounded by a little court of old friends – Hans von Twardowski, her leading man in Germany; the ever-attentive Erich Maria Remarque, author of *All Quiet on the Western Front*, and, latterly, *Flotsom*, who is a pretty consistent set visitor. It developed that Miss Dietrich is happy with her role in *Destry Rides Again* and that, war permitting, she will make a film in Paris for a gentleman named Charrell. It was at this moment that the set was again summoned to work.

I paused for a moment, talking to one of her worshippers. "She's so enthusiastic about this part," he said. "And her husband is here every moment, watching her, ready to help when she asks him for advice. I'll bet he's here right now, somewhere, unnoticed, retiring. Yes, there he is over there!"

The man he pointed to was the smallish, alert, urbanely handsome Erich Maria Remarque. Well, you can't be right all the time.

Dorothy Spensley was a prolific writer in the 1930s and 1940s. She was published in many of the entertainment magazines of the day such as *Movieland*, *Screenland*, and *Movie Magazine*.

"Saint or Devil?" by Elizabeth Wilson. *Screenland*, February, 1940

It was bound to happen. Every time a movie star in Hollywood changes her hair-do, her make-up, her manners, or something, we promptly have a New So-and-So. So when Marlene Dietrich, after a two-year absence, changed her studio recently I braced myself for a deluge of New Dietrichs.

Maybe it's Wishful Thinking, or maybe it's the Easiest Way. I don't know. But anyway, when a Glamour Girl starts a picture at a studio where she has never worked before, and a fresh batch of press agents are turned loose on her, the newspaper columns are quickly filled with all kind of stuff and nonsense about how she has changed – and always for the *better*, of course. (What must she have been!?) When *Destry Rides Again* got into production over on the Universal lot, I began to read endless paragraphs in all the columns about the "New Dietrich," and I must say that the more I read about the "New Dietrich" the bigger nostalgia I had for the "Old Dietrich." The new Dietrich, it seemed, was a regular paragon of virtue, sort of a potpourri of *Pollyanna, Elsie Dinsmore, Lady Bountiful*, and all the people I particularly disliked and distrusted, and hoped never to meet again. After days and days of reading about "Good Deeds" Dietrich in the morning and night editions, I began to long fervently for the old Paramount Dietrich – "Feathers" Dietrich, "Legs" Dietrich, "Narcissus" Dietrich, we used to call her. (That was before she was sainted by Universal.) Well, Universal can have its *Pollyanna the Glad Girl*, I growled, but I'll stick to Marlene the Mirror Girl. She was fun.

I was afraid to meet the new Dietrich, I'm allergic to saccharine, but I have my curiosity, so when the Universal press agents insisted that I come out ("You'll never know it's Dietrich," they said) and get a gander at Marlene-the-New, I took a little something to settle my estomac, and slung a big basket over my arm just in case Marlene started tossing trinkets around a la her publicity. It was the day that Una Merkel and Marlene were doing the famous fight sequence in *Destry*. When I saw the preview of the picture later the audience fairly shrieked their heads off as Una and Marlene tore into each other like a couple of hellions, and believe me, it was plenty exciting right there on the set. While they were waiting to go into their brawl, director George Marshall brought over two hefty dames and said that they would double for them and do all the fighting, except the close-ups. Marlene and Una exchanged glances. Said Marlene, "Una and I will do our own fighting. What do you think we are? Sissies?" And boy, they did!

At the end of the "take" where they roll off the table on top of each other with a loud *kerplunk*, I noticed that both girls rose painfully from the floor and said, simultaneously, with great concern, "Oh, I do hope I didn't hurt you." Bruises and scratches were looked over, and Marlene ran for the iodine with which she daubed Una up good. "You are so frail," she said. "I worry about you."

"See," said the press agent, fairly dancing with glee. "See how Dietrich has changed! Imagine a star worrying about the other fellow's bruises. She's so kind and considerate of everyone. And see how she can *take* it! No griping, no complaining. No time out to cry over skinned elbows. She's a new person entirely! I tell you she's not a Glamour Queen anymore! Why, she's swell!"

Marlene retired to her dressing room to dry out her hair – wait until you see Jimmy Stewart dump a pail of water on her head – and I stopped for a chat with Una, who, and I don't have to tell you that, is one of the best actresses in Hollywood. She too was full of the wonders of Marlene, except that Una is not concerned with whether it's a New Dietrich or an Old Dietrich, on account it is the first time she has ever met any Dietrich. "Her real charm," said Una, "is her complete sophistication. She has Eve written all over her. Someone should make a picture called The Garden of Eden and let Marlene play the part of Eve. The only trouble is that she'd be too clever to eat that apple."

For years, writers have been trying to solve the secret of Dietrich's charm, and I think that Una has hit the nail right on the bean. Marlene's charm is the charm of an Eve. A charm which all women desire but few possess. There isn't a feminine wile that Dietrich doesn't know. Not a trick that she has missed. There's a lot of honesty and goodness there, oh heck, yes – but there is also a lot of naughtiness. She's an extra smart Eve, that one, with more subtle sophistication in her finger-tip than most stars have in their entire anatomy.

My press agent friend was back. "See that girl over there?" he said. "That's her daughter, Maria. She's shot up something awful these last few years. Marlene doesn't try to conceal her, but has her on the set with her nearly every day. See that whistle the assistant director wears around his neck? Dietrich gave it to him. He called her one day and she didn't answer, and he said, "In the future, Miss Dietrich, I'll whistle for you." "All right," said Marlene, "whistle." And the next day she presented him with an expensive whistle, all monogrammed, from the best jewelers. And that fellow over there has a cigarette case she gave him that's a knock-out. He had to watch her words when she was doing her song recordings and so she had an impression of her mouth made in the inside of the case. The hairdressers are crazy about her and the waitresses in the

Marlene with Jimmy Stewart in Destry Rides Again, *1939.*

commissary – she eats right in there with everybody, none of this I-want-to-be-alone-in-my-dressing-room stuff about Marlene – practically shove and push each other down to wait on her. I'm telling you, she's a New Dietrich!"

And I'm telling *you*, my friends, that the press agent is full of soap. There isn't a New Dietrich. It's the same *Old* Dietrich, for which heaven be praised. She hasn't changed a bit. I admit that at first I was a little skeptical. Marlene hasn't made a picture in Hollywood in over two years – not since she mewed about the mystery of the desert and nearly choked herself to death with scarfs in *The Garden of Allah* – and two years off the screen is a long time in the career of a movie star. Also, it is reported that she used to get $150,000 for a picture, and that she made *Destry Rides Again* for $75,000. (If I know Marlene, and I think I do, she would have made *that* picture for nothing, so enchanted was she with the part of "Frenchie," the dance hall dame.) A drop in the exchange, and a drop in the box office, is certainly more than a drop in the bucket to a Glamour Girl. It has a very chastening effect. Yes, I admit. I was a bit wary at first.

Since I watched Marlene and Una scratch and pull and bite on the set that day, I have spent an afternoon with Marlene at her bungalow at the Beverly Hills Hotel, and I take great pleasure in announcing, and definitely, that Marlene hasn't changed. She hasn't any wings, or any halo. Why all this hoopla about the *New* Dietrich she doesn't know. She'll tell you that she's just like she always was, a little good, and a little bad.

Marlene always was the "easiest touch" in Hollywood. I've known her off and on for some seven years now, and with the possible exception of Joan Crawford she has paid more hospital bills and handed out more groceries, rent checks, and winter coats than any star in Hollywood. ("She'll die a pauper," her friends have said for years.) And I supposed with the exception of Barbara Stanwyck and Mae West, she has donated more watches, cigarette cases, bill folders, and bracelets to the people who work with her than any star in Hollywood. She gets a big kick out of giving expensive presents to people who can't afford expensive presents. She adores sending flowers to people to whom an orchid is an event. But she gets mad when you write about it. "I don't want to be known as Good Deeds Dietrich," she'll complain. "I do not give presents for the publicity." So she was always killing copy written by the publicity boys at Paramount. And that's how the rumor started that she was fussy, and that's how she got a bad name with the press.

After she left Paramount an annoyed writer fixed her up good with one of the weekly magazines in an article which described at length how the waitresses at the studio hated Dietrich. When the article appeared in print, Marlene felt all cut up in little pieces. But not for long – immediately she received letters from Paramount waitresses resenting the article and begging her to come back. One day recently she did "come back." She had to confer with a producer at Paramount in regard to a re-make of *Applause* (wouldn't she be wonderful in the old Helen Morgan role?) and instead of hiding away in a neighboring restaurant she insisted upon lunching right there in the commissary. When Dietrich entered the waitresses dropped their chicken sandwiches and Coca-Colas helter-skelter and with one accord gave her an ovation that brought tears to her eyes.

Despite a lot of spiteful talk to the contrary, Marlene has never made any effort to hide her fast-growing daughter, who fairly worships her. The first thing she did the afternoon I spent with her was to show me Maria's new pictures – Maria on horseback in a wild west outfit. "It's the *Destry* influence," says Marlene. "She is as crazy about the picture as I am. She rides beautifully. Maria, I suppose, is the only person who is enjoying the war in Europe. She was at school in Switzerland, but when the war broke out I had her brought to America at once. She loves it here."

Marlene has a "feeling" that the war will be over by Spring. Her hunches rarely fail her. She gets very excited when she talks about the war. She is very proud of the fact that she voted for the first time in the recent California elections. She knows much more about the Constitution and American history than you and I do, so don't tackle her on that subject. She thinks her meeting with producer Pasternak was quite the nicest meeting with any producer she has ever had. Mr. Pasternak, the most important producer in Hollywood at present, isn't the least concerned with his importance. He met Marlene when she got off the train in Pasadena, and as soon as he had her in the car, he said, "Can you roll cigarettes? I don't suppose you can. I brought you the makings. You might just as well try rolling one now. You'll have to do it in your new picture and the practice won't hurt you." From Pasadena to Beverly Hills they rolled cigarettes.

The New Dietrich, it seems, is supposed to be so unselfish, so interested in helping other people. There's nothing new about that. She's been helping young and ambitious actors and actresses get a foothold for years. She has started many of them off by giving them encouragement – and speaking to a director – when they needed it. At present, she is interested in Virginia Gilmore who is under contract to Sam Goldwyn. Virginia is being coached by Hans von Twardoski, a friend of Marlene's, who used to appear in German pictures with her before she came to America, and both Hans and Marlene are firmly convinced the girl has great talent. When a columnist came out recently with a headline that Virginia Gilmore's legs were far more gorgeous then Marlene's poor Virginia had a fit. "What will Marlene say?" she moaned. But she didn't have to worry about Marlene. As far as she is concerned every woman in Hollywood can have gorgeous legs and she won't lose a night's sleep. But Marlene never misses a chance to give you an eyeful of those priceless gams. When she talks with you she immediately draws them up in the chair. If she is on the set she will sit on a table, when possible, and cross them. Marlene likes those legs. She still likes her mirror, too, I was delighted to discover. She puts on her own makeup at the studio, and before every "take" spends a goodly time before her mirror. She is about the most meticulous actress I have ever known. If you don't like her, you can call it conceit.

She is still a devout Clark Gable fan, which is all right with me, and she still scribbles when she talks over the phone. She still adores well-tailored suits, dresses in them almost entirely, and when she gets a hat she likes she has the same model made up in a dozen or more colors. She still likes to cook and spent hours on the set of *Destry Rides Again* swapping recipes with Mischa Auer for Russian dishes. She still likes to bake cakes and bring them in to the crew on her pictures, and still gets annoyed when she reads that she is a good cook. She still goes dancing of an evening with one of Hollywood's attractive males – at present, it's Jimmy Stewart.

A lot of things have changed in the last two years – but not Dietrich. A *New* Marlene Dietrich, my eye!

Jimmy Stewart with Marlene in Destry Rides Again, *1939.*

"Dietrich Lure," by Irving Wallace. *Modern Screen*, March, 1940

Dietrich was angry.

It wasn't ordinary anger. She didn't throw anything, not even a tantrum. It was like Vesuvius, holding back its rage, seething. It began slowly, Dietrich's anger did, until her eyes sparked and her slender body stiffened.

She puffed her imported cigarette once, twice, quickly, and from behind the smoke screen, let blast, "You have come here to write a story about how Dietrich has changed. You think, just because I played a tough night-club girl in *Destry Rides Again*, and because I threw myself into the part and worked hard – that now I am different. Well, I am sick of the nonsense. I'm going to give you something to write – the *truth*!"

She leaned forward. Strands of hair fell over her eyes. She didn't mind. With great intensity, she spoke, "I have not changed. Not one single bit! Even if I wanted to, I wouldn't know how. I'm not enough the actress for that. I have not departed from my old roles. My characterization in *Destry* wasn't so startling and unusual as it's been played up to be. Merely, a throwback to my German film, *The Blue Angel*.

"I will be utterly frank with you. Wherever I go, whatever magazine I pick up to read, I learn, 'Dietrich is now different. A new person.' And then I pinch myself, and find I am exactly the same as always, physically and mentally. I think I should know better than anyone alive that I haven't changed. And believe me, I have told writers that, and critics, everyone – but no, they decide that since I sang and brawled in *Destry*, I must be a new Dietrich. They don't print what I really say. They need an angle for their stories, so they write about the transformed Dietrich."

"Okay," I say. "You haven't changed a bit. But can you account for this – that visitors to your set, during the making of *Destry*, reported you were friendlier than ever, less temperamental and were trying harder? How come?"

Marlene crushed out her cigarette. "Oh no, no, that's not so. In all the pictures I've made, I've always been the same. Can't people understand one thing – that I am human, that I have good days and bad days? I admit, in the past, there were times when I knew I didn't have good pictures, and I was in a poor temper. When you're disturbed, you can't wear a joking mask. At least I never could. But when I worked in *Destry*, I liked the script. I knew it was a good show. It put me in a fine humor, and I felt like laughing and talking. Do you understand?"

Marlene Dietrich paused, came up for air, and then sank back on the sofa with a sigh. I sat a trifle paralyzed and a little jarred. All publicity and gossip, in wake of the sexsational *Destry* convinced me that a new Dietrich was being born – a Dietrich who, inspired by her bawdy portrait of "Frenchy" and her own recent American citizenship, had acquired the star-spangled manner – sans make-up, accent, slink and continental mystery.

Ten minutes earlier, I had walked into the living room of her bungalow, situated in the rear of the Beverly Hills Hotel, certain I would find a Dietrich who had shed her glamour, and who was about as mysterious and exotic as your Aunt Sadie.

I was early for the interview. I studied her room. It was bright afternoon, and the sun sent dusky shafts down on an end-table where lay an open German language book and an astrology guide. On the mantelpiece was a cheap two-bit copy of Steinbeck's *Pastures of Heaven*, and bookmarked in the center, Hemingway's *Fifth Column and Other Stories*. And then Dietrich came into the room.

She didn't have much make-up on, and her copper-colored hair was mussed. She wore wrinkled brown suede trousers topped by a while silk blouse and a yellow sleeveless suede jacket. And I am here to report to all citizens and patriots, that Marlene Dietrich looked like an improved carbon of Venus De Milo. I decided on the spot that she was the only human on earth who could really look glamorous without make-up.

She was the same Dietrich who had come to Hollywood a decade ago for *Morocco*, and taught Americans the true meaning

Marlene with Jimmy Stewart in Destry Rides Again, *1939.*

of glamour. I knew the lady hadn't changed, and that all the inky-fingered lads were hoaxing the public.

Yes, slowly I began to understand, because Marlene was speaking in such throaty and energetic defense of herself, and with such conviction, I began to see for the first time that maybe – well – maybe everyone had her wrong. That sounds ordinary. And a trifle banal. But it answers a lot of items about Marlene.

I inquired about her future. "I am signed for two more pictures at Universal," she explained. "I'll take any roles they give me, from a countess to a scrub-woman, provided the stories are good. Despite what others say, I have no set ideas on the parts I desire to play. Most other actresses, I know, do possess firm ideas. But I'm not built that way."

She brushed the hair from her eye, and smiled. "Joe Pasternak, my producer at Universal, is a charming man. I trust him implicitly because he knows what he is doing. He has, more than anyone I have ever met, an instinct for the right thing. I want to cooperate. That is the only way to make a movie. You have to work with your producer, director and fellow actors. I know this. You can't succeed alone. Some try. But they usually fail. A person, alone, cannot acquire perspective."

I mumbled some question concerning her present ambitions. I asked, "Now that your latest show is box office, and you're on top, do you have any special ambition?"

Her reply was trigger-quick. "I have no ambition at all. No goal. I don't want to sound dull, but that's the way it is. No one has ever bothered to ask me before. And now that you have, this is my answer – Never in my entire life have I planned a single thing ahead. I wouldn't want my life that way, always fighting toward something. I never even desired to be famous. Never. When I landed in pictures, I wanted good parts. That's all. I've gone with the current, flexibly, without rigid aims in mind. This is not the *new* Dietrich talking. This is just the *real* Dietrich."

She paused, nibbled on her cigarette holder and said, "However, I recall there was one thing I did want, achingly, for nine long years. To be an American citizen. And that came true recently. I feel proud to be an American, at last. But frankly, I did not feel safe. And I still don't. One can't shut the European war, and the sorrow over there out of one's mind. It's all too big, too inclusive. Being an American doesn't make me feel that now at last I belong. I cannot feel safe when people everywhere are suffering, and the sensitive are weighed with moral worry. Many of my friends are in France and in Germany. It pains me deeply to see them suffer."

The phone rang. It was a good punctuation point. Someone was calling Marlene for a date. She replied in German that she already had an engagement for the evening. She argued over the phone.

And as all this went on, I sank back on the sofa, lit my briar, watched Dietrich curled in the armchair across the room and reflected on what a long way that strange German girl had come.

As I heard her voice, and her husky laugh, there was a drumming in my ears and the years were rolling back. She was born in Weimar, when Germany had a Kaiser, in 1904 and her name, at first, was Mary Magdalene von Losch. This later became Marlene by combining the first part of her first name and the latter part of her middle name.

Her father, a Prussian lieutenant, was killed on the Russian front in 1915. In remembering this, I realized, suddenly, why Marlene had been so disturbed by the European situation when we'd discussed it.

Her entire dramatic training had been obtained in Berlin, after the war, at Max Reinhardt's school. She toiled as an extra in German UFA films to get money for that school.

As an extra, she also got her break. She was one of the hundreds in a mob scene. A husky, blonde, assistant director named Rudolf Sieber spotted her, extracted her from the mob, handed her a lorgnette and told her to play a bit. That lorgnette changed Marlene's life. The glass reflected a spot of light on the camera lens. Technicians forgot to take this out. When the picture was shown, the reflection drew attention to Marlene's natural beauty – and she was on her way. A few months later, she married handsome Mr. Sieber. In 1925, they had a girl, christened Maria.

But now, across the room, Marlene had placed the receiver on the telephone hook and was coming back to the sofa. I dismissed my thoughts of the long-ago and returned to the delightful reality of our conversation.

I decided to ask Marlene a provocative question. I was probing for a hidden chapter in her life, so I inquired, "What person taught you the most about to act and how to live?"

Her answer came sharp and certain. "Josef von Sternberg." Then, without pausing, "He was the only person who ever taught me anything. He taught me all I know. Absolutely all – mainly how to produce and transmit my real self. I owe no human being more. I'll tell you a secret. I didn't originally come to Hollywood because it was fascinating. Berlin and Paris were as attractive. I came to Hollywood because Josef von Sternberg wanted me to. He sent for me to come. If he had been in Australia, believe me, I would have gone to Australia!"

She reclined on the sofa, silent – and I tried, in some psychic way, to imagine what she was recalling. What had the magic name – von Sternberg – conjured up? Maybe she was remembering the night she was a guest star at the Berliner Theatre, and von Sternberg, the mighty-mite, saw her, went backstage. He was planning a picture to be entitled *The Blue Angel*. He wanted a woman with beautiful legs to play opposite Emil Jannings. He signed Marlene Dietrich. In 1931, the Dietrich thighs, torso and talent were on display in *The Blue Angel*. It was a sensation. Von Sternberg went to the United States. He brought Marlene with him. He worked hard with her. Transformed her from a frail, awkward girl, touched with beauty, to a suave, full-grown woman. For twelve hours a day he hammered her, playing Svengali to her Trilby, forcing her to do single "takes" more than a dozen times over.

Sitting with Marlene, I remembered that von Sternberg was the only man she ever permitted to correct her in public. And he, at times, was brutal in his frankness. But it was under him that she earned $200,000 for making *Garden of Allah*. A fabulous and record sum.

Today, the two men who found her, nursed her to success, are down. Her husband, Sieber, is unemployed and in New York. Von Sternberg, her teacher, dwells in the valley, above Hollywood, obscure. Marlene Dietrich alone, ahead of them both, has come back today to a new fame, a brighter future and many tomorrows.

I asked her about her daughter, Maria.

"She's fifteen now," said Marlene. "I have no plans for her future. I couldn't make any if I wanted to, because she's utterly American, so independent." Marlene went to the piano, took down a picture of Maria on a bicycle. "Look, here she is. A pretty child, don't you think? But I've had so much trouble with her. That's the way with a child, I suppose. From the day of her birth, illness, kidnapping – worry, worry, worry. That's life."

Our conversation jumped from topic to topic, like a busy Mexican bean. We discussed, with detachment, Marlene's underpinnings. She said, "Frankly, I have never exploited my legs. When a part required I show my legs, I did. Never for any other reason. They have not helped or hindered me. But I suppose nice legs are a good thing."

It was getting late. And there was one more thing. In my pocket, on a slip of paper, was the report of a prominent movieland psychologist who had studied Marlene Dietrich's life. I had asked him for some "inside dope" on what made Marlene tick, and he had given it to me. Now, with Dietrich relaxed, I fished into my pocket, took out the slip, told her what I had, and then read it to her. Here is what I read –

"Miss Dietrich is psychologically interesting. Her early ambition to become a violinist was thwarted by an accident. But she wanted to become famous, so she turned to acting. To gain ease, she began staging situations in her private life. Do you know why Dietrich wears men's clothes? To hide an inferiority complex fostered by a girlhood of hardships and privations. Do you know why

Dietrich appears in night clubs with several escorts? It is an inner expression of her yearning for security."

I stopped reading. Glanced at Dietrich. Her face was an exclamation point. If she had been fed bombs for lunch, she couldn't have been nearer blowing up.

"It's wrong, all wrong!" she exploded. "That psychologist is as inaccurate as everyone else about me. For instance, that nonsense he writes about men's clothes hiding my so-called inferiority complex – dear me! Listen, I wear trousers and slacks and shirts because I find them more comfortable than anything else. And for no other psychological reason.

"And furthermore, am I the only woman ever to go out to night clubs with several escorts? Was that to hide my inner yearning for security? How silly! Why, I have never, never had a moment's desire for security. I think security is stale and awful. An artist, presuming that I am one, has too much imagination to worry about security. Why, if I had ever desired security, I wouldn't have become an actress. I'd have taken some other job, a steady, certain job, and worked until I was sixty, and then lived on the savings until I died. But, God, that's not the life I've lived or desired!"

I was on my feet. I had asked a million questions. There was still time for one more. "If you had it all to do over again, Marlene, what mistakes would you avoid?"

Her reply came clear. "None. I would do exactly the same thing over again. I would take the very same risks, the same crazy chances, the same blows. Because I don't believe in playing safe. And I'm not confessing this for publicity, but because I'm entirely sincere."

We were near the door. I stood across from her, and I looked into her eyes, briefly. They were deep blue – and honest.

"Thanks, Marlene," I said. "You were swell."

"I just had to get it all off my chest," she said.

I walked away. I was singing, not out loud, but in my head. I had seen the real Dietrich. And I'm here to shout it to the world. She's okay. A right guy. And she's going to be around a long, long time!

Irving Wallace (1916-1990) began selling stories to magazines when he was fifteen years old. He wrote fiction and non-fiction for numerous publications, including movie fan magazines. Wallace published more than a dozen non-fiction books, and many best-selling novels including *The Chapman Report*, *The Prize*, *The Man*, *The Plot*, and *The Fan Club*, among others. He wrote more than twenty-five screenplays and dramatic television episodes.

"Dietrich and Seven Sinners," by Nord Riley. *Hollywood,* November, 1940

Marlene in Seven Sinners, *1940.*

Universal's flicker, *Seven Sinners,* has some fetching moments all right. There is one right off that is calculated to make a shambles of human respiration and pulse. In it we see the extremely toothsome Miss Marlene Dietrich, slinking into the cabin of Albert Dekker. Dekker, a ship's doctor, has been examining the crew for East Indian diseases. He is tired and somewhat boiled, being by habit a somber rumpot in the film.

"Strip to the waist!" he bawls, not bothering to look up to see who it is.

The lady shudders some, but begins to peel off her clothes as directed. For a while the scene has a nice air of Gypsy Rose Lee at work. Just a button before the Hays office can let out a howl and raise its axe, Miss Dietrich's strip-tease is halted. It is a pretty interesting scene if you remember Miss Dietrich.

There are plenty of others in this sultry drama. For instance, we see Miss Dietrich shooting a very classy game of pool and picking up easy dough betting on her shots. Mischa Auer, the pencil-shaped Russian, and Miss Dietrich wriggle La Conga and at other times Miss Dietrich lets go with four songs in her hair-raising voice. Broderick Crawford, playing the part of a muscular party with a temper like a blitzkrieg, disembowels two cafes in his wild wrath. There is a practice "black-out" in which a magician of dubious morals pilfers a populace of its valuables. Besides all these catchy episodes there is a new dame that will knock your eye out, she is that nifty. She is Anna Lee, fresh from England, and prettier than a rose with dew on it. And, as if that weren't enough, John Wayne, who fast is becoming female America's favorite adrenalin, is to be seen, gotten up as a naval officer.

Lest you be misled, as many have been, we will put you wise to a little something. The name, *Seven Sinners*, doesn't mean that the picture is about seven miscreants; it merely refers to a café of that name on the imaginary island of Bomi-Komba. Writers Tugend, Fodor and Vodnoi, invented Bomi-Komba for their script. Nevertheless, it bears a certain similarity to our island of Guam in the south Pacific. Bomi-Komba is replete with a United States Navy base, brown natives and a tropical mien.

"It is not a good-woman role, thank goodness!" says Miss Dietrich, discussing her part. That "thank goodness!" means more than meets the eye. "Good-woman" roles almost finished Miss Dietrich's career as an actress. She was rescued just in time by Universal's champ producer, Joseph Pasternak, affectionately known as Uncle Joe. He ran a cagey optic over Miss Dietrich's past pictures, discovering that so long as she functioned as a disreputable lady, as she did in *Morocco* and *The Blue Angel*, she wowed the gentry, when she went respectable in her roles, gloom settled on the box office. Uncle Joe remedied all that by casting her as Frenchy in *Destry Rides Again*.

"This part is a little like Frenchy," Miss Dietrich explains, which means *Seven Sinners* has been cooked up according to Uncle Joe's favorite recipe for his blond gold mine.

As Bijou Blanche, Miss Dietrich plays a pretty tainted tomato. She seems to have a good heart, but she is all the time being deported from a series of islands in the East Indies group. Bijou is low and lovable – too lovable for insular tranquility. The flicker starts out with Miss Dietrich being deported by the Dutch authorities. Being given the bum's rush at the same time is a magician with a flair for kleptomania, named Sasha (Mischa Auer), and a stalwart American ex-gob named Little Ned (Broderick Crawford). On board the *S.S. Malacca*, Bijou meets Dr. Martin (Albert Dekker), who proposes marriage, and Dorothy Henderson (Anna Lee), who snubs her. Dorothy's father is the governor of Bomi-Komba, the American island on which all these characters, except Dekker, land. There Lieutenant Bruce Whitney (John Wayne) falls for Bijou. This makes Dorothy Henderson sore, because she, too, loves Lt. Whitney. She complains of Bijou to her father, the governor. He bawls out Bijou for swiping Lt. Whitney from the Navy, for Lt. Whitney has resigned his commission to marry Bijou. But Bijou sticks to her guns, refusing to change her mind. Then Little Ned, true to the dear old Navy, gives her a dressing-down for ruining Lt. Whitney's career. Bijou almost passes out trying to make up her mind. She decides to give up Lt. Whitney and starts a brawl in the Seven Sinner's Café to get herself deported. The last shot is of Bijou disappearing on the *S.S. Malacca*, presumably with designs on Dr. Martin. Lt. Whitney goes back to the Navy.

This plot antedates the Stone Age by some years and has been repeated to the joy of audiences ever since. So have most plots. What counts is the garnishing. Little things like Miss Dietrich playing pool.

Before *Seven Sinners* got under way, she wasn't much of a hand with a pool cue, but the lady is pretty artful with the tapered stick right now, because she has been practicing steadily for the pool-shooting scenes in which she whips the U.S. Navy at its favorite sport.

"I will," states Miss Dietrich in the midst of a number of gobs, "hit the seven-ball (the seven is blocked) and put the four-ball in that corner – and I will *bet*!"

"Two bits!" says a gob.

"Buck!" says another.

"Two bucks!"

Miss Dietrich smiles craftily. "Such easy money." She addresses the cue ball and lets fly. The ball caroms off the cushion, smacks the seven-ball, bounces off that and knocks the four-ball into the corner pocket as predicted. It is plenty hot shooting for a lady and your correspondent would very much like to take her down to Shorty's Billiard Parlor on the corner and lay a few wagers on her himself.

Frank Loesser and Frederick Hollander, who composed the songs for *Destry Rides Again*, have cooked up three brand new ones for *Seven Sinners*. Miss Dietrich's uncommon voice will deliver "I've Been in Love Before," "I Fall Overboard," and "The Man's in the Navy."

"My favorite leading man?" said Miss Dietrich, repeating our question. She rolled her eyes. "There is only one – Clark Gable." This is from a lady who has been heavily wooed by Gary Cooper, Charles Boyer, Robert Donat, and Jimmy Stewart. But it was expressed before the lady had engaged in any torrid scenes with John Wayne. She had then only met him at her champagne bust that traditionally celebrates the start of one her pictures. Tay Garnett, the director, was there, Joseph Pasternak, Wayne and Rudolph Mate, cameraman.

Mr. Wayne is likely to grow on Miss Dietrich, for Mr. Wayne has been growing outrageously fast as a young man who can harry the feminine pulse. It has not been long since this John Morrison, of Iowa, was spotted by director Raoul Walsh. Walsh took one gander at Mr. Wayne's walk and was so impressed by its ambulatory beauty he hung around a street corner for two hours just to get another glimpse of Mr. Wayne in stride. Mr. Wayne did considerable walking in *Stagecoach*, and managed to stroll from there into a good many leading man roles. Right now Mr. Wayne is so busy that he is harder to get for picture roles than wimmin at Little America. Give Mr. Wayne a chance and he may push Mr. Gable out of first place in the Dietrich league.

As Dorothy Henderson, the governor's dotter, Anna Lee gets her first crack at American cinema. The role of Dorothy Henderson isn't exactly lovable, for she is the gal who conspires to have Bijou deported in order to keep Lt. Whitney for herself. Actually, Anna Lee looks about as villainous as a Ming vase. But she is a sturdy sportswoman, and an exceptionally good shot. Once Miss Lee was out hunting in Egypt and had just drawn a bead on a jackal. She was about to rub out the beast when it stood up and became an Englishman named Robert Stevenson. Miss Lee married him.

When Mr. Stevenson came to America to direct *Tom Brown's School Days*, Miss Lee followed with their two-year-old progeny expecting to have a nice holiday in Hollywood. But Mr. Pasternak met her, signed her and cast her in *Seven Sinners*.

Miss Dietrich had a strong hand in getting Miss Lee her part. It happened when Miss Dietrich heard that Miss Lee was testing for the role and that Miss Lee was having a case of the jitters. Miss Dietrich stayed over a whole evening on the lot to help the young lady. She played opposite Miss Lee in the test, calmed her with advice. The result was that Miss Lee breezed through the test and into the part.

Some of the early scenes in *Seven Sinners* were shot during harrowing heat and some carnage resulted. The carnage hit Tay Garnett, the director, the hardest. Mr. Garnett was a surprising casualty, too, because he has been in hot places before. In fact, he was particularly qualified to handle *Seven Sinners* because he had sailed his 107-foot yawl, *Athene*, through the very South Seas he was filming. As a result, Mr. Garnett selected the native types for the flicker, even became an authority on what sort of merchandise should go into the native shops. It is a sad commentary on California climate that the dried Los Angeles river bottom should slap down a veteran like Mr. Garnett.

It happened whilst he was fixing to screen a street and waterfront scene. A full-fledged steamer sat on the dry sand, belching black smoke. A couple hundred coolies, assorted sepia-hued offspring, long-horned oxen, goats, chickens and naval officers roamed the muddy street. It was 100 degrees in the shade. Mr. Garnett, a stickler for long rehearsals, toiled stripped to the waist, but it didn't help. With a dismal exhalation, Mr. Garnett collapsed. Miss Dietrich, looking as cool as a stein of German beer, rushed to his side with a handkerchief filled with ice. With the ice on his brow and Miss Dietrich's cluckings in his ear, Mr. Garnett came around and finished the picture which had very nearly finished him.

Thomas "Nord" Riley (1914-2001) wrote for numerous periodicals and magazines including *Colliers*, *Saturday Evening Post*, *Esquire*, and *Cosmopolitan*, among others. He joined the U.S. Army after Japan bombed Pearl Harbor in December, 1941. He wrote numerous television program episodes during the 1950s including, *Schlitz Playhouse*, *My Favorite Husband*, *Celebrity Playhouse*, *General Electric Theatre*, and *The Many Loves of Dobie Gillis*. In the 1960s, his play, *The Armored Dove*, toured the U.S. His final major published work was *Nord Riley's Spain* (1989), a collection of humorous columns about the twenty years he spent as an expatriate in Spain.

"The Lady Is a Tramp," by Duncan Underhill. *Hollywood*, May, 1941

Marlene in The Flame of New Orleans, *1941.*

With loving tenderness, the studio rajahs bore the new Dietrich script into Marlene's dressing room, gleams of fond anticipation in their eyes. *The Flame of New Orleans* was the title and the author had striven for months to blend into it all the basic ingredients of Dietrich, *Destry* and *Seven Sinners*. Love, double-crossing, a suggestion of pleasant bawdiness and an action-charged background were all present.

Miss Dietrich flipped the pages idly, her brows elevated in a manner suggesting faint distaste.

"What have we here?" she inquired.

"A story," the spokesman assured her. "What a story! Ol' Man Ribber! Kidnapping! Raw passion in an opera box. Magnolia! Soft lights, sweet music…"

"The idea evades me," Miss Dietrich sighed. "There are no songs for me to sing. There are no trousers for me to wear. Without these *The Flame of New Orleans* is extinguished at the beginning."

So the boys went to work on her, and a masterful job of convincing they did. The first inducement was that the director they were prepared to provide for her was none other than Rene Clair, the French wonder boy, an old friend of Marlene's and creator of such internationally famous movies as *A nous la Liberte, Sous le Toits de Paris* and the English-made *The Ghost Goes West*, the last the film that made Hollywood conscious of Robert Donat.

Having pierced her armor of indifference, the committee showed Marlene the costume designs. They included blue-prints of lacy pantalettes, a fair substitute for pantaloons. They included gowns so decollete as to approach the vanishing point, opera-length hose of a length and sheerness never seen in an opera house, and an endless procession of filmy negligees and negligible nightgowns.

Marlene began to see the point. But still there were no songs for her to sing.

"Listen," pleaded the studio mouthpiece, "in this you are a great demimondaine, the Du Barry of the Bayous. You are too aloof and languid to exert yourself with singing. It would be out of character. Your sole function in life is to be an optical treat to rich and well-bred gentlemen."

With a flutter of sweet feminine submission, Dietrich accepted the script. Along with it she accepted certain rich and well-bred gentlemen named Roland Young, Mischa Auer, Raymond Walburn, and Franklin Pangborn. Not to mention a quartet of roughneck river-boat sailors named Bruce Cabot, Andy Devine, Frank Jenks, and Eddie Quillan.

As in all situations in which she has a hand, Dietrich became the queen of the party on the first day's shooting. This circumstance was owing not only to her 50,000 volt personality and the fact that she is one of the nation's flashiest box-office lures and therefore the pivot of every picture she appears in but also because she is a "good-egg" of premium quality, something that could not have been said of her when she was making between $250,000 and $450,000 a single picture.

Since the inception of her revamped career at Universal the lady has been the most lavish party-giver of the feminine stars, with her casts and working crews as favored guests. At the completion of a picture, and on holidays and birthdays, she hands out extravagant largesse in the form of gold and platinum watches, rings, studs and bracelets.

Out of the cast and crew of her current extravaganza, only one gave Dietrich the cold shoulder. This was a tough character named Junior, a monkey, who preferred a pert colored girl in *The Flame*.

Correctly for New Orleans of 1840, *The Flame* has a distinct French flavor. Marlene's character of "Claire Ledeux," described by herself as "an international tramp who has used up all the major European capitals and is now forced to try her luck in the bush league," is played with a slight French accent. This presents no difficulty at all for her, since, although her father was a general in the German Army, she is a thorough Francophile and before September, 1939, a part-time resident of Paris.

There are other French overtones in the company and cast. Bruce Cabot, the leading man, although American-born, bears the baptismal name of Jacques de Bujac and is descended from a family of French diplomats. Rene Clair is a native Parisian. His assistant, Gilbert Mendelik, was educated in France, served last year as an artillery officer in the French Army and escaped via Spain only after the Franco-German armistice. Cameraman Rudolph Mate speaks French better than English. Rene Hubert, the costume designer, is a Frenchman, and Mischa Auer, a polyglot, speaks all the better-known languages with an international accent.

With such a thick French atmosphere around the set it was natural during the first few days of shooting for everybody in the company who could speak French to lapse into that tongue.

Miss Dietrich, however, perceived that the members of the troupe who had no inkling of parlez-vous were annoyed by the unintelligible patter of the others. So she issued an edict.

"No more French on the set," she decreed. "Anybody caught speaking French, except to himself, will be fined ten cents and the proceeds given to British War Relief."

She appointed herself fine-collector and midway of the shooting period had amassed $10.90.

Director Clair, thanks to the enforced ban on French, is fast catching on to the American idiom. His favorite comment after a doubtful take is, "Hokay – wiz reservations."

The Flame of New Orleans gets off to a start in the romantic New Orleans Opera House, which has been faithfully reproduced inside and out as part of a whole Creole neighborhood of the epoch. Here Marlene, in her character of "international tramp" has gone to show herself off to the gentry and, if possible, make a connection before her slim bankroll expires.

In the cinematic version as conjured up by Joe Pasternak, the opera house was the acme of elegance, the shrine of all the gentlefolk of the glittering Crescent City. But in actuality it was slightly less than that, according to an old placard from the opera house which the Universal research department dug up, which admonishes, "No one will be allowed to throw or pretend to throw oranges or anything else at anyone on or off the stage."

At the opera Marlene manages to arouse the interest of Roland Young, the town's wealthiest bachelor, who calls at her home without invitation under the delusion that she is a member of European nobility, or better. While waiting to be received, he overhears Marlene in a tantrum during which she reveals herself as anything but the gently-reared blueblood he supposed she was.

When Marlene learns that she has been revealed in her true character, she blames the outbreak on a dissolute and incorrigible relative (non-existent). From that point on, to lend credibility to her lie, she plays the dual role of great lady and bawdy brawler.

In this way she acquires another suitor, the many-muscled Bruce Cabot, riverboat skipper.

Cabot after two years of unrelieved "heavy" roles, is distinctly a long shot as a sympathetic leading man opposite a glamour star. But Joe Pasternak is celebrated for betting on long shots. His signing of Dietrich when she was suffering from public apathy was an example of his sporting blood and the payoff a vindication of this judgement.

Bruce was cast in *The Flame* under odd circumstances. He had tentatively agreed to do a stage play in New York in which he had little confidence. On the way East, he stopped off at Dallas for the Cotton Bowl football game. In the lobby of his hotel after the game he heard a bellboy paging "Mr. Craddock." When the droning of the name got monotonous he called the boy over, only to learn that Hollywood wanted *him* on the telephone. The deal was set then and there.

When Bruce reported for work he was suffering from a dose of flu, described by the studio as "mild" but sufficiently tough to make him spend his nights in a hospital. He didn't squawk until he had licked the germs, fearful that absence might cause him to lose what appears to be his biggest chance in pictures to date.

The dual strain of being under the weather physically and on trial professionally would have been too much for a softer-fibered performer than Bruce. But his self-confidence didn't desert him. As the very first scene of the picture was being shot, something went haywire in the sound-making device as Cabot uttered his opening speech. A speech that sounded like a Bronx cheer emerged.

Not flustered in the least, Bruce remarked, for the benefit of everybody on the set, "Give a chance, *please*. It's too early yet for the razzberry."

Two seasons of playing magnificent heels, Cabot confessed, have twisted his normally pleasant smile into a combination leer-sneer. He had to practice in front of a mirror to erase the suggestions of evil from his grin.

Cabot's stature and athletic inclinations enabled him to outstrip Roland Young in the marathon event of *The Flame of New Orleans*. This was known as The One-Armed Catch of Dietrich. According to the plot, Marlene has a stock method of evading embarrassing situations and of attracting the attention of unattached gentlemen. This is to go, with all the grace of a swooning swan, into a slow-motion faint.

What with her boudoir, chaise-longue and fainting scenes, Marlene herself has confessed that she will win the horizontal championship of Universal City for 1941.

In her second role, that of her own no-good cousin, she manages to put in evidence the celebrated Dietrich legs, which have still to be matched by anything on film, contemporary or historical.

The jolly old Hays Office will have its annual convulsion when it sees the fadeout of *The Flame of New Orleans*. The situation is this: Cabot has kidnapped Marlene on her wedding day. The scene is an outside view of the cabin of Cabot's boat, narrowing down to the porthole.

Nothing happens for long, dreary seconds. Then Marlene's wedding dress, a resplendent confection of white moire, comes sailing out the window.

"Marlene Dietrich." Editorial, *Modern Screen*, September, 1941

She may be "Legs" to you and you – but Marlene Dietrich is "Mamma dear" to her 16-year-old daughter Maria. Maria can't remember when her famous mother came over from Germany in 1929 and started the vogue for emerald green fingernails and mannish suits – for zombie-like make-up and slinky foreign cars – but if she could, she'd just say, "How cute."

In Maria's eyes, Marlene – in spite of a 12-year separation from her husband, in spite of Mrs. Josef von Sternberg's $600,000 alienation of affections suit, in spite of innumerable studio feuds – can do no wrong.

She knows her too well; knows what good cookies she can bake and what fine stitches she can sew. She's seen her digging in the garden sans phony eyelashes, her two-inch nails covered with old gloves.

Marlene in Man Power, *1941.*

She's worried with her about the citizenship exams, been thrilled when Marlene got all the names of the Presidents straight on the test and became a full-fledged American in 1939. She knows she'd even break a date with Jean Gabin for the premiere of her Warner Brothers' killer-diller, *Man Power*, if Maria's school play were on the same night – which is going some – for there's a man, and *there's* a picture!

Marlene in Man Power, *1941.*

"Dietrich, No. 1 Woman Hater Picks the World's 10 Greatest Women," by Marlene Dietrich. *Hollywood*, March, 1942

From the moment Marlene Dietrich hit these shores, she was tagged a "femme fatale." An escape-you-never-sort of female whom men loved desperately in spite of themselves. With this inevitable postscript everyone who was fortunate enough to interview Dietrich lost no time in demanding what type of man she found fascinating. Why? No one ever thought to ask her about her own sex. It has been generally agreed that there is nothing about women which she either admires, envies or would seek to emulate.

Nonsense!

Once queried on the subject, Miss Dietrich lost no time in stating pointedly and intelligently what elements in a woman she finds most appealing, and who, to her mind, is the best example of that quality. Here are the ten selections of "Hollywood's No. 1 Woman Hater."

INTELLIGENCE:

Dorothy Thompson, the distinguished journalist, because she has finally proved that a woman's opinions concerning the troubled world in which we live can be as searching, profound and constructive as those of male minds; because her soundness has come to be generally recognized and her influence universally felt; and because she has managed to combine a successful career with successful motherhood.

COURAGE:

Helen Keller, because, despite the terrifying handicaps of being born without sight, speech, or hearing, she has become an international symbol of the triumph of the human will against all-out adversity; because she has turned her handicaps into assets; and because, above all, she is living a rich and useful life.

FEMINITY:

Queen Elizabeth of England, because she is attractive without intent, charming without effort, impressive without guile, and ladylike without apology, she is the most ultra-feminine woman in the world; and because she has always managed to be effacing enough to highlight the personality of her husband, the King.

VALOR:

Amelia Earhart, that slim, spare figure of a woman, because she set her compass on Life and never changed her course; because she lived for a purpose; and because she died heroically, a falling star plunging into an unchartered ocean and, surely, saluting with a smile and a wave of the hand the sun or the moon as her plane plummeted her to an unknown destiny.

MAGNETISM:

Alice Marble, the tennis champion, because she is the perfect embodiment of athletic femininity, healthy without being horsey; and because, in her capacity of National Director of Physical Training for Women she is using her gifts for the general good.

INSPIRATION:

Mme. Chiang Kai-shek, because she is one of the world's most brilliant women; because she is aiding her great husband, the Generalissimo, in preserving China in the face of unending peril; and because she is bringing a new freedom to the women of China.

CLEVERNESS:

Clare Booth, because she undeniably is one the most fascinating conversationalists; and because she knows women and had held up a mirror so we could see ourselves. (Or did you miss *The Women?*)

CHIC:

Eve Curie, because she is the bandbox type; because she can travel light and appear to be convoyed by a trailer filled with Schiaparelli; because she does not follow fashion but leads it – gently.

EXCITEMENT:

Greta Garbo, because where there's Garbo there's tension; and because she has proved that furbelows are foolish and mystery is marvelous.

SELF-REALIZATION:

Nellie Manley, my hair-dresser for eight years, not only because she does her job well but also because she has no apologies for its lack of luster; because she is neither amused by glamour, deceived by glitter and tinsel, or ravaged by ambition; because she is a true philosopher and can take life as it comes, and because, totally free from complexes and frustrations, she is at peace with herself and wouldn't change places with Marlene Dietrich for the Taj Mahal.

"What Hollywood Thinks About – Marlene Dietrich," by W. F. French. *Photoplay*, April, 1942

Fred MacMurray with Marlene in The Lady is Willing, *1942.*

Probably the most colorful and talked of star in Hollywood, Marlene Dietrich registers so positively upon all who come into contact with her that there's as sharp a contrast in the opinions of those who know her well and those who know her only casually as there is in the parts she has played in pictures.

As we haven't space to quote all those who helped paint this personality portrait of the original inspiration of Hollywood leg art, we pass on a representative cross section of the opinions they expressed.

According to the popular assistant director, "Chico," whose real name is Francisco Alonso, "Everybody has one opinion of Dietrich when he meets her and another when he leaves her. How different your second opinion is, depends on how long you've been with her."

"Chico" had more to say. "I'd always heard how tough Dietrich was," he continued. "That she was an ice-cold dame with a red-hot temperament. So I was plenty worried about working with her in *The Lady Is Willing*. An assistant's job is to have the cast, including the star, on hand in plenty of time, ready to shoot and willing to co-operate. The prospect of three months with Dietrich kept me awake nights.

"We shot for four months instead of three and Marlene worked with twins – when one baby on the set is usually enough to give a star the jitters. Then, she broke her ankle and had to hobble through five weeks of shooting.

"In spite of her pain and the heavy cast on her foot, Dietrich was always prompt. Which is more than you can say for a lot of stars. When I gave her an eight-thirty call she'd be there at eight-fifteen, made up and ready to work – and without that martyred air calculated to make the director go easy on her.

"One night when we were shooting late at the Columbia ranch, she had to walk rapidly along the New York street set. Because we were using two microphones and had to synchronize sound and action, and because bombers from the near-by Lockheed plant were zooming overhead and raising Ned with our sound track, the scene had to be shot eighteen times.

"Although her ankle was bothering her a lot that night, she never let out a whimper or a complaint. She'd take a deep breath and brace herself to walk without a limp – and then drop in a chair and grab her leg.

"I had never pictured Dietrich as being considerate. Yet she is one of the most unselfish people I ever worked with, always looking out for the other fellow. When we were doing a close-up of Aline MacMahon she suddenly stepped in front of the camera and wouldn't let us shoot until she had fixed Aline's hair. Another time she stopped the shooting to adjust the veil that was spoiling Arline Judge's close-up.

"Dietrich is so alert she sees everything. In a big sequence, when she was the busiest person on the set, she spotted an extra having trouble with her evening gown, sent out for tape and showed the girl how to fix it so it wouldn't slip down again. Marlene overheard wardrobe telling the colored girl who played her maid that they wouldn't replace the stockings she had torn on the set. Marlene sent out and got the girl a dozen pairs.

"Almost everyone has heard about Dietrich's breaking her ankle, but few people know how it really happened. She was doing a scene with the baby in her arms and got her foot caught in the toy fire engine. She was falling face down and to save the baby, she caught the sill of the door and twisted herself around. Her foot wouldn't turn and she knew she would probably ruin the ankle she had sprained in making the picture, *Manpower*, or maybe even break a leg. But she was too game to drop the baby or risk falling on it. And that's just one of the reasons she tops any list of favorite people."

Eleanor Broder, Director Mitchell Leisen's secretary, checked dialogue on *The Lady Is Willing*.

"Dietrich didn't turn out as I expected," Eleanor admitted frankly. "She had the glamour and the famous international air, as advertised, but instead of cold brilliance she had a warm sparkle. She wanted to have fun. Before her accident she was all over the place, mimicking opera singers, ballet dancers and old-time street musicians. We never knew what she would do next.

"But her various activities and interests didn't lessen her drive for perfection. She rehearsed endlessly, devoted unlimited time to her make-up, was satisfied with nothing less than the exact result she wanted in lighting and stood for fittings till she was ready to drop. Time and effort apparently mean nothing to her.

"Dietrich's self-control was positively amazing. No amount of irritation or annoyance can fuss her or make her raise her voice. What does bother her, though, is people not getting along together. She sensed there was friction between two of the girls on the set and managed to adjust their misunderstanding without seeming to be doing so. She's infinitely more diplomatic than the average star."

Not everyone your inquiring reporter interviewed cheered Dietrich. The magazine contact at one of the studios where Marlene made a picture doesn't clap hands at the mention of her name. This publicity worker said, "You can have my part of Dietrich.

I didn't think much of her when she came on the lot and less when she left. I've worked with too many stars to be impressed by snootiness. I went out on the set to arrange for an important magazine interview for her. It was an off-the-picture story and it didn't mean a thing to my studio or to me personally.

"But she let me stand for five minutes or more beside her make-up table without so much as glancing up. She couldn't help seeing me in the mirror, but she let me finally walk away without indicating she knew I was on earth. I tried again that afternoon, but she was telling the electrician how to light a scene and looked right through me.

"So in my very best English, I mentally told her to go to the deuce, and let it go at that. There were too many stars and players on our own lot who were willing to co-operate for me to stand around coughing and hemming in the hope Dietrich would finally notice me."

Walter Ruf, Columbia's publicity unit man on *The Lady Is Willing* unknowingly explained this magazine contact's experience with Marlene.

Marlene in The Lady is Willing, 1942.

"The first day or two on the picture," said Walter, "I thought Dietrich fancied herself a bit exclusive. But later I learned that her apparent aloofness was just concentration. When she's in the middle of something she won't give anybody a tumble. But the instant she finishes the job in hand she really extends herself to be friendly and gracious.

"Making-up is one of the things Marlene concentrates on. She takes longer to make-up than anybody I've ever seen. But when she's finished, gosh, how she's finished. Other stars continually rush back to a mirror for assurance or to adjust or add something. But not Dietrich. Once made-up she went through scenes, kidded with the boys, cuddled the babies and relaxed all over the place without once giving a thought to her make-up. And it was always perfect.

"Dietrich is very methodical. While in the Cedars of Lebanon Hospital with her broken ankle, she kept a complete record of every wire, letter and gift sent to her – and there were hundreds. Once they removed the cards before delivering her flowers and she had the whole hospital staff looking for them so she could make personal acknowledgements.

"She loves to use the telephone and one call seems to inspire another. She really had a field day with the phone in the hospital. She literally crawled under the bed covers and cooed into it."

A player who did a small part in one of Dietrich's pictures and who, for obvious reasons, doesn't want his name used, says, "Dietrich is too sure of herself and too officious for me. She wants to tell everybody how to do his job and has an exaggerated notion of her own importance. I also don't like her condescending way with bit players and extras. Nobody has to go out of his way to be nice to me, I just want to be treated as an equal, or let alone."

Joe Wald, a veteran cowboy and stuntman, says, "I sure never expected to be in a picture with 'Legs' Dietrich. And when us tobacco chewers did get the *Destry* call we figured we'd have to gentle down and not get too close to the glamour gal. We figured we'd have to muffle our spurs and hold our breath.

"But after we saw Marleenie tear into Una Merkel in that knockdown and drag-out cat fight, we kinda figured she was human, after all.

"And, by gum, she sure was. Before they got done with the big business sequence where we put on the roughhouse she had hog-tied the whole caboodle of us. Yes, sir, she was a full-fledged honorary member of our cowboy and stuntman's association. We liked teaching her to whirl a rope, but sure hedged when she wanted to start six-gun practice in the back lot.

"If Marleenie's what they call a glamour gal, I'd like to have me one out on my ranch."

Your reporter was told to contact George Raft's pal, Mack Gray, for an opinion on Dietrich. But when we called to see Mack, George was home alone. He said, "What do I think of Dietrich? Just that she's the swellest person I ever met. She's loyal, sincere, game and a good fellow. I don't understand how anyone can say she's stuck up. She's just the opposite of that. She was swell to everybody who worked on *Manpower* and at the end of the picture she gave them all watches – grips, juicers, wardrobe girls – everybody.

"In the scene where I was supposed to hit her, I wanted to fake it. But she made me do it legitimate. She said I'd look bad if I didn't. And she made me hit her so hard she fell and sprained her ankle.

"When she came limping back to work with her lips all swollen, I felt pretty bad. But she teased me out of it. That's the kind of a gal she is."

"It wasn't the big things Dietrich did, like taking care of all the expenses of the wardrobe girl who got hurt on *The Lady Is Willing* that won all of us," said Roselle Novello, who works in Columbia's wardrobe department. "It was the hundred little considerations she showed us. Like bringing home-baked cakes to the studio almost every day and giving birthday parties for Director Mitchell Leisen, for 'Chico' and for two or three others who had birthdays while working on the picture.

"Dietrich is an excellent cook and made the cakes she brought us, layer cakes and big, square fruit-filled cakes. One day she'd bring apricot cake, another day peach cake and another day pineapple cake – and everybody who ate lunch on the set got some.

"She made working on that picture a pleasure by always thinking up little ways to surprise and please us."

Harrold Johnson, a young man from Cincinnati out here to work in the Douglas plane plant, was interviewed as he left a Hollywood movie theater.

"I only know the Marlene Dietrich I've seen on the screen and read about in the papers," he said, after a little coaxing. "She's okay in pictures, but I don't think she's done the women of America much good by introducing the fad of wearing men's pants, shaving off their eyebrows and generally ruining their appearance.

"I met a fellow who works in a studio who says she's a regular fellow. But I say it's too bad she wasn't a regular woman when she came here first, instead of an extremist setting a screwy example for girls, just to get publicity."

Fred MacMurray, who co-stars with Dietrich in *The Lady Is Willing*, said, "Marlene was terrific – with her courage and performance before the camera and her sportsmanship behind it. I hope she gives the public as much pleasure in seeing the picture as she gave us in making it – and I'm sure she will."

Ruth Ford, one of Orson Welles' Mercury Players from New York, had her first movie part in Dietrich's picture.

"I watched Dietrich every minute of the six weeks I was on the picture," says Miss Ford. "I wanted to see what made her click; what gave her that peculiarly mysterious and sophisticated air, and what made her an international figure.

"I discovered she capitalizes the quality of restraint. If there is a scene of excitement or melodrama Dietrich lets the other fellow chew the scenery. She underplays it.

"That quality carries through into her personality. It awes people. I was afraid of Dietrich. (And I wasn't alone, for I learned that almost every worker on the picture, *The Lady Is Willing*, was afraid of the assignment with her.)

"I held Dietrich in awe. Usually I can talk with the best of them and never have had that 'at a loss in a crowd' feeling. But I was tongue-tied by Dietrich. Her aura frightened me.

"But the first thing she said to me when I came on the set to do off-stage dialogue was a lift. I had come from my home without make-up and with my hair brushed back. She said, 'Oh, how pretty you are,' and called people over to see me.

"Later, when I was more at ease, she showed me where my make-up was wrong. She told me to use just a base and a white shadow around my eyes. When I discovered how right she was, and asked her how she knew so much about it, she said that when they first made her up in Europe her husband came on the set and didn't recognize her. So she had to learn to make herself up in self-protection."

We talked to Nellie Manley, Dietrich's Girl Friday, and asked her what was Dietrich's most outstanding characteristic. She replied instantly, "Loyalty, loyalty to those close to her, loyalty to her work, loyalty to those who work with her.

"She has had Becky, her personal maid, for sixteen years. I have been with her for eight years. Miss Dietrich hired Becky in Europe as nurse for her daughter Maria. When she came to America, she brought Becky with her, and when she got an English-speaking governess for Maria she made Becky her own personal maid. When Miss Dietrich found it necessary to replace the governess with a private tutor, she found work for her, too.

"When she finishes a picture she gives everyone on it a present! But she doesn't merely tell someone to make out a list and give a wholesale order for the same item for everybody. She selects each present herself, choosing an article because, as she says, 'That looks like him,' or 'That looks like something that should belong to her.' I've seen her spend hours over a watch counter, picking heavy gold watches for publicity men and actors, dainty wrist watches for girls and then, fine models for sound men. She wanted to get the property boy at Universal a watch with all the gadgets on it he could need. So she shopped until she found one with a stop-watch arrangement, a special sweep second hand and other features that she knew would appeal to him.

"She spends days shopping for Christmas presents for Maria. She has a special table in Maria's room just for her presents. And it's always loaded down – and everything is made to order. And that same thoughtfulness marks what she does for others, too."

Because no woman can think of Dietrich without thinking of clothes and clothes sense, we asked Yolanda, the designer who has done a great deal of work for Marlene, to add a few lines to our personality sketch of the famous star.

"One thing you can mark down in your book," said this expert, "if she wanted to, Marlene Dietrich could be one of our greatest designers.

"I have never seen Dietrich wear anything that anybody made, no matter how famous the designer, that wasn't high-lighted by her own originality and personality.

"Marlene will let a designer work out anything she wants to, without interference. But Dietrich always picks up where she leaves off and adds a touch that makes it distinctive.

"I have designed for many women who have as much money, but never for one who has as much knowledge of what is smart and exclusive as Dietrich.

"Dietrich is generous and sympathetic to a fault. I have seen her take clothes off her back and give them to a woman who admired them. And I have seen her unhappy for days because of suffering in Europe. Once you know her, she is very easy to get along with. She is decidedly *not* snooty."

Stanley Dunne, property man at Columbia Studios, agrees that Dietrich is not "stuck up."

"Because I'd heard how exclusive and hard to get along with Marlene Dietrich was," explains Stanley, "we decided to beat her to the punch with a dressing room no glamour girl could object to.

"So we took two portable dressing rooms, built them together and spent a lot of money furnishing them exclusively. She had the classiest nest ever put on a set for a star.

"But aside from changing dresses inside a couple of times, she never used it. She used the set dressing table, out among the workers, instead. She insisted on mixing with the crew.

"Once, when I sat down at the piano to entertain the boys, she pulled a chair over beside me and joined in with a musical saw. And, boy, she could play it. She sang songs for us and kept things humming on the set. She served us coffee and her own home-made cake almost every day."

Margaret Teeter, waitress at Universal Studio's commissary served Dietrich every working day for seven weeks.

"I wish our average customer was half as easy to serve as Marlene Dietrich," mused Margaret. "She wasn't in the least fussy about her food, was always pleasant, was never in a hurry and didn't demand a lot of attention. She would eat anything. She ordered large luncheons and was very fond of roast beef, mashed potatoes and salads. She liked vegetables of all kinds. She didn't eat much dessert though she would occasionally have what she called a 'bust' of cake and ice cream. She drank a lot of coffee.

"One day she said to me, 'Margaret, people say I'm starving myself to keep my figure. But I always eat, don't I?' I said, 'And how!' and she laughed so you could hear her all over the commissary.

"During the making of *Destry* she and Jimmy Stewart ate lunch together and I waited on them every day. They had lots of fun and sometimes they would have as many as ten people crowded around that corner table with them.

"Jimmy loved our big hot turkey sandwiches with gravy and mashed potatoes. When he'd order one Marlene would ask if it was good, consider it and then she'd try the same. She would clean her plate. Next time Jimmy ordered his turkey sandwich she would go through the very same routine.

"They would bring all the foreign celebrities to her table and she could talk to them about anything, usually in their own language. When they'd all start talking a foreign language at the table Jimmy Stewart would ask me where an alien (meaning himself) should register."

Among others, we asked Bill Edward, publicity man who worked with Dietrich at Paramount and at Universal, to help us draw this pen picture of the famous blonde.

"Dietrich," Bill explained, "goes into everything wholeheartedly. But the most enthusiastic and proudest I've ever seen her was when she got her American citizenship.

"The first time she went to vote she spent hours dressing and arrived at the polls in a striking black and white creation and *very* photogenic. She gave the cameramen their field day.

"It was while the California "ham and eggs" campaign was hottest and we asked Marlene how she was voting on the issue. She replied, 'Doesn't the privilege of being an American citizen carry the obligation of not telling how you vote?' Leave it to Marlene always to have the right answer."

And that's what people think of Dietrich.

W. F. French was an entertainment writer.

"Dietrich Does a Strip," by Rex Edwards. *Hollywood*, March, 1943

Marlene Dietrich has shelved mystery and glamour for the duration. She no longer is the gay, glamorous figure of pre-war days, surrounded nightly by half a dozen adoring swains. Her nightclub appearances are a thing of the past.

Yes, Dietrich has buckled down to do her share of war work. Her name appears high on the lists of volunteers in every phase of war work in Hollywood. She is constantly in attendance for camp shows, benefits and canteen duty.

"I've never really been a mystery woman," she explains. "The whole idea is silly. Hollywood press agents built up that angle to sell pictures. I've spent a good deal of my time debunking it.

"Little 'eccentricities' confound Hollywood. Maybe they got off on that track about me because I never was in sight Thursday evenings. The first thing that astonished me about Hollywood was the Thursday night eating out fad. On cook's night out, a movie actress was not only expected to be taken to dinner, she had to be. She couldn't cook! Where I came from if a girl couldn't cook she wasn't ready for marriage. A cook book can fill in any gaps in home training. I've always regarded cooking as a great pleasure, never a tiresome task.

"No," laughed Marlene, "I'm not fantastic, I assure you. I am a woman, quite like any other woman, only my chosen profession happens to be acting. I didn't chance upon my career, either. I picked it and prepared for it. As my daughter is doing. I studied the rudiments of acting at Max Reinhardt's dramatic school abroad, as Maria has been doing in Hollywood. Then I started from the bottom. I did stage work before I was qualified to attempt film leads. There have been many moments when I have been severely discouraged."

Marlene still has her languorous movements, low voice, and unshakeable poise. But she disclaims an infallible knowledge of men. "I do not consider myself an expert on the male sex. My first studio built me up that way. A hangover from the wine, women, and song conception of the theater. They hushed my realistic side.

"If my true opinions about men, and not what press agents thought I thought, interest you, okay here goes! First of all, I don't agree at all with a song I sang in one of my pictures that love is merely a game. I think love is a most serious matter, and that it is bad to play at it as at a game. I don't think a girl should mature too fast, or ape her elders. The first long dress, the first big dancing party, all those steps in growing up ought to be great events in a girl's life. They were in mine. I was not allowed to cram thrills and excitement all at once, at sixteen."

Marlene's daughter, who is acting at the Reinhardt school under the assumed name of Maria Manton so she will progress on her own, does not mix with the young Hollywood set. She has no dates. Her concentration on mastering the fundamentals of acting is the direct result of her home life.

The old-fashioned mothering by such a sophisticate may seem amazing. But then the real life Dietrich does not even remotely resemble the screen Dietrich. "I don't think it is smart for a girl to experience too much too young and too fast," she continued. "I believe in good old-fashioned upbringing. I had it myself. Nor do I favor hasty marriages. Marrying too quickly, on fleeting attraction, is a major cause of divorce. The fact that you can rush into marriage doesn't mean you prove you have a man of your own; but a year's engagement may demonstrate you can hold him against all competition!

"On the screen I am the kind of woman who is imperious with her whims, and easily swept by emotions. But I am wise enough to realize that this is no way for a woman to be in real life. I have never met a 'siren' who was successful. Men don't like 'vamps.' I enact that type in my pictures because that brand of woman is not just like the woman next door and is, therefore, a diversion for an hour or so. Escape from the familiar. But be sure that making some man happy is what counts for every woman, including me!"

Marlene has little sympathy for the get-your-man rules ladled out.

"They're such poor psychology! The popular saying that a girl shouldn't show her love for a man is ridiculous. It is instinctive to be responsive. But that applies only after the man has made the advances.

"It is always a mistake to run after any man. Men are the hunters by nature. If a girl is healthy and natural the men will notice her. She shouldn't sit and wait for a man; she should go to work at something that interests her. And if she doesn't find a man thoroughly interesting, she should not have dates with him. It is better for her to stay at home and read, knit, cook, sew, or listen to music.

"I am," confessed Marlene, "personally suspicious of handsome men. They so seldom hold up. What a man thinks and feels is what counts.

"Because of my roles, I'm continually asked how to 'maneuver' men. My un-dressed-up answer is: be straightforward and honest and skip the attempt to maneuver them. Men have a keen instinct; they sense where they stand with a woman. What's more, men don't want suspense. They want to be sure of a woman. The woman who is temperamental is immature."

"And you," she was interrupted, "are never temperamental?"

Scorning evasion, Marlene retorted, "No! I am fatalistic about my life as a woman. But the opposite about my work; in one's work it is necessary to be always trying. I worry if everything isn't just right at the studio. I don't like half-way accomplishments there, and I tell them so. I work hard at acting and I want people's respect.

"If I've seemed freakish at times, blame it on the press agent build-up. If I haven't gushed to interviewers, remember there are some things too close to the heart to be blatantly broadcast. And reticence on my part should be credited to my notion of good taste, not to absurd temperament. I have had my share of bad hours."

She shrugged her shoulders. "But today, with what we have to do for America, why are we talking about me? There's work to be done – today, not tomorrow or next week. So let's all pitch in and finish the job in a hurry."

Rex Edwards was a prolific entertainment journalist.

Randolph Scott with Marlene in The Spoilers, *1942.*

"From Apple Strudel to Cheese Cake," by Constance Palmer. *Screenland*, March, 1944

Marlene in Kismet, *1944.*

The famous legs were gilded to the thigh. The feet were bare, toe-nails painted blood-red. The magnificent bone structure of the well-publicized torso was also bare and the blonde hair gilded and lacquered into a high, firm pin-cushion effect above hollow cheeks and slanting eyes, hard as flint.

Marlene Dietrich has done it again! Stars may rise and stars may fall, but the Dietrich can always be depended on to carry it off. Gloria Swanson and Pola Negri in their salad-days couldn't hold a candle to her when it comes to wearing the costumes studio designers dream up.

In *The Garden of Allah* she floated in Technicolor over an extremely sandy desert brushed by a well-controlled and becoming breeze, wearing pastel chiffons so delicate that they looked as substantial as fondant candy in a hot sun.

In *Destry Rides Again*, she was a way-out-West dance-hall girl, complete with spangles, feather boas, silks, satins, velvets and birds of Paradise that would have taxed the financial resources of Mrs. Astorbilt herself.

Now, in *Kismet* at Metro-Goldwyn-Mayer, she's undressed to the teeth. She does a sensuous Oriental dance to the blaring tones of the set recorder and succeeds in creating an atmosphere of provocative mystery that would do credit to a perpetrator of the Indian rope-trick.

First they did her up in tiny gold chains, but there were so many spectators around hoping the chains would break – which they did – that they changed the conception to voluminous folds of black chiffon through which the gilded legs shine satisfactorily.

But the Marlene Dietrich of the set is not the Dietrich of the Hollywood Canteen, the Government hospitals for wounded servicemen, the weekly broadcast in six different languages to countries under the Axis heel. The Marlene of the gilt, the chiffon, the small golden breastplates – the Marlene whose knitting needles click with furious efficiency between shots as she manufactures wristlets and scarfs, sweaters and mittens for soldiers and sailors and marines – is an entirely different woman.

Time was when she spent many hours being a good cook. Her coffee cake, her apple strudel melted in the mouth, as many a fellow-worker on the set and personal friend in the European contingent can bear witness. But now it's different.

This is the day of big things, organizations, War Bond tours, important public appearances and small, private, unheralded efforts. Every minute of the day must be budgeted and cared for as preciously as a jewel. There is time for work; time for rehearsal; time for speeches; time for traveling from Canteen to hospital to airport. There is no time for play.

"Every woman's life is so full now," she told me on the *Kismet* set, "that it seems only by forgetting oneself can one accomplish a small half of all the duties there are to be done."

She picked up her ever-present knitting and her strong fingers flew. The cold steel needles, moving so swiftly, fashioning the wool into something for a soldier to wear and perhaps die in, made strange contrast against the gold thighs, the chiffon, the sequins, the bracelets, and bangles. I asked her if she thought glamor still had a place in this war-torn world – if it was necessary to the morale of both fighting man and civilian.

Marlene pins the "Jump Wings" onto a paratrooper, 1944.

She most definitely thought it had not. "What I think we need here is more work on the part of everybody. Compared to the people of Europe and China we've been lucky – so far. And the small amount of rationing we've had, isn't even worth talking about."

She rose at the director's call, carefully laid down the sweater she was working on and went back into the scene.

She gets to the studio at seven every morning, as it takes four hours to prepare her for the set and almost as long at night to restore her to a reasonable facsimile of normal. Wood-alcohol is used to take the gilt from her legs and she wonders wryly if their present greenish tinge of an evening will be permanent.

The recorder blared raucous sounds you won't hear when you see the picture; Marlene hid behind a pillar at the top of a short rise of steps; technicians fussed with this, fiddled with that.

Finally, the clack of the marker and Marlene stuck her toe out from behind the pillar and the dance was on. She swayed sinuously down the steps, and waved her arms gracefully. The scene was completed without a hitch. She came back and sat down.

"American women," she went on, touching the black chiffon that cascaded in lovely folds from her marvelously-wrought and lacquered coiffure, "have thought too much in the past about making themselves beautiful. They have the reputation of being the best-groomed women in the world. More and more magazines are published teaching them taste about dressing, methods of beautifying the body.

"Motion pictures have helped. The habit of beauty is so deep-seated now that scarcities and the demands of the war-effort are possibly upsetting to the woman accustomed to having plenty of time to work out her own glamorizing routine. But with all there is to be done, they should not forget the importance of keeping themselves healthy. And the best way for them to retain beauty is for them to use the simplest means to present an attractive appearance."

She believes that meat and butter shortages will work wonders for our complexions because we are eating, perforce, more fruit and vegetables. Happy and good thoughts bring beauty to an otherwise plain face, so – to the girl whose features are not too perfect – she says, "Don't worry. Don't brood over fancied slights. Think with all your might that things are good – and they *will* be good!"

She is all for hard work during the day because she says it makes us go to bed early enough to get a full night's sleep, which makes naturally for bright eyes and an alert brain.

When I asked her what her advice was about the buying of finery and embellishments during war-time, her reply was oblique – like her eyebrows.

"There is an ancient saying that is very wise." She smiled a little. "It goes, 'I went to the market today and admired so many beautiful things I couldn't use.' Isn't that wonderful? It's so good to remember. For instance, before rationing we thought nothing of buying three or four pairs of shoes at a time. It was so much easier to pick out the season's supply all at once. Now we know that one sturdy, comfortable, well-fitted pair, of good leather and workmanship, will have to do until the next shoe-stamp is good.

"Now it's doubly necessary to shop wisely. Some women seem to make a life's work of shopping. They shop by the hour, six days a week. They wander up and down the aisles of every department store, from floor to floor, fingering, pricing, picking up, laying down articles they can't possibly need or use. They'll buy anything – just for the satisfaction of being able to choose, pay for and say, 'It's mine!' Better – much better to spend this time at the Red Cross or Canteen or U.S.O. where you can be of service to your fellow man who's perhaps giving his life for you."

Marlene at the Front, 1944. For her work during WWII, she received the Medal of Freedom from General Maxwell D. Taylor in a ceremony at West Point in 1947.

It used to be a studio legend that she almost never arrived empty-handed for work. Sometimes it was a batch of cookies she'd baked for the crew, or a cake for the birthday of somebody's little girl, or a wad of bills in an envelope to help an electrician with a sick wife. Now her generosity is taking on bigger scope. While, in the past, she's given away fortunes to the needy, today her largess goes to the starving children in stricken lands.

Because she knew hunger in her native Germany after the end of the first World War, she intends – when this war is over – to go back to Europe, not as an actress, but as a simple woman, working among those starving and tragic little ones to bring back into their lives what measure of happiness and comfort she can.

Constance Palmer (1897-1979) was a freelance writer for newspapers and movie magazines. She retired in 1925 after marrying character actor Lucien Littlefield, whom she met on the set of Rudolph Valentino's 1921 film, *The Sheik*. After raising two children, she returned to entertainment journalism in the 1940s. She remained married to Littlefield, who appeared in more than 250 films, until his death in 1960.

The couple's daughter recalled her mother in a 2006 interview with Anthony Slide. "All the editors were in New York, so she would make a list of suggested stories, send them to Delight Evans or whoever it was in New York, and maybe the editor would pick out one. Then she would go to the studio and get permission from the publicity office. Usually a publicity person would come along to the interview, maybe the star would change the content or the publicity department would change something. By the time it got back to the editor, maybe it wasn't the same angle the editor wanted. Maybe she would sell it and maybe she wouldn't."

Marlene, 1947.

"Dietrich – The Body and The Soul." Collier's, May, 14, 1954

Anyone who sets out to do an article on Marlene Dietrich is confronted by three facts: (1) there has already been a great deal written about her, all of it tending to make her a legend ("the fabulous grandmother," "the eternal glamor queen," and so on); (2) few people agree about her; and (3) her friends and non-friends have banded together generally in a conspiracy to say nothing but good about her – at least when quoted directly.

Miss Dietrich ridicules the legend, but it grows in spite of her, because of the difficulty of pinning her down and classifying her.

While it is certain, for example, that she was born Maria Magdalene Dietrich in Berlin, Germany on December 27th, the year is open to debate (and has been widely debated). She has appeared in more than 25 movies, and few of them have been very good – yet she ranks with the outstanding film personalities of the century. Her primary asset on the screen, the smoky-eyed allure that drives men wild, has also affected a number of men (many of them very well known) off the screen – yet there is abundant testimony that her main ambition is to be simply a housewife and a mother.

Miss Dietrich has always evidenced a sincere dislike for publicity, yet last winter she played for three weeks at the Sahara Hotel in Las Vegas in a $6,000 dress made of a material which has been described as rhinestones-and-nothing, thus

Marlene in "that" gown.

getting her picture on page one of an astonishing number of newspapers.

What follows is an effort to present the first full portrait of Dietrich. A number of *Collier's* reporters spent several months interviewing close friends, chance acquaintances and Miss Dietrich herself – more than 100 people in all – at the main sources of the legend: Europe, California and New York. Most of this article has been turned over to those who were interviewed, some of whom preferred to remain anonymous.

HOLLYWOOD DIRECTOR HENRY KOSTER: Whatever you say about Miss Dietrich, there's always a story to disprove it.

A FRIEND: Tell me, does anyone really know how old she is? I've heard estimates ranging from forty-seven to fifty-seven; I admit I'm curious.

MARLENE DIETRICH: I've decided the best idea, when people ask my age, is to say I'm seventy-one and let it go at that. Someone told me that the Encyclopedia of Names has my right age. I don't know; I haven't see it.

NEW CENTURY CYCLOPEDIA OF NAMES: Dietrich, Marlene. b. at Berlin, Dec. 27, 1904 – American Actress.

A PROFESSIONAL ASSOCIATE: I think most of her close friends will tell you she'll be fifty this year. I've known her about as long as any; I first met Marlene in 1927 in Berlin, when she was unknown (she still has a sister living there). Marlene was something of an ugly duckling in those days...

REPORTERS SEYMOUR FREIDIN AND WILLIAM RICHARDSON (*in Berlin*): The German police have no record of a sister, but they report Miss Dietrich's mother died in Germany in 1948.

A CLOSE FRIEND: I understand Marlene's sister was held in a Nazi concentration camp in World War II.

PROFESSIONAL ASSOCIATE (continuing): ...and only her success made her beautiful. When Nicholas Farkas, then Germany's foremost cameraman, heard she was to appear in a picture he was filming he threated to quit. She looked as bad in that picture as he had predicted. But director Josef von Sternberg saw rushes of the film, and picked her to star in *The Blue Angel*, the picture that made her. It took him 20 minutes to figure out how she should be lighted – from the right, high above, the ways she has insisted on having her lighting ever since – and from that moment Marlene became a beautiful woman...first on the screen, then in life. She was beautiful because she *wanted* to be beautiful.

A HOLLYWOOD DIRECTOR: She had a falling out with von Sternberg later. He had created a robot – and then, along the classic lines, the robot destroyed its creator.

A CRITICAL ACQUAINTANCE: Before he met her, von Sternberg had a reputation for shooting his pictures under the budget. After he met her, he began shooting her scenes 20 to 60 times. His pictures began costing a fortune.

JOSEF VON STERNBERG (*now in the United States*): Anything I have to say about Miss Dietrich I've said in my films.

A GIRL IN BERLIN: I knew her 27 years ago and even then she walked and talked like Cleopatra – except that Dietrich was more dangerous. She could make any woman look like a dumpy *Hausfrau*.

MOVIE DIRECTOR WILLIAM DIETERLE: She had just turned eighteen when I first met her in Germany. She has never changed. With anyone else, you run into a mutual acquaintance and say, "How is so-and-so?" Not with Marlene; you *know* how Marlene is, no matter how long it's been since you last saw her. Others have their dreams behind them or before them; Marlene carried her dream with her and used it for a halo. In Hollywood, they made a big thing about her legs. If someone had suggested playing up the legs to another actress who took herself seriously, she'd have slapped his face, knowing it would have ruined her. Marlene just said, "If it's legs they want, it's legs they'll get." Her secret? She is always herself. She'll never change.

THE CRITICAL ACQUAINTANCE: The secret of Dietrich is that she believes she is the most beautiful and glamorous woman in the world – and she has sold the public her own picture of herself.

SONGSTRESS ROSEMARY CLOONEY: One night Marlene suggested going to a night club to hear Johnnie Ray – just she, Billy Wilder's wife and I. I thought it might not be nice, three women in a night club without escorts, but she said, "Three women as lovely as we? If we are alone, it is naturally because we want to be alone."

LEO LERMAN (*contributing editor of Mademoiselle, and a close Dietrich friend*): She knows she's beautiful, and is aware it's a good thing, but she does nothing to take care of her beauty.

MARLENE DIETRICH: Beauty comes from within. It sounds horrible, but it's true.

CLARA BIANCHI (*ladies' room attendant at New York's Colony Restaurant*): In twenty years I've never see her replenish her make-up – even her lipstick.

A DIRECTOR: There's a lot about her I'd criticize – but if it's super-glamor you need in a picture Marlene is simply impossible to replace. Nobody, nobody ever came up to it.

STILL PHOTOGRAPHER RAY JONES (*chief of the Universal-International portrait gallery*): What Monroe is to sex Dietrich is to glamor. With that woman, just one light, and a photographer

Marlene in Stage Fright, 1950.

has a priceless piece of sculpture – the high forehead, the arch between the eyes, those soft lips slightly parted…What a sight!

DIRECTOR ALFRED HITCHCOCK: Miss Dietrich has that spark that transmits itself visually. It's rare.

ACTOR MAURICE CHEVALIER (*in Paris*): I knew her best in the early thirties – and in those days she could make any man fall in love with her just by looking at him.

ACTRESS EVA GABOR: I am her number one worshiper. She is the real glamor. Marlene stretches her leg and a whole roomful of people jump!

MRS. WALTER REISCH (*wife of the film writer*): If she were at a masked costume ball and nobody knew who she was, all eyes would still be on her.

MOVIE COLUMNIST HERBERT STEIN: When she comes into a night club it just lights up the joint.

BROADWAY COLUMNIST EARL WILSON: I once interviewed her in a famous restaurant, and I noticed the headwaiter watching us. Afterward he asked me, "Are her legs really beautiful? I never thought to look at them." Quite a tribute to her personality.

FRENCH POET-DRAMATIST JEAN COCTEAU: …the most exciting and terrifying woman I have ever known.

PAUL ROSE (*a New York furniture restorer*): I have done a lot of work for her. Her voice alone is enough to drive you crazy. Once she called to give me her phone number so I could call back about something, and that voice, just speaking a telephone number, was…well, it was…it was like another woman talking of love. You know? And still, though she's the absolute female, she has a completely masculine mind.

SIR ALEXANDER FLEMING (*the discoverer of penicillin, who met Dietrich only once, but corresponds with her and has her picture hanging in his outer office in London*): I don't know what people mean by glamor. But Miss Dietrich is incredibly intelligent and brilliantly witty.

PLAYWRIGHT-COMPOSER-ACTOR NOEL COWARD: She may be the greatest woman of our age…but so *damned* intelligent for a woman.

A HOLLYWOOD DIRECTOR: Dietrich has had many men friends, but I think it's significant that her greatest interest was an intellectual, Erich Maria Remarque, the German novelist. He'd recommend books for her to read – she reads widely, and not just trash – and she was supposed to be the heroine in his novel, *Arch of Triumph*.

REPORTER JOSEPH LAITIN (*in Hollywood*): I interviewed Miss Dietrich and asked who her greatest and closest friend had been. That all depends, she said, on what I meant by "greatest" and "closest"; did I mean the person she saw most now, or a long time ago; did I mean the person she loved the most, the person she'd most like to be with, the one who loved her most…? "I just can't answer the question," she said, and changed the subject. But just before I left her, the conversation turned back to her friends and I carefully raised the question again. She sat silently for a moment, staring straight ahead, then said in a very small voice: "Mr. Remarque…but I don't see him very often now."

ERICH MARIA REMARQUE (*author of All Quiet on the Western Front, and the new novel A Time to Love and a Time to Die*): She is a very great and generous artist and a very great personality. That is all I can say.

A HOLLYWOOD FRIEND: Dietrich and Remarque saw a great deal of each other for seven or eight years. I was present, I believe, when it ended. She had given him an aquarium full of tropical fish – including three she especially admired, which she called the French Fleet, because they had the French tricolor on their tails. Remarque treasured the gift; he would clean the aquarium every day. Then, after some time, it began to show signs of neglect. One night, at a dinner party at his place, she looked at

Marlene with Erich Maria Remarque, 1957.

the aquarium and saw some fish floating on the surface, dead – including the French Fleet. The dinner went very badly; she kept referring to the fish, and everybody at the table could feel the tension. We all left immediately after dinner. I don't think she and Remarque saw much of each other after that.

A MOVIE DIRECTOR: I believe her relationship with her husband, Rudy Sieber, may have been a little strained for the only time in her life when she was going around with Remarque. Nothing ever came of it, of course. She and Sieber are still married, after 30 years.

A FRIEND: She married Sieber when she was still unknown; in fact, there's a story that he got her her first movie job in Germany, when he was an assistant director. They still spend a lot of time together, and apparently are very fond of each other. He's running a chicken farm in California now.

RUDOLPH SIEBER (from his California chicken farm): I'm sorry, but I make it a rule never to make public statements about my wife.

ACTRESS MERCEDES MCCAMBRIDGE: You should really hear her tell the story of her funeral.

WRITER-PUBLICIST IRVING HOFFMAN: I wrote a column on the funeral story in the *Hollywood Reporter* a few years ago. Miss Dietrich tells the story at parties, reciting it in script form. According to the script, only men who have known her well will be permitted to attend the Dietrich rites – and her husband, equipped with a list, will be posted at the door to keep out gate crashers…the many men who have falsely insisted they have been her friend.

LAITIN: Her friends told me that the funeral story gets longer and longer as time goes on – and more hilarious, as she caricatures the men who will be admitted. Douglas Fairbanks, Jr., she indicates, will show up in a full-dress Navy uniform, bearing a wreath from the Queen of England; French actor Jean Gabin (who is said to have ranked next to Remarque in her esteem) will be leaning against the church door, a cigarette dangling from his lips, disdaining to join the other mourners; Remarque, with characteristic vagueness, will be at the wrong church, mourning at the wrong

Dietrich in Las Vegas.

funeral. Other men get similar treatment in the story – British actor Michael Wilding, Gary Cooper, James Stewart, John Wayne and many more.

A DIRECTOR: For everybody else, falling in love is a tiring experience, but not for her. It keeps her alive. Marlene has the romantic immaturity of a girl of sixteen.

A STUDIO EXECUTIVE: No one I know has had more men friends – and by that I mean men she has seen steadily for months or years. If she is with a man, she acts as if there's never been another before him and never will be another again. She's his cook, agent, secretary, astrologer, partner. She never compares him to another man, never thinks of another. When she senses that the friendship has reached an end, she withdraws gracefully before the man knows what it's all about.

A HOLLYWOOD ACTRESS: Once Marlene said to me, "When you change men, if the last one liked classical music, make sure the next one likes jazz…" You know, in spite of the way men feel about her, she has the admiration and friendship of many, many women. I don't know how to explain it, but if a man preferred Marlene to me, I'd understand.

EVA GABOR: She's the only woman whom a man could prefer to me without making me angry.

A MOVIE DIRECTOR: Marlene will still be looking beautiful – and falling in love – when she's eighty.

DIRECTOR WILLIAM DIETERLE: When I first met her, she had a kind of provincial air about her – but with such nonchalance, such tongue-in-cheek. You felt that where she came from, you had to go through the kitchen to reach the living room. And yet you knew she was the *grande dame*. She is the same today: the *grande dame*, and yet the *Hausfrau*.

SONG WRITER HAROLD ARLEN: Everyone talks about Marlene as a *Hausfrau* – and I can see why. There's a wonderful peasant quality about her, an earthiness…

MARLENE DIETRICH: If the people who call me a *Hausfrau* mean that I like to work around the house, they're right.

CARROLL RIGHTER (Miss Dietrich's astrologer): I can't talk about her; it wouldn't be ethical. But I'll say one thing: she'd rather cook than do anything else.

MICHAEL WILDING: …a superb cook.

MAURICE CHEVALIER: …magnificent.

ACTRESS TALLULAH BANKHEAD: One night in Las Vegas I got hungry and she walked into the kitchen of the Sands Hotel, dressed in white evening gown and furs, and cooked scrambled eggs for four.

DIRECTOR BILLY WILDER: People joke about scrambled eggs being easy to make, but actually it's the most difficult dish there is. Marlene is the best egg scrambler the world has ever known.

MME. TATIANA DE PLESSIX (*custom hat designer, Saks Fifth Avenue*): I have dined at Miss Dietrich's home and I'd say her greatest dish is *pot-au-feu*, a beef soup.

JOHN MARKLE (*twelve-year-old son of Mercedes McCambridge and television producer John Markle*): She just makes a mess out of the kitchen – but she sure can cook!

MARLENE DIETRICH: Of course I like to cook. Before I was well known, the studio publicity people put out a lot of untrue releases; they didn't think it was glamorous for a movie star to

Marlene in Las Vegas.

cook, or smoke, or have children. That was nonsense, and when I became important enough, I put a stop to it.

ROSEMARY CLOONEY (*who has made two recordings with Miss Dietrich*): She once cooked a meal for Joe (Miss Clooney's husband, actor Jose Ferrer) and me. She's one of the most generous people I know. You can say, "Don't bother" to her a million times, but if she thinks you need something, nothing will stop her. Any time you have an ailment, she's right there with a remedy she claims is better than the one you're using. Quite often it is, too.

TALLULAH BANKHEAD: If I were sick and couldn't get Florence Nightingale, I'd get Marlene.

DIRECTOR BILLY WILDER: Telling her your troubles is as good as having a psychiatrist.

RADIO DIRECTOR MURRAY BURNETT: In many ways she's an old-fashioned lady. She accepts some modern things but rejects others. Aureomycin she'll take; psychoanalysis she won't. She's very loyal – which is also old-fashioned.

MARLENE DIETRICH: If the basic values are old-fashioned, then I'm old-fashioned. Good taste, these basic things, they never change.

LEO LERMAN: She'll do anything for her friends. Don't go shopping with her. If she sees something she thinks you'd like, she'll buy it for you.

MOVIE COLUMNIST HERBERT STEIN: When it comes to helping people, this gal is always there. Before Gloria Swanson made her comeback, while she was still looking for work, a nightclub photographer asked Dietrich if she'd mind having Swanson come to her table to pose for a picture together. Dietrich got to her feet and said, "For Swanson, I'll go to *her* table."

A HOLLYWOOD WRITER: When the singer Richard Tauber was dying, broke, in London, she gave him money for medical treatments – though he wasn't really one of her close friends.

MARLENE DIETRICH: Someone once wrote that I was kind because I give people presents. That's superficial. Because I like to give presents doesn't tell what kind of woman I am. If I cook for someone who's ill, and scrub his floor, why should anyone be surprised? Millions of women do that daily.

ANN KEELLAN (*attendant in the ladies' room at Manhattan's El Morocco night club*): She's a good tipper; usually leaves me a dollar.

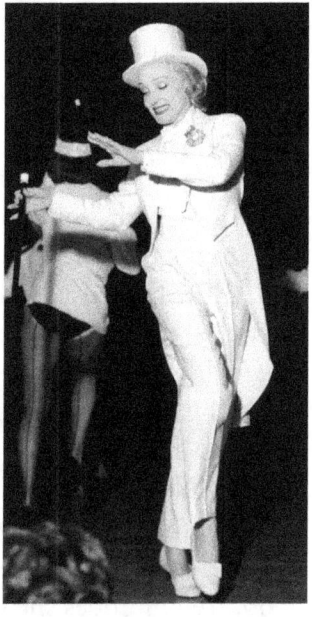

Marlene in Las Vegas.

PRODUCER IRVING ASHER: I had lunch with her a couple of days ago and she picked up her own check and left her own tip. It was a 60-cent check – and a two-dollar tip. Funny it never occurred to me to pick up *her* check. She pays her own. And on the way out she remembered she'd forgotten something – and ran back for it herself. She even lights her own cigarettes – with an old beat-up cigarette lighter that a GI made for her out of a wrecked plane's tank or something, when she was touring the fronts in World War II.

MARLENE DIETRICH: I don't prefer lighting cigarettes myself; it's faster that way. Same thing with opening doors: I do it myself because it's faster.

TALLULAH BANKHEAD: During the war, many people entertained the troops briefly and then came home to make movies. Dietrich went with the troops and stayed with them. She said she loved it because "no woman can please one man; this way you can please many men."

ASHER (a former colonel): After the war, the Pentagon gave her the Medal of Freedom; many men had written in asking why she hadn't received an award. She also got the French Legion of Honor medal.

GENERAL OF THE ARMY OMAR N. BRADLEY: Many of us came to admire her spirit and to appreciate her contribution because she was so much interested in entertaining our soldiers over a long period of time and because she quite often visited very close to the front lines.

HAROLD ARLEN: I first met her at the Hollywood Canteen in the early forties. She's a great personality. That is what the theater used to be full of – great personalities, not great actresses…

DIETERLE: She's the last of the great performers. There'll never be another personality like her.

ARLEN: …I think she'd have been a far better actress if she hadn't been typed. A great actress? No, I don't think so.

A DIRECTOR: She's adequate as an actress, but not really good. Tell me, does she know that?

MARLENE DIETRICH (*quoted by a friend*): I'm no actress…

ANOTHER DIRECTOR: Of course, she's no actress; everybody in the industry knows that. Yet off the screen, she's always acting. If she's alone in a room and a cat walks in, she starts acting. She almost doesn't know herself any more.

ACTOR BURGESS MEREDITH: She's a woman of many masks. She can take any part she wants and believe it implicitly – and she seems to enjoy all parts and all masks.

MARLENE DIETRICH: I don't see why anyone would say I ever act off stage. To do that, I would have to pretend to be something I'm not – something false, something someone else expected me to be.

MURRAY BURNETT (*formerly director of her current CBS radio show, Time for Love*): One source of the Dietrich legend is that she appears different to different people. She knows what's right for her, though; she constantly rewrites radio scripts to suit her particular requirements.

RADIO EXECUTIVE: The radio show is her package. She got the idea for it – based on the role she played in *The Blue Angel* – and she hires the actors and writers with her own money. She has turned down a fortune in TV. She feels – so far, at least – that it's not right for her.

MARLENE DIETRICH: If I do television it will have to be something special. People expect something special of me.

RADIO EXECUTIVE: She's a real student of the dollar in business, though – even if she hasn't succumbed to television.

LEO LERMAN: She wrote an article for a women's magazine not long ago and got $20,000 for it. The magazine wanted a writer to work with her, but she insisted on doing it herself, and actually did it, every word of it.

MARLENE DIETRICH: Writing is so easy, easier than acting or singing. I really do not want to write – or to make movies, or to sing; I have no ambition. I work because I need the money. I wish I didn't have to work. I lead a full life; not working would give me more time for it.

Marlene in The Room Upstairs, *1946.*

RADIO EXECUTIVE: She's pleasant and easy to work with. She gets along with everybody – with the possible exception of the publicity people.

PUBLICIST RUSSELL BIRDWELL: She hired me once – but for a sort of general public-relations function…not to get her picture on page one. I don't believe she ever consciously did anything to get her name in the papers.

MARLENE DIETRICH: I never paid anyone to get publicity for me. I have never begged for attention; I am not that kind of person who will say, "Look at me; this is what I really feel inside." If I had to write the story of my life, in the third person, I would say, "Marlene Dietrich has never emptied herself."

I have never been on my knees to the press, and they respect me for it; my relations with the press have always been good.

A MOVIE DIRECTOR: Sure, it's easy to get along with Marlene. All you have to do is acknowledge her superior position.

THE CRITICAL ACQUAINTANCE: She's as much in love with herself as it's possible for a human being to be. A magnificent symphony wouldn't mean a thing to Dietrich unless it were dedicated to her.

A CLOSE FRIEND (chuckling): The symphony crack isn't bad. Marlene *has* a certain egotism. Of course, she wouldn't accept the dedication unless it was a *good* symphony!

ANOTHER CLOSE FRIEND: What other woman could refer to the Arc de Triomphe as "my arch" and get away with it – in a room full of Frenchmen?

DIRECTOR MITCHELL LEISEN: She loves realism. Before playing a gypsy in *Golden Earrings* she saw gypsies eating fish heads, eyes and all, so she did the same. She put so much dirt on her face that I had to tell her to stop.

STILL PHOTOGRAPHER RAY JONES: I was taking some publicity stills for the film *Destry Rides Again* and she suggested some of her and Jimmy Stewart in a hay wagon. She said she wanted them realistic – so she began nibbling at his ear. They were realistic…

ACTOR JIMMY STEWART: Yeah, I remember. She was pretty realistic, all right.

DIRECTOR ALFRED HITCHCOCK: She's a professional. A professional cameraman, a professional dress designer…

ACTOR EDWARD G. ROBINSON: Playing opposite Marlene, I developed a new respect for her. She seemed to know as much about the technical side of the work as the director, the cameraman and the prop man.

MERCEDES MCCAMBRIDGE: Marlene is really an authority on everything.

REPORTER MARTHA WEINMAN: People in every field cite her as an expert.

MARY NETTER (*New York antique dealer*): That woman knows more about antiques than just about any other customer I have.

MME. DE PLESSIX (*hat designer*): She can tell me where a certain seam is misplaced, why a certain facing is good.

EDITH HEAD (*chief dress designer at Paramount Pictures*): You don't design clothes for Dietrich. You design them *with* her.

MOVIE WRITER WALTER REISCH: She's an accomplished violinist, with a sensational ear for music.

MARLENE DIETRICH: Perhaps people say I know something about everybody's job because I never say anything or do anything unless I know. So many people talk and make pretenses about things they know nothing about.

PAUL ROSE (*furniture restorer*): Once we argued about the color of something she wanted. I lost the argument, and I was sure the color would look very bad. I was wrong. Incidentally, her apartment is all soft beiges and pinks and gold – a perfect background for her. There are no pictures of her in the place.

A HOLLYWOOD FRIEND: You ought to see her bedroom in the New York apartment. Indirect lighting comes out from under the bed.

A NEW YORK FRIEND: The lights are operated by buttons built into the bed – and they don't just go on and off; they go from dim to bright. The chandelier over the bed is the same; it lights up in stages, and it can be operated from the bed.

LEO LERMAN: The apartment is a small living-room-bedroom-kitchen affair; with the living room made to look larger by a mirror on one wall.

MARLENE DIETRICH: When I decided I wanted mirrors in my apartment, to make it look bigger, some of my friends said: "Mirrors? Isn't that a little Hollywood?" What's wrong with Hollywood?

Marlene in Around the World in 80 Days, *1956.*

LEO LERMAN: There are some paintings on the apartment walls by great French artists, and a few photographs – including one of her good friend Ernest Hemingway, and one of Maria Riva and Miss Riva's older child, John Michael, five. The other Dietrich grandchild is John Peter Riva, aged three. The youngsters call their grandmother Missy. Marlene acts as a sort of combination maid, sitter and cook for Maria, helping out whenever Maria or her husband Bill, a television director, needs her.

SONGWRITER MAX COLPET: One day in 1949 she asked me to meet her in Central Park. When I arrived, she was sitting on a bench rocking her grandchild's baby carriage – and talking to Greta Garbo. They had just happened to run into each.

DIRECTOR BILLY WILDER: Her great dream was to do a picture with Garbo, but she never did.

ANOTHER DIRECTOR: Marlene has this great love for her daughter Maria – too much love, almost.

MERCEDES MCCAMBRIDGE: All her friends get wires from Marlene whenever Maria is on television, giving the time, the day and the network.

A FRIEND: …and if she tells you to watch, you'd better watch.

MANAGER OF A NEW YORK RESTAURANT: Miss Dietrich and her daughter come in here often, sometimes together, sometimes not. Miss Riva quiets down a lot when her mother is around.

MME. DE PLESSIX: Miss Dietrich picks a great many of her daughter's clothes.

EVA GABOR: I ran into her one day on Fifth Avenue. She had a newspaper clipping in one hand, and ad for flat-heeled shoes. She was hurrying to a store to get them for Maria.

PAUL ROSE: One day, Miss Dietrich showed me her wardrobe. There weren't many clothes, but there were hundreds of shoes, all beautiful. She apparently collects them.

MME. DE PLESSIX: Miss Dietrich sticks largely to black, simple suits and dresses, but sometimes wears beige – as close as possible to the color of her hair – and sometimes light blue. Although she buys perhaps a dozen hats a season, and never wears them a second season, she wears many of her dresses several years.

EVA GABOR: Marlene once told me, "When you buy good basic gowns, you can wear them and wear them. You don't need many."

MARLENE DIETRICH: Sometimes I won't see reporters because I have nothing to say, and then all they can write about is what I wear. What I wear is not important. I hate that kind of story.

JEAN LOUIS (*chief dress designer for Columbia Studios*): All my life, I wondered what it would be like to design a dress for her – and then one day I got a phone call from her. She wanted a dress for her Las Vegas show – "furs, spangles and diamonds," she told me. Fifteen seamstresses worked three months on the dresses – there were actually three gowns – tearing them apart and putting them together as she suggested alterations. Each dress had 200 rhinestones – at a dollar a rhinestone.

Marlene in Foreign Correspondent, *1948.*

PRODUCER IRVING ASHER: She discussed the Las Vegas gown with me beforehand. "There isn't anything new I can do with an evening gown," she told me, "except cut the neck a little lower than everyone else, and I don't want to do that. No, I'll give them a costume – the kind all women like to dream of themselves in and men like to dream of their women wearing."

HARLOD ARLEN: She told me, during her Las Vegas engagement, "It's ridiculous. I get out there, and all those women keep sighing, 'She's beautiful! She's beautiful!' Well, after all, it's just lo-*gic*." (That's a favorite expression of Marlene's: its lo-*gic*.) "What do they expect?" she said. "I should come out here for $30,000 a week and just say 'allo," and not be beautiful?"

LEO LERMAN: Her younger grandson saw a picture of her in the glittering Las Vegas dress and said, "You look just like a Christmas tree."

MARLENE DIETRICH: The news pictures of my Las Vegas dress were misleading. It was not transparent; those flash-bulb shots, they shoot right through the dress. They could shoot through a black sweater.

THE CRITICAL ACQUAINTANCE: She sure couldn't have worn that gown in the early days of her career. She looked like a horse in those days. My lord, the double portions of goulash that woman put away.

A GERMAN FILM PRODUCER: She made a potato-dumpling figure popular. A good trick.

AN AMERICAN FILM EXECUTIVE: She still eats like a truck driver, but it never seems to affect her figure.

LEO LERMAN: Sometimes, when she's busy, she'll go a whole day without eating a bite.

COLUMNIST EARL WILSON: Her favorite late-at-night snack is champagne and kosher frankfurters.

BRUNO CARAVAGGI (*co-owner of the swank New York restaurant Quo Vadis*): She eats slowly, and she is always the central figure at her table. Yet she always speaks in a very soft voice.

MURRAY BURNETT: She never shouts. She has a temper, but she keeps it under control. When she's angry, the tip of her nose turns white.

HAROLD ARLEN: Her anger is frosty.

IRVING ASHER: She never says anything that can't be said in front of children – partly, I think, because she's deeply religious… although I've never known her to go to church.

PHONE OPERATOR IN A HOLLYWOOD STUDIO: About other actresses, you'd hear complaints: bad manners, foul language, temper. About Miss Dietrich you heard only nice things. Once I peeked into her dressing room. On her table was a big crucifix, a foot and a half high, and a statue of the Virgin Mary.

A DIRECTOR: I don't know about her religion, but I do know she believes in astrology.

A STUDIO EXECUTIVE: She always calls her astrologer long-distance before taking a trip, to see if the date is a good one for her to travel on. Her friends in Hollywood often call him to see when she'll be in town; he's usually the first to know.

MARLENE DIETRICH: Astrology? Of course. After all, everyone knows that the moon pulls the sea away from the land, and farmers don't plant when the moon is wrong – why should we humans escape; why shouldn't we be affected too? If you have something big to do and the stars are with you, then I think you should follow them. But I don't believe in this business of not leaving the house when the stars are wrong; I guess I'm too practical.

A FRIEND: How do you assess a woman like Dietrich? She believes in astrology, yet she impresses scientists with her keen mind. She's the world's most glamorous woman, yet she's most at home in the kitchen. She's the essence of soft femininity, yet with a will like iron. I have known her 20 years, and I confess she stumps me.

A DIRECTOR: There's a lot of Jekyll and Hyde in Dietrich.

TV PRODUCER FLETCHER MARKLE: You might call your article "The Housebroken Goddess."

ACTOR-PRODUCER MEL FERRER: The word for Marlene is Erda – the earth goddess.

A HOLLYWOOD DIRECTOR: She once told me she wanted to be always "a little unhappy" – a line from one of her songs.

A NUMBER OF PEOPLE: She's one of the loneliest figures in the entertainment world – but don't tell her I said so.

A MOVIE EXECUTIVE: Dietrich is a tragic figure.

PHONE OPERATOR IN A HOLLYWOOD STUDIO: Did you ever know someone you could look in their eyes and see their soul? That's Miss Dietrich.

A CLOSE FRIEND: I think she's happy.

A SCREEN WRITER: Nothing breaks her heart.

WILLIAM DIETERLE: She is one of the most self-controlled, self-disciplined people I know.

MARLENE DIETRICH: I don't believe in being controlled by anything or anyone but myself.

MOVIE ACTOR: She's a legend because she dares to lead a natural life. Most of us haven't the courage to do likewise, but we get a vicarious thrill out of watching someone else do it – and in such good taste!

RAY JONES: Marlene is reckless, but she makes you feel there's a difference between recklessness and carelessness.

MAURICE CHEVALIER: Dietrich is something that has never existed before and will never exist again. That's a woman…a real, ripe woman.

A HOLLYWOOD OBSERVER: Essentially, Dietrich is a rather old-fashioned girl. Everything about her seems somewhat quaint and Germanic – including her Wagnerian self-love. There is always a sort of fascination about people who manage to exist beyond the period in which they were appropriate symbols…a little like the Walt Disney animals who run off a cliff and walk on the air for a few moments before they discover it.

A MOVIE DIRECTOR: I am not one of her admirers. She hasn't much ability as an actress, her singing leaves much to be desired, her beauty has been largely a state of mind, and it's leaving her now. She has hurt many people – usually, to be sure, while trying to help someone else. But one fact remains; you cannot eliminate Marlene Dietrich from the history of the motion picture. (*Pausing, with an air of bewilderment.*) In fact, you cannot even eliminate Marlene Dietrich from a history of our time.

MARLENE DIETRICH: Everything there is to say about me has been said. I'm not much: nothing spectacular. A director once said to me when I was making a picture, "Come now, give me Marlene!" What is *Marlene*, I asked him. I do not know…

Marlene in Las Vegas.

Marlene Dietrich Has the Last Word

After renouncing her German citizenship, Dietrich became an American citizen in 1939. The United States entered World War II following the Japanese attack on Pearl Harbor in 1941. Dietrich was deeply moved by the horrors of war, and toured the United States from January 1942 until September 1943 selling war bonds. In 1944 and 1945, she performed for Allied troops during two extended tours for the USO, often putting herself in dangerous situations on the ground. After the war ended, she returned to Hollywood, but her film career never fully recovered. She had enjoyed performing for live audiences, and decided to turn her attention to pursuing a new career as a cabaret singer.

Marlene entertains Allied troops during World War II.

In 1953, she made a spectacular debut at the Sahara Hotel in Las Vegas to standing-room only, appreciative audiences. She hired Burt Bacharach to craft her stage show. The two had a prolonged affair while they worked together. Dietrich polished her one-woman show, and triumphantly toured the world until 1975. She performed on Broadway in 1967, and again in 1968. That year she won a special Tony Award.

Despite her international success, she kept the press at arm's length. She granted only a few interviews, always for the sole purpose of promoting an upcoming singing engagement. She never enjoyed interviews, and wearied of answering the same questions for more than thirty years. She questioned her movie achievements, mocked her public characterization of being a "sex symbol," wondered why anyone was interested in her private life, and even dismissed the adulation of her fans. Nevertheless, her blunt, unemotional answers to questions never deterred her fans, the prying press or invasive photographers. Instead, they were more and more intrigued by the legend's thoughts.

Marlene in Paris, 1964.

In August, 1965, she performed an extended engagement in England. She was in the midst of a long, and tedious concert tour. When she was asked by journalist Clive Hirschhorn why she continued to work – why she worked so hard, her response was surprisingly abrupt. "For the money," she said. "Yes, for the money. What else for? It's hard work! And who would work if they didn't have to? I work because I pay taxes to the American Government. I enjoy living in that country and one pays for one's pleasures. So. I work. And as long as people want me, and I have them eating out of my hands, I shall continue to do so."

Her success in motion pictures, and later on stage, was long speculated upon by journalists. She felt there was no "secret" to her success, and laughed at the idea there was any mystery to it. "Secret?" she mused. "No secret at all. I work hard, that is all! People say that I have some sort of *quality* – well, maybe I have. How am I to know that?

"I think it is Dietrich the woman they like – rather than Dietrich the singer. They pay to see me for what I am. Particularly the English audiences, who are marvelous and warm. To me they are the most emotional, and also the most un-phony people I know. And as I am that way too, we get along just fine. They know that I do not take myself seriously, and the whole thing is a joke, and that I am laughing at myself all the time. And when I laugh, they laugh. I am a unique performer and my audiences realize this."

When she was asked what lead to her transition from movie star to stage performer, she said simply, "The War. I realized that if I was to be a useful person in it, doing a job of work that was worth doing – the best thing to do would be to entertain the troops. And that's how it all happened. Which is just as well, because films I find too technical really to enjoy – and much more personal."

Dietrich said she never thought about retirement, but speculated that wealth would give her the opportunity to walk away from a public life. "I have an awful lot of private life to catch up on, which, at this rate, I don't think will be possible," she pondered. "When you're in the public eye as conspicuously as I am it is conceivable to maintain a private life – but the trouble is you can only devote half your time to it. My private life, which no one knows anything about, nor ever will, needs more than just half my time if it is to be a success."

Her "private life" was the worst kept secret in Hollywood. She married Rudolf Sieber in Germany in 1923. They lived separate lives. Dietrich was bisexual, and entertained many lovers of both sexes. Sieber had a mistress most of his life. He died of cancer on June 24, 1976. He lived on a California farm the actress had purchased many years before. The couple had one child, actress Maria Riva. Mother and daughter endured a tumultuous, strained relationship.

Since her early years in Hollywood, Dietrich had the reputation for being difficult and temperamental. Her reluctance to talk with the press, and refusal to accommodate studio publicists, and determination to lead her personal life on her own individual terms, contributed to the mythologizing of the actress. She was bored with such talk, and shrugged off any suggestion that her behavior was calculated for best effect. And her advanced age did not temper her willingness to speak her mind.

"I do not change my face for my public," she stated. "I have not tried to create an image or a myth about myself; I am as quiet and placid off-stage as I am when the bright lights are on me. No temperaments, no periods of dark, gloomy despair. I am easy going and the only thing I cannot stand is stupidity – in any form. Stupidity is the one thing I'm intolerant about. And the only thing that breaks me up. Stupid people annoy me. There are fans of mine who worship and idolize me, and who are in awe of me. They are stupid people. Who am I to be held in awe? What have I accomplished? If one is to be in awe of anyone, let it be a doctor or a brilliant scientist. Not a performer. I could never be friends with anyone stupid enough to worship me."

She considered being characterized as a "Hollywood Sex Goddess" equally ridiculous. "I'm not a sex goddess and I never have been. Not in the 1930s – and not now. I don't get annoyed, because one comes to expect people to confuse glamour with sex, which is a different thing altogether. This is the price one pays for being famous.

"People, particularly Americans, love to create myths which later become legends. And if sex – which means money – comes into it, they'll go out of their way to play God and create something out of nothing. For example – magazines – the biggest myth-creators of all! You must never, never read American magazines. And if you're sitting in a waiting room and cannot help it – don't believe a word of any of them."

The End

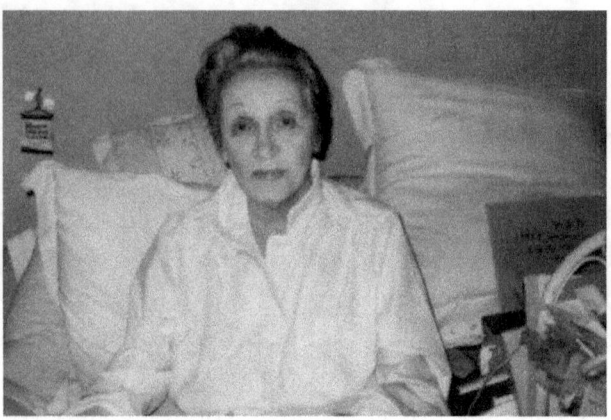

Marlene in her Paris apartment, 1991.

"Oh, I got another one of those *professor* books," Maria recalls her mother said to her on one of her visits to Marlene's Paris apartment near the end of her reclusive life. "Some American fan sent it. Again, full of *deep* meanings. What Jo really meant with a 'shot,' what I really meant with a 'look'! The usual crap. Where do they *get* all these ideas? They all think they have discovered something new. All this 'to-do' about *deep* meanings and Freud. We made a film – then we did another. Now they all think it is *art*. Such stupidity! You get paid to make a film – if it makes money, you get to make another film. If it doesn't, you are suddenly not so la-di-da important. It's a business, not art."

(From *Marlene Dietrich*, the brilliant biography written by her daughter Maria Riva. This revealing book has recently been reissued, and is well worth the read for fans of Dietrich.)

Dietrich's Bienenstich (Bee's Nest Cake)

Bienenstich is a traditional German dessert. This is a lightly sweetened yeast cake with a honey-almond-caramel crunch topping. The single-layer cake is split and filled with pastry cream.

CAKE
2 ¼ teaspoons instant yeast (not active dry yeast)
¾ cup whole milk, room temperature
¼ cup granulated sugar
2 cups all-purpose flour
¾ teaspoon salt
2 large eggs, room temperature
4 tablespoons unsalted butter, room temperature

HONEY-ALMOND-CRUNCH TOPPING
6 tablespoons unsalted butter
1/3 cup granulated sugar
3 tablespoons honey

2 tablespoons heavy cream
1 ½ cups sliced almonds
2 pinches of sea salt

PASTRY CREAM FILLING
1 cup whole milk
1 teaspoon pure vanilla extract
3 large egg yolks
¼ cup granulated sugar
3 tablespoons all-purpose flour
2 pinches of sea salt
2 tablespoons unsalted butter

To prepare the cake: Combine all the cake ingredients in a medium-sized mixing bowl, stirring until the mixture becomes cohesive, then stirring for two minutes more. In a stand mixer, you can mix this with the paddle attachment at low-medium speed for 2 to 3 minutes. Scrape down the sides, cover with plastic wrap and let rise for 60 minutes, until it's a little puffy. (It will not double in size.) Butter a 9-inch round cake pan. Stir the batter a few times to deflate it slightly, then scrape it into the prepared pan and nudge it until it fills the bottom. Cover again with plastic wrap and set aside for 30 minutes. (Do not let the wrap touch the top of the dough.) Heat oven to 350 degrees.

To make the honey-almond-crunch topping: In a small or medium sized saucepan over medium heat, heat the butter, sugar, honey, cream and salt until the butter is melted. Bring to a simmer and let it boil for 3 to 5 minutes, until the mixture becomes a shade darker (it should go from a yellowish tone to a light beige), stirring frequently. Stir in the almonds. The mixture will thicken. Set it aside to cool slightly.

To finish the cake: Once the cake has finished its "second" rise, use a small spoon to scoop out small amounts of the almond topping and distribute it over the top of the cake. It's going to be thick, but it will smooth out evenly in the oven. Bake the cake on a foil-lined tray to catch any caramel drips, for 20 to 25 minutes, until top is bronzed and a toothpick inserted into the center comes out batter-free. Transfer to a cooling rack and let it sit in the pan for 10-15 minutes. Run a knife along the outside of the cake, making sure no places are stuck and invert the cake onto the cooling rack. Reverse it back onto another rack to finish cooling. Place any almonds that fell off back on the top.

To make the pastry cream: Warm milk in a medium sized saucepan. Pour into a small bowl, set aside. In a clean saucepan whisk the egg yolks and sugar vigorously for a minute. Whisk in flour and salt until smooth. Drizzle in warm milk, a small amount at a time, whisking constantly. Put the saucepan on the heat and cook on medium-high heat until it bubbles, then simmer for 2 to 3 minutes more, constantly whisking. Remove from the heat and whisk in the butter and vanilla extract. Cool the pastry cream filling completely.

To assemble the Bienenstich: Once the cake and cream are fully cooled, place the cake on a serving platter and cut it horizontally into two layers with a serrated knife. Spread all the pastry cream over the bottom half evenly. Place top half of the cake on the pastry cream. Refrigerate leftovers.

The Films of Marlene Dietrich

Marlene in Judgement at Nuremberg, *1961.*

Dietrich first appeared on screen in Germany in 1919. She made twenty films before moving to the United States to begin her Hollywood career. Although *The Blue Angel* was filmed in Germany, it is considered her first "Hollywood" film. The now classic film was directed by Josef von Sternberg and produced by Paramount Pictures and UFA, Paramount's sister studio in Germany. The movie was shot simultaneously in German and English language versions. *The Blue Angel* was released in the United States in late 1930. During the following forty-eight years, Dietrich made thirty-five feature films.

1930 *Morocco*, directed by Josef von Sternberg for Paramount Pictures.

1931 *Dishonored*, directed by Josef von Sternberg for Paramount Pictures.

1932 *Shanghai Express*, directed by Josef von Sternberg for Paramount Pictures.
1932 *Blonde Venus*, directed by Josef von Sternberg for Paramount Pictures.
1933 *The Song of Songs*, directed by Rouben Mamoulian, for Paramount Pictures.
1934 *The Scarlet Empress*, directed by Josef von Sternberg, for Paramount Pictures.
1935 *The Devil Is a Woman*, directed by Josef von Sternberg, for Paramount Pictures.
1936 *Desire*, directed by Frank Borzage, for Paramount Pictures.
1936 *The Garden of Allah*, directed by Richard Boleslawski, for Selznick International Pictures.
1936 *I Loved a Soldier*, directed by Henry Hathaway, for Paramount Pictures.
1937 *Knight Without Armor*, directed by Jacques Feyder, for London Film Productions.
1937 *Angel*, directed by Ernst Lubitsch, for Paramount Pictures.
1939 *Destry Rides Again*, directed by George Marshall, for Universal.
1940 *Seven Sinners*, directed by Tay Garnett, for Universal.
1941 *The Flame of New Orleans*, directed by Rene Clair, for Universal.
1941 *Manpower*, directed by Raoul Walsh, for Warner Bros.
1942 *The Lady Is Willing*, directed by Mitchell Leisen, for Columbia Pictures.
1942 *The Spoilers*, directed by Ray Enright, for Universal.
1942 *Pittsburgh*, directed by Lewis Seiler, for Feldman Group/Universal.
1944 *Follow the Boys*, directed by A. Edward Sutherland, for Universal.
1944 *Kismet*, directed by William Dieterle, for MGM.
1946 *The Room Upstairs*, directed by Georges Lacombe, for Alcina.
1947 *Golden Earrings*, directed by Mitchell Leisen, for Paramount.
1948 *A Foreign Affair*, directed by Billy Wilder, for Paramount.
1949 *Jigsaw*, directed by Fletcher Markle, for Tower Pictures, Inc.
1950 *Stage Fright*, directed by Alfred Hitchcock, for Warner Bros.

1951 *No Highway in the Sky*, directed by Henry Kosher, for 20th Century-Fox.

1952 *Rancho Notorious*, directed by Fritz Lang, for Fidelity Pictures, Inc./RKO.

1956 *Around the World in 80 Days*, directed by Michael Anderson, for Michael Todd Co./United Artists.

1956 *The Montecarlo Story*, directed by Samuel A. Taylor, for Tan Films, Inc./United Artists.

1957 *Witness for the Prosecution*, directed by Billy Wilder, for Edward Small Productions/United Artists.

1958 *Touch of Evil*, directed by Orson Wells, for Universal International Pictures.

1961 *Judgement at Nuremberg*, directed by Stanley Kramer, for Roxlom Films, Inc./United Artists.

1964 *Paris When It Sizzles*, directed by Richard Quine, for Richard Quine Productions/Paramount.

1978 *Just a Gigolo*, directed by David Hemmings, for Bayerischer Rundfunk.

1984 *Marlene*, directed by Maximilian Schell, for Bayerischer Rundfunk.

Marlene Dietrich was a movie star, but by her own admission, she was not a good actress. She was acknowledged by the Academy of Motion Picture Arts and Sciences with an Oscar nomination for Best Performance by an Actress in the 1930 film, *Morocco*. She was acknowledged again in 1958 by the Hollywood Foreign Press with a Golden Globe Award nomination for Best Performance by an Actress in the film, *Witness for the Prosecution*.

Marlene in her final film role, Just A Gigolo, *1978.*

MARLENE DIETRICH ON THE AIR

Dietrich worked frequently on national radio broadcasts between 1936 and 1954, usually performing as a guest-star on numerous hit shows. She also acted in a number of dramatic radio productions.

June 01, 1936 "The Legionnaire and the Lady," Lux Radio Theater
March 15, 1937 "Desire," Lux Radio Theater
December 20, 1937 "The Song of Songs," Lux Radio Theater
February 06, 1938 Special Guest Star, The Chase and Sanborn Hour
March 16, 1942 "Manpower," Lux Radio Theater
May 13, 1942 "National Association of Broadcasters Show," Command Performance
August 11, 1942 Special Guest, Command Performance
April 14, 1943 "The Mayor Tries to Spend a Quiet Night at Home," Mayor of the Town

September 09, 1943 Special Guest, Command Performance
November 16, 1943 Special Guest, Burns and Allen
December 25, 1946 "1946 Christmas Special with Bob Hope, Part I," Command Performance
December 25, 1946 "1946 Christmas Special with Lionel Barrymore," Command Performance
December 25, 1946 "1946 Christmas Special with Bob Hope, Part II," Command Performance
December 11, 1947 "Broadway Melody," Hollywood's Open House
June 29, 1948 "Arabesque," Studio One
October 08, 1948 "Madam Bovary," The Ford Theater
March 06, 1949 "A Foreign Affair," The Screen Director's Playhouse
March 09, 1949 "Archie Writes A Television Play (With Marlene Dietrich)," Duffy's Tavern
March 11, 1949 "The Lady From The Sea," The Philip Morris Playhouse
March 17, 1949 "George Has A Cold," Burns and Allen
November 18, 1949 "Citadel," MGM Theater Of The Air
December 09, 1949 "Anna Karenina," MGM Theater Of The Air
February 16, 1950 "Murder Strikes Three Times," Suspense
January 07, 1951 Special Guest, Big Show
March 01, 1951 "A Foreign Affair," The Screen Director's Playhouse
March 21, 1952 Special Guest, Martin & Lewis Show
April 28, 1952 "No Highway In The Sky," Lux Radio Theater
May 07, 1952 Special Guest, Bing Crosby Chesterfield Show
July 07, 1953 Special Guest, Martin & Lewis Show

In 1951, Dietrich worked with producer Leonard Blair to create a dramatic radio serial based on the role she played in *The Blue Angel*. Titled, *Café Istanbul*, the story, filled with foreign intrigue and adventure, was set in Café Istanbul, a cabaret located somewhere in the Far East. Dietrich played the role of Mademoiselle Madou, a sultry singer, who becomes involved with international spies, criminals, and the Secret Police. Actor Ken Lynch played her love interest, Christopher Gard, a young American man with mysterious connections. Veteran actor Arnold Moss played the role of Police Colonel Raul Felki, who didn't know whether to romance Mlle. Madou, or lock her up. Directed by Marx Leebe, the series premiered on the American Broadcasting Company on January 6, 1952. The series concluded with a final broadcast on December 28, 1952.

The actress returned to the airwaves two weeks later in a new dramatic radio serial. The setting was changed, but otherwise the newly named series, *Time for Love*, seemed like little more than a remake of *Café Istanbul*. Dietrich played the role of Dianne La Volte, "a globally famous vocal performer who crusaded for law and order across the continents." Actor Robert Readick played the role of Dianne's love interest, Michael Victor, an American journalist who always arrived in the nick of time to rescue her. The series was directed by Murray Burnett and Ernest Ricca, and produced by Dietrich. The program's theme song, "Time for Love," was recorded by the actress and Percy Faith and his orchestra. Jergens hand cream was the sponsor. *Time for Love* was first broadcast on January 15, 1953. The final episode was broadcast on May 27, 1954.

Notes and Sources

Marlene with her daughter Maria, 1947.

"The Politics of Acting." "Miss you." Maria Riva, *Marlene Dietrich* (New York: Knopf, 1993) pg. 80; "Well, the 'Great Find of the Century'" Ibid, pg. 84; "Liesel would cry in sympathy" Ibid, pg.18-19; "During the war" Ibid, pg. 24; "I am starting to love" Ibid, pg. 26; "My heart is set on fire" Ibid, pg. 27; "considering her exaggerated" Ibid, pg. 32; "Both of them are so dry" Ibid, pg. 33-34; "Saturdays and Sundays" Ibid, pg. 36; "If only someone" Ibid, pg. 37; "I went to his house" Ibid, pg. 375; "He groaned" Ibid, pg. 375; "He looked at me" Ibid, pg. 44; "Only pansies" Ibid, pg. 44; "That von Sternberg" Ibid, pg. 69; "Why don't you let me" Ibid, pg. 73; "Papi, you made me" Ibid, pg. 69/70; "But the song" Ibid, pg. 67; "In English" Ibid, pg. 70; "Papi, it is still" Ibid, pg. 73; "That was the first time" Ibid, pg. 73; "MARLENE DIETRICH" Ibid, pg. 75; "To be courteous" Ibid, pg. 87; "Tomorrow we begin shooting" Ibid, pg. 89; "Gary Cooper is pleasant" Ibid, pg. 91; "All Cooper can do" Ibid, pg. 244; "First I am called" Ibid, pg. 110; "Not bad, honey, not bad at all" Ibid, pg. 140; "She reall took one out" Ibid, pg. 151; "YOU SHOULDN'T GO" Ibid, pg. 152; "That hoity-toity" Ibid, pg. 148; "I must force myelf" Ibid, pg. 159; "SITUATION BERLIN" Ibid, pg. 187; "There is one fact" Ibid, pg. 232; "I don't know what is wrong" Ibid, pg. 232; "He was in love with me" Ibid, pg. 781; "I saw" Brian Aherne, *A Proper Job* (Boston, Houghton Mifflin, 1969) pg. 208; "SVENGALI & DIETRICH" Maria Riva, Marlene Dietrich (New York: Knopf, 1933) pg. 342; "Applause for Marlene" Ibid, pg. 343.

Libraries are the greatest free source of reliable information and research. Grateful acknowledgement to all the wonderful librarians who assisted me. Support your local library.

Los Angeles Public Library, Los Angeles, California

Margaret Herrick Library of the Academy of Motion Picture Arts and Sciences, Beverly Hills, California

New York Public Library, New York, New York

New York Public Library for the Performing Arts, New York New York

SELECTED BIBLIOGRAPHY

Aherne, Brian. *A Proper Job*. Boston: Houghton Mifflin, 1969

Bach, Steven. *Marlene Dietrich: Life and Legend*. New York: William Morrow and Co., 1992

Chandler, Charlotte. *Marlene Dietrich, A Personal Biography*. New York: Simon & Schuster, 2011

Chevalier, Maurice. *With Love*. Boston: Little, Brown and Co., 1960

Dickens, Homer. *The Complete Films of Marlene Dietrich*. New York: Citadel Press, 1992

Dietrich, Marlene. *Marlene Dietrich's ABC*. New York: Frederick Ungar Publishing, 1987

Dietrich, Marlene. *My Life*. London: Weidenfeld & Nicolson, Ltd., 1989

Higham, Charles. *Marlene: The Life of Marlene Dietrich*. New York: W.W. Norton & Co., 1977

Riva, J. David. *A Woman at War: Marlene Dietrich Remembered*. Detroit: Painted Turtle Books, 2006

Riva, Maria. *Marlene Dietrich*. New York: Knopf, 1992

Spoto, Donald. *Blue Angel: The Life of Marlene Dietrich*. New York: Doubleday, 1992

Walker, Alexander. *Dietrich*. New York: Harper & Row, 1984

Marlene, 1970.

About the Author

Author photo by James Gavin.

MICHAEL GREGG MICHAUD is the author of the critically acclaimed, best-selling, Lambda Book Award nominated *Sal Mineo, A Biography* (Crown Archetype, 2010). The biography was a pick of the month in *Los Angeles Magazine* and by Turner Classic Movies, appeared on Leonard Maltin's recommended holiday list in December 2010, and later adapted for the screen as a feature film, *Sal*, by James Franco. Michaud is the co-author, with actress Diane McBain, of *Famous Enough, A Hollywood Memoir* (BearManor Media, 2014). He wrote the *Classic Images* 2017 Best Book of the Year, and two-time 2018 Next Generation Indie Book Award nominated biography, *Alan Sues, A Funny Man* (BearManor Media, 2016). He edited and annotated, *Mae West: Between the Covers* (BearManor Media, 2018), which was a finalist for the 2019 Next Generation Indie Book Award for Best Anthology, and wrote *Mae West: Broadcast Muse* (BearManor Media,

2019). Michaud writes about Hollywood, and has contributed to numerous books about show business and the arts. He updated and edited Tippi Hedren's book, *The Cats of Shambala* (Shambala Press, 1992) and contributed to Linda Blair's book, *Going Vegan* (SHA, Inc. 2001). He appears in the 2012 Biography Channel documentary, *Hollywood's Most Notorious Crimes* (Sharp Entertainment), and the 2019 feature length documentary film, *Steven Arnold: Heavenly Bodies*. He is also a contributor to the 2020 PBS American Masters feature documentary, *Mae West – Dirty Blonde*. Follow him on Facebook.

www.ingramcontent.com/pod-product-compliance
Lightning Source LLC
Chambersburg PA
CBHW061922220426
43662CB00012B/1778